Stability Economics

The Economic Foundations of Security in Post-conflict Environments

General Editors

Nathan W. Toronto and Dan G. Cox

Combat Studies Institute Press

Fort Leavenworth, Kansas

I0120281

Meeting of the Minds (cover photo)

US service members meet with a member of a local Kuchi tribe residing in Bawka district in Farah province, Afghanistan, June 12, 2010. The service members, assigned to the Provincial Reconstruction Team Farah, visited three villages in the district to gather information on the needs of the village residents and to promote the importance of seeking government assistance to help resolve those needs.

US Air Force photo by Senior Airman Rylan K. Albright

Contents

Introduction

by

Nathan W. Toronto

In the years after invading Iraq and Afghanistan, the US military realized that it had a problem: How does a military force set the economic conditions for security success? This problem was certainly not novel—the military had confronted it before in such diverse locations as Grenada, Haiti, Bosnia, and Kosovo. The scale and complexity of the problem, however, were unlike anything military planners had confronted beforehand. This was especially the case in Iraq, where some commentators expected oil production to drive reconstruction.[1] When the fragile state of Iraq's infrastructure and a rapidly deteriorating security situation prevented this from happening, the problem became even more vexing: Should a military force focus on security first, or the economy? How can it do both? This is the challenge of Stability Economics.

One answer to this problem in Iraq was the Commander's Emergency Response Program (CERP) and using money as a weapon system.[2] The notion was that commanders could target funding at projects that would contribute to improvements in the economy and the security situation simultaneously. Beyond sparking an ongoing debate about CERP effectiveness,[3] the evolution of money as a weapon system occurred under the shadow of a larger debate over whether the US military should prepare the future force for population-centric counterinsurgency operations or for large-unit combined arms maneuver operations.[4] A force prepared for population-centric counterinsurgency would presumably also be better positioned to set the economic conditions for security success in a post-conflict environment. In very general terms, what one observer playfully called COINdinistas[5] would favor the building of military doctrine and competencies to prepare the force to build economies in the future, the expectation being that facing such challenges are inevitable for the US military. Thus, the debate over how good the military should be at economic development influenced and was influenced by the debate over force structure and the character of future warfare.

These debates arose in Afghanistan, as they did in Iraq, but at a later date. One important reason for this was the gap in resources that the US military dedicated to Iraq as opposed to Afghanistan. While the scale of US involvement in Iraq ballooned in 2006 and 2007, the problem of Stability Economics came into sharp focus. The force used some of the solutions learned in Iraq in Afghanistan, including CERP and using money as a weapon system, but the decidedly primitive nature of Afghan infrastructure placed limits on the transferability of such lessons. So, as the US military surged forces and resources to Afghanistan after the election of President Barack Obama and the winding down of operations in Iraq, military planners searched for solutions to new problems of Stability Economics.

One solution to these new problems was expeditionary economics, sponsored by the Ewing Marion Kaufmann Foundation.[6] Consistent with its mission to "help individuals attain economic independence by advancing educational achievement and entrepreneurial

1

success,"[7] then-President and CEO Carl J. Schramm saw an opportunity to spur economic growth in the aftermath of military conflicts and natural disasters.[8] In addition, he advocated the development of an economic development capability organic to the US military, akin to the School of Government that trained military commanders and staff officers for civil governance in post-World War II Germany and Japan.[9] In May 2010, the Foundation held a conference at its Kansas City, Missouri, headquarters to spur a debate on these ideas. There were two follow-on conferences—held at the US Military Academy at West Point, New York, in February and May 2011—to further develop and convey these ideas. Then the momentum stalled. The Foundation published a few occasional papers,[10] but after Schramm's quiet and quite unexpected departure in January 2012 the Foundation decided to begin no more expeditionary economics initiatives, arguing that the idea, in the words of a person familiar with the situation, had "taken on a life of its own" and no longer needed support from the Foundation.

Suspicion lurks, however, that the tongue was firmly in the cheek. At least one of the co-editors of this volume attended all three expeditionary economics conferences and had repeated interaction with individuals from the Foundation, both in person and over the phone. Rarely did the conversation move beyond whether the US military could—or should—be involved in economic development, much less reach the level of operational detail required to make expeditionary economics a military planning reality. In fact, at the first follow-on conference in February 2011, one of the editors of this volume asked when the conference would discuss such operational details, but was told that developing those details was the purpose of the second follow-on conference, in May 2011. Such operational specifics did not materialize then, either. Furthermore, repeated requests for the Foundation to comment on expeditionary economics-related work by operational planners at the US Army School of Advanced Military Studies (SAMS) went largely unrequited. Not only has the US military failed to develop an organic economic development capability—per Schramm's objective—but the theory and knowledge to do so is still unavailable. By all reasonable accounts, then, the expeditionary economics movement had only limited success.

This volume on Stability Economics begins to fill the gap that expeditionary economics did not: the operational details. What is the theoretical relationship between economics and security? What strategic, political, and environmental contexts do military planners need to consider in order to write economic development lines of effort into operations? At what point do economic development efforts pass from being necessary to achieve the security mission to being humanitarian aid mission creep?

Stability Economics also puts the CERP effectiveness and force structure debates into their proper operational context. With respect to CERP effectiveness and money as a weapon system, Stability Economics recognizes that setting the economic conditions for security success entails more than targeting money effectively; it also entails a thorough appreciation of the social, political, and geographic conditions of the fight in which a military unit is engaged. In fact, armed with a robust theory of how economies grow in turbulent post-conflict environments, commanders could recognize that there are times when it is actually better to *not* spend money. By broadening the theoretical aperture,

Stability Economics gives commanders and planners the perspective they need set the economic conditions for security success. It is about more than spending money. It is about understanding the unique characteristics of post-conflict economies.

The proper operational context for the force structure debate—should the force prepare for counterinsurgency or major combat or something in between?—is as a political condition for the conduct of Stability Economics. Individual military planners rarely, if ever, have the luxury of determining the structure of the force that will conduct the military operations they plan. They may influence this structure, but only in an indirect, diffuse way, through contributions to professional military discussions or in such forums as the Quadrennial Defense Review. More often than not, military planners take the force structure given in the context of the forces available and the political end states desired. For example, determining whether the force should include a 20,000-man advisor corps seems ancillary to setting the economic conditions for security success. Better to have a clear idea of how a commander might use *any* force to achieve economically-relevant goals. This is the gap that this volume on Stability Economics begins to fill.

We present herein five SAMS monographs, as an effort to understand Stability Economics from the perspective of theory, history, and practice. The first two monographs review the theory related to Stability Economics. The first, "Entrepreneurial Expeditionary Economics and the United States Military: Right Task, Wrong Tool?" by Major Thomas Archer-Burton (United Kingdom Land Forces), provides a critical review of expeditionary economics. The second monograph, "Expeditionary Economics and Its Implications for the United States Army," by Major Marc Pelini (United States Army), is more receptive to concepts in expeditionary economics, although it also offers a wider review of theory related to economics in war zones and highlights the need to develop some sort of Stability Economics capacity. The third monograph, "Expeditionary Economics in Turbulent Times," by Lieutenant James Connally (United States Army), presents a historical case of a government applying Stability Economics principles: the Peruvian government combating Shining Path guerrillas. In doing so, it also emphasizes the importance of understanding the political and social context of an economy; some principles of Stability Economics may exhibit stability over time and space, but rarely are these principles truly immutable.

The final two monographs begin to delve into the operational details of Stability Economics. The fourth monograph, "Comparing Models for the Restoration of Essential Services during Counterinsurgency Operations," by Major Anthony Barbina (United States Army), examines the dominant model for restoring essential services—sewer, water, electrical, academics, trash (SWEAT)—against experience in Iraq and Afghanistan, and concludes that a more flexible Factor-Precedence Model provides a more robust framework for restoring essential services. The fifth and final monograph, "*Shari'a* Compliant Finance: The Overlooked Element for Developing an Effective Financial System in Afghanistan," by Lieutenant Colonel Jan Willem Maas (Kingdom of the Netherlands Army), evaluates an alternative financial system model for Afghanistan, questioning as it does the appropriateness of Western modes of finance. While these final two monographs hardly cover the gamut of what doctrine on Stability Economics could entail, establishing a financial system and restoring essential services figure to be two critical pieces of the puzzle. Furthermore, they contribute practical, operational details to add to the history and theory of Stability Economics.

Military commanders and staffs will need to understand the theory, history, and practice of Stability Economics because they will undoubtedly confront this simple: How does a military force set the economic conditions for security success? In an increasingly globalized world economy, this is especially the case for the US military, since the United States has global interests and global reach. Furthermore, this question will likely obtain in a wide variety of different conflicts, from small advise and assist operations as in Uganda and the Philippines to larger-scale operations as in Iraq or Afghanistan. The scale and scope of the question may be different, but the need to understand the unique characteristics of economics in a combat zone will be the same.

Notes

1. See, for example, Kenneth Pollack, *The Threatening Storm: The Case for Invading Iraq* (Random House, 2002).

2. See Leonard J. DeFrancisci, "Money as a Force Multiplier in COIN," *Military Review* (May–June 2008), 21–8; Center for Army Lessons Learned, *Commander's Guide to Money as a Weapon System*, Handbook no. 09-27 (April 2009); Jason W. Condrey, "The Commander's Emergency Response Program: A Model for Future Implementation" (Master's thesis, School of Advanced Military Studies, Ft. Leavenworth, KS, 2010).

3. Eli Berman, Jacob N. Shapiro, and Joseph H. Felter, "Can Hearts and Minds Be Bought? The Economics of Counterinsurgency in Iraq," *Journal of Political Economy*, vol. 119, no. 4 (August 2011), 766–819; Michael Fischerkeller, "The Premature Debate on CERP Effectiveness," *PRISM*, vol. 2, no. 4 (September 2011), 139–50.

4. Gian P. Gentile, "Freeing the Army From the Counterinsurgency Straightjacket," *Joint Force Quarterly*, iss. 58 (3rd Quarter 2010): 121–2; John Nagl, "Learning and Adapting to Win," *Joint Force Quarterly*, iss. 58 (3rd Quarter 2010): 123–4; Gian P. Gentile, "A Strategy of Tactics: Population-centric COIN and the Army," *Parameters* (August 2009), 5–17; Elisabeth Bumiller, "West Point Divided on War Doctrine's Fate," *New York Times* (27 May 2012). See also Frank G. Hoffman, "Future Threats and Strategic Thinking," *Infinity Journal*, vol. 1, no. 4 (Fall 2011); Hoffman; Dan G. Cox, Thomas Bruscino, and Alex Ryan, "Why Hybrid Warfare is Tactics Not Strategy: A Rejoinder to 'Future Threats and Strategic Thinking,'" *Infinity Journal*, vol. 2, no. 2 (Spring 2012).

5. "A Few Random Thoughts on COIN Theory and the Future," *Small Wars Journal*, accessed on 29 May 2012 at http://smallwarsjournal.com/blog/a-few-random-thoughts-on-coin-theory-and-the-future.

6. Carl J. Schramm, "Expeditionary Economics: Spurring Growth after Conflicts and Disasters," *Foreign Affairs* (May/June 2010), 89–99; Carl Schramm, "Institutionalizing Economic Analysis in the U.S. Military: The Basis for Preventive Defense," *Joint Force Quarterly*, issue 61 (2d quarter 2011): 32–8.

7. Ewing Marion Kaufmann Foundation, "Vision, Mission, and Approach," accessed at http://www.kauffman.org/about-foundation/vision-mission-and-approach.aspx on 30 May 2012.

8. Schramm, "Expeditionary Economics."

9. Schramm, "Institutionalizing Economic Analysis."

10. See, for example, Rebecca Patterson and Dane Stangler, "Building Expeditionary Economics: Understanding the Field and Setting Forth a Research Agenda," *Kaufmann Foundation Research Series: Expeditionary Economics* (November 2010); Jake Cusack and Erik Malmstrom, "Bactrian Gold: Challenges and Hope for Private-Sector Development in Afghanistan," *Kaufmann Foundation Research Series: Expeditionary Economics* (February 2011).

Entrepreneurial Expeditionary Economics and the United States Military Right Task, Wrong Tool?

by

Major Thomas J. Archer-Burton RHG/D - British Army

Abstract

Should the United States military alter current development practices by entwining entrepreneurial expeditionary economics into a new approach to the successful delivery of aid? This study explores whether the military is the right actor to deliver the policy of entrepreneurial expeditionary economics. Focusing on the current operational environment, evidence suggests that frustrations exist within the military over the progress of nongovernmental organizations and other government agencies in counterinsurgency environments, and this has resulted in a blurring of the military civilian relationship; this goes some way to explain the move towards the militarization of aid that is inherent within the concept of entrepreneurial expeditionary economics, which is at a pivotal point of inception. Much work is required to place entrepreneurial expeditionary economics in context with governance, political, social, and security efforts before the military should ascribe to the concept in its' current form. Notwithstanding the study's findings that entrepreneurial expeditionary economics has much potential in its' relevance to current and future military operations, there is little evidence that the military is the credible owner of the tools to engage in this form of development and weaknesses arise in both the conceptual realm and the practical reality of the entrepreneurial model as the driver for developmental change in counterinsurgency operations.

Introduction

Expeditionary economics is a concept first developed by the Kauffman Foundation in 2010. No definition of the concept yet exists, not least by the Kaufmann Foundation and the United States Military, yet as a tool to help commanders in post-conflict operations, it has received much positive attention. There is a movement developing to create an addendum to FM 3-24 in order to incorporate expeditionary economics, and studies are being conducted by West Point, The Kauffman Foundation, and the Council for Foreign Relations, to ensure buy-in from senior military leaders in accepting the relevancy of expeditionary economics and its' doctrinal importance.[1]

The concept is at a pivotal point of inception and much work is required to place the concept in context with governance, political, social, and security efforts. Expeditionary economics needs to be relevant to current and future operations, and be justified that the military is a credible owner of the tools to engage in this form of development.[2]

Expeditionary economics' background is traced to the economic models of Keynes and Hayek, and these must be understood to form any basis for combating economic crisis and implementing potential solutions. Although these two economists disagree on the fundamental nature of why economies collapse, the essential point is that both Hayekian and Keynesian frameworks assert that once an economy has collapsed, recovery takes a long time. For Hayek, recovery from a crisis caused by over-consumption and under-saving has to run its course, and cannot be speeded up by a Keynesian fiscal or monetary stimulus. It requires time before consumers recover from under-saving and business gains confidence that profitability can be restored. [3]

Keynesians believe that, once aggregate demand has subsided, a fiscal and monetary boost is the only way to get the economy growing again. Post-conflict environments are very different to the formal structures of the economies that Keynes and Hayek witnessed, and economic collapse in countries that have experienced conflict trace the roots not to the economic, but in the security and political sphere. Nevertheless, the model implied by expeditionary economics focuses on a western view of economic markets; how to impose this model into a non-Western framework is challenging, and arguably counterproductive. Essentially, the first part of the monograph will seek to define what expeditionary economics is, and why it is important.

FM 3-24 would appear to be the right document to express expeditionary economic doctrine. Current experience in Iraq and Afghanistan has shown that Soldiers are increasingly forced to rebuild economies without proper doctrinal or institutional support. Commanders on the ground are often left with little guidance as to how to develop post-conflict economics and the concept of expeditionary economics is thus designed to encompass the instances in which military and civilian expeditions must implicitly rebuild an economy. Fostering economic success, the third leg in the stool of diplomacy, defense, and development, needs clarification in doctrinal form in order to become an effective dimension of American expeditionary capacity. The second section of the monograph will seek to define who the players are in expeditionary economics, and specifically, their capabilities, limitations, and roles. The Commander's Emergency Response Program and other development programs will be analyzed as well as it relates directly to the expeditionary economics movement.

Expeditionary economics encompasses and informs many larger ideas about national security, strategy, and the exercise of power, and leaves itself open to the criticism of being a form of militarization of foreign policy. In trying to operationalize the concept, the final part of the monograph will seek to explore whether the military is the right actor to deliver the policy of entrepreneurship in a post-conflict environment, and is the main reason why this current study is being conducted.

The Importance of Economic Development

Why should the United States military be concerned and tasked with economic development? The military has been engaged equally, if not greater, in non-kinetic operations in the counterinsurgency efforts in Afghanistan and Iraq and the most recent case of Haiti is truly an attempt at a non-kinetic, humanitarian aid/economic development operation, all within the framework of delivering strategic success, yet economic progress within the countries that current operations focus upon has been limited. More than a decade after the United States and her allies entered into the Balkans, the social and economic dimension of conflict provides sparse evidence of strategic success. No less so in the current fight. The foundation of expeditionary economics promotes post-conflict economic entrepreneurial development and seeks to operationalize the concept by providing doctrine at the non-kinetic level.

From a historical stance, military involvement in economic entrepreneurial development is consistent with post-conflict circumstances. The Marshall Plan centered upon economic activity in rebuilding a war-ravaged Western Europe, and economic planning was at the heart of the strategic formulation of the United States' foreign policy. Underpinning this strategy was the notion that growth "provides the central basis for secure and stable countries, helping to strengthen the security of surrounding nations and the United States."[4] In an article in Foreign Affairs, Carl Schramm, the Chief Executive Officer of The Kauffman Foundation, argues that the United States military does not have these skills to partake successfully in the realm of economic development. He asserts:

> Post conflict economic reconstruction must become a core competence of the US military... It is imperative that the US military develops its competence in economics. It must establish a new field of inquiry that treats economic reconstruction as part of any successful three-legged strategy of invasion, stabilization or pacification, and economic reconstruction. Call this 'expeditionary economics.'[5]

Whether or not expeditionary economics is a new field of inquiry is dependent on how one perceives the role of the United States military, from a historical perspective, in its' role in nation-building. Engagement with economic activity has been an essential role of the military within, after, and contemporaneously with conflict, as was seen respectively with the Marshall Plan in Europe post World War II, the Balkans, and more recently in Afghanistan and Iraq. There is historical precedent for economic development to coexist as a mechanism to provide stability and security, but there has been little effort to provide a consistent approach to what the military's role should be when approaching economic development.

The recently produced National Security Strategy describes how the "Joint Force will redefine America's military leadership by enabling whole-of-nation approaches to address national security challenges."[6] The strategy states, "Military power complements economic development, governance, and rule of law – the true bedrocks of counterterrorism efforts."[7] It continues to define a mutually sustaining relationship between defense, diplomacy, and development, by claiming, "We will support whole-of-nation deterrence approaches that blend economic, diplomatic, and military tools to influence adversary behavior."[8] The whole-of-nation, or until recently termed whole-of-government approach, is viewed suspiciously by many within the United States military. Patterson and Stangler write, this "approach touted by the United States has usually meant an increase of bureaucracy as well as a focus on what can be measured: namely, the rate at which budgeted funds can be spent, irrespective of outcomes."[9] Furthermore, the military has undertaken the role of development under the backdrop of conflict, often referred to as opposed development: defined by the United State Institute for Peace as "development activities undertaken in the presence of an armed opposition."[10]

Expeditionary Economics as an Economic Concept

The majority of foreign aid is distributed through the means of government-to-government transfers. The services that this money is intended for not only seeks to affect intangible ideas, such as good governance, and the rise of civil society, but more importantly, seeks to contribute to economic growth. Foust demonstrates the skepticism concerning the practice of transfers of money to aid economic growth

> In practice… these money transfers tend to evade the reform of public services—negating their purpose. Studies of government behavior in aid relationships indicate that, often, the leadership of both donor and recipient governments instead tend to seek policies that protect their hold on power.[11]

Foust suggests that a way to alter the current modus operandi of developmental aid is to focus upon bottom-up, or community centered aid. Current models, focusing on top-down aid, support the host government and translate into intangible and ill-defined projects focusing on capacity building or major infrastructure projects. One such way of viewing the current developmental impetus is to categorize its focus on economic inputs as opposed to outputs. But a bottom-up approach can fall into the same trap; by continuing to measure success of community activity in terms of money spent over time devoted to a project, this approach misses a crucial element of considering areas such as the empowerment of civil society, and the needs of the non-politically aligned population. Ultimately, it is a truism to categorize the current thought on aid development, certainly in areas of the world in which there is a presence of United States forces, as being "driven by donor concerns and political arrangements in the recipient capital."[12]

Working through established institutions, such as host nation governments, local and international based non-government organizations, is where the provision of services is offered, denies civic and formal institutions the ability to engage fully with economic development and entrepreneurship. Little effort is made to allow these fringe organizations, who are politically autonomous, to become an effective enabler to economic growth and developmental partners. Expeditionary economics fundamentally challenges the current thinking of aid and suggests that at the heart of economic growth is the entrepreneur and that the existence of this actor predicates economic growth, which in turns, translates into fulfilling the national security aims and outcomes and promotes the security agenda of American politics.

Expeditionary economics challenges traditional thought that growth stems form that capacity and the good governance of a political system, but that individuals and businesses within a society can generate the outputs necessary for economic growth and the fulfillment of United States foreign policy. Under the concept of expeditionary economics, localized business development and entrepreneurial incentivizing replaces the international community and the host nation governments.

Carl Schramm loosely defines expeditionary economics as a new field of study that focuses on the delivery of assistance within a neatly defined threefold military strategy of invasion, stabilization, and economic reconstruction. He purports to the view that "The US military is well placed to play a leading role in bringing economic growth to devastated countries."[13] Carl Schramm is the President and CEO of the Ewing Marion Kauffman Foundation, a non-profit organization charged with pursuing the field of entrepreneurship. Schramm is perhaps the first to suggest the concept of expeditionary economics, and he has steered clear of in-depth attempts to formulize a doctrine for the military or a clear modus operandi for policy makers to incorporate this concept in to a meaningful method of delivering foreign policy aims. The Kauffman Foundation continues to explore this concept in conjunction with officers and academics aligned to the Department of Defense and a clear and unambiguous challenge has been given to the United States military in particular:

> The US military must therefore formulate a doctrine of expeditionary economics designed to spur solid growth as rapidly and effectively as possible. For this, it should draw on some of the more recent wisdom of the international development community -- a growing number of scholars are rejecting the decades-old doctrine of big plans and dictated reforms and turning instead to more modest yet more effective projects. Some military officers, in fact, have already been doing work along these lines. The military could then use the various means of influence at its disposal to steer international development practices in the direction of the new doctrine.[14]

What is interesting about Schramm's gauntlet, thrown to the military, is the implicit notion that the United States military are in the position, or more accurately, should be in the position, to alter current development practices and to weave expeditionary economics into a new approach to the successful delivery of aid. Schramm is cynical in regards to the comprehensive approach in the post-invasion of Iraq; he cites an example of the United States Agency for International Development as bypassing local civilians in the quest to hire American contractors for development projects. Although the Coalition Provincial Authority in Iraq sought to promote free trade and the development of a market economy, current developmental practice precluded an approach that created jobs and companies – the basis of his economic understanding of entrepreneurship.

Other economic areas which have failed to promote entrepreneurship lie in the field of micro-finance, which although creating individual employment, fails to generate the type of high-growth economy that Schramm seeks, and in developing economics, Schramm dismisses the view that micro-finance, as well as venture capital, is effective in inducing and sustaining entrepreneurship. The need for a new approach to development is highlighted by Schramm's dismissal of the Commander's Emergency Response Program, used by Commanders in Iraq and Afghanistan to rapidly disperse funds to infrastructure projects, often to rebuild infrastructure damaged by coalition war fighting activity. Employment is created by the Commander's Emergency Response Program, but at the neglect of long-term priorities, and creates a culture of dependency within the local populace.

Although it is difficult to discern what expeditionary economics ultimately calls for, it fundamentally rejects the notion that it is a blueprint for direct foreign investment by the United States. Ownership of businesses and the economic environment is implicitly tied to the local population, and although the presence of foreign direct investment and the positioning of multi-national corporations in host countries may provide an economic backdrop, it denies the chances of local businesses to exist by creating barriers to entry removing incentives for entrepreneurial activity. Schramm is also critical of previous attempts to boost the prospects of an economic recovery in areas of conflict by citing the example of Operation ADAM SMITH in Baghdad in 2004. CNN, reporting on this operation, highlight that that local Iraqis who actually participate in this operation were "within the embrace of US security and sell primarily to Americans," not who "the US government have in mind when they talk about rebuilding the country 'one business at a time.'"[15] The concept of expeditionary economics not only eliminates the need for the formalization of economic planning, but implicitly preludes the use of top down authoritarian initiatives, instead relying upon the local communities to have the knowledge and expertise to promote economic growth through their own initiative rather than that of a foreign entity.

Unlike in Operation ADAM SMITH, the concept of expeditionary economics rejects the need to dictate the process of privatization and to dictate best practices. Expeditionary economics fundamentally seeks to create economic growth by removing the current developmental tools, which provide barriers to economic growth. Inherent in Schramm's argument, is that current development models need to withdraw from the areas of aid in which support to business activity are delivered, and let the natural processes of economic growth occur, and focus development to those who conduct business, and support the entrepreneur.

It is equally important to understand what is implicitly missing from Schramm's ideas surrounding the concept of expeditionary economics. Of note, is the lack of "details necessary to pragmatically integrate 'expeditionary economics' into a working doctrine relevant and useful to military leaders."[16] Thus, for the military to embrace the idea of expeditionary economics, not only has it to agree on the strategic and operational relevance of the concept, but also to identify the "specific conditions under which the military might conduct 'expeditionary economics' and the specific objectives toward which the military applies the use of 'expeditionary economics.'"[17] The military face many challenges in both understanding of the concept and integrating the principles to the operational environment. If the United States military are to embrace Schramm's ideas, then doctrinal integration at the strategic, operational, and tactic level will be fundamental to the success of applying this development model.

The Military as an Expeditionary Economic Actor – a Path to Victory?

If the United States military is to take the lead during conflict for the imposition of expeditionary economics, as Schramm indicates, the question that should first be asked, is whether the military is the right actor to fulfill these developmental objectives? The evidence from recent stability operations point to the fact the United States military is already engaged in development and thus further questions must arise as to how to better use and adjust the current military practices?

In the post-Cold War environment, humanitarian, security, and peacekeeping operations became more prevalent, and the geographical footprint of the United States military expanded. A debate as to whether the military's involvement in operations other than war were a distraction to their main role of full combat operations, was ongoing when the events of 9/11 altered the parameters of the argument. Threats from unstable and weak states were directly addressed in the 2002 National Security Strategy. The strategy called upon the need for development to work side by side with diplomacy and defense to achieve the nation's security aims. The counterinsurgencies in Iraq and Afghanistan that followed the events of 9/11 created the operational tool of the Commander's Emergency Response Program (CERP) and Provincial Reconstruction Teams (PRTs). As Johnson, Ramachandran and Walz acknowledge:

The US Military responded diligently, incorporating the use of seized Iraqi funds to create a program that was designed to fund projects that would help stabilize military units' operating. This program evolved into the Commander's Emergency Response Program, which was formally initiated in late 2003, utilizing US appropriated funds, for both Iraq and Afghanistan. Units consisting of both civilian and military officials termed Provincial Reconstructions Teams (PRTs) were established in Afghanistan and later in Iraq, designed to enhance inter-agency cooperation, improve stability, and build capacity by working closely with local officials.[18]

Stability Operations subsequently became recognized as being a core mission for the United States Military, incorporating the need to provide security, to restore essential services, and to meet the humanitarian needs of the local populace, whilst fostering the long term development of indigenous capacity, promoting a viable market economy, democratic institutions, and the rule of law. "In short, in a span of just over 15 years, the US Military significantly altered its operational framework, increasing its responsibilities and requirements in an effort to improve stability where it is employed and engaged."[19]

The Commander's Emergency Response Program – Funding and Entrepreneurship

The use of financial aid in current operations in Afghanistan is realized in CERPs, which are a discretionary pool of money that the commanders on the ground can use in order to fund projects that improve the security environment in their area of operations. Security gains are paramount when commanders assess potential projects to inject capital, yet the assumption that security and economic growth are mutually reinforcing suggest that CERPs have a continued role in providing economic development within Afghanistan. Patterson and Robinson give an example of the usage of CERPS:

During the invasion of Iraq, US forces seized approximately $900 million from various locations across Iraq. In a brilliant military innovation in the aftermath of the invasion, many of the US military's first reconstruction projects used these seized funds in what was the genesis of the Commander's Emergency Response Program. The initial success of CERP was in large part due to its flexibility and responsiveness to the unique situations commanders faced on the ground. Over time, CERP has been increasingly burdened by process (the new standard operating procedure is 165 pages), degrading some of its early benefits. Its usage also expanded from smaller scale projects that could be effectively overseen by the military to larger scale development efforts that outstripped the military's oversight ability.[20]

In Iraq, the practice of using CERPs has expanded, and by 2010, the program received nearly four billion dollars in appropriations, and had become a fundamental tenant of counterinsurgency campaigns.[21] The ability to choose projects with CERP funding that fosters long-term economic growth is challenging, and a gap exists within the military in terms of expertise—creating problems with implementation and project oversight. The projects too, had to be aligned with the COIN objectives in the commander's area of operations. With increased understanding, fueled by experience, CERP has evolved to meet not only the emergency and security needs, but to encapsulate spending on water and sanitation infrastructure, food production and distribution, agriculture, electrical power generation and distribution, health care, education, telecommunications infrastructure, transportation infrastructure, rule of law and governance improvements, irrigation, civic cleanup activities, repair and construction of civic and cultural facilities, as well as incentivizing entrepreneurship and small businesses formation.[22]

Crucially, a centrally managed process has not brought about obvious success to within the delivery of aid through CERPs'. Rather, commanders on the ground have used their judgment to determine which projects are likely to aid security, and in turn, harness the potential for the entrepreneurial economic progress that Schramm posits in his quest to have the United States military embrace expeditionary economics. The evidence from CERPs suggests that there is not the entrepreneurial vacuum that Schramm postulates.

Schramm's ideology has an important role to play when assessing CERPs, and his insight gives those commanders who are involved with CERPs the opportunity to reevaluate the long-term implications of the projects that are identified. Schramm's view of expeditionary economics is a useful conceptual tool to impose upon commanders when aspiring to make the programs as effective as possible. His theory also correctly asserts that the role of the military in economic development should not be limited to the current fight, and the current CERP model has inherent internal flexibility to be used in future conflict. As Johnson, Ramachandran, Walz, rightly assert, "The US Military is already substantially engaged in the development realm beyond stability efforts, and it is likely that the military will continue conducting development-like projects in parts of Afghanistan, the Philippines, and in other areas of the globe, for years to come." [23] The discussion of whether the United States military is involved in development is not disputed, and the examination of how to make this involvement as effective as possible is inherent within the debate surrounding expeditionary economics.

The Center for Army Lessons Learned in the United States have gathered a comprehensive set of data on CERPs and advises upon what works and what is likely to fail in the provision of security and economic development. A thorough evaluation of the data is needed, with statistical quantitative analysis brought into the economic development realm. Until this effort is achieved, and further research carried out, it will be difficult to draw tangible lessons from Iraq and Afghanistan, and subsequently apply them to future conflict areas where CERP is administered.

Opposed Development

Whilst we have asserted that the United States military already practice expeditionary economics to some degree in Afghanistan and Iraq, other scholars have coined the current approach by the military in engaging with economic development, as that of opposed development. Kilcullen is a leading counterinsurgency expert and served as Senior COIN Advisor to General David Petraeus, Commanding General, Multi-National Force, Iraq. Kilcullen coined opposed development as the scenario that faces coalition forces in Iraq and Afghanistan.[24] Opposed development incorporates an operational environment where not only is there an active presence of terrorist actors, but these actors compete for our own development programs, thus offering the target population a choice between the development procedures and objectives as the coalition effort, and those offered by the insurgents.

Kilcullen's theory of opposed development is relevant to the debate over expeditionary economics for the principle reason that it challenges the notion that development and stability work in harmony. This challenge, in turn, questions the philosophical underpinnings of CERPs and the current modus operandi of the United States military in Afghanistan and Iraq. His arguments resonant with the logic of General Rupert Smith who argues:

> There is no such thing as impartial governance or humanitarian or humanitarian assistance. In this environment, every time you help someone, you hurt someone else.[25]

Smith accurately pinpoints the problematic nature of development in the midst of an insurgency. Development, especially in the form that CERPs currently practice, creates winners as well as losers, which has the potential to fuel destabilization.

If development is to be successful, then the practitioners, no matter which theory provides the fundamental philosophical basis of their development model, must realize that the actions, be it of non-government organizations, government development workers, or militaries, exist as a direct challenge to the grass-roots control of the local population, and their efforts will necessarily react with the ensuing violence. Regardless of the cognitive backdrop to any development activity, there is a complex interaction between the political characteristics of the insurgents' movement, the population, the local and national governance, the counterinsurgent, and all other external actors, which drive the characteristics of a particular counterinsurgency campaign.

There is a fundamental difference between conducting counterinsurgency operations in a hostile or occupied foreign country, and conducting counterinsurgency operations in a territory one seeks to control. Kilcullen describes counterinsurgency operations as "an armed variant of domestic politics in which numerous challengers compete for control over the population."[26] Galula seeks to codify the military's role in counterinsurgency by asserting that essentially, "A revolutionary war is 20 per cent military action and 80 per cent political"[27], thus placing military action as secondary to political action, and relegating the military's role as primarily being within the realm of affording the political power enough freedom to work safely with the population. Galula expounds on this idea by arguing that in giving the soldier authority over the civilian, would contradict one of the major characteristics of this type of war. In practice, it would inevitably tend to reverse the relative importance of military versus political action and move the counterinsurgent's warfare closer to a conventional one. Were the armed forces the instrument of a party and their leaders high-ranking members of the party, controlled and assisted by political commissars having their own direct channel to the party's central direction, then giving complete authority to the military might work; however, this describes the general situation of the insurgent, not of his opponent. [28]

Kilcullen notes that in 2006, United States spending in Iraq for the year 2003 to 2006, accorded to 1.4 percent civilian, and 98.6 percent military.[29] This seems out of kilter with the fundamental tenants of counterinsurgency warfare as laid out by David Galula. Although much of the military spending in Iraq was, and continues to be, directed at political programs and military operations supporting political objectives, thus distorting the statistic, 1.4 percent spending on civilian programs is an alarming figure, no matter how one interprets the data or Galula's ratio for the successful prosecution of counterinsurgency warfare.

Furthermore, if the fundamental requirements for a successful counterinsurgency campaign, as identified by United States Field Manual 3-24, is that of control, then the current development practices of the United States military, in its' use of CERPs, engages in a much wider set of objectives that it seeks to influence; CERPs are currently used to legitimize some of the US military's actions, and are also designed to create local population good will as well as development assistance.

The multiple objectives for CERPs underline the cognitive tension that exists between stability and development. This tension is embodied by the relationship between United States Agency for International Development and the United States military, and described by Johnson et al, as a continuum of activities.

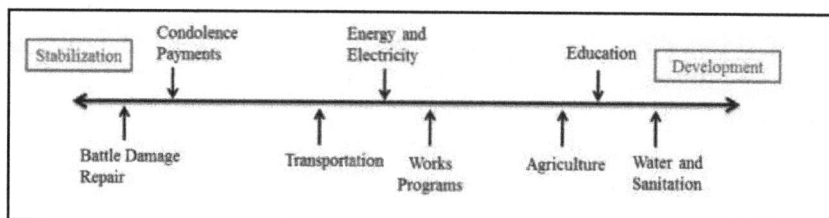

Figure 1: The Stabilization-Development Continuum.[30]
Source: Author.

The continuum identifies that there is no clear delineation between stability and development activity and as a result, the activity of the United States Agency for International Development and the United States military operate concurrent of time, space, and purpose.

Another way of understanding this cognitive tension is by describing the tension that exists between visibility and viability, as suggested by Andrew Natsios, a former administrator of United States Agency for International Development.[31] Natsios suggests that visible development projects, such as road construction and food aid, identified as being direct from the United States government, aid the process of legitimization, and are designed to win the hearts and minds of the local population. These projects are easily identifiable by the insurgents, and as such, the local population will become inevitable targets. Development aid projects that are not visible to the local population, *de facto* the insurgents, blend into the local economy, and the identification of the intended and realized recipient becomes difficult. The invisibility of aid tackles General Rupert Smith's aforementioned dilemma of every time you help someone you hurt someone else.

The continuum does not seek to resolve this cognitive tension between development and stabilization; rather, it seeks to make practitioners aware of the challenges that CERPs and other development projects face in a counterinsurgency environment, in which control is the underlying principle. The challenges presented by this cognitive tension run through the heart of Galula's definition of victory in counterinsurgency:

> A victory is not [just] the destruction in a given area of the insurgent's forces and his political organization… A victory is that plus the permanent isolation of the insurgent from the population, isolation not enforced upon the population but maintained by and with the population.[32]

Operationalize or Decouple? Other Actors in Expeditionary Economics

Some of the major doubts about the concept of expeditionary economics occur in the realm of the practical realities of operationalization. Whether or not the United States military should expand upon its' current role within Afghanistan and Iraq, to incorporate Schramm's ideas, and harness its capabilities to include taking on the role of developing economies as a central part of their activities, lies at the heart of the debate over expeditionary economics.

The 2011 National Military Strategy affirms, "Our military power is most effective when employed in support and in concert with other elements of power as part of whole-of-nation approaches to foreign policy."[33] The Chairman of the Joint Chiefs of Staff emphasizes in the document that whilst there is continual refinement of how we counter violent extremism and deter aggression, the is emphases on military power as most effectively employed when in concert with other elements of national power. Reinforcing a whole-of-nation approach to foreign policy, the strategy cites that civilian leadership is appropriately at the helm, as is fundamental to addressing the complex characteristics of the security challenges faced.

The National Security Strategy was updated in 2011 for the first time in seven years. The whole-of-nation approach is designed as a broad strategy, which not only includes security forces to counter specified and non-specified security challenges, but also incorporates the diplomatic and development communities too. In a sweeping rebuke of the employment of United States Agency for International Development, Kori Schake argues:

> The military is the only part of the 'whole-of-government operations' that is doing its job well… When the country has Soldiers, sailors, airmen, and Marines in

harm's way, the nonmilitary agencies have an ethical responsibility as well as a practical need to get good at their jobs, and fast.[34]

For Schake, the civilian arms of our government must engage with the world as they are central to the successful delivery of the tasks American national security policy outlines. Rather than encapsulating the United States military into conducting tasks that are in the realm of the United States Agency for International Development, civilian agencies should realize their capacity and engage with the challenges of the current security environment instead of leaving the military to do what is essentially the responsibility of civilian agencies. In essence, Schake argues that instead of making the United States military the United States Agency for International Development, civilian agencies should become good at they are designed to do.

Schake's argument does not imply that the military should take on more responsibility because of its successes. Rather, the whole-of-nation approach, as identified in the 2011 National Security Strategy, should be reinforced at the operational level. The problem with Schake's stance, is that explicit within the argument, is the assertion that "Economic development is not the work of the Department of Defense."[35] This disregards the cognitive tension that exists between stabilization and development, and implies that the two conceptual realms are mutually exclusive, rather than mutually reinforcing, as has been shown through Johnson, Ramachandran, and Walz's continuum. Furthermore, it is equally problematic to assess that the Department of Defense's current practices that engage with economic development occur as a direct result of nonmilitary agencies, in particular United States Agency for International Development, having failed to "deliver on their responsibilities of creating a foundation for economic prosperity."[36]

Nevertheless, Schake invokes the right question: should the United States military be the agents to deliver Schramm's concept of expeditionary economics. If economic development is an aid to victory in a counterinsurgency, then military participation, heightened understanding of the principles governing economic aid, and an acute awareness of what contextually works and what does not, is fundamental to success. However, this does not necessarily imply a lead role for the military. If Schramm is correct in his assertion that the "US military planners and US troops on the ground often turn to US and international development agencies or nongovernmental organizations (NGOs) for practical guidance on improving local economic conditions only to find that the putative experts are little help,"[37] then perhaps what is being identified, is the cognitive tension between stabilization and development, rather than a call to arms for the military to autonomously conduct development.

Schalke is right to question Schramm's notion that:

it is not enough merely to restore the economy to a level resembling the pre-crisis status quo. The economy is part of the problem.[38]

The implication of Schramm comments here suggest that the military should engage in development tasks long after the security environment is stable. Heightened military engagement in economic development could, however, led to what Kilcullen describes as the kiss-of-death scenario. This scenario depicts the military surging into areas and introducing civil programs, which, in turn, exposes moderates and cooperative leaders to insurgents. As security improves, the military reduce their presence, and consequently, the insurgents kill those who cooperated with the initial military surge.[39]

The use of existing power structures in Iraq and Afghanistan, combined with other government agencies are more likely to avoid the kiss-of-death scenario. In Iraq, evidence suggests that the Sheik's proactive stance discourages Sunni insurgent activity, and in Afghanistan, warlords are also in a position to prevent Taliban incursions.[40] This suggests that there may be better-suited actors than the military to set the conditions for both stabilization and development; it does not purport to Schramm's notion that the military are the key players to set these conditions.

Schramm goes much further than suggesting that the military should be the prime actor in the stabilization and development continuum. Schramm states:

The US military must therefore formulate a doctrine of expeditionary economics designed to spur solid growth as rapidly and effectively as possible. For this, it should draw on some of the more recent wisdom of the international development community—a growing number of scholars are rejecting the decades-old doctrine of big plans and dictated reforms and turning instead to more modest, yet more effective projects. Some military officers, in fact, have already been doing work along these lines. The military could then use the various means of influence at its disposal to steer international development practices in the direction of the new doctrine.[41]

The notion that the military will be in a position to demonstrate both practice and procedures, to not only the development community and nongovernmental organizations, but to agencies such as the World Bank and the IMF, is stretching to the limit, the realms of operational and conceptual possibilities It also places an unnecessary burden on the United states military, whom possess limited technical, strategic, or operational experience, and renders non military organizations as periphery and unimportant to the current operational environment. This would further challenge the assertion that the whole of nation approach in the newly updated National Security Strategy is out of kilter with how the operational environment in counterinsurgency should be orchestrated.

The military should not be seen in isolation within the whole-of-nation approach. Neither should the military be ignorant to other government agencies and nongovernmental organization's capability and capacity to serve as the mechanism for coordinating "unique departmental activities, correcting for the current militarization of activity in theaters of military operations."[42]

Blurring the Civil-Military Divide

There has been criticism of the United States strategy in Afghanistan that points to the heart of the debate surrounding the militarization of aid. Following the initial intervention in Afghanistan in 2001, stabilization and development objectives were arguably sidelined in favor of pursuing Islamic terrorists.[43] If indeed, the "consequent lack of success in developing a functional and effective Afghan government, and in promoting development, especially in rural areas, has… contributed to the deterioration in security conditions," then it follows that Schramm's emphasis in using the military as the solution to the counterinsurgency fails to match the opinion that military solutions alone are unable to create long term economic development and stabilization in Afghanistan. There is little agreement about how and whom the actors involved should orchestrate operations in Afghanistan, yet the international focus has tended to lean heavily on the military capabilities, or perceived capabilities, at the expense of other worthy actors. The existence of community defense initiatives, and the expansions of PRTs, suggests that there is a creeping militarization of aid. An Oxfam report highlights that overall United States spending on current military operations in Afghanistan is twenty times that of spending on development; the US military currently spends $35 billion a year, nearly $100 million a day, whilst spending for USAID is $1.6 billion a year, $4.4 million a day.[44]

Further opposing Schramm's view on the military as the prime conductors of expeditionary economics is the evidence from Afghanistan's recent checkered past, where foreign militaries have yielded only short-term security advances and have failed in the quest for long term stability. A truly comprehensive strategy, or to use the National Security Strategy parlance, whole of nation approach, to the long-term development and security of the current counterinsurgency fight in Afghanistan, is surely the right approach to enable the stabilization and development continuum to permeate all activities by coalition nations operating in Afghanistan.

This view reinforces ISAF's approach to acknowledging the inherent limitations to the suitability and legitimacy of their prosecution of operations in Afghanistan. The military's prime focus should be on providing security; civilian actors should, in partnership with security operations, focus on the implementation and long-term ownership of reconstruction, development and humanitarian challenges that are mutually reinforcing to the stabilization of the country. There exists the further complexity of regional stability that both directly and indirectly affects the strategy in Afghanistan.

Just as military and civilian tensions exist in Afghanistan, so too is the tension in Pakistan. As Auil Shah argues that although Pakistan is unlikely to collapse, the imbalance of power between its civilian and military branches must be addressed if it is to fulfill security demands and become a normal functioning modern state that is able to effectively governing its territory. "For its part, the United States must resist using the generals as shortcuts to stability, demonstrate patience with Pakistan's civilian authorities, and help them consolidate their hold on power."[45]

This does not negate the need for reform, and further suggests that much of Schramm's philosophy should be embraced within the civilian organizational realm. Nongovernmental organizations and other government agencies must enhance the effectiveness of aid, thereby diminishing the dependency effect. They must also allow for governance reform that both supports the stabilization and development continuum, and achieves Afghan accountability and transparency at all levels. In sum, policy-makers must recognize the lack of clarity and coherence in the existing international approach to Afghanistan, especially in the pursuit of critical development, governance and stabilization objectives. "In order to succeed, a comprehensive strategy urgently requires a substantial, coordinated and long-term international commitment, both in terms of resources and political will."[46]

Civil Military Synchronization

There are guidelines for civilian and military agency interaction endorsed by the Commander of ISAF and the United Nations. Waldman et al cite that these guidelines maintain, "A clear distinction between the role and function of humanitarian actors from that of the military [which] is a determining factor in creating an operating environment in which humanitarian organizations can discharge their responsibilities both effectively and safely."[47] Due in part to the frustrations of the military over progress that nongovernmental organizations and other government agencies are making in counterinsurgency environments, a blurring of the military civilian relationship has occurred. These frustrations, felt on behalf of the military, may explain to a certain degree, the militarization of aid that is contained within Schramm's concept of expeditionary economics.

The frustration is not just borne by actors in the military community; in the nongovernmental organizations and other government agencies, there is a suspicion of the relevancy and effectiveness of military progress within Afghanistan. One such "egregious example of military forces acting contrary to the Civil-Military Guidelines is the use by military personnel of certain contingents, apparently including the US, France and Spain, of unmarked, white vehicles, conventionally used by humanitarian organizations."[48]These actions breach the guidelines of civil military activity as well as a potentially more serious breach of international humanitarian law, which demand that combatants must distinguish themselves from civilians in conflict. These accusations underline the friction between the military and their civilian partners.

If this friction is to lead to the military taking on the prime responsibility to deliver economic developmental aid in the current counterinsurgency environment, the operational reach of nongovernmental organizations and other government agencies will diminish, and attempts to implement the direction of the National Security Strategy will falter. Furthermore, ISAF's current understanding of the shared responsibility for delivering stabilization and development in partnership with nongovernmental organizations and other government agencies should become more transparent if other actors outside of the military were more, rather than less, involved in an integrated approach to operations that seek to deliver the framework of expeditionary economics.

Identifying Success – Comprehensive Economic Development

Expeditionary economics' call for harnessing an entrepreneurial environment lacks an accompanying practical implementation model, but addresses some of the military failures of operational conduct over the previous ten years of conflict. One example of this is identified by Riegg, who states that in Iraq:

The Army not only put $10.8 billion into infrastructure, and only a pittance toward entrepreneurial stimulation, it also gave everything to the Iraqi government (or to ill-structured local cooperatives) at no cost and with no conditions attached. Such largesse simply breeds contempt. It conveys the impression that the United States owes Iraq restitution for the invasion and undermines the message that countries that act the way Iraq acted under Saddam Hussein will suffer the consequences. Also, by simply giving everything away, we missed a great opportunity to help Iraq develop a more powerful private, entrepreneurial sector within its economy.[49]

Conditionality attached to aid has been practiced by the development community for many years and is enshrined within the Washington Consensus approach to developmental assistance.

Giving away aid, with little accountability of conditions attached, circumnavigates potential opportunities to strengthen local economic environments. The Provincial Reconstruction Teams are not immune from criticism in this regard, even with the imbedded civilian actors that are currently employed. Provincial Reconstruction Teams have employed a method in Iraq of asking village and community leaders what infrastructure they need to improve economic conditions:

> The Army or USAID then goes in, builds what is needed, and simply turns it over to the local community, free of charge. If instead we insisted that the community pay for some or all of these projects, we might get more respect and more active participation by the community in them.[50]

These program have the capability of stimulating the development of municipal bonds and bond markets, allows for charging adequate user fees, properly maintains new infrastructure, facilitates more efficient, cost-effective approaches to construction, and critically, uses local talent and resources.

Capital dispersed through Provincial Reconstruction Teams may undermine the local economy's ability to provide such goods and services and undercut the natural efficient markets that Schramm is so keen to foster. These projects may serve to also build upon the culture of dependency and entitlement, undermine the work ethic, and build the illusion that the Afghan government will be in a situation to continue to provide many services which expeditionary economics would rather encourage through pure entrepreneurial capitalism, that feeds back to the government through taxation, and provides revenue for the host country to provide essential public provision.

In addressing the debate surrounding the activity of Provincial Reconstruction Teams, eight non-governmental organizations, currently working in Afghanistan (and have been for up to fifty years) have written a report highlighting the dangers of the militarization of aid.[51] The report goes further than Riegg in criticizing Provincial Reconstruction Teams, and calls for their complete, though gradual, removal from theater. The report states that, Military-dominated institutions, such as Provincial Reconstruction Teams, often:

> lack the capacity to manage effective development initiatives, even where civilians are inserted into these structures. They are unable to achieve the level of local trust, engagement and community ownership required to achieve positive and lasting improvements to Afghan lives.

In so many cases, Provincial Reconstruction Teams in insecure environments rely on local contracting companies who have limited capacities, and weak links to communities. They are often wasteful, ineffective and corrupt.

Inherent within the report is the suggestion that the military approach to aid in Afghanistan focuses directly on winning the loyalty of the local populace rather than incorporating the alleviation of poverty and other humanitarian focuses. The report cites a

United States army manual for troops in Afghanistan and Iraq, to highlight the military's definition of aid as a nonlethal weapon that is utilized to "win the hearts and minds of the indigenous population to facilitate defeating the insurgents."[52] Criticisms of the current military approach are levied at the unintended consequences for governance reform and the validity and sustainability of Afghan institutions. "In assuming some of the responsibilities that the Afghan government should be fulfilling, PRTs may weaken government accountability to the Afghan people."[53] Perhaps the most damning conclusion of the report, is the assessment that "There is also increasing evidence that military involvement in development activities may be putting Afghans on the frontlines of the conflict."[54] The British and Irish Afghanistan Group (BAAG) that monitor activity in Afghanistan endorse this view. [55]

As a sweeping rebuff to the suggestion by Schramm that expeditionary economics should be seized by the military as a tool to provide economic development, the BAAG recommends the phasing out of Provincial Reconstruction Teams whilst simultaneously increasing the capacity and funding of civilian organizations and increasing the footprint on the ground. Furthermore, the coordinating authority for economic development is suggested as being most beneficial under the auspices of the United Nations.

The opposition to the militarization of aid comes not only from the development community, who stand much to lose if the path to increased military power over developmental aid is affected, but also from the United Nations. The Special Representative of the Secretary-General, Kai Eide, asserts that the international community needs to demilitarize their overall approach in Afghanistan if it is to reverse the current trend of unsuccessful economic developmental aid.[56] Speaking to journalists in Kabul, Eide said: "We have to get into a mode where our strategy is politically driven and not militarily driven, where the political and civilian components become an appendix to a military strategy," Eide is skeptical of the increase in military forces in Afghanistan, especially where military forces engage in the political, civilian and humanitarian realms:

> When you have an increased number of troops coming in, there will always be a trend for those forces to demonstrate quick results and take upon themselves political tasks. That leads to quick impact… quick impact very often becomes quick collapse.[57]

Eide's concern regarding the military engaging in the political, civilian, and humanitarian realm, are explicitly addressed in the new Field Manual 3.0 (FM 3.0), Operations. This Field Manual presents the United States military's overarching doctrinal guidance and direction for conducting operations. FM 3.0 states:

> The foundations for Army operations are contained in its operational concept—full spectrum operations. The goal of full spectrum operations is to apply land power as part of unified action to defeat the enemy on land and establish conditions that achieve the joint force commander's end state. The complexity of today's operational environments requires commanders to combine offensive, defensive, and stability or civil support tasks to reach this goal. Commanders direct the application of full spectrum operations to seize, retain, and exploit the initiative and achieve decisive results.[58]

Within the area of stability or civil support tasks, the engagement in the political, civilian, and humanitarian realm is both necessary and prescribed.

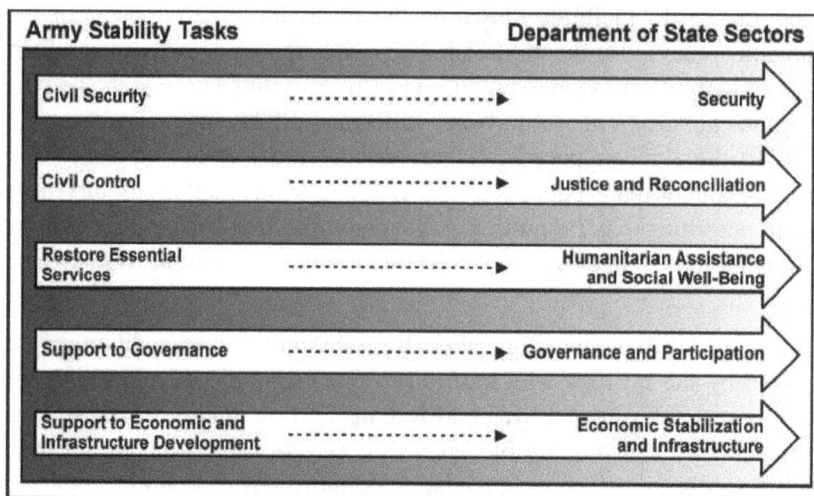

Army Stability Tasks		Department of State Sectors
Civil Security	·····················▶	Security
Civil Control	·····················▶	Justice and Reconciliation
Restore Essential Services	·····················▶	Humanitarian Assistance and Social Well-Being
Support to Governance	·····················▶	Governance and Participation
Support to Economic and Infrastructure Development	·····················▶	Economic Stabilization and Infrastructure

Figure 2. Stability Tasks and Department of State Technical Sectors
Source: Author.

Figure 2, from FM 3.0, demonstrates that the core army stability tasks are linked to that of the Department of State's post-conflict reconstruction and stabilization technical sectors, security, justice and reconciliation, humanitarian assistance and social well-being, governance and participation, and economic stabilization and infrastructure:

Normally, Army forces act to support host-nation and other civilian agencies. However, when the host nation cannot provide basic government functions, Army forces may be required to do so directly.[59]

Full spectrum operations conducted by the United States military in accordance with FM 3.0 require continuous, simultaneous combinations of offensive, defensive, and stability (for operations outside of the United States) or civil support tasks (for operations inside the United States). The practice of the simultaneous combination of offensive, defensive and stability elements require military officers to work within the political, civilian, and humanitarian realm. United States military officials must put aside the Special Representative of the United Nations Secretary-General's criticism of their approach during this current insurgency, if they are to follow the tenants of FM 3.0.

This continual tension that remains between the military planners and those in civilian authority are charged by the National Security Strategy to practice a comprehensive approach to operations, and any debate that calls for more civilian input, or more military input, into the realm of economic developmental aid, too often miss the central and partnered ground that a comprehensive approach offers.

In forming a comprehensive approach to the implementation of expeditionary economics, the military, nongovernmental organizations, and other government agencies, may partner to determine priorities for a free market system that operates conceptually within a counterinsurgency environment. How much integration is needed will depend upon at what stage of the campaign the current environment dictates; yet within the framework of full spectrum operations, simultaneous comprehensive effort is always required.

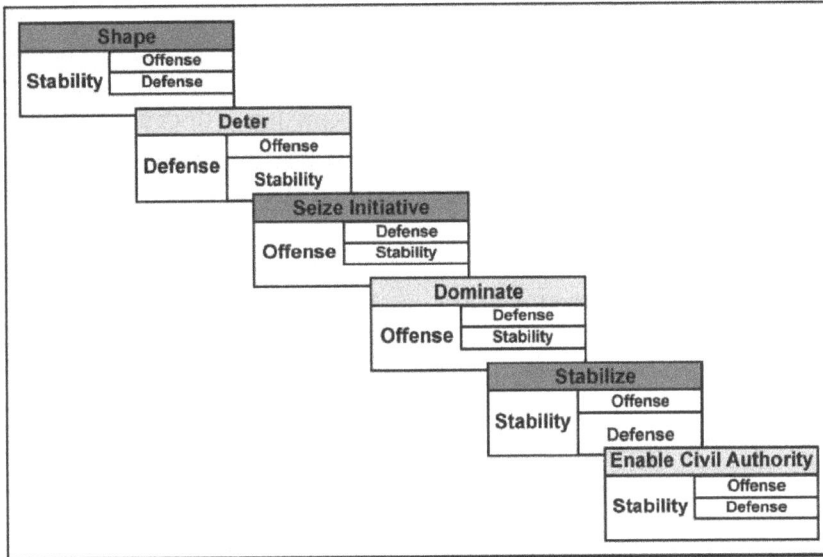

Figure 3. Example of combining the elements of full spectrum operations in a notional campaign.[60]
Source: Author.

As figure 3 depicts, from a purely military stance, conducting a notional full spectrum operation that involves more than just simultaneous execution of all its elements. In addition, it requires commanders and staffs to consider their own particular capabilities and capacities relative to each element. This is true of all nongovernmental organizations and other government agencies involved across the stabilization and development continuum, and not just for the military.

Conditions are fluid in any counterinsurgency campaign, and actors at all levels should consider the concurrent conduct of each element. As is shown in figure 3, the offensive, defensive and stability (or civil support) combinations are weighted differently across the phases of a campaign. The phases in the notional example will necessarily be tailored differently for every unique scenario, and it is in the application of operational art in full spectrum operations that determines when, and if, simultaneous combinations are appropriate and feasible.

Incorporating stability operations into full spectrum operations in a counterinsurgency environment needs the United States military to embrace the comprehensive approach and seek the expertise of nongovernmental organizations and other government agencies whose partnership will be the enabler for success. One example of how the army can use these other elements of national power is in the understanding of the operational environment and how to best administer economic developmental aid to facilitate stabilization within full spectrum operations. A thorough conceptual understanding of this theory will lead to a hesitation to identify specific doctrinal solutions to a given counterinsurgency environment.

For example, the economic aid that is necessary in Iraq, differ greatly from that of Afghanistan. The degree of free market economic principles that can allow for fulfilling the maximum potential of rational economic actors need different forms of governance in order to address different host country challenges.

One such example is the foreign exchange position of Afghanistan, which differs from Iraq; export industry is nonexistence in the former, save for the illegal opium and poppy market. To industrialize an economy, the host nation has to reform its economic structure and develop an export-orientated market that is labor intense, and focused on manufacturing. Entrepreneurial private sector expansion may be needed more in Afghanistan than is the case in Iraq, where economic structures already focus on export led growth. Conversely, the government in Afghanistan may have to employ more Keynesian style economic principles to facilitate growth, and develop state owned enterprises, especially as there is no current significant tax income for the government, or residual accumulated wealth. Although Afghanistan necessarily relies upon the private sector and entrepreneurial expeditionary economics that lead to prosperity, Afghan government led control will also facilitate meaningful economic development.

Riegg accurately portrays the situation by drawing attention to the interrelationship of development and security:

> Whether Afghanistan will be able to follow an entrepreneurial path to development will depend on a couple of noneconomic factors, as well as the usual needs of good property and commercial law, functioning labor markets, a stable currency, and so on. In particular, society, its tribes and clans, will have to end their fighting and establish real peace and adequate security. Society will also have to embrace factory culture, probably including the legitimacy of young, unmarried women working in factories where occasionally male supervisors might check on the quality of their work. The alternative may be to develop and rely on women supervisors, possibly brought from other cultures where they are permitted to interact with men. If these societal issues can be worked out, Afghanistan will still have to compete with other countries to attract investment capital. Investors will need a reason to choose Afghanistan versus, for example, Kenya, Nicaragua, or Bangladesh.[61]

Conclusion

Reigning in an Isolated Concept

A full-scale push to implement expeditionary economics, not just by the military, but also by nongovernmental organizations and other government agencies, will limit the type of Keynesian response to governing the economic backdrop that long-term growth demands. Far from a rejecting the conceptual premise of expeditionary economics, there is a realization that weaknesses arise in both the conceptual realm and the practical reality of the entrepreneurial model as the driver for developmental change in counterinsurgency operations. These weaknesses occur in time, space, and thought. Entrepreneurial firms, many of whom fail, need a great amount of time in order for large-scale production to develop and tangible influence on the wider economy is realized; time creates a vacuum, with little external control to prevent unethical and unproductive economic governance of the economic environment, and an opportunity for the insurgent to dominate. This lack of governance, if remained unchecked, will increase the monopolization of firms in the market place, and drive barriers to entry, which dampens subsequent entrepreneurial activity, and weakens the competitive market.

The successes in Iraq to build an entrepreneurial economy, led to the privatization of many state-owned enterprises. This effort combined with building infrastructure, has not seen many positive signs of rousing an entrepreneurial revolution. Notwithstanding the obvious limitation to successful entrepreneurial developmental aid within the midst of an insurgency, far too much developmental aid has been given away unattached to any form of conditionality. This has created a degree of dependency and dampened the conditions for a successful entrepreneurial economy to flourish.

So too in Afghanistan, where there are seldom links between good governance and economic developmental aid; consequentially, this has inhibited the capacity and capability for the entrepreneurial environment. Unquestionably, Iraq and Afghanistan, and many other counties too, would benefit from adopting more entrepreneurial approaches to development, and the effects of neglecting this necessary approach to developmental aid permeates not only in the economic realm, but also into the political and social environment. An exclusive concentration on entrepreneurial expeditionary economics as a concept, and the rate of entrepreneurial growth as a judgment of success, has a most damaging effect. Entrepreneurial expeditionary economic growth offers the opportunity to improve people's lives in a counterinsurgency environment, but single-minded emphasis on developmental aid from the United States military has limitations that need clear understanding.[62]

In seeking an answer to whether the military is the right actor to deliver the policy of entrepreneurship in a post-conflict environment, this work acknowledges the benefits of expeditionary economics in a post-conflict environment, but raises concerns over whether the military should be the actor to deliver this policy. If a whole-of-nation strategy is to be realized, then other government agencies must become serious about employing their expertise and resources to complement the military. The development community posses the necessary intellectual and authoritative capability to engage upon expeditionary economics, but must avoid giving the military reason to doubt this capacity. In addition, both military and civilian actors must not seek to blur the distinction between military and civilian roles. Although complex counterinsurgency environments will challenge the ability to impart a military-civilian divide, expeditionary economics is a concept that can help to ensure the appropriation of agencies that allows for the military to do less than they imagine they can do, and for the development community to do more than they fear.

In trying to build a bottom-up approach to spurring economic growth, expeditionary economics (regardless of whom the actor) must avoid a fundamental approach through top-down implementation. Cognizant of a top-down approach to governance and security reforms such as building military capacity, judicial systems, and police forces in Iraq and Afghanistan, the approach to expeditionary economics must invert current capacity building thought to encapsulate the bottom-up approach to effect entrepreneurial activity and capacity.

Furthermore, the absence of specific literature that affirms the success of implementing the broad themes of expeditionary economics within a post-conflict or counterinsurgency environment, should provide the United States military with the good judgment to be cautious about embracing an unknown, in a field they are, as yet, ill-equipped to encounter.

In sum, the question of whether expeditionary economics is the right task remains unanswered, amongst the backdrop of insufficient literature and statistical analysis of the environment. Whether the military, by default or not, is the right tool to implement expeditionary economics, is cautiously refuted.

Notes

1. Ideas in Action, "Is DOD the New AID? Tasking Soldiers with Economic Development," http://www.ideasinactiontv.com/episodes/2010/10/is-dod-the-new-aid-tasking-Soldiers-with-economic-development.html (accessed January 22, 2011).

2. "In 2010, Carl Schramm, the president and CEO of the Ewing Marion Kauffman Foundation, published a paper in Foreign Affairs entitled "Expeditionary Economics." Arguing that the economies of Iraq and Afghanistan have shown few signs of progress, Schramm makes the case for the US military to engage broadly in mid-conflict and post-conflict reconstruction, using a variety of tools. Economic reconstruction must be a part of a three-legged strategy along with invasion and stabilization. To do reconstruction, the US Military needs to expand its areas of competence, rid itself of its central planning mentality and become a more flexible force that can facilitate economic growth at the same time that it is trying to stabilize the regions in which it is engaged. Schramm argues for modest yet effective projects, saying that "job diversity" in the private sector is very important and requires a wide range of interventions, well beyond the relatively narrow set of activities that the US Military currently funds in places like Iraq and Afghanistan. "Messy capitalism" requires the military to allow and even foster various forms of entrepreneurial activity to emerge, in an uncontrolled and even chaotic manner, from which a robust private sector can be created." Gregory Johnson, Vijaya Ramachandran and Julie Walz, "The Commanders Emergency Response Program in Afghanistan & Refining US Military Capabilities in Stability and in Conflict Development" USMA Senior Conference XLVII http://www.dean.usma.edu/sosh/senior_conference/sc_papers/Ramachandran%20EE%20final%205%2019%202011.pdf (accessed 12 June 2012).

3. This idea is expanded upon by Yergin, Daniel, and Stanislaw, Joseph. *The Commanding Heights: the Battle for the World Economy*. (New York: Simon & Schuster, 2002), ch. 4.

4. Command and General Staff College *Entrepreneurship and Expeditionary Economics: Towards a New Approach to Economic Growth following Conflict or Disaster*, proceedings, Command and General Staff College, Ft. Leavenworth, Kansas http://sites.kauffman.org/eee/resources/ee_summit_proceedings.pdf (accessed 1 April 2011).

5. Carl J. Schramm, "Expeditionary Economics: Spurring Growth after Conflicts and Disasters," *Foreign Affairs* 89, no. 3 (April/May 2010): 89.

6. US Joint Chiefs of Staff. *National Military Strategy of the United States of America 2011—Redefining America's Military Leadership*. Washington, DC: US Joint Chiefs of Staff, February 8, 2011. http://www.jcs.mil//content/files/2011-02/020811084800_2011_NMS_-_08_FEB_2011.pdf (accessed 25 April 2011).

7. US Joint Chiefs of Staff. *National Military Strategy of the United States of America 2011—Redefining America's Military Leadership*. Washington, DC: US Joint Chiefs of Staff, February 8, 2011. http://www.jcs.mil//content/files/2011-02/020811084800_2011_NMS_-_08_FEB_2011.pdf (accessed 25 April 2011).

8. US Joint Chiefs of Staff. *National Military Strategy of the United States of America 2011—Redefining America's Military Leadership*. Washington, DC: US Joint Chiefs of Staff, February 8, 2011. http://www.jcs.mil//content/files/2011-02/020811084800_2011_NMS_-_08_FEB_2011.pdf (accessed 25 April 2011).

9. Rebecca Patterson and Dane Stangler, *Building Expeditionary Economics: Understanding the Field and Setting Forth a Research Agenda*, (Kansas City: Kauffman Foundation, 2010), 6.

10. United States Institute of Peace "Opposed Development: Concept and Implications." http://

www.usip.org/events/opposed-development-concept-and-implications (accessed 4 April 2011).

11. Joshua Foust. "Expeditionary Economics: A New Approach to Post-Crisis Development." American Security Project. http://americansecurityproject.org/wp-content/uploads/2011/04/ Expeditionary-Economics-ExpEcon-Part-One.pdf (accessed 20 May 2011).

12. Joshua Foust. "Expeditionary Economics: A New Approach to Post-Crisis Development." American Security Project. http://americansecurityproject.org/wp-content/uploads/2011/04/ Expeditionary-Economics-ExpEcon-Part-One.pdf (accessed 20 May 2011).

13. Carl J. Schramm, "Expeditionary Economics: Spurring Growth after Conflicts and Disasters," *Foreign Affairs* 89, no. 3 (April/May 2010).

14. Carl J. Schramm, "Expeditionary Economics: Spurring Growth after Conflicts and Disasters," *Foreign Affairs* 89, no. 3 (April/May 2010), 90.

15. Arlyn T. Gajilan "Entrepreneurs in Iraq Tangle in US Red Tape" *CNN* 1 November 2004, http://money.cnn.com/magazines/fsb/fsb_archive/2004/11/01/8190934/index.htm (accessed 6 March 2011).

16. Jeff Peterson and Mark Crow "Expeditionary Economics: Towards a Doctrine for Enabling Stabilization and Growth" USMA Senior Conference XLVIII http://www.dean.usma.edu/sosh/ senior_conference/sc_papers/USMA%20February%20Conference%202011-Paper.pdf (accessed 5 June 2012).

17. This idea is expanded upon on by Jeff Peterson and Mark Crow "Expeditionary Economics: Towards a Doctrine for Enabling Stabilization and Growth" USMA Senior Conference XLVIII http:// www.dean.usma.edu/sosh/senior_conference/sc_papers/USMA%20February%20Conference%20 2011-Paper.pdf (accessed 5 June 2012).

18. Gregory Johnson, Vijaya Ramachandran and Julie Walz, "The Commanders Emergency Response Program in Afghanistan & Refining US Military Capabilities in Stability and In-Conflict Development." USMA Senior Conference XLVIII http://www.dean.usma.edu/sosh/senior_ conference/sc_papers/Ramachandran%20EE%20final%205%2019%202011.pdf (accessed 12 June 2012).

19. Gregory Johnson, Vijaya Ramachandran and Julie Walz, "The Commanders Emergency Response Program in Afghanistan & Refining US Military Capabilities in Stability and in Conflict Development" USMA Senior Conference XLVII http://www.dean.usma.edu/sosh/senior_ conference/sc_papers/Ramachandran%20EE%20final%205%2019%202011.pdf (accessed 12 June 2012).

20. Rebecca Patterson and Jonathan Robinson. "The Commander as Investor: Changing CERP Practices." *PRISM* 2, no. 2 (March 2011): 115-26. http://www.ndu.edu/press/lib/images/prism2-2/ prism_toc.pdf (accessed April 1, 2011).

21. CERP has three primary components: reconstruction, death benefits/battle damage payments, and economic development. Reconstruction includes repair or reconstruction of hospitals, clinics, power transmission and distribution networks, water or sewer systems, police and fire stations, schools, telecommunications systems or infrastructure, roads, bridges, and civic or cultural buildings/facilities. Death benefits/battle damage payments include condolence payments as a means of expressing sympathy and repair of damage resulting from military operations that cannot be compensated under the Foreign Claims Act. Economic development includes protective measures

for critical infrastructure sites, micro grants to disadvantaged small businesses and entrepreneurs, job promotion, and civil cleanup activities. Rebecca Patterson and Jonathan Robinson. "The Commander as Investor: Changing CERP Practices." *PRISM*, no. 2 (March 2011): 115-26. http://www.ndu.edu/press/lib/images/prism2-2/prism_toc.pdf (accessed April 1, 2011).

22. As highlighted by Rebecca Patterson and Jonathan Robinson. "The Commander as Investor: Changing CERP Practices." *PRISM*, no. 2 (March 2011): 115-26. http://www.ndu.edu/press/lib/images/prism2-2/prism_toc.pdf (accessed April 1, 2011).

23. Gregory Johnson, Vijaya Ramachandran and Julie Walz, "The Commanders Emergency Response Program in Afghanistan & Refining US Military Capabilities in Stability and In-Conflict Development." USMA Senior Conference XLVIII http://www.dean.usma.edu/sosh/senior_conference/sc_papers/Ramachandran%20EE%20final%205%2019%202011.pdf (accessed 12 June 2012).

24. David Kilcullen argues that there is a threefold framework in which development activity occurs: in environments of peace or post conflict, environments where active terrorist organizations exist, and environments where an added layer of complexity is introduced by the terrorists vying for population support through their own development activity. This framework draws from the comments of Gregory Johnson, Vijaya Ramachandran and Julie Walz, "The Commanders Emergency Response Program in Afghanistan & Refining US Military Capabilities in Stability and In-Conflict Development." USMA Senior Conference XLVIII http://www.dean.usma.edu/sosh/senior_conference/sc_papers/Ramachandran%20EE%20final%205%2019%202011.pdf (accessed 12 June 2012).

25. As cited by David Kilcullen "Counterinsurgency in Iraq" Noetic. http://www.orgsites.com/va/asis151/CounterinsurgencyinIraqTheoryandPractice2007.pdf (accessed 20 February 2011).

26. As cited by David Kilcullen "Counterinsurgency in Iraq" Noetic. http://www.orgsites.com/va/asis151/CounterinsurgencyinIraqTheoryandPractice2007.pdf (accessed 20 February 2011).

27. David Galula, Counter-*Insurgency Warfare: Theory and Practice* (New York: Oxford University Press, 1964), p. 63.

28. David Galula, Counter-*Insurgency Warfare: Theory and Practice* (New York: Oxford University Press, 1964), p. 63.

29. David Kilcullen, "Small Wars Center of Excellence Counterinsurgency Seminar 07" Small Wars Center. https://jko.harmonieweb.org/coi/iwt/IWed/Document%20Library/Report%20-%20Counterinsurgency%20in%20Iraq%20-%20Theory%20and%20Practice%202007.pdf (accessed 5 May 2011).

30. Gregory Johnson, Vijaya Ramachandran and Julie Walz, "The Commanders Emergency Response Program in Afghanistan & Refining US Military Capabilities in Stability and In-Conflict Development." USMA Senior Conference XLVIII http://www.dean.usma.edu/sosh/senior_conference/sc_papers/Ramachandran%20EE%20final%205%2019%202011.pdf (accessed 12 June 2012).

31. Andrew Natsios, "Opposed Development: Concept and Implications." Event at the United States Institute of Peace, June 16, 2010. As cited by Gregory Johnson, Vijaya Ramachandran and Julie Walz, "The Commanders Emergency Response Program in Afghanistan & Refining US Military Capabilities in Stability and In-Conflict Development." USMA Senior Conference XLVIII http://www.dean.usma.edu/sosh/senior_conference/sc_papers/Ramachandran%20EE%20final%205%2019%202011.pdf (accessed 12 June 2012).

32. David Galula, Counter-*Insurgency Warfare: Theory and Practice* (New York: Oxford University Press, 1964), p. 54. David Galula further states that *victory is not just the destruction in a given area of the insurgent's forces and his political organization,* for if either or both are destroyed, it will be re-created either from within, or by insurgents from outside. He cites the numerous examples of mopping-up operations by the French in the Plain of Reeds in Cochinchina throughout the Indochina War. A complete victory, *the isolation of insurgents maintained by and with the population,* is exemplified by David Galula in the defeat of the FLM in the Oran region in Algeria (1959-1969).

33. Barack Obama, *National Security Strategy 2010*. http://www.whitehouse.gov/sites/default/files/rss_viewer/national_security_strategy.pdf (accessed 5 February 2011).

34. Kori Schake "Operationalizing Expeditionary Economics," *Entrepreneurship and Expeditionary Economics: Towards a New Approach to Economic Growth following Conflict or Disaster*, Command and General Staff College, Ft. Leavenworth, Kansas, http://sites.kauffman.org/eee/resources/ee_summit_proceedings.pdf (accessed 1 April 2011).

35. Kori Schake "Operationalizing Expeditionary Economics," *Entrepreneurship and Expeditionary Economics: Towards a New Approach to Economic Growth following Conflict or Disaster*, Command and General Staff College, Ft. Leavenworth, Kansas, http://sites.kauffman.org/eee/resources/ee_summit_proceedings.pdf (accessed 1 April 2011).

36. Kori Schake "Operationalizing Expeditionary Economics," *Entrepreneurship and Expeditionary Economics: Towards a New Approach to Economic Growth following Conflict or Disaster*, Command and General Staff College, Ft. Leavenworth, Kansas, http://sites.kauffman.org/eee/resources/ee_summit_proceedings.pdf (accessed 1 April 2011).

37. Carl J. Schramm, "Expeditionary Economics: Spurring Growth after Conflicts and Disasters," *Foreign Affairs* 89, no. 3 (April/May 2010): 90.

38. Carl J. Schramm, "Expeditionary Economics: Spurring Growth after Conflicts and Disasters," *Foreign Affairs* 89, no. 3 (April/May 2010): 90.

39. Described by David Kilcullen, "Small Wars Center of Excellence Counterinsurgency Seminar 07" Small Wars Center. https://jko.harmonieweb.org/coi/iwt/IWed/Document%20Library/Report%20-%20Counterinsurgency%20in%20Iraq%20-%20Theory%20and%20Practice%20 2007.pdf (accessed 5 May 2011).

40. As cited by Kori Schake "Operationalizing Expeditionary Economics," *Entrepreneurship and Expeditionary Economics: Towards a New Approach to Economic Growth following Conflict or Disaster*, Command and General Staff College, Ft. Leavenworth, Kansas, http://sites.kauffman.org/eee/resources/ee_summit_proceedings.pdf (accessed 1 April 2011).

41. Carl J. Schramm, "Expeditionary Economics: Spurring Growth after Conflicts and Disasters," *Foreign Affairs* 89, no. 3 (April/May 2010): 95.

42. As cited by Kori Schake "Operationalizing Expeditionary Economics," *Entrepreneurship and Expeditionary Economics: Towards a New Approach to Economic Growth following Conflict or Disaster*, Command and General Staff College, Ft. Leavenworth, Kansas, http://sites.kauffman.org/eee/resources/ee_summit_proceedings.pdf (accessed 1 April 2011).

43. As suggested by Matt Waldman, "Caught in the Conflict – Civilians and the International Security Strategy in Afghanistan" *A Briefing Paper for the NATO Heads of State and Government Summit, 3-4 April 2009.* http://www.oxfam.org.uk/resources/policy/conflict_disasters/downloads/bp_caught_in_conflict_afghanistan.pdf (accessed 03 March 2011).

44. *Country Profile*, USAID Afghanistan, 11 May 2008, as cited by Matt Waldman, "Caught in the Conflict – Civilians and the International Security Strategy in Afghanistan" *A Briefing Paper for the NATO Heads of State and Government Summit, 3-4 April 2009.* http://www.oxfam.org.uk/ resources/policy/conflict_disasters/downloads/bp_caught_in_conflict_afghanistan.pdf (accessed 03 March 2011).

45. Auil Shah in the new Foreign Affairs edition on Pakistan

46. Matt Waldman, "Caught in the Conflict – Civilians and the International Security Strategy in Afghanistan" *A Briefing Paper for the NATO Heads of State and Government Summit, 3-4 April 2009.* http://www.oxfam.org.uk/resources/policy/conflict_disasters/downloads/bp_caught_in_ conflict_afghanistan.pdf (accessed 03 March 2011).

47. Matt Waldman, "Caught in the Conflict – Civilians and the International Security Strategy in Afghanistan" *A Briefing Paper for the NATO Heads of State and Government Summit, 3-4 April 2009.* http://www.oxfam.org.uk/resources/policy/conflict_disasters/downloads/bp_caught_in_ conflict_afghanistan.pdf (accessed 03 March 2011).

48. Matt Waldman, "Caught in the Conflict – Civilians and the International Security Strategy in Afghanistan" *A Briefing Paper for the NATO Heads of State and Government Summit, 3-4 April 2009.* http://www.oxfam.org.uk/resources/policy/conflict_disasters/downloads/bp_caught_in_ conflict_afghanistan.pdf (accessed 03 March 2011).

49. Nicholas H. Riegg, "Implementing Expeditionary and Entrepreneurial Economics: Iraq and Afghanistan," *Entrepreneurship and Expeditionary Economics: Towards a New Approach to Economic Growth following Conflict or Disaster*, Command and General Staff College, Ft. Leavenworth, Kansas, http://sites.kauffman.org/eee/resources/ee_summit_proceedings.pdf (accessed 1 April 2011).

50. Nicholas H. Riegg, "Implementing Expeditionary and Entrepreneurial Economics: Iraq and Afghanistan," *Entrepreneurship and Expeditionary Economics: Towards a New Approach to Economic Growth following Conflict or Disaster*, Command and General Staff College, Ft. Leavenworth, Kansas, http://sites.kauffman.org/eee/resources/ee_summit_proceedings.pdf (accessed 1 April 2011).

51. The signatories to this report are: Action Aid, Afghanaid, CARE, Christian Aid, Concern Worldwide, Norwegian Refugee Council, Oxfam and Trocaire.

52. US Army Combined Arms Center, "Commanders' Guide to Money as a Weapons System: Tactics, techniques and Procedures," April 2009.

53. Oxfam "Quick Impact Quick Collapse: The Dangers of Militarized Aid in Afghanistan," *Oxfam Research*. http://www.oxfam.org/en/policy/quick-impact-quick-collapse (accessed 20 April 2011).

54. Oxfam "Quick Impact Quick Collapse: The Dangers of Militarized Aid in Afghanistan," *Oxfam Research*. http://www.oxfam.org/en/policy/quick-impact-quick-collapse (accessed 20 April 2011).

55. BAAG provides regular information on the political, economic and security situation in Afghanistan and is an effective network for international NGOs operating in Afghanistan. The BAAG project was set up by British NGOs in 1987 as an umbrella group to draw public attention to the humanitarian needs of the population of Afghanistan and of Afghan refugees in Iran and Pakistan. BAAG's endorsement of Oxfam's views is found in An Alternative View: Afghan Perspectives on Development and Security, http://www.baag.org.uk/news/7-latest-news/31-live-video-streaming-

of-an-alternative-view-afghan-perspectivves-on-development-and-security

56. As reported by Aditya Mehta, UNAMA, http://unama.unmissions.org/Default.aspx?tabid= 1741&ctl=Details&mid=1882&ItemID=7100 (accessed 20 May 2011).

57. As reported by Aditya Mehta, UNAMA, http://unama.unmissions.org/Default.aspx?tabid= 1741&ctl=Details&mid=1882&ItemID=7100 (accessed 20 May 2011).

58. US Army, *Field Manual (Interim) 3, Operations, 2008* (Washington: Headquarters, Department of the Army, 2008).

59. US Army, *Field Manual (Interim) 3, Operations, 2008* (Washington: Headquarters, Department of the Army, 2008).

60. US Army, *Field Manual (Interim) 3, Operations, 2008* (Washington: Headquarters, Department of the Army, 2008), 3-20.

61. Nicholas H. Riegg, "Implementing Expeditionary and Entrepreneurial Economics: Iraq and Afghanistan," *Entrepreneurship and Expeditionary Economics: Towards a New Approach to Economic Growth following Conflict or Disaster*, Command and General Staff College, Ft. Leavenworth, Kansas, http://sites.kauffman.org/eee/resources/ee_summit_proceedings.pdf (accessed 1 April 2011).

62. Conclusion needs work. You need to have some punch at the end and clearly indicate what the US military, especially the Army, should do in regard to EE. Also, go back to your introduction and ensure you address all your initial questions with forceful answers here.

Expeditionary Economics and Its Implications on the United States Army

by

Major Marc E. Pelini - United States Army

Abstract

Since the end of the Cold War, the United States government has increasingly deployed its Army forces in support of global stability and support operations. Based on the 2010 Department of Defense Review and the Department of Defense Directive 3000.05, this trend is likely to continue for the foreseeable future. These documents, as well the national security documents at every level of the US federal government place a mandate on the military to develop, institutionalize, and resource economic stability and development capabilities to reduce both global instabilities and to prevent regional and global insurgencies. While the Army has begun to adapt in response to these directives, it remains institutionally ill-prepared to deal with the economic issues presented in stability operations. This monograph investigates two influential economic theories that could serve as fundamental approaches towards economic development in stability operations; analyzes what and how effective the "whole-of-government" approach has been in stability operations in Iraq and Afghanistan; examines how the Army is trying to change its institutional approach to stability operations; and identifies areas in the Army force structure, doctrine, training and education, and organization that could increase its overall effectiveness in future stability operations.

Acronyms

AAB	Advise and Assist Brigade
AC	Active Component
ACS	Advanced Civil Schooling
ARFORGEN	Army Force Generation Model
ASI	Army Skill Identifier
BCT	Brigade Combat Team
BDE	Brigade
BOG	Boots on the Ground
CA	Civil Affairs
CARD	Center for Agriculture and Rural Development
CCC	Captains Career Course
CCJO	Capstone Concept for Joint Operations
CCP	Contingency Command Post
CGSC	Command and General Staff College
CERP	Commander's Emergency Relief Program
DoD	Department of Defense
ePRT	Embedded Provincial Reconstruction Teams
FM	Field Manual
GCC	Global Combatant Command
HBCT	Heavy Brigade Combat Teams
ILE	Intermediate Level Training
JOE	Joint Operating Environment
NDS	National Defense Strategy
NGO	Non-Government Organization
NSS	National Security Strategy
OBC	Officer Basic Course
OEF	Operation ENDURING FREEDOM
OIF	Operation IRAQI FREEDOM
PRT	Provincial Reconstruction Teams
QDR	Quadrennial Defense Review
RC	Reserve Component
S/CRS	Department of State Office of the Coordinator for Reconstruction and Stabilization
USAID	United States Agency for International Development
USAFRICOM	United States Africa Command
USAR	United States Army Reserve
USCENTCOM	United States Central Command
USEUCOM	United States European Command
USPACOM	United States Pacific Command
USSOUTHCOM	United States Southern Command

Introduction

But I have spoken thus far only of the military challenges which your education must prepare you for. The nonmilitary problems, which you will face, will also be most demanding. . . In the years ahead, some of you will serve as advisors to foreign aid missions or even to foreign governments. . . . Whatever your position, the scope of your decisions will not be confined to the traditional tenants of military competence and training. . . . You will be involved in economic judgments, which most economists would hesitate to make.[1]

- President John F. Kennedy
Remarks to the United States Military Academy Graduating Class of 1962

Since the end of the Cold War, the US government has become increasingly dependent on its military to support its global political objectives. During this time, the US military has deployed in support of over 110 contingencies throughout the world.[2] These contingencies have ranged from peacekeeping operations in Kosovo and Bosnia to combat and later stability and reconstruction operations in Afghanistan and Iraq. Because of these operations, the US has gained significant experience and insights into conducting operations across the full spectrum of conflict. While some would argue that the challenging experiences in Afghanistan and Iraq would make politicians less prone to deploy the military in the future, these pundits are not properly considering the current geopolitical environment.

The United States exists in a world that is interconnected more than at any other time in history. Globalization, global terrorism, and regional instability have significantly increased the complexity of the world. They have not only placed greater demands on resources, but have placed disparate cultures in direct confrontation with each other in areas or regions that possess critical US economic and military interests. As a result, the United States is committed to ensuring these interests remain secure by achieving long-term stability of these states and regions. Yet, unlike the pre-Cold War environment, which viewed the Soviet threat as linear and to an extent predictable, the asymmetrical environment and threats that the United States faces today and for the near future are more lethal, adaptable, and irregular.

The *2010 Joint Operating Environment* (JOE), a document that provides a strategic framework and forecasts threat trends that will challenge the US Armed Forces in the future, states that the US will continue to face numerous multidimensional challenges to its security. The US will continue to confront challenges posed by increasing proliferation of technology, globalization, urbanization, and weak or failing states, as well as competing international narratives. The prospects provided by these trends may increase the necessity to deploy US Forces to secure our global interests. They will present unique challenges to our military capabilities by growing conventional, irregular, or hybrid threats that operate in both urban and austere environments.[3] As a result, the US military must develop capabilities and expertise that not only focuses on defeating these potential threats, but also create an environment that prevents their reoccurrence.

While the first priority of the US military must always be the safety and security of its population, it must face the fact that the nature of warfare is ever changing and evolving. The military must shed the paradigm of focusing solely on the lethality of the military instrument of power and recognize that in order to protect the US interests in the long-term, it must be willing to possess and sustain innovative security assistance and stability operations capabilities. It must be willing to instill and institutionalize many of the ad hoc security assistance, stability, reconstruction and peacekeeping capabilities that were painfully borne out of Operation ENDURING FREEDOM (OEF) and Operation IRAQI FREEDOM (OIF).[4] While both of these conflicts demonstrate that the US military is extremely capable of providing short-term stability while its troops are on the ground, the underlying challenge remains – how can the US military establish long-term security so it does not have to return? One avenue to potential success is simple to identify, it is even harder to solve – economic development. Despite this avenue for long-term stability, the US Army is currently ill-prepared to deal with economic issues presented in stability operations.

According to Paul Collier, a former Director of the Development Research Group of the World Bank, economic disparity is the root cause of conflict. Contrary to many previous assertions, social grievances such as inequality, lack of democracy, and ethnic and religious divisions are not the root cause of conflict. Rather, Collier identifies economic conditions such as dependence on commodity exports and low national income as the main contributive factors to conflict.[5] He ascertains that there is a strong correlative relationship between the risk of conflict and the population's level of income. This relationship is important because he demonstrates that a decline in per capita income is directly proportional to the increase in risk of conflict in that nation.[6] Given this fact, a primary question remains: Does the US military need to create an economic development capability as part of its stability and reconstruction portfolio or should it remain the responsibility of another US agency?

According to Kori Schake, a research fellow at the Hoover Institute, the responsibility for economic development is not a military one. Rather, Schake argues that the lines of authority for economic development "lie with the Department of State, the US Agency for International Development, the Export-Import Bank of the US Trade Representative, the Department of Commerce and the Department of Treasury."[7] Yet, experiences in Iraq and Afghanistan have demonstrated that these departments and agencies have not adequately fulfilled their statutory requirements. This, in turn, creates operational voids that the Department of Defense (DoD) typically has to fill without any level of expertise or preparation. These voids occur because of the environments in which these civilian agencies are required to operate and not a result of their expertise. Because many stability and reconstruction operations occur in hostile[8] or uncertain[9] environments, where the risk for armed conflict is present, civilian servants are less likely to deploy to these areas. The difficulties of deploying civilian servants was evident in 2007 when Department of State employees balked at calls to serve in Iraq during the troop surge and when violence in Baghdad was high.[10] While Secretary of State Condoleezza Rice eventually filled these vacancies with some direct intervention, the question remains if the embassy received the right level of expertise to fill these positions.

In 2004, the US federal government attempted to address the requirement for an economic development capability as well as others needed during the period in which operations change from "sustained combat operations to stability operations," [11] or commonly referred to as Phase IV operations. During this phase, it is expected that the host country will have a limited or lack of a legitimate government. To prevent the country from falling into further chaos, the US military must be prepared to perform limited government functions and to coordinate and integrate other government, non-government organization (NGO) and international government efforts until a legitimate government is functioning.[12] In its attempt to address this essential capability outside the military, the US federal government established the Civilian Response Corps. This agency, which is part of the Department of State Office of the Coordinator for Reconstruction and Stabilization (S/CRS), is authorized to hire 4,250 people to fill this gap. Yet, these civilians do not receive the necessary security training to protect them in either a hostile or an uncertain environment. The resulting threats from these environments and a lack of security training may drive some of these experts to respond in the same way their peers did in 2007 when faced with the prospects of being assigned to the US Embassy in Iraq. Based on this assertion, it is likely that the US Army will be compelled to fill any vacancies if it is going to effectively and successfully garner the support of the local population and establish the conditions for long-term success. With this is mind, former United Nations General Dag Hammerskold's statement remains relevant today that, "peacekeeping is not a job for Soldiers, but only a soldier can do it."[13]

In dealing with the complex economic problems present in stability operations, there are no easy solutions. Yet the solutions that we implement must be done with some basic understanding and expertise of both the economic theories that describe and provide a fundamental understanding of economics. Without this knowledge, hidden economic effects that could have been identified through education may worsen the problem and change the course of the whole strategy that the United States is pursuing. Rather than simply spending money to achieve short-term symptomatic solutions, the US military should address the economic causes and help define and implement long-term solutions that resolve the underlying economic causes of instability.

While there is a general sense that the military is beginning to develop approaches to deal with the overall challenges of stability operations, comprehensive tools to analyze and constructively develop recommended solutions to the economic issues on the battlefield are insufficient. The Army must look at the way that it is constructed if it is going to be able to really reframe the problem and develop innovative capabilities that are able to address the economic challenges that are present within stability operations. One argument is that the Army should develop numerous peacekeeping units that are solely responsible for stability operations. While this is an appealing method, the current and projected rotational requirements for supporting the numerous global contingencies make this option untenable. This is because the reliance on the Reserve Component, consisting of the Army National Guard and Army Reserve is becoming less sustainable when their Soldiers are removed from their civilian occupations on a routine basis.

The Army has taken considerable steps forward in another approach by institutionalizing the modular Brigade Combat Team (BCT). The modular BCT is unique because it is versatile enough to adapt and transform into an Advise and Assist Brigade (AAB) during stability operations. The BCT accomplishes this transformation by integrating critical enabling capabilities such as Civil Affairs (CA) and others into is organizational structure. Yet, the transformation into BCT modularity is still not enough to adequately deal with the economic challenges faced during stability operations. This is because many of the enabling capabilities that help transform the BCT into an AAB during OIF and OEF have not been institutionalized into the Army's force structure to the level necessary to provide a sustainable solution.

This monograph will attempt to bring resolution to some of these issues. It will examine why economic development is essential to our nation's strategies and what economic theories could provide guidance for future Army operations. It will then examine proven techniques and procedures that are currently being employed throughout the world to facilitate economic development and promote stability. This monograph will then examine, in more depth, the effectiveness of the whole of government approach and areas in which the Army can provide assistance. It will then examine areas in which the Army is lacking the necessary economic expertise and capabilities to facilitate economic growth and then provide manning, training, and force structure recommendations. In addressing these areas, this monograph will also examine the impacts, if any; that result from the development of an expeditionary economic capability will have on the operational force and its deployment cycles.

The Mandate for Economic Development Capability

Economic development, along with security and diplomacy, is one of the three pillars of a successful counterinsurgency or stability and support strategy.[14] Every level of the US federal government recognizes economic development capabilities and expertise as a key planning component to reduce both global instabilities and to prevent regional and global insurgencies. From the national strategy to the departmental strategies, economic development expertise is an enabling capability that not only aids in the establishment of long-term security, but also assists in defeating potential terrorist organizations. In his *2010 National Security Strategy* (NSS), President Barrack Obama codifies this premise by providing the strategic underpinnings for the establishment of an economic development capability for the US government. The NSS, provides executive agencies with guidance to create budgets and develop capabilities that pursue the US national objectives through the employment of its national instruments of power.[15] This national strategy states that the federal government must create and maintain development capabilities that "prevent conflict, spur economic growth, strengthen weak and failing states, lift people out of poverty . . . and strengthen institutions of democratic governance."[16] It places development capabilities as a strategic, economic, and moral imperative that "can strengthen the regional partners we need to help us stop conflicts and counter global criminal networks . . . and position ourselves to better address key global challenges by growing the ranks of prosperous, capable, and democratic states that can be our partners in the decades ahead."[17]

The *National Defense Strategy* (NDS) serves as DoD's capstone strategy document. It provides guidance to the military for the development of global contingency plans as well as direction on how to best man, train and equip the Armed Forces to fight and win the nation's wars.[18] Like the NSS, the NDS postulates that the DoD will continue to participate in a protracted war against violent extremism for the foreseeable future. These types of conflicts will require the DoD to employ the military instrument of power skillfully to establish security while using the diplomatic, economic, and information instruments of power to achieve long-term success.[19] While this assertion is based on an uncertain future, it is grounded by the DoD's experiences in Iraq and Afghanistan where it has executed several non-traditional military tasks of long-term reconstruction, development, and governance. While the DoD recognizes and encourages other federal agencies to develop expeditionary capabilities to support these missions, the NDS calls for the US Armed Forces "to institutionalize and retain these capabilities."[20]

In addition to the NDS, the DoD issued a directive in September 2009 that further solidified the requirement for an economic development capability within the military. Department of Defense Instruction 3000.05 ordered the department to make stability operations a core competency of the Armed Forces. For that reason, stability operations and conventional combat operations are co-equals with respect to planning, staffing, training, and equipping. The purpose of this policy directive is to ensure that the military is prepared to conduct future stability operations in all phases of conflict and across the range of military operations, to include both combat and non-combat environments. It supports the fielding of capabilities:

> aimed not only at rebuilding infrastructure, developing local governance structures, and fostering security, but also in fostering economic stability and development and building of indigenous capability for such tasks."[21] In supporting this requirement, the instruction directs the DoD to "revive or build the private sector, including encouraging citizen-driven, bottom-up economic activity and constructing necessary infrastructure.[22]

The call for the creation of an economic development capability later matured with the publication of the *2010 Quadrennial Defense Review* (QDR) in February 2010. The 2010 QDR identified the increase of counterinsurgency, stability operations, and counterterrorism competency in the general-purpose force, or conventional Army, as one of its six key initiatives.[23] In pursing this initiative, the 2010 QDR recommended the growth of Army Civil Affairs forces to serve as the vanguard for the DoD in supporting the federal government's efforts to assist partner governments in the field of economic stability as well as other stabilization and support activities.[24]

Finally, the *2009 Capstone Concept for Joint Operations* (CCJO), which is the Chairman of the Joint Chiefs of Staff's guidance for joint force development and employment, directs the joint force to optimize across nine domains; one of which is to improve the ability to operate in urban environments. In identifying urban conflicts as a common environment of future conflict, the CCJO articulates the requirement of the joint force to conduct economic engagement activities in support of reconstruction or development activities.[25]

When the US military occupies an operational area, both the NDS to the CCJO clearly state that it must be prepared to handle the economic development and stability activities that derive from stability operations. According to *Joint Publication 3-07.3: Peace Operations*, these activities include "restoring employment opportunities, initiating market reform, mobilizing domestic and foreign investment, supervising monetary reform, and rebuilding public structures."[26] In examining these requirements, the Army commissioned a study in 2010 to identify the types of tasks and challenges it could face when executing these economic stabilization activities. Table 1 lists the tasks, definitions, and respective subtasks.

When the military approaches these economic stabilization and development tasks, it is important that it does so using accepted economic theory. Although there are several economic theories that could be used based on their specific mission and the environment in which the Army is operating within, this monograph will examine two of the more influential theories: Classical and Keynesian economic theory. Understanding these two theories is important for two reasons. First, it provides the foundation for understanding how the US Army can approach economic development at the local level as well as possible ramifications that could emerge from such activities. Second, these theories can serve as a cornerstone or theoretical foundation for providing informed recommendations to the host nation or to the Department of State that may render long-term ramifications for the host nations stability, security and overall economic viability during Phase IV operations.

Foundational Economic Theory

Classic economic theory was developed in 1776 by Adam Smith with the publication of the *Wealth of Nations* and is considered the first recognized theory on economics. In the *Wealth of Nations*, Smith denounced the mercantilist practices of his time, which encouraged the government's obtaining wealth at the expense of its population in order for it to project military or political power. He fundamentally disagreed with the mercantilist approach that encouraged the population to buy only domestically produced goods, set price and maximum wage laws, predetermined the society's production specialties, and directed the professions of its population. Smith believed that such government policies were inefficient and limited the nation's true production capability.[27] Instead, he believed that the population as a whole, and not the government, was wise enough to plan the economic affairs of the nation. This concept was rooted in the faith that the production capability of the nation resided in its population and could be harnessed through laissez-faire capitalism, or with little government intervention.[28] He thought that the role of the government should be limited to three roles: defense, justice, and public works. Defense is a necessary role of the government to provide the required security and defense to protect its people and their property in order for free trade and commerce to flourish. Justice, or a legal system, is required to regulate contracts and arbitrate commercial disagreements. Finally, public works are necessary to provide public goods such as roads, bridges, and post offices as well as issuing a common currency, enforcing property rights and education that further the overall well-being of the society.[29]

Smith and other classical economists such as David Ricardo, Thomas Malthus, and John Stuart Mill favor laissez-faire economics because it eliminates special privileges, arbitrary restrictions, and ineffective use of resources that limit the growth of an economy.[30] By eliminating government sponsored monopolies or other economic hindrances in favor of individual economic freedoms, these economists believe the economy and the nation as a whole is more apt to flourish. By leveling the economic playing field, individuals have the opportunity to prosper over their previous generations by allowing them to maximize their profits by specializing in production and exploiting comparative advantages in the marketplace. The effects from these limitations on government policy would, over time, result in a more effective and efficient allocation of the nation's finite resources.[31]

Classical economic theory represents a supply side model by proclaiming that the overall economic well-being of a country is directly proportional to how fast demand for labor increases over time.[32] It considers the price of goods, cost of labor, and interest rates as fixed or constant at the existing market price in the short-term, and argues they are flexible or capable of going up or down, in the long-term.[33] Classical economists contend that the economy is based on a self-correcting mechanism, referred to as the "invisible hand", which pushes prices, labor costs, and interest rates towards its "natural" or equilibrium point in the long-term. Because of the influence of the invisible hand, any unemployment that may arise from higher labor costs is temporary and will be eliminated as the cost of labor drops in response to lower costing labor in the marketplace.[34]

Say's Law, which states supply constitutes or creates its own demand, is a critical component of classical economic theory. Say's Law maintains that the total supply of goods and services will always equal the total demand for goods and services. This means that the production for goods only occurs if people receive satisfaction from that good and are willing to pay for it, thus creating its own demand.[35] Similarly, this assertion also contends that any excess or shortages of total supply or demand of a good is eliminated as its price decreases or increases over time.[36]

Finally, classical economists maintain that the level of a country's money supply is neutral to its economic prosperity. If there is excess money on the market, prices increase proportionally. In the end, the country's total output or its employment rates do not change because of the rise in prices. Classical economists also say that economic growth is determined by the relationship between savings and capital investment. Savings, or any excess purchasing power that is not spent on consumption, will support capital development by creating demand for capital investment by affecting the market's interest rates. When there is excess capital due to "over saving", interest rates, which serves to equalize savings and capital investment, will decline. As interest rates decline, it will encourage more capital investment. If, on the other hand, there is "over investment" interest rates will increase and restrict further expansion of production opportunities by firms by making it more costly to acquire the necessary capital. These counter-balancing weights serve as a self-correcting system for interest rates which results in a long-term "natural" interest rate for the market. Based on this explanation, it is understandable why classic economists argue that in economic downturns, countries should choke off potential depression by increasing saving, reducing their debts, reducing government expenditures, balancing their budgets, and reducing wages to achieve economic growth.[37]

Table 1. Economic Development Tasks for Stability Operations

DoD Major Mission Element - Support Economic Development		
Essential Task	**Working Definition**	**Subtasks**
Generate Employment	The ability to design, fund, and implement public work initiatives, to stimulate micro and small enterprise and foster workforce development programs that will rapidly provide employment for the indigenous population	• Public works jobs • Micro and small enterprise stimulation • Skills training • Counseling
Develop Monetary Policy	The ability to develop mechanisms and institutions, including the ability to set and control interest rates that allow the government to manage the economy by expanding or contracting the money supply	• Central bank operations • Macroeconomic policy and exchange rates • Monetary audit • Monetary statistics
Develop and Apply Fiscal Policy and Governance	The ability to develop and apply sustainable, efficient, and transparent fiscal policies that can generate the resources required to sustain key public functions. This includes the ability to establish revenue and expenditure structures and to manage the economy through the expansion and contraction of government spending and to design and administer public expenditure systems that are transparent and which lend themselves to the equitable and timely formulation of budgets and which can plan for the needs of the entire population	• Fiscal and macroeconomic policy • Treasury operations • Budget • Public sector investment • Revenue generation • Tax administration • Customs reform • Enforcement • Tax policy • Fiscal audit
Promote General Economic Policies	None	• Strategy/assessment • Prices and subsidies • International financial assistance – donor coordination • Public sector institutions
Establish, Develop, Regulate, and Sustain a Well-Functioning and Equitable Financial Sector	The ability to establish, develop, regulate, and sustain a well-functioning and equitable financial sector	• Banking operations • Banking regulations and oversight • Banking law • Bank lending • Asset and money laundering • Non-banking sector • Stock and commodity markets
Manage and Control Both Foreign and Domestic Borrowing and Debt	The ability to manage and control both foreign and domestic borrowing and debt	• Debt management • Arrears clearance
Develop Trade	The ability to establish, develop, sustain, and enforce trade policies, laws, regulations, and administrative practices that support	• Trade structure • Trade facilitation
Promote a Market Economy	The ability to support the establishment or re-establishment of a functioning market economy	• Private sector development • Small and micro-enterprise regime • Privatization • Natural resources and environment
Promote Legal and Regulatory Reform	The ability to support the development of a legal and regulatory framework supportive of a market economy	• Property rights • Business/commercial law • Labor • Economic legal reform • Competition policy • Public utilities and resources regulation • Economic enforcement and anti-corruption
Promote Agricultural Development	The ability to support the establishment or re-establishment of a viable agricultural sector capable of long-term growth	• Agricultural land and livestock • Agricultural inputs • Agricultural policy and financing • Agricultural distribution
Establish a Social Safety Net	The ability to support the establishment of social safety net programs	• Pension system • Social entitlement funds • Women's issues

Source: Author Created based on data from Jefferson P. Marquis, *Developing an Army Strategy for Building Partner Capacity for Stability Operations* (Arlington, Virginia: RAND Corporation, 2010), 154-156.

While Classical Economic theory provides some important insights into how to approach economic development, another theory rose to prominence because of the Great Depression. In 1936, John Maynard Keynes challenged classical economic theory with the publication of *The General Theory of Employment, Interest, and Money*. In the publication of his book, Keynes challenged nearly all of the basic principles of classical economics, which believed that the economy would automatically adjust itself to maximize a society's output and employment. Keynes argued that insufficient demand was the main obstacle to economic growth, which directly contradicted the classical economic notion that insufficient supply was the culprit. To establish sufficient demand in unstable times, Keynes argued that the government must play a central role in keeping the economy going to allow private enterprises to survive.[38]

Unemployment was a central point of contention between Keynes and his classical economist peers. Whereas classical theorists consider unemployment as temporary and to some extent, voluntary, Keynesian theorists are concerned with the problem of involuntary unemployment. In examining unemployment, Keynes understood that there were three major types of unemployment present in all economies: structural, frictional, and cyclical.[39] Structural unemployment occurs when the main industry of the nation cannot support the entire workforce. Frictional unemployment occurs when workers move from their current job to another or into a new industry. Finally, cyclical unemployment, or depression related unemployment, occurs when the economy goes through a cyclical downturn. Cyclical unemployment was Keynes' primary focus in his *General Theory*.[40]

At the center of Keynes' argument was uncertainty. He believed that uncertainty "loosens all of the 'tight' relationships assumed by classical theory which produce a smooth flow of demand and supply and validate Say's Law."[41] Keynes argued that capital investment only occurs when there are high expectations that the investment will grow. When the market is in decline, uncertainty increases, consumption will naturally decline, and savings will increase. Yet, unlike the classical theorists who argue the increase in savings will result in higher capital investments as interest rates decline, Keynesian economists argue that people will forgo investing because they are uncertain that their investment will provide a positive return. This unwillingness to invest and consume, known as a "paradox of thrift", will push the economy further into a depression, create higher unemployment, and leave the economy worse off.[42]

To counterbalance the paradox of thrift, Keynesian economic theory argues that the government must act to offset market declines with increased deficit spending. Keynes argues in the short-term, total supply is constant and the volume of output, employment, and income is reliant on total demand.[43] Therefore, the government should focus on increasing total demand by increasing governmental expenditures to stimulate consumption and create an environment that is favorable to capital investment. By instituting these policies, the government is able to stabilize the economy through its fiscal policies. It is able to restrict rapid economic growth when the economy is strong by restricting demand for goods through taxation and it is able to promote economic growth when the economy is weak by borrowing and spending on government projects. This explains why Keynesian economists argue that in economic downturns the government should increase spending, increase debts, increase government expenditures, and unbalance the government's budget.[44]

While neither classical or Keynesian economics provide a one size fits all solution for conducting economic development, they both provide some useful insights for how the Army can use or recommend the implementation of various parts of these theories to help stabilize a country's economy and prevent further conflict. For instance, the Army can recommend a policy, based on its local observations and assessments, to increase governmental spending to create short-term demand for a particular good or service that is essential to the maturing of the economy. Whether the good is private or public, stimulation of demand as argued by Keynes may restart the country's economy in the uncertain environment created in Phase IV operations by promoting the necessary investment in firms, even if it is for a short period. In contrast, the Army can help ensure the long-term viability of the country by recommending or imposing a classical economic model. By assisting the local population to establish a diverse supply of goods that are desired by the population through the infusion of investment capital, long-term economic stability can occur by creating demand for goods that are desired by the population. In pursing this mode, the Army could help identify entrepreneurs and provide them with the necessary expertise and funding to begin the path of long-term economic growth. Yet, to accomplish these goals, there have to be certain conditions that must be set for these theories to work effectively in the long- run.

Conditions for Implementation

The three primary conditions that must be present for any economic stabilization or development strategy to succeed are security, good governance, and the rule of law. Security is the most important condition in stability operations because it serves as the foundation for all other areas of stabilization such as governance, civil control, infrastructure development, and economic development to succeed. If individuals and the collective population feel that they are threatened, they are less likely to allow comprehensive reform to occur.[45] Furthermore, a threatening environment creates uncertainty, which will discourage the population from returning to their everyday activities. Uncertainty will also compound the economic decline of the country, as Keynes argues, because people will not consume goods or invest in businesses at a level, which they otherwise would. To accomplish a safe and secure environment, large scale-violence has to cease, pubic order has to be restored, illegal armed groups have to be disarmed, physical security has to be instituted, and territorial security has to be established.[46]

The second condition that is essential for any level of long-term stability to occur is good governance. In 1998, Kofi-Annan, the former United Nations Secretary General stated, "good governance is perhaps the single most important factor in eradicating poverty and promoting development."[47] While the definition of good governance is broad and can be interpreted in many ways, the G-8 in 2001 identified six key components of good governance as being:

> (1) Accountability and transparency in the public sector, (2) legal frameworks and corporate governance regimes to fight corruption, (3) safeguards against the misappropriation of public funds and their diversion into non-productive uses, (4) access to legal systems for all citizens, independence of the judiciary, and legal provisions enabling private sector activity, (5) active involvement of civil society and non-governmental organizations (NGOs), and (6) freedom of economic activities.[48]

Together, security and good governance serve as the foundation for economic development in stability operations because they provide the necessary elements for the rule of law to occur. Rule of law is a state in which "all individuals and institutions, public and private, and the state itself are held accountable to the law, which is supreme."[49] Rule of law is a necessary component for economic recovery and prosperity because it provides a systematic and legitimate way of ensuring freedom of movement to access public services such as education and health and ensures the safety and security of individuals, families, businesses and property.[50]

While security, good governance, and the rule of law are the critical conditions for laying the foundation for economic development to come to fruition, Carl Shramm, the President of the Kauffman Foundation, argues that there are three additional requirements that help create long-term stability through economic development. The first is the existence of a financial system that is capable of providing capital funding to entities trying to start a business. The second element is government policies that avoid "rent seeking" or charging entities a fee or bribe in order to establish a business. Finally, the third element is government policies, which encourage entrepreneurial activity through the provision of government incentives for local businesses to innovate, adapt, and ultimately grow.[51] These are all areas that the US military can affect when deployed in support of a stability operation.

Finally, economic development policies and regulations must always consider the cultural norms of the host nation. Consideration of cultural norms is critical because without it, the military will never achieve the intended effect of the policy it is pursuing. According to Professors Steven Cornell of the University of Arizona and Joseph P. Kalt of Harvard University, any economic development policy must be adequate and appropriate in that it must adequately address the realities of the economic situation while being sensitive to the cultural norms of the society.[52] During their research on American Indian economic development challenges, they discovered that:

> [E]conomic development can take hold in the face of a wide range of cultural attitudes on such matters as the sanctity of natural resources or the propriety of individuals trying to make themselves wealthier. However, unless there is a fit between the culture of the community and the structure and powers of its governing institutions, those institutions may be seen as illegitimate, their ability to regulate and organize the development process will be undermined, and development will be blocked. Without a match between culture and governing institutions, tribal government cannot consistently do its basic job: creating and sustaining the "rules of the game" that development in any society requires.[53]

While there, the research focused primarily on American Indian economic development issues, their findings are relevant to any of the stability operations that the US Army has conducted in the past and will continue to conduct in the future.

What Has the United States Done So Far?

In 2005, President George W. Bush signed Presidential Directive 44. The purpose of Presidential Directive 44 was to "promote the security of the United States through improved coordination, planning, and implementation and stabilization assistance for foreign states and regions at risk of, in, or in transition from conflict or civil strife."[54] It directed the Department of State to coordinate, integrate, and lead the US Government's efforts to prepare, plan for, and conduct stabilization and reconstruction activities and to ensure "harmonization" with military operations across the spectrum of conflict.[55] This directive also solidified the role of the S/CRS created in June 2004 to coordinate and synchronize the US government's civilian response to reconstruction and stabilization efforts.

The S/CRS is a unique governmental organization that is intended to serve as the "hub" for the "whole of government" approach to stability and reconstruction operations. It is charged with forming a readily responsive Civil Response Corps that is globally deployable. The 4,250 member Civilian Response Corps will contain three distinct groups once it is fully formed: the Active, Standby and Reserve. The Active group will consist of 250 personnel who would be ready to deploy globally within 48-hours in support of a stability operation. The Standby group will consist of 2,000 federal employees and will be available to deploy within 30 days of a large crisis occurring for periods of 90 to 180 days. [56] The Reserve group, which is yet to be pursued, consists of 2,000 non-federal employees who would enlist for a year deployment during their four-year enlistment. By July 2010, the Civilian Response Corps had 100 Active and 900 Standby members and had deployed to twenty-eight countries to conduct assessments and conflict prevention focused primarily on the national or strategic level issues.[57] It also started planning for a "whole of government" approach in future contingency operation by participating in strategic level exercises with the Geographic Combatant Commands. An example of this was S/CRS' participation in US Africa Command's (USAFRICOM) civilian-military exercise *Judicious Response 2010/2011*. During this exercise, S/CRS worked with USAFRICOM to identify ways in which the military could support the Civilian Response Corps on the African continent.[58]

While the Civilian Response Corps is a great idea to coordinate an overall "whole of government" approach for stability operations, there are three major concerns about its ability to execute its mission given its current resourcing. The first concern is its ability to deploy an adequate amount of personnel to conduct stabilization operations properly based its current 4,250-person structure authorization. If a contingency or group of contingencies lasting a year or more occurred, the Civilian Response Corps could only mobilize and deploy approximately 1,750 members from all three manning groups on a sustained basis.[59] This equates to a little more than one US Army CA Brigade to coordinate all stability and reconstruction activities for the US government.[60] This could prove to be greatly inadequate if the Civilian Response Corps is required to solely coordinate and conduct large-scale contingencies similar to those in Iraq and Afghanistan as well as other ongoing responses. Tackling these types of missions with their limited personnel availability could result in the Civilian Response Corps adopting the US Agency for International Development's (USAID) model, which relies heavily on contractors to supplement their mission. This is dangerous because it could in essence morph the Civilian Response Corps into a "contracting" and "oversight" agency rather than an agency that brings critical knowledge and expertise to stabilization operations.

The second area concerns the Civil Response Corps' ability to respond rapidly to a situation based on its logistics capability. Because it lacks the robust logistical and security capability necessary to support its operations, it is clear that the Civilian Response Corps will likely not be as responsive as the military, particularly in austere environments that have uncertain or hostile populations. As a result, it is unlikely that the Civilian Response Corps will serve as the first responder to those global emergencies, which would leave an operational gap for the military to fill.[61]

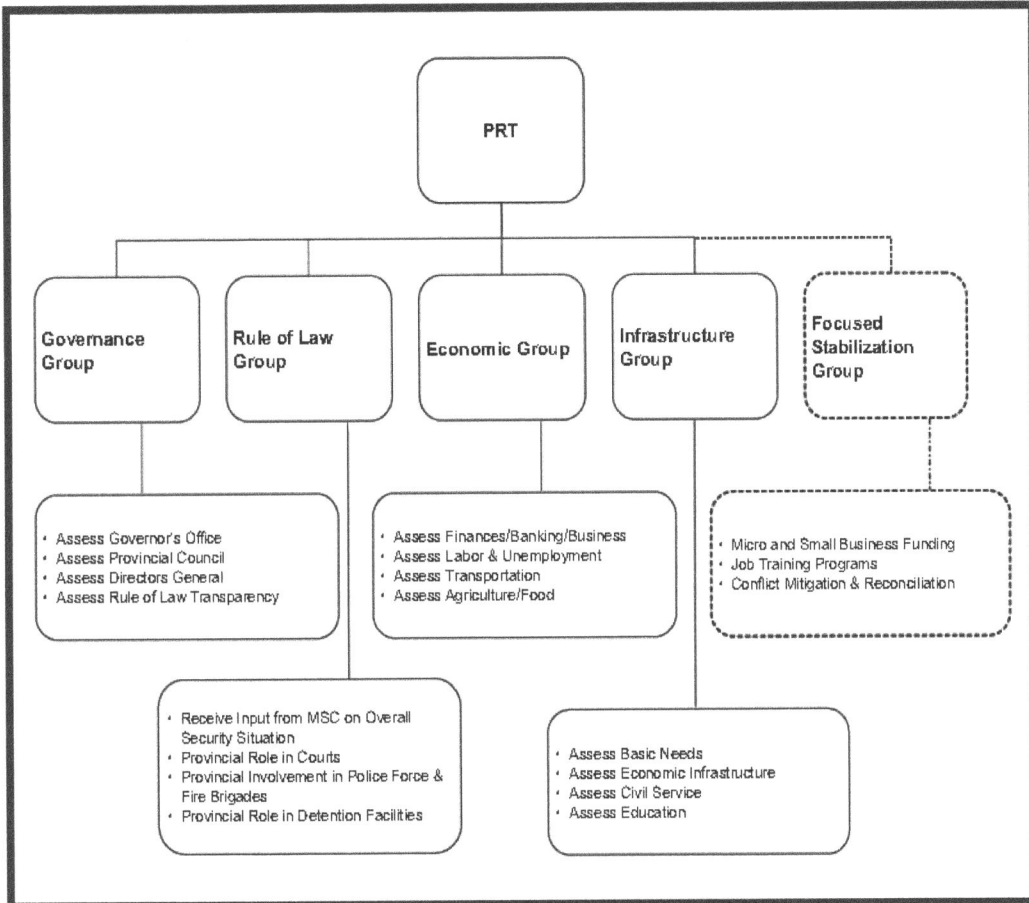

Figure 1. Recommended Organization of a Provincial Reconstruction Team

Source: US Army Combined Arms Center, "Provincial Reconstruction Teams: Tactics Techniques and Procedures" *Center for Army Lessons Learned Playbook* (2007), 69.

The final area of concern revolves around the willingness of civilian personnel to deploy to unstable areas. While the 2007 Iraq example provided earlier in this monograph highlights this concern, there has been little to no movement by the federal government to rectify this issue. While there are penalties such as the repayment for any education and expenses the member incurred during their training as part of the Civil Response Corps, unlike the military, there is no way to compel someone to deploy into a less than stable location.[62] Furthermore, once the civilian is deployed, it is hard to ensure that they will leave the security of their bases to execute their jobs responsibilities if security declines. In Iraq for example, "in particularly dangerous areas, civilian officials [would] frequently not leave military compounds for weeks or even months . . . [were] therefore almost completely ignorant of their surroundings, and rel[ied] heavily on the military or intelligence agencies for information on local events."[63] While some of the operational policy restrictions placed on civilians by their agencies exacerbate these shortfalls, the lack of in-depth security and response training and supporting capabilities also serve as a major contributive factor inhibiting success.

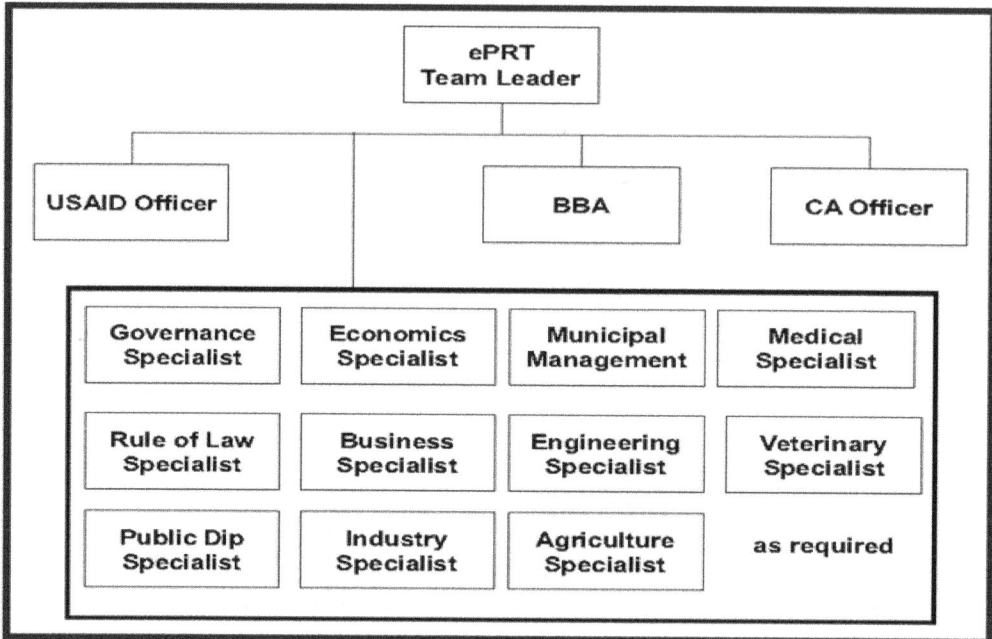

Figure 2. Embedded Provincial Reconstruction Team Organization
Source: US Army Combined Arms Center, "Provincial Reconstruction Teams: Tactics Techniques and Procedures" *Center for Army Lessons Learned Playbook* (2007), 70.

Another area where the US has taken considerable efforts to increase its ability to conduct economic development in stability operations is the Provincial Reconstruction Team (PRT). Created in 2002 to support Operation ENDURING FREEDOM in Afghanistan, the PRT is an organization that has membership from the Department of State, Department of Defense, and other federal agencies such as the Departments of Agriculture and Justice. The PRT assists in coordinating the efforts of these different agencies to address the regional reconstruction efforts in both Afghanistan and Iraq at the provincial level. They assist in the development of "a transparent and sustained capability to govern, promoting increased security and rule of law, promoting political and economic development and providing provincial administration necessary to meet the basic needs of the population".[64] Figure 1, outlines the recommended organization of the PRT.

To support reconstruction efforts below the provincial level and to assist the BCT, the concept of the Embedded Provincial Reconstruction Teams (ePRT) was developed in 2008. The ePRT concept provides the Brigade Commander with eight to twelve additional Department of State contractors and financial resources that can focus solely on the reconstruction and development efforts in his area of responsibility. In addition to its civilian membership, the ePRT also has a CA Officer to help coordinate the localized stability and development efforts.

While PRTs have received numerous accolades from the field for assisting in the success in Iraq, some significant concerns remain about their long-term viability. The first concern revolves around the regional and cultural knowledge that a member of a PRT brings, particularly now that the Department of State is beginning to rely more heavily on contractors to fill its personnel requirements. According to a study conducted by the United States Institute of Peace, "many of these contractors did not have previous field experience in the Middle East or had not previously worked on overseas development projects."[65] Thus, it typically took time for the ePRTs to understand the culture to a level where it could initiate economic development projects and provide governmental policy recommendations that fit Cornell and Kalt's standards for being both adequate and appropriate. The second major concern is that the PRT is an ad hoc organization. The assignment of military officers to fill these crucial positions is often based on their availability and not on any sort of development expertise or educational background, they may have. Additionally, the failure to institutionalize the PRT organization fails to establish effective long-term training programs and exercises similar to those that other institutionalized organizations complete such as rotations at the Army's National Training Center. Finally, the operational availability of civilian experts remains a major concern. Because there is such a heavy reliance on the civilian sector to provide the necessary development expertise, many of the concerns about their willingness to leave the safety and security of their bases remain. The US Marine Corps realized this concern in the summer of 2009 during Operation PANACHAI PALANG in Afghanistan when they cited a near total absence of civilian reconstruction experts to support their efforts into Helmand Province, forcing them to shift personnel from other areas to fill this personnel void.[66]

To support the reconstruction efforts in Afghanistan and Iraq, military units and PRTs have access to different funding sources. One of the unique sources is the Commander's Emergency Relief Program (CERP) that the Coalition Provincial Authority in Iraq created in 2003.[67] The Commander's Emergency Relief program enables "local commanders in Afghanistan and Iraq to respond to a non-lethal weapon to urgent, small-scale, humanitarian relief, and reconstruction projects and serves that immediately assist the indigenous population and the local population or government can sustain."[68] While CERP was originally intended to be used as a stabilization tool after the US toppled Iraq's Ba'ath Party in 2003 and was funded using seized assets from the Saddam Hussein regime, it has, over the years, become an integral part of the US approach to funding projects during Phase IV operations in both Iraq and Afghanistan. Since 2003, the United States Congress has appropriated more than $3.8 billion for CERP funding to support operations in Iraq.[69] While CERP only equates to approximately seven percent of the $53.8 billion in total US reconstruction appropriations for Operation IRAQI FREEDOM, it has forced the DoD to become involved in all aspects of stability operations, to include economic development.[70]

Within the $3.8 billion appropriated, approximately sixty percent, or $2.28 billion of the funds spent had direct ramifications on the economic development efforts in Iraq.[71]

The purpose of CERP is to allow Army units the ability to conduct small-scale projects that are less than $500,000 that produce a positive and recognizable impact in a unit's area of responsibility.[72] Projects funded with CERP should focus on improving local security, restoring essential services, reconstructing infrastructure damaged by combat operations, or conducting economic development in an area. While these areas are generally broad, the DoD has limited CERP expenditures to eighteen primary areas. Table 2 provides a description of those areas, the aggregate amount and associated percentages of CERP fund obligated to each area through July 2010.

Table 2. CERP Expenditures through July 2010

Authorized Area	Purpose	Amount of CERP Obligations through July 2010 (millions)	Percentage of CERP Obligations through July 2010
Water and sanitation	Repair or reconstruct water or sewer infrastructure, including water wells.	$690.2	20.3%
Protective measures	Fences, lights, barrier materials, berms over pipelines, or guard towers. Includes Temporary Contract Guards to guard critical infrastructure.	$476.8	14.0%
Electricity	Repair or reconstruct electrical power or distribution infrastructure, including generators.	$381.5	11.2%
Transportation	Repair or reconstruct transportation systems, roads, bridges, or transportation infrastructure.	$357.2	10.5%
Education	Repair or reconstruct schools, purchase school supplies, or equipment.	$339.9	10.0%
Civic cleanup activities	Remove trach, clean up the community, or perform beautification.	$207.5	6.1%
Other humanitarian or reconstruction projects	Repair collateral damage not otherwise payable because of combat exclusions or condolence payments.	$174.0	5.1%
Economic, financial and management improvments	Improve economic or financial security.	$137.2	4.0%
Agriculture	Increase agricultural production or cooperative agricultural programs. Includes repair or reconstruction of irrigation systems, including canal cleanup.	$122.3	3.6%
Rule of law and governance	Repair or reconstruct government buildings such as administration offices, courthouses, or prisons.	$120.6	3.6%
Healthcare	Repair or reconstruct hospitals or clinics or to provide urgent healthcare services, immunizations, medicine, medical supplies, or equipment	$112.6	3.3%
Repair civic and cultural facilities	Repair or restore civic cultural buidings or facilities.	$104.5	3.1%
Condolence Payments	Compensate for death, injury, or property damage resulting from U.S., coalition, or supporting military operations. Includes Survival payments to compensate surviving spouses or next of kin of Afghan or Iraqi defense or police personnel who were killed as a result of U.S., coalition, or supporting military operations.	$50.8	1.5%
Battle Damage Repair	Reoaur damage that results from U.S., coalition, or supporting military operations that is not compensable under the Foreign Claims Act.	$44.1	1.3%
Telecommunications	Repair or reconstruct telecommunications systems or infrastructure.	$32.6	1.0%
Civic support vehicles	Purchase or lease vehicles to support civic and community activities.	$24.6	0.7%
Food production and distribution	Increase food production or distribution processes.	$17.4	0.5%
Detainee Release Payments	Payments to individuals upon release from detention (only applies to Major Subordinate Commands) non-theater internment facility holding areas).	$1.4	0.04%

Source: Author Created based on data from Special Investigator General for Iraqi Reconstruction (SIGR), *Quarterly and Semi-Annual Report to the United States Congress* (Washington, DC: Government Printing Office, 2010), 39, and US Army Combined Arms Center, "Commander's Guide to Money as a Weapon System," *Center for Army Lessons Learned Handbook* 09-07 (2009), 17.

Despite the fact, there are several uses for CERP funds, economic development and reducing unemployment are two central goals for its use. By funding humanitarian relief and assistance projects with CERP funds, the US military is not only providing basic needs to the population, it is helping the host nation avoid the phenomenon Keynes coined as "paradox of thrift." The military accomplishes this through infrastructure investment and by creating short-term demand for goods and services needed to support humanitarian relief and assistance efforts. While this approach is critical in the early phases of a post-conflict environment, the US Army should also facilitate long-term economic stability by helping individuals gain access to capital markets. In pursing this goal, the DoD developed the Micro-Grant Program, which is a variant of micro-financing. Although microfinance is ineffective in resolving conflicts in active war zones, it does play an important role in Phase IV operations. The importance of micro-financing during the transition from conflict is articulated in a 2007 USAID study in which, micro-finance, "in the early phases of post-conflict stabilization and reconstruction can provide an effective means of both providing direct support to some of those most affected by conflict and laying the foundations for building permanent local financial institutions that will serve the poor in the long-term."[73] The purpose of the CERP Micro-Grant Program is to help disadvantaged entrepreneurs who are pursuing small or micro-business activities, which support humanitarian relief or reconstruction efforts. It provides individuals who do not have the necessary capital with access to funding that they otherwise would not be eligible for if they had to apply in the commercial market.[74]

While some consider the micro-grant program as one of the most successful components of CERP, the current program fails to maximize its true long-term potential. This is because it limits access to capital to only those entrepreneurs that provide goods and services to the traditional humanitarian relief and assistance sector. It discounts other viable economic sectors that provide innovative or imitative goods and services that could otherwise thrive if it had the necessary investment capital. The micro-grant program also fails to realize its long-term potential because it is relies solely on grants and not on loans or even a mixture of the two. Because there is no repayment of a micro-grant, the US military's long-term, economic development potential essentially stops and relies solely on the success of the business that received the grant. If the business fails, the money is lost. On the other hand, a micro-loan program would allow the long-term development potential to continue growing by continuing the financing of additional small businesses using the money repaid from the initial investment. This ultimately would expand the long-term development potential of the investment. Nobel Laurite Muhammad Yunus demonstrated the success of this type of program when he founded the Grameen Bank in India.

In his use of micro-loans, Yunis established a socially accepted structure that was relatively simple, relied on mutual trust, and was culturally sensitive. First, the structure or terms of Grameen Bank's loans was simple in that they lasted for only one year and borrowers were expected to pay weekly installments that equated to approximately two percent of the total loan starting one week after the loan was issued.[75] Second, it required that each prospective borrower join a group of like-minded people from similar economic and social backgrounds to create a support network and to make each borrower more reliable through peer pressure. Peer pressure was a key component because it provided incentive for those in the group to repay their loans. If a member of the group failed to pay, future loans to others in the group would be rejected until the original loan was repaid.[76]

This type of organization has resulted in a 97.2 percent repayment rate.[77] Third, it was culturally sensitive in that it operated within the constraints of Sharia Law which forbids banks from charging borrowers interest. Since each borrower was part of a group that was formally recognized by the bank, they were viewed as part owners.[78] Furthermore, because the Grameen Bank established policies that were both culturally acceptable and adequate, the bank eventually grew to serve more than 8.3 million people, ninety-seven percent of which are women, in over 100 countries.[79]

While this monograph is not advocating that the US Army enter into the banking business system, it is arguing for more effective use of CERP funds. Rather than simply using grants, the Army could foster a micro-loan program by helping the host nation establish an organization similar to the Grameen Bank and later provide it with the necessary starting capital. The Center for Agriculture and Rural Development (CARD) in the Philippines serves as a salient example of this type of arrangement. This organization initially faced difficulties finding organizations that could provide for financial sourcing. Yet, once CARD secured financing, the program took off. In less than seven years, ninety-seven percent of CARD borrowers invested in income-generating activities that created on average 163 days of employment for its borrowers and an eighty-four additional days for their family members. It has also resulted in an approximate 36 percent increase in wages over the prevailing local rate.[80] By approaching economic development in this manner will help to ensure that economic development efforts have a lasting effect.

Army Support to Stability Operations

In *The Utility of Force: The Art of War in the Modern World,* British General Rupert Smith argues that there is not a generic "military force." Rather, there are components of specialized forces that can be selected for specific purposes.[81] This statement is especially true when it comes to dealing with many of the complex civilian problems a military unit faces in stability operations. In dealing with this problem, some advocates argue that the US Army's force structure should be bifurcated to contain "warfighters and peacekeepers." While this type of approach would resolve many of the tensions within the Army regarding training focus and resourcing, the financial costs of this option and the domestic economic realities of today make this option largely untenable. Rather, adroitly focusing Army units in the Army Force Generation Model (ARFORGEN) as well as comprehensively reforming the Army's organizational structure, doctrine, and education system, to address many of the stability challenges of tomorrow within the current budgetary and force structure allocations.

One way that the Army is attempting to approach increasing its effectiveness in stability operations is through the regional alignment of BCTs with each of the five overseas Global Combatant Commands (GCC).[82] To understand this approach, one has to understand how the Army goes about identifying, training, manning, and equipping its forces using the ARFORGEN model first. The ARFORGEN model is "the structured progression of increased unit readiness over time, resulting in recurring periods of availability of trained, ready, and cohesive units prepared for operational deployment in support of civil authorities and combatant commander requirements."[83] The intent of this supply side model is to provide the nation with a continuous and predictable amount of trained and ready forces to deploy in support of global contingencies.

In this model, every unit's life cycle begins in the Reset Pool. When a unit is in this pool, it begins to build its organization through the reception of new personnel and equipment and begins to train on individual tasks. Once the unit receives key personnel and equipment, it moves to the Train/Ready Pool. In this pool, the unit continues to receive personnel and equipment and begins to train on collective tasks that affect the entire unit. The unit remains in the pool unit it is proficient for its future mission and completes culminating collective training exercise, validating its readiness to deploy. Once validated, the unit moves into the Available pool where it either deploys or is remains ready in the United States to support a global contingency.

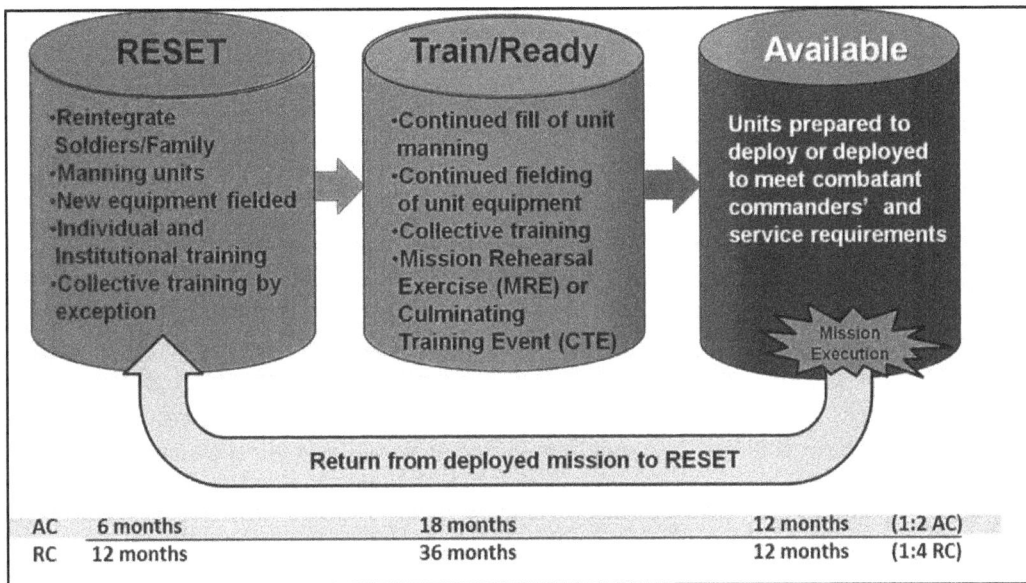

RESET
- Reintegrate Soldiers/Family
- Manning units
- New equipment fielded
- Individual and Institutional training
- Collective training by exception

Train/Ready
- Continued fill of unit manning
- Continued fielding of unit equipment
- Collective training
- Mission Rehearsal Exercise (MRE) or Culminating Training Event (CTE)

Available
Units prepared to deploy or deployed to meet combatant commanders' and service requirements

Mission Execution

Return from deployed mission to RESET

AC	6 months	18 months	12 months	(1:2 AC)
RC	12 months	36 months	12 months	(1:4 RC)

Figure 3. Army Force Generation Model

Source: Headquarters, Department of the Army. *2010 Army Posture Statement.* (Washington, DC: Government Printing Office, 2010), F-1.

Because the ARFORGEN model is cyclic in nature, the speed that the units move through the model can vary based on the operational demand. It is measured using boots on the ground (BOG) to time at home, or dwell, ratio. For instance, in the 2007, the global demand for BCTs was approximately 27 out of the 72 total BCTs to meet the operational requirements for all global contingencies, to include OIF, OEF, Korea, Horn of Africa missions, etc. Within the total twenty-seven BCT demand, nineteen were from the Active Component (AC). As a result, the AC BCT BOG-to-Dwell ratio was one-to-one.[84] This meant that for every twelve months deployed, a BCT, on average, would receive approximately twelve months at home. A one-to-one BOG-to-Dwell ratio is highly unsustainable for the protracted conflicts the US is currently operating within for numerous reasons such as unit preparedness, individual stress, and equipment availability. To alleviate the stress on the force, the Secretary of Defense, through the QDR has established goals of a one-to-two

BOG-to-Dwell ratio for Active Component units and a one-to-four BOG-to-Dwell ratio for Reserve Component (RC) units.[85] The Army has increased the time at home by stating in 2010 Army Posture Statement that its goal is to achieve a sustainable BOG-to-Dwell ratio of one-to-three for the AC and a one-to-five BOG-to-Dwell ratio for the RC.[86]

The implementation of regionally aligning BCTs would require identification of the BCT while it was in the Reset pool. In this pool, the BCT could receive unique equipping, manning, and training to either conduct stability operations, security forces assistance, or participate in partnership exercises in each of the GCC's area of responsibility. They will receive mission unique equipment and cultural and language skills that will help ensure the BCT is trained to maximize its effectiveness. Additionally, the BCT regional alignment plan receives further enhancement through the re-alignment of a Special Forces Group to each of the GCCs.[87] While it is apparent that the regional alignment strategy should not be implemented until demand in OIF and OEF is reduced, this type of strategy will greatly enhance the GCC's ability to employ the best led, staffed, and equipped forces in pursuit of their regional strategic objectives.

In his 2007 white paper "Adapting our Aim: A Balanced Army for a Balanced Strategy," the Army Chief of Staff, General George Casey Jr., outlined six defining qualities that will enable the US Army to meet the operational challenges of the twenty-first century: versatile, expeditionary, agile, lethal, sustainable, and interoperable. In outlining these qualities, he states, "versatility is the central organizing principle of a balanced Army, for it is this quality that will enable our forces and institutions to effectively execute operations across the spectrum of conflict."[88] In pursuit of this goal, the US Army has taken considerable steps in trying to adapt its force structure. Since 2004, the Army has "taken between 175,000 and 200,000 [personnel] spaces away from skills that were very necessary in the Cold War and have converted them into skills that are more relevant today."[89] This equates to the conversion of approximately 200 tank, air defense, and artillery units to a corresponding number of CA, Psychological Operations, Special Forces, and Engineer units.[90] Yet, there are several organizational, doctrinal, training, and personnel challenges that continue to impede the Army's forward momentum in fully developing institutionally supported stability capabilities.

Organization

The majority of the Army's specialized stability and reconstruction capabilities reside within CA because it is responsible for providing the military commander with expertise in areas ranging from foreign humanitarian assistance to on nation assistance and support to civil administration.[91] After the Vietnam War, political and fiscal factors drove former Chief of Staff of the Army General Creighton Abrams to place the majority of the Army's CA capability into the reserve component, where it remains today.[92] The RC force structure consists of four Civil Affairs Commands (CACOM) that support four of the five overseas GCCs: US European Command (USEUCOM), US Central Command (USCENTCOM), US Southern Command (USSOUTHCOM), and US Pacific Command (USPACOM). The RC also has eight CA Brigades, twenty-eight CA Battalions, and 112 CA Companies. The AC force structure consists of two Brigades. The 95th CA Brigade consists of three battalions and supports US Special Forces Command. The 96th CA Brigade supports the general-purpose force and consists of four battalions to provide some level of regional alignment, similar to the CACOMs. In addition to these two AC CA Brigades, the Army recently decided to build the 86th CA Brigade to support the general-purpose force. While superficially this force structure appears adequate, there are several areas, which, if adjusted, could greatly improve the overall effectiveness of the Civil Affairs Branch to conduct economic development.

The distribution of AC and RC units must be re-balanced to ensure long-term readiness and responsiveness of the CA units. The problem with having majority of CA force structure in the Reserve Component is that they are not as responsive as active duty organizations. Typically, a reserve unit requires approximately sixty days to mobilize upon notification, which may delay their arrival until long after they are needed during Phase IV operations. Another concern is the high demand of these units is requires increased disruption to the civilian lives of its Reserve Soldiers, which in the long-term is politically untenable. In Fiscal Year 2010, the United States Army Reserve (USAR) CA BDE Headquarters cycled through the ARFORGEN cycle at a one-to-one point one BOG-to-Dwell ratio; meaning that units received only thirteen months and six days at home for every year they were deployed.[93] This ratio is well below the QDR stated BOG-to-Dwell goal of one-to-four. It is evident by the current trends projected in the Joint Operating Environment that operational demands for the military will not decline as land forces continue to focus on engaging more countries to help them build capacity to deny insurgents areas to operate.[94] General Casey reiterated this belief in April 2010 when he stated that the Army would have approximately 50,000 to 70,000 troops deployed for the near future.[95] This equates to approximately ten BCTs. Therefore, it is safe to assume that there is going to be a sustained demand for the unique stabilization capabilities that CA units provide. In 2010, Major Samuel Kyle Simpson examined this question and concluded the annual aggregate demand for supporting expected global contingencies for CA units would equate to 16.8 Company equivalents, 4.8 Battalion Headquarters, and 1.3 Brigade Headquarters.[96]

To meet the anticipated future global CA demands and to reduce reliance on the RC, the Army should grow four additional AC CA Brigades. Because the Army's Active Component end-strength is limited to 547,000 personnel, the Army can accomplish this growth by converting more expensive and conventional capabilities into RC capabilities to free up personnel spaces. This monograph advocates accomplishing this task through the conversion of two Heavy Brigade Combat Teams (HBCT) from the AC to the RC and converting four CA Brigades and other critical enabling capabilities such as Engineers from the RC to the AC. This type of conversion will also do three things. First, it will relieve the stress on the Reserve Component by allowing the Active Component to shoulder more of the operational demand requirements for Civil Affairs. Second, it will provide enough AC force structure to allow each AC CA Brigade to focus its training, education, and recruiting efforts regionally. It will also allow the AC CA Brigade to provide the necessary continuity needed to oversee long-term development projects within these regions. Finally, it will provide the additional AC personnel slots to develop and build additional economic stability sections that will be discussed later in this section.

Table 3. Alternative BCT Force Mix

Approved 2013 BCT Force Mix					Proposed BCT Force Mix			
	Active Component	Reserve Component	Total			Active Component	Reserve Component	Total
HBCT	18	7	25		HBCT	16	9	25
IBCT	20	20	40		IBCT	20	20	40
SBCT	7	1	8		SBCT	7	1	8
Total	45	28	73		Total	43	30	73

Source: Author created.

The HBCT is an excellent candidate for this type of conversion because it accomplishes four things. First, it does not change the total number of HBCTs that would be available to deploy in support of a large-scale contingency such as OIF. Second, it does not greatly diminish the US Army's global responsiveness. Because the HBCTs are reliant on strategic sealift to deploy, the amount of time that it would take for the flotilla to return to the US after delivering the initial entry forces would provide adequate time for these RC HBCTs to prepare to deploy. Third, it has a negligible effect on how many HBCTs are produced in the ARFORGEN cycle. At a one-to-three AC BOG-to-Dwell cycle, the Army can still produce four HBCTs. Finally, at a ten BCT demand, the Army can still meet its one-to-three AC and one-to-five RC BOG-to-Dwell rates if this conversion is executed. It will degrade the AC BCT dwell by approximately ninety-three days[97] while increasing the RC BCT dwell by approximately 162 days.[98] While this will reduce the deployment of reserve CA personnel who will deploy and bring with them critical experience and expertise that could help in economic development, long-term utilization of these personnel will become more politically untenable if the US remains in a protracted conflict as predicted by the national strategies.

Table 4. BOG-to-Dwell Implications

BOG:Dwell based on Operational Demands Using Proposed 2013 BCT Force Mix					BOG:Dwell based on Operational Demands Using Proposed 2013 BCT Force Mix			
	BCT Demand	Active Component	Reserve Component			BCT Demand	Active Component	Reserve Component
2007-like (Peak)	27 (19 AC/8 RC)	1:1.1	1:1.3		2007-like (Peak)	27 (19 AC/8 RC)	1:1 -34 days	1:1.5 +61 days
2010-like (Current)	22 (15 AC/7 RC)	1:1.7	1:1.7		2010-like (Current)	22 (15 AC/7 RC)	1:1.6 -43 days	1:1.9 +70 days
2012-like (Post Iraq)	10 (7 AC/3 RC)	1:4.8	1:5.3		2012-like (Post Iraq)	10 (7 AC/3 RC)	1:4.5 -93 days	1:5.8 +162 days

Source: Author created.

To help it integrate itself within the Army organizational structure, CA aligns itself organizationally within the various levels of the Army command structure. The Civil Affairs Commands (CACOM) provide theater-level CA planning, coordination, policies, and programs to support stability operations through their alignment with the

Combatant Command.[99] Below the CACOM, the CA Brigade supports the Corps and the Battalion supports the Division. While this type of support structure is beneficial at the Combatant Command Level, it does not provide the same level of operational fidelity at the Operational level where strategic guidance is translated into tactical actions. One way to increase operational fidelity is to allow the CA Brigade to support the Army Service Component Commands, or Theater Armies, directly. This will not only provide greater situational awareness for the CA Brigade (BDE), but it will also help facilitate and operational deployment. When an operation occurs and the Army Service Command employs its deployable Contingency Command Post (CCP), the CA BDE can deploy a fully integrated contingency planning cell that has full understanding of the country as well as the operational plan.[100]

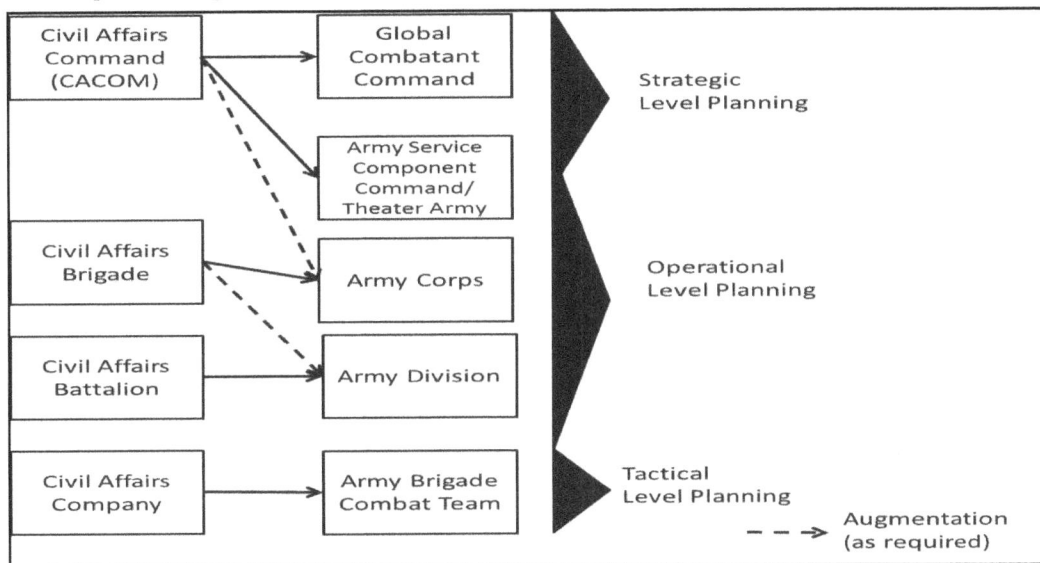

Figure 4. Army Civil Affairs Support Relationship

Source: Adapted from figure 2-2, Headquarters, Department of the Army, *Field Manual 3-05.40: Civil Affairs Operations* (Washington, DC, 2006) 2-5.

Within each of the four CACOMs, there are three functional specialty cells split into six sections. One of these sections is an economic stability section. The economic stability section is important because it provides the Geographic Combatant Commander with critical insights of the economic situation of a country. Manned with economic and business specialists, the economic stability section provides critical economic insights for the development of plans, policies, and procedures for establishing economic and commercial systems. The sections are capable of providing technical expertise to assist in the identification and assessment of food and agriculture systems, provide advice on the reestablishment of budgetary systems, monetary policy, treasury operations, and counter-inflationary measures such as price control and rationing programs.[101]

While this cell provides the Geographic Combatant Commander with economic advice to help in the development of strategic level policies, this essential capability is not present at either the tactical level or the operational level where strategic guidance is translated into tactical actions. As a result, the commands at these levels have to create ad-hoc organizations, typically by moving personnel with some level of economic background from their military specialty to fill this void. While this approach may work in some situations, there are two significant downsides to this approach. The first is that the Commander may not always have someone with the necessary expertise to understand the economic development challenges that the unit faces, which over time may worsen the problem. The second downside is by taking personnel from their assigned responsibilities, the Commander is assuming some inherent risk to his operation in areas from where they pull people. A way to mitigate this risk is by establishing an economic stability section in each of the CA Brigades, Battalions and Companies to integrate with the other four specialty cells. Executing this course of action would require approximately 600 additional AC personnel spaces, which would be within the personnel authorizations of this conversion strategy.[102]

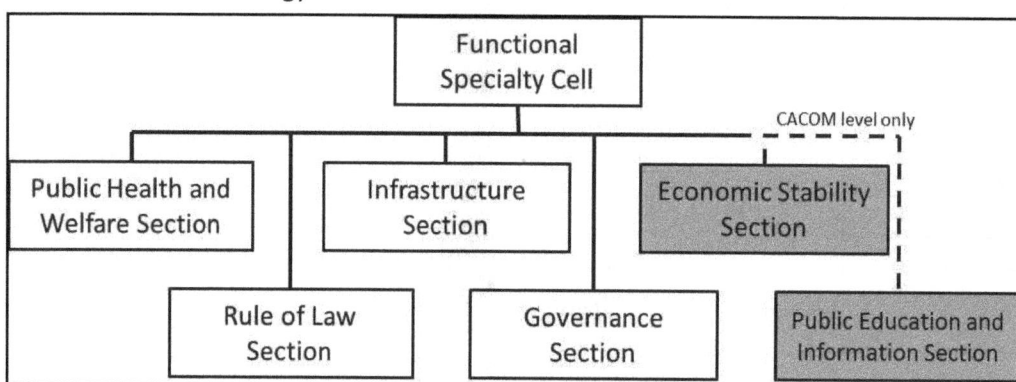

Figure 5. Functional Specialty Cell Organization

Source: Adapted from figure 2-4, Headquarters, Department of the Army, *Field Manual 3-05.40: Civil Affairs Operations* (Washington, DC, 2006) 2-7.

Doctrine

Joint Publication 1-02: Dictionary of Military and Associated Terms defines doctrine as the:

> fundamental principles by which the military forces or elements thereof guide their actions in support of national objectives. It is authoritative but requires judgment in application.[03]

Doctrine is important because it provides the Army with guidance, a common understanding, and a generalized way of approaching a situation. First, it helps guide the Army in determining what type of force structure and technologies to purse. Second, it provides a forum in which lessons from past operations can be recorded and disseminated. Third, it provides a foundation for how the Army conducts business in an operation by providing standardized approaches to a problem.[104] The purpose of doctrine should be to give a baseline understanding of how to approach a mission. Doctrine should not direct specific solutions or be prescriptive in providing solutions for specific problems. Rather, it should be generalized and provide abstract conceptual understanding for how to approach a problem. Prescriptive solutions and understanding should occur through mentorship or professional military education, which gives the individual the necessary experience to be reflective and approach the problem from different perspectives.

While the need for economic development is identified in nearly all of the Army's major doctrinal field manuals to include *Field Manual* (FM) *3-0: Operations, FM 3-28: Counterinsurgency,* and *FM 3-05.40: Civil Affairs Operations, FM 3-07: Stability Operations* provides the greatest conceptual insights into how an Army unit should go about conducting economic development. It provides military personnel with a generalized understanding that economic development efforts should integrate with efforts in governance and security, particularly at the local level. It highlights the importance of restoring the physical infrastructure of the host nation to facilitate the transfer of goods and services as well as the need to support the host nations central monetary institutions and treasury operations. Finally, *FM 3-07: Stability Operations* also discusses the importance of supporting private sector and agricultural programs. Yet, unlike other field manuals that help provide both detail and general understanding, *FM 3-07: Stability Operations* focuses solely on the general description at the strategic or national level. It provides little insights into how a BCT, CA Brigade, or any Battalion should approach economic development in their area of operation. As a result, military personnel seeking to understand how they can lead their units in an economic development mission are forced to look elsewhere.

One place where individuals can look is to the Center for Army Lessons Learned. This organization periodically publishes Handbooks and Playbooks that disseminate tactics, techniques, and procedures in areas ranging from the establishment of a Provincial Reconstruction Team to Agribusiness Development Teams. Although the Handbook 10-10 Agribusiness Development Teams, provides some excellent insights on areas to train prior to deployment, the majority of these books focus on administrative tasks such as filling out paperwork, approval cycles, and funding rules versus providing insights on best business or employment practices.

Although some critics of economic development believe the Army should not invest time or resources in writing this type of doctrine in favor other manuals that could have greater value, or because they believe the US Army should not have a part in economic development, they are failing to recognize the increasing use of the military for stability operations. Because the US Army is not going to untangle itself from stability operations that include an economic development aspect for the foreseeable future, it is critical that the Army develop a field manual that fills this void. While there is never a "one size fits all" approach to economic development, a manual that provides insights into economic development is significant. First, it provides the necessary detail and understanding to implement the national level economic development tasks outlined in Table 1 successfully. Second, it will provide guidance on how to approach entrepreneurial economic development at the local level. Third, it will significantly influence the bureaucracy and funding authorities that enable this type of mission. Finally, it will codify many of the lessons and economic development approaches borne out of nine years of stability operations in Iraq and Afghanistan.

Training and Education

In examining some of the lessons learned from Iraq and Afghanistan, more commanders and senior officers highlighted the significance of economic development and its importance on the national and local economies.[105] Lieutenant General Robert Caslen Jr., a former Commander of the 25th Infantry Division cogently summarized this belief when he stated:

> [f]rom a division commander who had responsibility for the seven northern provinces of Iraq here recently, we had an economic line of effort and we put a lot of energy into the development of the economy through CERP or starting new businesses . . . if I had had this background, and if our officers had had this training, this was exactly the kind of thing we need to go into these kinds of operations.[106]

Over the past nine years, the Army has taken some considerable steps in trying to educate its force on the importance of good governance and cultural awareness, which as discussed earlier, are critical components for successful economic development. It has established the West Point Center for the Rule of Law, which is dedicated to promulgating the idea of rule of law in both peacetime and conflict. It has established the Judge Advocate General's Legal Center and School to provide members of other federal agencies with an academic understanding of the rule of law. The Army also established the Center for Law and Military operations to collect the lessons learned from past operational experiences with the rule of law in order to publish them to those deploying in support of a contingency operation.[107]

Culturally, the Army has taken some positive steps as well. To begin developing future leaders who are culturally sound and have a strong foundation for high demand languages, the Army has begun to give incentives to Reserve Officer Training Corps cadets to take language courses as part of their undergraduate studies. It has also begun to institute and encourage enrollment in online language programs such as Rosetta Stone©. Finally, Officers identified for deployment in OIF or OEF are required to take language training if they are attending one of the Army's professional development schools.

While these schools have provided insights into the cultural and governance aspects of stability operations, a void remains when it comes to teaching economic development to the overall officer population. In examining the officer professional development system there is little to no economic development education for company grade and field grade officers who are the most likely to encounter economic development at the local and province level. When an officer is commissioned after the completion of their undergraduate studies, they attend the Officer Basic Course (OBC). The OBC is intended to provide specialty and some general training to prepare the officer for their future jobs as a Platoon Leader. Once the officer is selected for the rank of captain, they attend the Captains Career Course (CCC) which builds upon the education they received in OBC by providing the officer with more in-depth specialty training as well as some non-branch specific they will need to execute their future job as a company commander. This training typically includes equipment accountability and instruction on the Uniform Code of Military Justice. Once the officer attains the rank of major, they attend Intermediate Level Training (ILE) at the Command

and General Staff College (CGSC). Intermediate Level Training provides the officer with a broad level of non-branch material instruction that focuses on Joint and Army operational planning, history, leadership and tactics.

At all of these schools, there is an emphasis on conducting stability operations but primarily focus on the security or military aspect. For example, the economic development education that majors attending the ILE program received during their core instruction focused solely on the bureaucratic rules of how to request, dispense, and account for funds from the CERP.[108] While this is important for accountability, the failure to provide some basic instruction on entrepreneurism or business development is a huge missed opportunity. Recently, CGSC developed some classes such as "Expeditionary Economics" and "Economic Instrument of Power" to provide exposure to economics. Although the enrollment opportunity for these classes was limited to approximately three percent of the population based on resourcing, this is a step in the right direction.[109] The Army and CGSC can take this to the next level by developing an economic development program of instruction similar to the joint planner, space activities, or strategist programs already taught to expose the general officer population to economics.

One way that this can be accomplished is through the development of a generalized economic development Army Skill Identifier (ASI). The ASI is a way that the Army trains and later identifies Soldiers with skills beyond their basic military specialty. There is currently a 6C "economist" ASI, but it focuses primarily on those serving within the specialty functional cells of a CA unit. It requires a "[m]asters degree in economics, finance, international business, or business administration and/or a minimum of 5 years civilian experience in economics, banking, public finance, or foreign/domestic development or a related field". [110] While these types of qualifications are critically important for CA personnel, particularly in the economic specialty cells, it fails to provide the general officer population with the opportunity to gain tangible economic development understanding in order to improve their units' capabilities and performance in stability operations. To fill this void, the Army should develop a "tactical economic developer" ASI program that provides basic understanding entrepreneurial and small business development strategies, innovative and imitative economic development strategies, and neighborhood development strategies. All of these types of courses can be taught at CGSC similar to the three programs discussed earlier. Doing so will increase the number of officers with the basic skills, insights, and approaches for tacking economic development issues at the tactical or local level.

Economic development training should also be a focal point for the Civil Affairs CA School to ensure that all active and reserve component Civil Affairs Soldiers are certified to some level. According to Edward Burke, a researcher at the Spanish think tank Fundación para las Relaciones Internacionales y el Diálogo Exterior or FRIDE, Reserve CA officers "often lack training in political and linguistic skills, as well as an advanced knowledge of their local environment upon deploying to Iraq and Afghanistan."[111] In conjunction with the formal military education provided by the Civil Affairs School, the Army should also focus the type of education Soldiers receive when pursuing a master's degree as part of its Advanced Civil Schooling (ACS) program. While there are some branches in the Army that direct the study program for its participants, the majority of them do not. As a result, educational experience that would be mutually beneficial to both the officer and could provide the Army with broader economic or business development knowledge is lost.

In trying to improve its Soldiers understanding of the interagency and the private sector, the Army has instituted several strategic relationships with other federal agencies, think tanks and private institutions. Examples of these include fellowships at the Department of State, Arroyo Center, and the United States Congress. While these opportunities are greatly beneficial to those officers that attend, participation is limited to a small handful of officers. To rectify this problem, the Army should further expand these opportunities by establishing standing assignments that qualified Civil Affairs Soldiers can fill which directly related to economic development. By expanding training opportunities with federal agencies such as USAID and the Departments of Commerce, Trade, Agriculture, and Treasury and with private and non-governmental organizations such as the Grameen Bank, US Chamber of Commerce, Kauffman Center, and the International Agency for Economic Development, Soldiers will gain critical economic development insights that they can bring back to the Army.

Conclusion

The current environment that the United States exists is one, which will require greater commitment to stability operations if it is going to secure its interests abroad adequately. Doing so will require a greater understanding and ability to skillfully employ economic development as a way to achieve long-term stability. Since the end of the Cold War, the United States Army has clearly demonstrated that it understands and can effectively conduct conventional operations. Yet, the conflicts the Army currently faces and will for the foreseeable future will require non-conventional understanding to effectively execute stability operations or counterinsurgency operations. These types of missions are less familiar and require understanding of factors other than military force to include governance, information, tribal influence, religion, history, culture, and economic development.

In a 2010 article discussing the military's attempts to cope with the complex operational issues presented in stability operations, the Chairman of the Joint Chiefs of Staff, Admiral Michael Mullen stated, "[t]his just strikes at the heart of something I've thought for a long time: It's all about economics." [112] Yet, the Army is currently ill-prepared to deal with this central issue because it is apprehensive to formalize, institutionalize, and build upon the lessons that it has gained over the past nine years in the conflicts in Iraq and Afghanistan. As a result, extensive familiarity and understanding of the complex environments presented in both counterinsurgency and stability operations could be lost. Instead, the Army seems to be relying on the "whole of government" approach as a silver bullet solution so it can disengage from developing and institutionalizing many of the "uncomfortable" capabilities in favor of traditional military capabilities.

While the "whole of government" approach is a lofty one, the realities of large-scale contingencies indicate that organizations such as the Civilian Response Corps will not absolve the US Army from an economic development role in stability operations. Experiences with this type of approach demonstrate that it will not achieve its full expectations until a fully secure environment is established. As demonstrated in both Iraq and Afghanistan, while civilian economic development experts bring significant expertise to a stability operation, they are continually apprehensive about venturing into uncertain or hostile environments. Therefore, it is incumbent upon military to fill this operational gap in order to seize and exploit potential opportunities to lay the foundation for long-term economic development in these situations.

While the Army has taken some considerable steps in adapting its force structure to provide better cultural awareness and focus for its BCTs to conduct security forces assistance under the regional alignment plan, it must also do so in its non-traditional military capabilities as well. By developing doctrine that addresses many of the economic development questions presented in local and by providing officers and non-commissioned officers with some basic understanding of economic theory and development approaches in their professional education, the Army can improve its overall effectiveness in stability operations. The Army can take another significant leap in establishing a balanced force for the twenty-first century that is able to respond to global contingencies by growing its active CA capabilities. By converting two HBCTs from the AC to the RC and converting four CA brigades and other critical enablers from the RC to the AC, the Army will be able to shoulder more operational demands while developing and sustaining the necessary regional expertise and long-term development oversight necessary to support the Geographic Combatant Commands more effectively.

In their book *Military Misfortunes*, Eliot Cohen and John Gooch identify three kinds of failure that military organizations encounter: failure to learn, failure to anticipate, and failure to adapt. They argue that when two or more failures occur at the same time, it is an aggregate failure that can have catastrophic effects.[113] It is apparent, based on the current trends and projections provided by the CCJO, that technology, globalization, urbanization, and weak or failing states, as well as competing international narratives that will require the military to possess in-depth knowledge and experience in each of the instruments of power; to include the economic instrument of power. Although the Army has anticipated this requirement, continued reluctance to learn and adapt its organization could result in the Army relearning these lessons the same way it did in both Iraq and Afghanistan – the hard way.

Notes

1. John F. Kennedy, "Remarks at West Point to the Graduating Class of the US Military Academy," John F. Kennedy Library, June 6, 1962. http://www.jfklibrary.org/Asset+Tree/ Asset+Viewers/Audio+Video+Asset+Viewer.htm?guid={71B1B505-C400-4CA5-8CE8- 2C36BC2618F0}&type=Audio (accessed December 7, 2010).

2. Richard F. Grimmett, CRS Report for Congress: Instances of Use of United States Armed Forces Abroad, 1798-2007 (Washington, DC: Congressional Research Service, 2008), http://www. au.af.mil/au/awc/awcgate/crs/rl32170.pdf (accessed December 7, 2010).

3. United States Joint Forces Command, Joint Operating Environment: 2010 (Suffolk, VA: Government Printing Office, 2010), 3.

4. Robert M. Gates, "Helping Others Defend Themselves." Foreign Affairs 89, no. 3 (May/June 2010): 2. In this article, Secretary of Defense Robert M. Gates stated that the types of threats that the US will encounter will require many of the ad hoc security assistance, stability, and reconstruction capabilities that the Department of Defense (DoD) created during the prosecution of the wars in Afghanistan and Iraq.

5. Paul Collier, "Economic Causes of Civil Conflict and their Implications for Policy" (University of Oxford, 2006), http://users.ox.ac.uk/...econpco/research/pdfs/EconomicCausesofCivilConflict- ImplicationsforPolicy.pdf (accessed December 7, 2010), 6.

6. Collier, "Economic Causes of Civil Conflict and their Implications for Policy", 6.

7. Kori Schake, "Operationalizing Expeditionary Economics" (Hoover Institution, 2010), 2.

8. Joint Staff, Joint Publication 1-02: Dictionary of Military and Associated Terms: As Amended Through 31 July 2010 (Washington, DC: Government Printing Office, 2010), 212. A hostile environment is an "operational environment in which hostile forces have control as well as the intent and capability to effectively oppose or react to the operations a unit intends to conduct."

9. Joint Staff, Joint Publication 1-0: Dictionary of Military and Associated Terms: As Amended Through 31 July 2010 (Washington, DC: Government Printing Office, 2010), 212. An uncertain environment is an "Operational environment in which host government forces, whether opposed to or receptive to operations that a unit intends to conduct, do not have totally effective control of the territory and population in the intended operational area."

10. National Public Radio, "Diplomats Pushed to Serve in Iraq," National Public Radio, http:// www.npr.org/templates/story/story.php?storyId=15939537&ft=1&f=1012 (accessed December 7, 2010).

11. Joint Staff, Joint Publication 3.0: Joint Operations: Incorporating Change 2 (Washington, DC: Government Printing Office, 2010), IV-29.

12. Joint Staff, Joint Publication 3.0, IV-29.

13. Conrad C. Crane, "Phase IV Operations: Where Wars are Really Won," Military Review (May-June 2007): 19.

14. Keith Mines, "E-Notes: Economic tools in Counterinsurgency and Postconflict Stabilizations: Lessons Learned (and Relearned) in al Anbar, Iraq, 2003-04," Foreign Policy Research Institute, http://www.fpri.org/enotes/20060928.military.mines.economictoolscounterinsurgency.html (accessed September 17, 2010).

15. The Department of Defense categorizes the national instruments of power into four areas:

66

diplomatic, information, military, and economic.

16. Office of the President of the United States, The National Security Strategy of the United States of America (Washington, DC: Government Printing Office, 2010), 15.

17. Office of the President, The National Security Strategy of the United States, 15.

18. Department of Defense, National Defense Strategy (Washington, DC: Government Printing Office, 2008), 1.

19. Department of Defense, National Defense Strategy, 7-8.

20. Department of Defense, National Defense Strategy, 17.

21. Department of Defense, Department of Defense Instruction 3000.05 (Washington, DC: US Department of Defense, 2009), 2-3.

22. Department of Defense, Department of Defense Instruction 3000.05, 1.

23. Department of Defense, Quadrennial Defense Review Report (Washington, DC: Government Printing Office, 2010), 24.

24. Department of Defense, Quadrennial Defense Review Report, 24.

25. Joint Staff, Capstone Concept for Joint Operations [Version 3.0] (Washington, DC: Government Printing Office, 2009), 32-33.

26. Joint Staff, Joint Publication 3-07.3: Peace Operations (Washington, DC: Government Printing Office, 2007), IV-9.

27. Gerald P. Driscoll, Adam Smith and Modern Political Economy: Bicentennial Essays on the Wealth of Nations (Ames: Iowa State University Press, 1979), 5.

28. Driscoll, Adam Smith and Modern Political Economy, 5.

29. D.P. O'Brien, Classical Economists (Oxford: Oxford University Press, 1975), 32.

30. Gerald P. Driscoll, Adam Smith and Modern Political Economy: Bicentennial Essays on the Wealth of Nations (Ames: Iowa State University Press, 1979), 5.

31. Driscoll, Adam Smith and Modern Political Economy, 24.

32. Driscoll, Adam Smith and Modern Political Economy, 12.

33. Driscoll, Adam Smith and Modern Political Economy, 10.

34. Sayali Bedekar Patil, "Classical Economics vs. Keynesian Economics," Buzzle Web Portal: Intelligent Life on the Web, http://www.buzzle.com/articles/classical-economics-vs-keynesian-economics.html (accessed December 7, 2010).

35. Harlan M. Smith, Understanding Economics (Armonk, N.Y.: M.E. Sharpe, 1999), 110.

36. Smith, Understanding Economics, 110.

37. Anatol Murad, What Keynes Means: A Critical Clarification of the Economic Theories of John Maynard (New York: Bookman Associates, 1962), 184.

38. Murad, What Keynes Means, 17.

39. Murad, What Keynes Means, 21.

40. Murad, What Keynes Means, 21.

41. Robert Skidelsky, Keynes: The Return of the Master (New York: PublicAffairs, 2009), 120.

42. Anatol Murad, What Keynes Means: A Critical Clarification of the Economic Theories of John Maynard (New York: Bookman Associates, 1962), 171-172.

43. Murad, What Keynes Means, 27.

44. Murad, What Keynes Means, 187.

45. Headquarters, Department of the Army, Field Manual 3-07 Stability Operations, (Washington, DC: Government Printing Office, 2008), 4-8.

46. United States Institute of Peace and US Peacekeeping and Stability Operations Institute, Guiding Principles for Stabilization and Reconstruction (Washington, DC: United States Institute of Peace Press, 2009), 6-38-6-39.

47. United Nations Development Program (UNDP), Human Development Report 2002 (New York: Oxford University Press, USA, 2002), 51.

48. "UT G8 Info. Centre. Genoa Summit 2001. COMMUNIQUÉ." G8 Information Centre. http://www.g8.utoronto.ca/summit/2001genoa/finalcommunique.html (accessed December 7, 2010).

49. United States Institute of Peace and US Peacekeeping and Stability Operations Institute, Guiding Principles for Stabilization and Reconstruction (Washington, DC: United States Institute of Peace Press, 2009), 7-0.

50. United States Institute of Peace, Guiding Principles for Stabilization and Reconstruction, 7-65.

51. William J. Baumol, Robert E. Litan and Carl J. Schramm, Good Capitalism, Bad Capitalism, and the Economics of Growth and Prosperity (New Haven: Yale University Press, 2009), 7-8.

52. Stephen Cornell and Joseph P. Kalt. "Reloading the Dice: Improving the Chances for Economic Development on American Indian Reservations." (Los Angeles: American Indian Studies Center, UCLA.1992), 46.

53. Cornell and Kalt, "Reloading the Dice, 46.

54. Office of the President of the United States, National Security Presidential Directive/ NSPD-44 (Washington, DC: The White House, 2005), 1.

55. Office of the President, National Security Presidential Directive/NSPD-44, 2.

56. United States Department of State, "Standby Component Opportunities," US Department of State. http://www.crs.state.gov/index.cfm?fuseaction=public.display&shortcut=4FPI (accessed December 7, 2010).

57. United States Department of State, "Secretary Clinton Announces Civilian Response Corps Reaches 1,000 Members at Its Two-Year Anniversary Mark," US Department of State. http://www. state.gov/video/?videoid=114750580001 (accessed December 7, 2010).

58. Matt Treadgold, "Fit to Exercise: S/CRS and AFRICOM's Judicious Response Exercise," Civilian Response no. 11 (Summer 2010): 24.

59. The 1,750 deployable personnel figure based on a contingency that is longer than one year and that the Civil Response Corps is fully available; meaning all three groups are fully manned. It is calculated using 250 members of the Active Group, 1,000 members of the Stand-by Group deployed for 180-days, and 500 members of the Reserve Group deployed for one year out of their four-year

contract.

60. Department of the Army, G-3 Force Management Memorandum "Organizational Design Paper for Active Army Conventional Forces CA Brigade (Washington, DC, February 22, 2010), 4. The current force structure design for the 96th Civil Affairs Brigade (General Purpose Force) 1,431 personnel. This equates to one Civil Affairs Brigade headquarters, five Civil Affairs Battalions, and thirty Civil Affairs Companies.

61. Robert Hoekstra, "Adjusting to Stabilization and Reconstruction Operations," PRISM 1, no. 2 (March 2010): 23.

62. United States Department of State, "Reserve Component, Civilian Response Corps," US Department of State, http://www.crs.state.gov/index.cfm?fuseaction=public. display&shortcut=4B5C (accessed December 7, 2010).

63. Edward Burke, "Leaving the Civilians Behind: The 'Soldier-diplomat' in Afghanistan and Iraq," Prism 1, no. 2 (March 2010): 35.

64. US Embassy Iraq, "PRT (Provincial Reconstruction Team) Fact Sheet 2008," (March 2008).

65. United States Institute of Peace, "Embedded Provincial Reconstruction Teams United States Institute of Peace," United States Institute of Peace, http://www.usip.org/publications/embedded-provincial-reconstruction-teams (accessed December 7, 2010).

66. Rajiv Chandrasekaran, "Marines seek foothold in Helmand," The Financial Times, (July 8, 2009), 8.

67. Donald P. Wright and Timothy R. Reese, On Point II: Transition to the New Campaign: The United States Army in Operation IRAQI FREEDOM, May 2003-January 2005 (Fort Leavenworth, KS: Department of the Army, 2008), 519.

68. US Army Combined Arms Center, "Commander's Guide to Money as a Weapon System," Center for Army Lessons Learned Handbook 09-07 (2009), 13.

69. Special Investigator General for Iraqi Reconstruction (SIGR). Quarterly and Semi-Annual Report to the United States Congress (Washington DC: SIGR, July 2010), 22.

70. Special Investigator General for Iraqi Reconstruction Quarterly and Semi-Annual Report, 22.

71. Special Investigator General for Iraqi Reconstruction Quarterly and Semi-Annual Report, 36.

72. US Army Combined Arms Center, "Commander's Guide to Money as a Weapon System," Center for Army Lessons Learned Handbook 09-07 (2009), 16.

73. The Louis Berger Group, Inc. and The Services Group, Inc., Iraq Private Sector Growth and Employment Generation: The Iraq Microfinance Strategy (Washington, DC: United States Agency for International Development, 2007), 2.1.

74. United States Forces Afghanistan (USFOR-A). USAFOR-A Publication 1-06: Money As A Weapon System. (Kabul, Afghanistan: 2007), 45.

75. Muhammad Yunus, Banker To The Poor: Micro-Lending and the Battle Against World Poverty, Revised and updated for the paperback edition (London: PublicAffairs, 2008), 68.

76. Yunus, Banker To The Poor, 71.

77. Grameen Bank, "Grameen Bank At A Glance: September 2010," http://www.grameen-info.org/index.php?option=com_content&task=view&id=26&Itemid=175 (accessed December 7, 2010)

78. Muhammad Yunus, Banker To The Poor: Micro-Lending and the Battle Against World Poverty, Revised and updated for the paperback edition (London: PublicAffairs, 2008), 110.

79. Grameen Bank, "Grameen Bank At A Glance: September 2010," http://www.grameen-info.org/index.php?option=com_content&task=view&id=26&Itemid=175 (accessed December 7, 2010)

80. Muhammad Yunus, Banker To The Poor: Micro-Lending and the Battle Against World Poverty, Revised and updated for the paperback edition (London: PublicAffairs, 2008), 160.

81. Rupert Smith, The Utility of Force: The Art of War in the Modern World (Vintage) (New York: Vintage, 2008), 20.

82. United States Forces Command. "National Guard Association of the United States" (presentation at the National Guard Association of the United States conference, US Forces Command, Fort McPherson, GA, August 23, 2010), http://www.ngaus.org/ngaus/files/ccLibraryFiles/Filename/000000006899/thurman.pdf (accessed December 7, 2010).

83. United States Forces Command. "Infantry Warfighting Conference" (presentation at the Infantry Warfighting Conference, US Forces Command, Fort Benning, GA, September 14, 2010), https://www.benning.army.mil/iwc/2010/...Gen%20Thurman.ppt (accessed December 7, 2010).

84. Headquarters, Department of the Army. The Army Strategy 2008. (Washington, DC: Government Printing Office, 2008), 21.

85. Department of Defense, Quadrennial Defense Review Report (Washington, DC: Government Printing Office, 2010), xii.

86. Headquarters, Department of the Army. 2010 Army Posture Statement. (Washington, DC: Government Printing Office, 2010), 13.

87. United States Forces Command. "National Guard Association of the United States" (presentation at the National Guard Association of the United States conference, US Forces Command, Fort McPherson, GA, August 23, 2010), http://www.ngaus.org/ngaus/files/ccLibraryFiles/Filename/000000006899/thurman.pdf (accessed December 7, 2010).

88. "Adapting our Aim: A Balanced Army for a Balanced Strategy". (Washington, DC: United States Army, 2009), 7.

89. George Casey Jr., "SITREP on the Army" (lecture presented at the Command and General Staff College, Fort Leavenworth, KS, April 16, 2010), MP3 file, https://courses.leavenworth.army.mil/webapps/portal/frameset.jsp?tab_id=_18_1 (accessed December 7, 2010).

90. Casey Jr., "SITREP on the Army".

91. Headquarters, Department of the Army, Field Manual 3-05.40: Civil Affairs Operations (Washington, DC: Government Printing Office, 2006), 3-2.

92. Lawrence J. Kolb, "Fixing the Mix," Foreign Affairs 83, no. 2 (March 2004), 2.

93. United States Forces Command. "Infantry Warfighting Conference" (presentation at the Infantry Warfighting Conference, US Forces Command, Fort Benning, GA, September 14, 2010), https://www.benning.army.mil/iwc/2010/...Gen%20Thurman.ppt (accessed December 7, 2010).

94. George Casey Jr., "SITREP on the Army" (lecture presented at the Command and General Staff College, Fort Leavenworth, KS, April 16, 2010), MP3 file, https://courses.leavenworth.army.mil/webapps/portal/frameset.jsp?tab_id=_18_1 (accessed December 7, 2010).

95. Casey Jr., "SITREP on the Army".

96. Samual Kyle Simpson, "Restructuring Civil Affairs For Persistent Engagement" (US Army Command and General Staff College, 2010), 37.

97. Active Component BOG-to-Dwell is calculated using the following equation where 1.11 in the denominator accounts for 40 days associated with the relief in process activities in country.

$$AC\ BOG:Dwell = \frac{Total\ number\ of\ AC\ BCTs}{(Total\ BCT\ demand)(1.11)} - 1$$

98. Reserve Component BOG-to-Dwell is calculated using the following equation where .75 in the numerator equates to nine months of availability and 1.11 in the denominator accounts for 40 days associated with the relief in

$$RC\ BOG:Dwell = \frac{(Total\ number\ of\ RC\ BCTs)(0.75)}{(Total\ BCT\ demand)(1.11)} - 1$$

process activities in country.

$$RC\ BOG:Dwell = \frac{(Total\ number\ of\ RC\ BCTs)(0.75)}{(Total\ BCT\ demand)(1.11)} - 1$$

. Dwell days are calculated using the following equation: Dwellx12 (months)x30 (days).

99. Headquarters, Department of the Army, Field Manual 3-05.40: Civil Affairs Operations (Washington, DC: Government Printing Office, 2006), 2-2.

100. A Contingency Command Post (CCP) is composed of approximately 100 personnel and serves as the deployable headquarters of the Theater Army/Army Service Component Command. It is designed to provide the Theater Army/Army Service Component Commander with an immediate, but limited, command and control capability for low to medium scale contingency operations. With additional enabling command and control capability, the CCP can serve as the foundation for a Joint Task Force Headquarters.

101. Headquarters, Department of the Army, Field Manual 3-05.40: Civil Affairs Operations (Washington, DC: Government Printing Office, 2006), 2-10.

102. The strategy would provide each AC CA Brigade with an Economic Stability Section consisting of 20 personnel at the Brigade level, eight personnel at the Battalion level, two personnel at the Company level, one person in each of the Contingency-A Teams and one person in each of the Civil Military Operations Centers within the CA Brigade.

103. Joint Staff, Joint Publication 1-02: Dictionary of Military and Associated Terms: As Amended Through 31 July 2010 (Washington, DC: Government Printing Office, 2010), 143.

104. Clinton J. Ancker II, "How Ideas Become Doctrine: The Evolution of Military Thought in an Era of Complex, Rapid Change" (Fort Leavenworth, KS: Combined Arms Doctrine Directorate, US Army Combined Arms Center. 2010), 6-7

105. Bernard Carreau, "Lessons from USDA in Iraq and Afghanistan," Prism 1, no. 3 (June 2010): 139-50.

106. John J. Kruzel, "Economic Training for Junior Ranks Resonates with Military Chief," Official Homepage of the United States Army, http://www.army.mil/-news/2010/03/05/35363-economic-training-for-junior-ranks-resonates-with-military-chief/ (accessed December 7, 2010).

107. Jefferson P. Marquis, Developing an Army Strategy for Building Partner Capacity for Stability Operations (Arlington, Virginia: RAND Corporation, 2010), 57-58.

108. Special Investigator General for Iraqi Reconstruction (SIGR). "SIGR Accomplishments," March 2010, http://www.sigir.mil/files/about/SIGIRaccomplishments.pdf (accessed December 7, 2010). Audits conducted in 2006, 2009, and 2010 demonstrated that US Army lacked adequate numbers of contracting officer representatives and personnel trained to manage CERP funds; increasing the likelihood of fraud waste and abuse. Since the reporting of these findings, the US Army increased the numbers of contracting officer representatives and trained personnel through CERP-focused training and certification prior to deployment.

109. "CGSC ILE Graduation", Fort Leavenworth Lamp, June 17, 2010. http://www. ftleavenworthlamp.com/community/x1224666916/Eikenberry-discusses-interagency-ops-at-ILE-graduation-Intermediate-Level-Education-course-2010-01-awards-announced (accessed December 7, 2010). The total student population that graduated from the Command and General Staff School Class 10-01 was 985. The available seats in A516 (Economic Instrument of Power) and A982 (Expeditionary Economics) was limited to 16 seats respectively for Class 10-01.

110. Department of the Army, Pamphlet 611-21: Personnel Selection and Classification, (Washington, DC: Government Printing Office, January 22, 2007), Table 4-3. This ASI is also restricted to the ranks of captain to colonel or grade of O-3 to O-6. There is no economic related ASI for enlisted or warrant officer ranks.

111. Edward Burke, "Leaving the Civilians Behind: The 'Soldier-diplomat' in Afghanistan and Iraq," Prism 1, no. 2 (March 2010): 30.

112. Jeff Chu, "Joint Venture," Fast Company, May 2010, 78.

113. Eliot A. Cohen and John Gooch, Military Misfortunes: The Anatomy of Failure in War, Illustrated. ed. (New York: Anchor, 1991), 26.

Expeditionary Economics in Turbulent Times

by

Lieutenant Colonel James R. Connally - United States Army

Abstract

The United States today finds itself in a turbulent era of failing and underdeveloped states. When a population either threatens or undertakes an overthrow of their government, the government will often request United States assistance for post-conflict stabilization. Often this assistance will extend past a normal security function and into the realm of economics. This monograph explores the term expeditionary economics and the importance of contextual understanding by military planners and commanders prior to intervening in another state's economic system. Additionally, analysis of the economic development of Peru provides examples of both successful and unsuccessful economic interventions. Lessons learned from Peru's defeat of the Shining Path provide an example of how a flawed approach fueled an insurgency while a perceptive approach helped eliminate the source of grievances within a population. While these lessons will not provide a formulaic answer to conducting future expeditionary economics, such knowledge provides better judgment in how to approach future interventions. Only through contextual understanding will military commanders and planners influence a state to change laws and economic practices in order to eliminate the source of economic grievances within a population and to increase economic growth.

Introduction

Since the end of World War II, many states of the world experimented with various forms of economics. Overall, the economic systems that allowed for a capitalistic approach succeeded whereas those who relied upon central planning ultimately failed. Although numerous reasons exist for the multiple failures of centrally planned economies, the overriding cause for such failures often stems from the lack of economic opportunity. Additionally, when the system of the state excludes individuals and groups from access to legitimate economic opportunities, the system drives these individuals and groups either to work outside the legal system or to take extreme actions against legitimate governments.

When violence erupts from within a populace against a government, governments often focus on eliminating the symptoms rather than the underlying causes for the violence. Military intervention initially restores some semblance of stability, but normally it fails to address the long-term catalysts of violence. During such pivotal moments, tremendous opportunities emerge to initiate economic growth through an acceptable set of economic policies. United States Army doctrine addresses the important development tasks of establishing economic policies, securing natural resources, engaging the private sector, encouraging trade, rebuilding economic governance institutions, and building essential economic infrastructure; however, it fails to discuss the tremendous issue of the exclusion of individuals and groups from legitimate economic activity.[1]

Military doctrine acknowledges the importance of an engaged labor force, but there exists an overreliance upon intergovernmental organizations to set up economic policies and establish conditions for long-term development and investment. By relying on such entities, the United States government misses an opportunity to influence the initiation of needed economic policy changes and often fails to support lower level sectors that comprise the engine of growth.

According to Carl J. Schramm of the Kauffman Foundation, the United States needs to develop an ability to conduct expeditionary economics given that the current attempts at rebuilding economies after conflict or disasters fall short.[2] Dr. Schramm identifies that economic growth is critical to establishing social stability and attributes many of the recent failures of development economics to the shortcomings in the current doctrine on international development. He further suggests that the United States' entrepreneurial model provides an example for future expeditionary economic endeavors.

Though the term expeditionary economics lacks a universally accepted definition and few authors write concerning the topic, historical examples exist that assist in the formation of an accepted doctrine. For instance, the Peruvian government's economic development process during the 1990s provides an example of how changes in law and economic practices helped eliminate the source of grievances within a population. Lessons learned from Peru's defeat of the Shining Path provide an example that should facilitate greater understanding of the proper use of economics to support the defeat of future enemies or resurrect the economy of a country after a disaster. However, such a historical example will not provide a predictive method for future leaders and planners to apply to future problems. Rather, the understanding gained by future leaders and planners from such instances illustrates how changes to policy influenced economic systems. This knowledge provides better judgment when attempting to influence a country's economy in future post-conflict situations.

Certain development economic advocates, such as David Landes and Paul Krugman, argue that a country's confined culture, isolated geography, deficient education, unattainable finance, or undemocratic government represents the true issues experienced by faltering economies. Although extremely important, these variables are not critical elements that drive the economy of a country. Additionally, other development economists, such as Jeffery Sachs and John Maynard Keynes, advocate for plans that either focus on rapid changes within a country's economic system or place unnecessary requirements that support a utopian or special interest goal. While many of the changes support a commonly desired outcome, tremendous or unnecessary changes to a system often cause it to fail and revert to a more centrally controlled economy.

A state's economic system exists in a vulnerable and sensitive condition. Prior to entering a conflict, consideration of the state's post-conflict economy must take place. Therefore, when approaching another state's economic system, planners and commanders must approach another country's economic system with extreme caution. Military commanders and planners must concentrate on understanding the environment in order to successfully influence the state's economy. Most environments require understanding four essential areas. First, commanders and planners must possess a deep understanding of the successes and failures of past economic development attempts to improve the domestic economic system of the state. Second, commanders and planners must understand the need to suppress the appetite for immediate changes to a country's economic system. This requires extreme patience and a long-term view of influencing the economic system of another country to reach an acceptable outcome of a new form of capitalism that facilitates access to its people. Third, commanders and planners must understand that the complexity of dealing with an economic system cannot be solved through simple solutions or a large central plan. Fourth, commanders and planners must understand the historical background of the area, cultural issues, economic systems, and the legal difficulties that facilitated the specific grievances. Through contextual understanding, commanders and planners can influence a state to change laws and economic practices in order to eliminate the source of economic grievances within a population and to increase economic growth.

Structure

This monograph does not examine the appropriateness of the United States military conducting expeditionary economics. Rather, the monograph examines the difficulties of intervening in the economics of another state and the importance of contextual understanding when performing expeditionary economics. This monograph is arranged in five major sections. The first section provides background on development economics and relevant history of Peru. The second section discusses the rise of the Shining Path. The third section examines the causes of the legal and extralegal activities. The fourth section provides analysis on development economic successes and failures. Finally, the fifth section provides essential areas for military commanders and planners to focus upon when conducting expeditionary economics.

Expeditionary Economics Defined

The term expeditionary economics does not possess a universally accepted definition. However, one may analyze the term's meaning by disassembling it, defining the individual words, and reassembling the term to create a suitable meaning. *Expeditionary*, as defined by the Oxford English dictionary, means "of or forming an expedition, especially a military expedition." [3] Additionally, the Oxford English dictionary defines *economics* as a noun, meaning "the branch of knowledge concerned with the production, consumption, and transfer of wealth."[4] After reducing the term to its basic elements, one may begin to understand the term's true meaning. Adding *expeditionary* to the word, *economics*, gives the term a military connotation – that is when a military is deployed to a foreign country. Although expeditionary economics intertwines itself with the military, the focus of this type of economics sounds comparable to the field of development economics. Therefore, for the purposes of this monograph, the term expeditionary economics defines a type of economics similar to development economics that a military performs or supports when they intervene in another country's economic system.

Background on Development Economic Approaches

The field of economics contains almost as many economic theories as it does economists. This paper does not examine the debate between various economic theories such as how world markets have emerged from the Keynesian system of macroeconomic policies to the Chicago School of economics promoting free markets. Rather, the monograph centers on the ill-defined term of expeditionary economics and associating that term to existing economic thought. Since the field of development economics encompasses a comparable type of economics to the concept of expeditionary economics, an examination of development economics will prove helpful. Development economics focuses on economic growth, but consists of two very different approaches in developing a country's economic structure. First, the top-down approach, focuses primarily on policy changes performed by the central government. Secondly, the bottom-up approach supports the local individuals or groups. Both have their bevy of vocal advocates, yet, neither extreme has produced successful changes within any country in recent history.

Some economists fervently argue that successful examples of intervention exist. However, most examples consist of the post World War II Japanese and German recovery and the resulting successes of the Marshall Plan. Unfortunately, both of these examples are not true instances of expeditionary economics or even radical economic intervention. In fact, many individuals fail to understand that the Marshall Plan focused on reindustrialization instead of financial planning.[5] Prior to the war, the German and Japanese governments possessed advanced economies. During the post-conflict period, both economies were reconstructed by their own citizens and not by Americans or a big American plan.[6] Without these two highly touted examples of development economics, the argument for intervening with a big plan falls short. Additional examples of successful economic interventions by another state do not readily exist. Yet, the fact remains that when states fail, and the United States government possesses enough interest to intervene, the intervention will require the United States government to normally call upon its military to intercede. Post-conflict intervention requires the military to provide security, support governance, and supply economic assistance.

However, such intervention causes a great deal of concern among many Americans. In the field of economics, economists, such as William Easterly, believe that "military intervention to overthrow evil dictators and remake other societies into some reflection of Western democratic capitalism is the extreme of contemporary utopian social engineering."[7] However, the failing state will, nevertheless, request the visiting state's military to begin developing the state's economy. The military normally enters the failing country first, possesses the greatest ability to plan, and maintains the largest amount of manpower within a foreign country. As a result, the burden to prevent the country from slipping into economic chaos, falls directly on the visiting state's military. Consequently, with an understanding of the complex nature of an economic system within a state, military leaders and planners must carefully determine the best approach to the situation. Although planners do not have a wealth of examples from which to choose, they can analyze Peru as a case study in both a successful and unsuccessful intervention. Peru provides an excellent example of a country that possessed both civilian and military leadership, experienced a Maoist insurgency within its borders, struggled with economic solutions, and eventually succeeded in forming acceptable solutions that eliminated many economic grievances and prevented an insurgency from flourishing within its borders.

Economic Background on Peru

Outsiders may never fully understand the nuances of any society, however, if one is to influence the economy of another state, it is essential to understand the background of the state, its economy, its politics and its people. In the case of Peru, although insiders attempted for decades to correct the economic azimuth of Peru, it was not until the 1990s that Peru set a course to truly provide economic opportunity for its people. Peru possesses a rich and diverse political and economic history. Once known as the cradle of the Incan civilization and the center of Spain's Empire in South America, Peru was one of the last Latin American countries to gain its independence from Spain. While Peru experienced almost 300 years of Spanish rule and gained its independence in 1824, it was not until 1895 that a stable elected civilian government was formed with the establishment of the "Aristocratic Republic."[8] Prior to the Aristocratic Republic's establishment, the leadership of Peru simply continued many of the colonial systems inherited from Spain. Although the Aristocratic Republic enacted many changes, the Peruvian government continued two main elements of Spanish control: authoritarian political institutions and mercantilist economic institutions.[9]

Authoritarian rule continued until 1895 and Peru maintained mercantilist economic policies with Great Brittan. Consequently, many emerging Peruvian entrepreneurs acted as agents for British interests.[10] Many of these entrepreneurs became the elites within Peruvian society and exerted influence to protect their interests and exclude competition. Political leaders attempting to change the status quo did not last. In fact, few leaders lasted to serve a full term. Although there were some enlightened military leaders such as Ramon Castilla (1845-1851, 1854-1862), who worked to change the existing system, Peru's political divisions did not arise from a typical conservative-liberal split (like much of Latin America during the nineteenth century), but more by the issue of military or civilian rule.[11] Regardless of the party controlling the politics, mercantilist economic practices remained relatively untouched by the various governments. Such economic practices led to the economic difficulties within Peru.

Throughout Peru's history, the mercantilist economic system oppressed most Peruvians rather than communism or democratic capitalism. The Peruvian experience with mercantilism is an important aspect of Peruvian society that spanned from Peru's time as a Spanish colony to the 1990s. Peruvian economist, Hernando de Soto, defined mercantilism "as the supply and demand for monopoly rights by means of laws, regulations, subsidies, taxes, and license."[12] In other words, within Peruvian society, there existed state-sanctioned monopolies that protected the few from the competition of the many. Although most western states engaged in mercantilist economic practices until the late 1700s, some nations, like Peru did not undergo the economic evolutions that developed nations experienced. In fact, whether Peru's colonial heritage or to the lack of a destabilizing attack upon the central government, mercantilism lasted in Peru at least a century longer than in Europe. However, after World War II, an emergence of informal activity, frequent property invasions, widespread lawbreaking, the first elements of a market economy, the anarchy resulting from negotiating for laws and bureaucratic favors, and many of the factors that preceded and shaped the European Industrial Revolution occurred that fought the restraints of a mercantilist economy.[13]

Prior to World War II, Peru's mercantilist economic policies did not appear to harm the state's economy or stability. Throughout the majority of the 1800s, Peru enjoyed an economic expansion spawning from an abundance of natural resources (especially the extremely large and rich deposits of guano on islands off the coast). However, Peru's economic tide contracted with the outbreak of the War of the Pacific (1879-1883). Although this war with Chile resulted in Peru's defeat that humiliated and demonstrated the weakness of the Peruvian government, and caused the loss of the costal department of Tarapaca (with its immense nitrate deposits) to Chile, the war successfully ushered in a period of social and political change under a limited civilian democracy.[14] However, economically, the war was a disaster for Peru. It increased Peru's economic dependency on foreign markets, foreign entrepreneurship, and foreign loans. It also "set the pattern for a limited state (i.e. small budgets) and private enterprise (i.e., large foreign investment) that most Peruvian governments tried to follow until the 1968 military coup."[15]

Although the War of the Pacific caused Peru to lose a significant portion of its economic resources, the war did not change Peru's overall economic system. Peru's political leaders dealt with the challenges of balancing the desires of the military and the elites. In the war's aftermath, the elites and the military concentrated on maintaining the status quo. As the only elected civilian to complete a full term between 1914 and 1984, Manuel Prado (1939-1945; 1956-1962) was one of the few Peruvian leaders able to maintain the status quo and satisfy the desires of both the elites and the military. Prado accomplished this difficult task by being a part of the elite and by providing the military with the desired military and budgetary requirements.[16]

Economic difficulties continued to plague Peru. However, it was not until Peru began to experience the post WWII migrations to urban areas and the emerging problems with the mercantilist economic system, that caused the government to recognize the need for reform. The majority of the reforms focused on integrating labor, students, and the more marginal middle sectors. Although the government initiated many important reforms between 1963 and 1968, the failure to fully carry out any reform initiatives and meet the development challenges in the 1960s, caused the military to intervene on October 3, 1968 with a bloodless coup.[17]

The military's control over the Peruvian government marked a pivotal time in the state's history. For the first time, the state's leadership focused on reforming the state and not on maintaining the status quo. Remarkably, the military looked to create changes that supported the majority of Peruvians. The reforms concentrated on diversifying its economy to reduce the country's economic and political dependency and institute large-scale agrarian reforms to eliminate large private landholdings. The policies did not try to redistribute the existing share of the market. Rather, it focused on generating economic growth, improving the distribution of this growth, and garnering the support of economic elites to redirect their wealth toward new productive activities.[18] However, established laws and economic practices did not always support the changing reality occurring at the grass-roots level. Individuals emerged from rural areas and had to work outside the law to engage in activities normally accepted by formal society in other states. This behavior revealed that Peru could no longer follow a mercantilist economic path.

Many of the reforms focused on directing the economic evolution away from mercantilism. General Velasco Alvarado's agrarian reforms in the 1970s helped to dismantle the socio-economic system that dominated and isolated the rural population.[19] However, the military's inability to quickly adapt to both Peru's evolving internal problems and those within the global economy increased discontent and dissatisfaction among the people. By 1977, mounting economic and political pressures prompted the military regime to initiate a gradual return to civilian rule.[20] The return to civilian rule corresponded to the Shining Path's people's war on the eve of the national election of May 18, 1980.[21]

During the 1980s, Peru witnessed increasing terrorist violence and continued economic strife. In many cases, the government's action only exacerbated problems and increased the hardships on the Peruvians. However, many outside agencies share the blame with the Peruvian government. During the debt crisis of the 1980s, the IMF and World Bank possessed a great amount of leverage over developing countries and instituted many policy requirements and conditions that were not generally in the interests of the developing countries.[22] For example, the International Monetary Fund (IMF) imposed onerous, restrictive and controversial requirements on the domestic economic policies. These restrictions crippled Peru's eligibility to receive new external resources and debt refinancing.[23] Although Peru made such required changes, Peru continued to experience economic woes and terrorist violence. Such hardships led a majority of Peruvians to crave dramatic change away from what the traditional political parties had to offer and to gamble on an individual that would represent a "new Peru."[24] In June 1990, a relatively unknown politician, Alberto Fujimori, won the Peruvian national election by running on a platform focusing on alleviating economic hardships and eliminating guerilla violence.

During the campaign, Fujimori's platform was not as extreme as his challenger's, Vargas Llosa. However, once in power, Fujimori immediately initiated an economic shock program even more severe than Llosa proposed during his campaign. This economic shock program (known as "Fujishock") implemented drastic measures which dramatically accelerated inflation, further reduced domestic economic activity, and pushed several million more Peruvians below the poverty line (approximately 14 million, or 60 to 70 percent of the population).[25] Fujimori implemented such draconian measures in an attempt to reestablish international credit and create a foundation for future economic growth. Throughout this period, the Washington Consensus heavily influenced many of the policies Fujimori implemented.

American economist John Williamson initially coined the term Washington Consensus to describe a set of economic policies imposed by the World Bank and the International Monetary Fund during the 1990s.[26] The Washington Consensus established a list of ten specific macroeconomic policy prescriptions for developing countries to implement in order to recover from the economic and financial crisis of the 1980s. The policy prescriptions outlined in the Washington Consensus became synonymous with neo-liberalism and centered on trade liberalization, liberalization of inflows of foreign direct investments, deregulation and privatization.[27] Economists and policymakers alike consider this a controversial list as it requires adherence to a set of rules instead of allowing the state to find its own path to development and reform. The ten macroeconomic policy prescriptions are: 1) fiscal discipline, 2) redistribution of government funds on the basis of need rather than politics, 3) broadening of tax bases and reduction of marginal tax rates, 4) liberalization of financial markets (absence of entry and price controls for institutions, national treatment for foreign firms, and absence of capital controls), 5) competitive exchange rates, 6) replacement of trade quotas with tariffs, 7) removal of barriers to product market competition, 8) privatization of state-owned enterprises, 9) abolition of barriers to foreign direct investment, and 10) strong and effectively enforced property rights.[28]

Although extremely painful for Peru, Fujimori's "Fujishock," with the inclusions of select Washington Consensus prescriptions, began to turn the economy around. However, since Fujimori lacked a congressional majority and did not desire to continue negotiating through democratic channels, on April 5, 1992, he temporarily suspended democracy by suspending the Peruvian congress, the judiciary and the constitution.[29] This autoglope (coup against oneself) received domestic and international condemnation, however Fujimori easily continued to effectuate reforms. The autoglope only lasted until December 1992, during which, Fujimori facilitated economic stabilization and centralized, thus increasing, the power of the presidency.[30] The success of market-oriented economic policies coupled with the capture of the Shining Path's leader, Abimael Guzman, in late 1992 set the Peruvian state on an excellent economic path and permitted Fujimori to bring together the technocrats, business elites and personal loyalists to collaborate on economic reforms.[31] The lasting effects of the economic reforms within Peru are still in question. However, early indications suggest that Fujimori's approach set Peru on a sustainable development path.

The Shining Path

The violence in Peru, between the years of 1980 and 1993, claimed over 30,000 lives and resulted in more than 24 billion dollars in direct and indirect property damages (over half of Peru's Gross National Product).[32] Many reasons for social discontent existed in Peru during this time. However, the dissatisfaction with Peru's government does not explain the rise of one of the most brutal insurgencies in the Western Hemisphere. While Peru faced many of the same difficulties of other Latin countries, how did a young philosophy professor named Abimael Guzman, create the violent organization known as Sendero Luminoso, or the Shining Path?

Origins of the Shining Path

To understand the Shining Path, one must start at the genesis of the organization. The origins of the Shining Path began in 1959 when Abimael Guzman joined the Peruvian Communist Party (PCP). Guzman further developed the organization in 1962 when he took a job at the newly reopened San Cristobal de Huamanga University in Ayacucho, Peru.[33] Both the Andean department of Ayacucho and the Huamanga University were instrumental in the growth of the Shining Path. In this remote, poor and backward Andean region, Huamanga University provided the only school for higher learning and represented a path of upward mobility. This institution gave hope of an education to a people where until midcentury, bankrupt landowners persisted in the serf-like exploitation of "their" Indians.[34]

As with many universities around the world, students at Huamanga University began to question their previously held beliefs. Inequalities observed outside the campus coupled with the economic reality that few jobs existed for recent graduates caused students to protest government policies and form various political groups. Although the PCP existed at Huamanga University, Guzman formed a Red Faction group within the party. He further aligned this group with the Maoist followers that eventually created a split within the PCP between pro-Soviet and Maoist followers.[35]

When examining his background, Guzman's path toward leading the Shining Path does not seem predestined. However, Guzman's experiences of organizing, debating, and political infighting while at the university prepared him to create and lead the Shining Path. Additionally, Guzman gained other valuable experiences from outside Peru. Although Guzman's Maoist PCP did not support the 1965 pro-Cuban, communist insurgency within Peru, Guzman's arrest appeared imminent nonetheless. Consequently, the PCP sent Guzman to cadre school in China where he gained valuable experience.[36] After an enlightening time in China, Guzman returned to a changed Peru. The government takeover by the Peruvian military concerned Guzman and many of the pro-Chinese communists since the military desired to implement many of the reforms advocated by the Peruvian left winged parties. Guzman and the pro-Chinese communist strongly opposed the military government for they feared being forced out if the military succeeded in such reforms.[37] However in 1970, Guzman was expelled from the Maoist PCP after an internal struggle within the party. Guzman's expulsion provided a path on which the Red Faction would travel towards becoming the Communist Party of Peru – The Shining Path.[38] From this point forward, the Shining Path's identity and belief system spawns from the mind of one person, Professor Abimael Guzman Rynosos.

Shining Path's Maoist Approach

Although Abimael Guzman claimed that his ideology was the "fourth sword of Marxism," his actions were overwhelmingly Maoist.[39] Like Mao, Guzman identified three key phases of guerrilla war: "defensive," "equilibrium," and finally, "offensive."[40] Additionally, in Maoist tradition, and in order to justify armed insurgency, Guzman defined Peru's society as semifeudal and semicolonial.[41] Although Peru's society did not fit neatly within this Maoist construct, such a view enabled Guzman to define his approach. Guzman believed that he had to start the war from the rural base with the aid of peasants. Once he created the revolutionary base in the rural areas, Guzman believed that he would have enough forces to then encircle the cities. However, Guzman's dogmatic insistence on this misguided approach lasted until the Shining Path's first congress in 1988, where the Maoist prioritization of the countryside was modified to one focused on the cities.[42]

While many reasons exist to explain this misguided approach, the primary reason for the failure of this approach originates from Guzman's inflexible adherence to a guerilla model and his lack of understanding of the situation in Peru. The Shining Path did not start out as a peasant rebellion, but was derived from the university.[43] In fact, one of the first groups that the Shining Path recruited came from teachers and students. Although many of these individuals were the first in their family to receive an education, economic struggles had led many not to be able to provide for their families' basic needs.[44] Additionally, not until the late 1980s, did Guzman comprehend the difficulties experienced by peasants migrating to the cities. Prior to that time, Guzman viewed Peru as a larger example of what he witnessed in the Peruvian state of Ayacucho.

Building Political Base

In the 1970s, Guzman started building his base in Ayacucho. This time period in Ayacucho heavily influenced the Shining Path and caused the leadership to form many of its ideals around problems facing Peru with what was seen within Ayacucho: poor, provincial, isolated, and Indian.[45] This experience, coupled with the influences of Guzman's stay in China, led to the Shining Path ideology's three key elements: (1) characterization of society as "semi-feudal," implying that the peasantry will be the primary social base of the revolution and that democracy is impossible; (2) the fundamental role of political violence in the revolutionary process; and (3) Gang-of-Four Maoism as an invariable truth.[46] Although Guzman garners support through the addressing of grievances, the extreme nature of this form of communist ideology created future difficulties for the Shining Path.

When the military government was in power, the Shining Path garnered considerable sympathy and support among the Ayacucho population by addressing grievances that the military initially raised when first assuming power.[47] However, the military did not see the importance of some of Peru's rural departments since such areas did not typify the main issues that the central government faced. The central government concentrated on problems generated by large urban populations and the massive migration to urban areas. Therefore, the Shining Path took advantage of the government vacuum in Ayacucho, addressed the people's needs and consequently, garnered their support. The lack of government focus and inability to exert control in many of the rural areas helped support the Shining Paths' ideology and plan for Peru's future. The Shining Path's leadership created a strategy that initiated a People's war in order to gain control of the countryside for the purpose of encircling the cities.[48]

While the Shining Path grew in strength in areas where the government held little influence, they continued to struggle outside of their home base of Ayacucho. In order to compensate for its weakening impact on society, the Shining Path built increasingly well-organized cadres steeped in the ideology of destroying society in order to build a new society.[49] Subsequently, when the deteriorating economic conditions forced down the wages on which many peasants depended, and continued lack of access to land for economic security pressed them further, the Shining Path possessed a ready stable of hardened believers to move into other areas to reinforce the organization. The Shining Path simply transformed the power structure with itself at the top and with the peasant masses, which it considered in need of leadership and instruction, at the bottom. The Shining Path admonished villagers to refrain from participating in the capitalistic market and to remain autonomous.[50] During this period, the local realities of the peasant economy served to maintain sympathy for the Shining Path.[51] Such sympathy helped to subvert the reforms the military government often attempted. The initial actions were all political until the eve of the elections in 1980, when the Shining Path's leadership decided that the time was ripe to introduce the military arm of their movement.

The Peruvian government did not take seriously the Shining Path's initial disruptions. Interestingly, the government's response, or lack thereof, caused problems with the local population. It angered the local population, when, in December 1982, the government used massive and indiscriminate military force, instead of selective force, against the Shining Path.[52] The Shining Path continued to exert themselves and increased their strength where the government was weak. The Shining Path established a foothold in areas where coca eradication caused ill-will and created a financial windfall for the organization, providing millions annually.[53] Any place where the government lacked power and influence only created more opportunity for the Shining Path. The Shining Path acknowledged this opportunity in their 1986 war plan by starting to title land, homes and businesses throughout Peru to win the favor of the people.[54] The Shining Path experienced immense support when they focused on the grievances of people. However, the Shining Path failed when they attempted to impose a set of procedures and controls that appeared to exert the same structures of domination most local communities were trying to escape. Interestingly, this helped individuals conclude that the government, not the Shining Path, could better respond to their needs.[55]

Sources of Grievances

Grievances are often caused when groups are excluded from legitimate activities. The Shining Path failed to provide the spark to enflame Peru into a true revolution. This failure stemmed from a flawed ideology and lack of understanding concerning the grievances held by most Peruvians. In Peru, exclusion from the formal legal system, land disparity, and lack of access to education were the three major sources of grievances. These grievances caused the disenfranchised to search for other sources for relief, which, in turn, undermined any existing support for the local government. As Peruvians migrated from rural areas, seeking a better life, they had to rely on their entrepreneurial abilities to earn a living. This group of entrepreneurs worked in the informal or extralegal sector and made up sixty to eighty percent of the population.[56] These entrepreneurs desired to live under the rule of law in order to have their homes and businesses recognized. However, when they existed outside of the rule of law, in the extralegal sector, their security could only be assured through an extralegal arrangement not recognized by legitimate law. Extralegal arrangements produce many difficulties for the entrepreneur. Primarily, by not having their assets within the legal system, these entrepreneurs could not use the assets to guarantee credit, and thus did not possess any incentives to initiate long-term projects.[57]

The disparity of legal land ownership continued as a source of grievance for many Peruvians. Historically, the Peruvian elites drove many indigenous people from their lands so that the elites could establish large haciendas.[58] Although the government recognized the disparity of land as a legitimate grievance, rising population growth and the state's failed agrarian reforms only increased the divide. Land reform solutions came from a grass-roots level, but unfortunately the state failed to acknowledge the legitimacy of such solutions and dismissed the power of reforms originating from the local level. The state's failure to incorporate a grass-roots movement for land reform coupled with an imposition of a bureaucratic cooperative structure, created cooperatives that lacked accountability and drew resentment from the peasants.[59]

Lack of access to education became an increasing source of grievance for the peasantry. Peasants migrated to urban areas seeking out education to take away the elites monopoly on Spanish, reading and writing in order to provide opportunity for upward mobility.[60] In 1969, the military government attempted to restrict free high school education to students with passing grades, and caused the peasants of Ayacucho to create a social movement that defended free education.[61] In this instance, the government heeded to the desires of the people. Although such movements caused the government to discontinue such attempts at limiting education, it did not motivate the government to improve the education opportunities for the peasants in the rural areas. For the peasantry, education continued to provide upward mobility, remained highly desired and became the catalyst for many to migrate to the city in order to provide brighter future and more opportunities for their children.[62]

However, migration did not meet the expectations of many of the Peruvians. Once in the city, the Peruvians found themselves forced to work in the extralegal sector. The migrant's inability to receive legal recognition and public services (light, water, sewage, transport, and education) from the government caused them to create community organizations that employed an arsenal of pressures, from marches to bribes, in order to stimulate government action.[63] The government's inability to respond to the basic needs of their citizens often led to individuals forming local solutions outside the legal domain. Consequently, since the government did not sanction such local solutions, the government viewed such actions as illegal. However, a distinction must be drawn between what is truly illegal and extralegal.

Legal and Extralegal Activity

Legal economic activities consists of economic activities occurring within a state that the state permits and governs by law. Extralegal activity consists of any activity that does not fall within the realm of legally sanctioned activity by the government. Black market activities or underground activities are additional terms used for extralegal activity that occurs outside of the law of the state. Regardless of the term used, such activity persists around the world and provides a source of income for many individuals. States often have the misconception that the extralegal sector exists only to provide cover for those avoiding taxes. Extralegal activity does not always equate to illegal activity. For example, when a government fails to provide a service such as public transportation for a community, entrepreneurs will often step in to fill the need. However, once the state changes the law to prohibit such activity, the extralegal activity now becomes illegal from the purview of the state.

Additionally states wrongly believe that solutions to land titling problems lie with building better databases, or that the current laws are sufficient, or the costs of compliance are at an acceptable level.[64] States should search for inclusive solutions and must understand the necessity of high-level political leadership to incorporate extralegal arrangements. When states fail to fully understand the extralegal sector's causes and effects, the existing grievances are further exacerbated. While severe problems exist with extralegal activity, individuals charged with reforming the system must understand that macroeconomic reforms are not enough.[65] Even if the macroeconomic reforms meet international standards, it does not equate to sustained economic growth in a society. Each state provides a unique set problems that require a distinctly different approach from other states. For example, until the recent entrepreneur expansion that changed the entire economy, India exemplified how state guidance hindered economic growth.[66] Although India followed a protectionist industry-building strategy for about fifty years, true economic growth did not occur until they were exposed to freer trade.[67] In the majority of cases, a heavy-handed, centralized approach to economic growth undermines entrepreneurial ability to create growth.

Economic Growth

The majority of states desire to increase their economic growth. Although onerous economic policies often reduce such growth, this does not mean that economic policies lack merit. Prudent fiscal and monetary policies keep inflation low, prevents economic downturns, and fuels economic growth.[68] States reduce grievances by facilitating economic growth opportunity. When a state lacks economic opportunity, they are prone to political instability and backlashes.[69] It is important not to confuse economic growth with economic activity. Economists typically measure the economic growth of a country by the increase or decrease of the gross domestic product (GDP) that traditionally comprises a country's output of goods and services.[70] However, GDP only measures legal activities and fails to account for the majority of economic activities in non-Western states. This aspect provides one of the greatest opportunities for a state to change their economy. States can transform their economy through facilitating an environment that encourages economic growth in the legal economy. Key elements that facilitate growth for entrepreneurs are the ability to easily form a business and the legal enforcement of property and contract rights.[71]

Law

The importance of law to encouraging economic growth cannot be overstated. In developing countries, laws often focus on protecting ownership and opportunities for a small group of elites.[72] For the majority, laws determine if they work within the formal sector or are forced to operate in the extralegal sector. Individuals in developing countries continually evaluate the cost of access to and the cost of remaining within the formal sector.[73] States should not arbitrarily create or enforce laws that only benefit the few. The state's laws must represent the society and their grievances. When a state understands the true sources of societal grievances, it is better prepared to create effective and unbiased law. Such laws reflect what is occurring in society and provide incentives for people to abide by the law.[74]

When a state faces rapid changes associated with mass migration to urban areas, the state often becomes overwhelmed and needs to re-evaluate its laws. The complex nature of these societal changes requires effective legal institutions able to enact changes in a timely manner. Peru provides an excellent example of the importance of creating effective laws and how a state must discard ineffective ones. In Peru's case, the debilitating laws of mercantilism sought to regulate every issue, every transaction, every property, but the state found efficient laws to replace the existing system and promote the desired ends.[75] Such a process is iterative and emerges unpredictably.

The Formal Sector

Commanders and planners must understand the importance of enabling and assisting individuals to operate within the formal sector of a state's economy. When individuals operate within the formal economy, their assets become live capital that is recognized and used globally. Formal property provides a primary mechanism to increase a state's economic growth. When the state's formal sector recognizes property, it effectively protects ownership, secures transactions, and encourages citizens in advanced countries to respect titles, honor contracts, and obey the law.[76] Although protection of ownership is important, the key aspect of the formal property lies in the ability to represent something other than its physical state. The ability of an individual to leverage property provides a catalyst that generates economic growth. In essence, formal property improves the flow of communications about assets and their potential.[77]

The Informal Sector (the excluded)

Individuals existing in the extralegal sector do not enjoy the protections of the law. In Peru, the existing dominant groups in the legal sector viewed the new migrants to urban areas as competition. To limit the competition from such migrants, these dominant groups used Peru's legal institutions to bar migrants from establishing social and economic activities, sought means to maintain the elite privileges, and isolated the peasants in rural areas.[78] When individuals realize that the laws do not support their needs and excludes them from participation, they invariably seek alternatives to the legal system that provides protection.

The Peruvian economist, Hernando de Soto, describes informality as existing "when individuals and firms carry out economic activities that are inherently constructive – such as building homes, selling goods and services, and so on – but in ways that are technically illegal because they lack the requisite official approvals, licenses, or, in the case of land, titles."[79] In many countries, the extralegal sector provides the majority of economic activity by its citizens. In fact, the International Labor Organization reports that during 1990s, eighty-five percent of all new jobs in Latin America and the Caribbean were created in the extralegal sector.[80] Although the extralegal assets of individuals become dead capital and lose the ability to generate economic growth in the legal arena, the cost associated with obeying the law are too onerous and outweigh any benefit of working within the legal sector. However, options do exist for individuals charged with creating economic growth. The United States' expansion into the West provides an example of a state generating economic growth by successfully incorporating the extralegal sector. Although analysis of Western expansion does not provide an exact parallel, history reveals that when those in power accept and ratify established extralegal contracts, they provide a way to successfully transition from the extralegal to the legal sector.[81] This does not imply that legal systems should look to absorbing all extralegal arrangements. Rather, voluntary compliance will only occur if the system is relevant and efficient.[82]

Social Contract

In creating a system that engenders compliance, the state absorbs social contracts into the legal sector and creates a national social contract with its citizens. To accomplish a national social contract, the state must understand the beliefs, desires, intentions, customs, and rules that are contained in these local social contracts.[83] Through this understanding, the state can begin to transition individuals into the legal sector. By creating a legal and political bridge from existing extralegal arrangements into a new social contract, the state gains the support of the people and individuals enjoy the benefits under formal law. The new contract brings the extralegal into the legal framework and gives them a stake in the capitalist system. However, this is a major political task since it tampers with the status quo.[84]

A state failing to incorporate the extralegal sector within its borders exposes itself to potential internal threats. Since extralegal assets are extremely hard to move without being connected to the legal sector, individuals have to rely on their extralegal social contracts. This reliance upon extralegal social contracts causes individuals to view the law and the government that was trying to enforce the law, as hostile to their interests.[85] It is extremely dangerous for a government to rely on established laws that exclude a significant portion of its populous. Failure to incorporate the excluded provides an opportunity for radical and subversive individuals and groups to gain the excluded's support, by providing asset protection, championing their causes, and providing a violent alternative to their present situation. Extralegal activity is not inherently subversive to the state. However, when the state limits the opportunities to only the politically well-connected, fatalism and despair occur, causing emigration or revolution.[86]

Costs

People naturally follow rules that protect their assets. When the legal order fails to keep pace with economic and social upheaval, people invent informal, ad hoc business arrangements that do not always best serve their interests.[87] People tend to follow the laws that directly protect their assets. Hernando de Soto noticed that when laws were consensual, extralegal groups preferred the formal titles over continuing previous arrangements.[88] This results from the cost associated with the extralegal sector. Contrary to popular thought, when individuals build a house outside the legal process, they pay a very high price for the land they occupy.[89] Additionally, any investment made to build or improve on that piece of land becomes dead capital since it exists in the extralegal sector. Both the individual and the state lose when this occurs. Hernando de Soto calculated that approximately $9.3 trillion worth of real estate is held, but not legally owned, in the third world and former communist countries.[90] The primary reasons for individuals to hold their assets outside the legal sector stems from their inability to pay the costs of obtaining property. These are high costs in both time and money. Prior to changes in the government, it took a Peruvian more than three hundred days (working six hours a day), thirty-two times the monthly minimum wage, and seven hundred and twenty-eight bureaucratic steps to have an asset set up in the legal sector.[91]

Capital

To obtain capital from their assets, an individual cannot remain in the extralegal sector. The importance of understanding how capital drives economic growth is vital when conducting expeditionary economics. Economists generally define "capital" as that part of a country's assets that initiates surplus production and increases productivity.[92] Understandably, this can be difficult for those outside the field of economics to visualize. Capital is not money or accumulated stock of assets, but the potential it holds for new production.[93] An asset cannot be easily leveraged if it does not exist legally. One cannot put up their house as collateral for a loan if the bank is unsure of the legality of the asset. Therefore, capital can be seen as a title, a security, a contract, or other such record that represents the asset.

This is why capitalism works in the West and has difficulties elsewhere. Imitating capitalism by imitating Western economics through macroeconomic or structural reforms does not create wealth. Rather, states need to produce capital, which requires a legal property system.[94] This formal property system should represent assets in a way to allow individuals to understand each other, make connections, and synthesize knowledge about the assets to enhance productivity. Although many entrepreneurial individuals already possess the assets they need for success in a capitalistic system, the major stumbling block that keeps the rest of the world from benefiting from capitalism is its inability to produce capital.[95]

The Importance of Entrepreneurs

Once the state provides mechanisms to unlock the economic potential of extralegal assets, entrepreneurs can tap into trillions of dollars of real estate in order to produce, secure, or guarantee greater value in the expanded market.[96] The key for the success of economic growth in the state is unlocking the potential of entrepreneurs. Entrepreneurs are any entity, new or existing, that provides a new product or service or that develops and uses new methods to produce or deliver existing goods and services at lower cost.[97] Entrepreneurs assume a tremendous amount of risk and initiative when they migrate from a rural to an urban area. This, coupled with the ability to identify and satisfy other's needs, creates wealth from knowing how to use resources, not from owning them. This entrepreneurial ingenuity creates wealth on a vast scale far exceeding the holdings of the government, the local exchanges, and foreign direct investment; they are many times greater than all the aid from advanced nations and all the loans extended by the World Bank.[98] However, when the wealth exists in the extralegal sector, it is essentially dead capital. By transferring this dead capital into the legal domain, entrepreneurs can utilize the new resources to accumulate much more wealth. Although a local community may view the rapid accumulation of wealth by an entrepreneur as a source of friction within a community, entrepreneurs are the solution for economic growth.

Entrepreneurship triumphed in the West because the law integrated everyone under one system of property, giving them the means to cooperate and produce large amounts of surplus value in an expanded market.[99] Capitalism provides the system for entrepreneurs to succeed and provides individuals the incentive to take risks. Individuals are more likely to come up with and implement good ideas than any group of planners or experts, and the very "un-plannedness" of a free-market economy, which might seem to be a great weakness, turns out to be a great strength.[100] The global economy is not a "zero sum game" where some countries "win" and others must "lose."[101]

Failure and Success of Development Economics

Countries and organizations with the best of intentions to improve the state's economics fail on a regular basis. Many development economists tout that their list of requirements provides states with a plan that will create economic growth. However, the prerequisites that economists provide to states usually only apply to a small portion that have had some success. For instance, Jeffery Sachs lists the preconditions of basic infrastructure (roads, power, and ports) and human capital (health and education) coupled with foreign assistance as ingredients to create economic success.[102] Yet, economic growth occurs throughout the world without such preconditions or ingredients. Although no formula exists for the improvement of economic growth within a country, one can gain better understanding from looking at past successes and failures. Peru exemplifies a case where one can view both the successes and failures of economic development. By borrowing from this and other countries' successes and failures, commanders and planners can facilitate a better approach to future operations. The international community provides many examples that demonstrate the challenges and difficulties associated with changing a society's economic path. However, the two main obstacles to creating economic growth are free market reform and outside government intervention.

Free Market Reforms

Financial markets provide a great source of free market efficiency and create opportunities for individuals to get rich by borrowing and investing.[103] While free markets do work, free markets reforms often fail as a result of the state taking a centralized approach to reform. The need to democratize the reform process constitutes one of the main challenges of institutional reform.[104] In order to get the local level to function in a free market requires the state to understand the reality at the local level. The ability to understand that poverty is a complicated tangle of political, social, historical, and institutional factors should cause a state to search for homegrown solutions.[105] This is where the system of state-driven capitalism differs from central planning. In centrally planned economies, the state picks the winners, owns the means of production, sets all prices and wages, and provides no incentives for progress.[106] This does not insinuate that all state-driven capitalism economies work. For instance, oligarchic capitalism thrives on corruption and stymies economic growth. The attempted privatization in Russia displays the failure of state-driven capitalism to incorporate a participatory process that that included homegrown solutions.[107] However, states can promote growth and move toward a healthy form of capitalism if they understand the complexities of their society.

The state must find out what works at the local level. Failure to do so leads to one of the three main problems that create opposition to free markets. First, free market reforms that do not regulate profit-seeking behavior, allows opportunists to benefit at the expense of others.[108] Such regulation can be extremely difficult in disparate societies. For example, the state must provide enough protection for the wealthy or they will not accept the reforms. However, if the poor are excluded, they will revolt. Checks and balances are as important to economic development as is the existence of free markets.[109] The second challenge to free markets is failing to understand the local custom and its effect on the existing, working extralegal arrangements. For example, when aid agencies recommend to build computer databases to catalogue land titles as a solution to land ownership conflicts, they fail to understand the local challenges and potentially create more problems. Complex problems do not present simple solutions. The last challenge to free markets are rapid introduction of reforms designed to change all the rules at once. This drastic change disrupts the established order and causes such turmoil that the weak new arrangements are unable to make the free market work well.[110] An abrupt change to an economic system creates confusion and often causes individuals to revert to something more familiar.

Since the state does not have the ability to possess all the required information to create lasting change, all reforms are partial. Rather than trying to accomplish everything at once, policy makers need to pursue inclusive ways that give the majority access to the free market. Too often, policy makers believe that their role is complete once they stabilized and adjusted the macroeconomic level, allowing legal business and foreign investors to prosper and orthodox economists to control the treasury.[111] The exclusion of the majority through free market reforms leads to future problems. Policy makers need to advance with gradual, experimental steps toward free markets.[112] This allows individuals to adopt reforms that work and states to better adapt to the changing requirements.

Outside Intervention

Many observers outside of the state do not always believe that the state is capable of righting its own ship. Outside intervention normally consists of either military invasion or foreign aid. Although liberals may prefer big state-led effort to fight global poverty and conservatives prefer benevolent imperialism to spread Western capitalism and subdue opposition to the West, neither type of intervention works.[113] Macroeconomic plans fail despite the best of intentions, when outsiders fail to understand local customs and challenges. When outside government intervention attempts to design a comprehensive reform for a country that creates benevolent laws and forms new institutions to make markets work, it actually tends to exacerbate the problem.[114]

Commanders and planners must strive to understand the true causes of the local economic climate. The United States government promotes economic development as a part of its global war on terrorism, but the military is often insulated from being able to understand local interests.[115] Lasting change only occurs through homegrown solutions that embody local customs. Historically, at best, the majority of interventions by the military, IMF, World Bank and others produce mediocre results for the host country. Remarkably, countries lacking outside intervention will normally develop themselves regardless of the perceived inability to create positive change.

For example, without outside intervention, foreign aid, or even international recognition, the breakaway Republic of Somaliland in the north of Somalia enjoys peace, economic growth, and democratic elections.[116] Finding solutions to one's own problem is often easier than finding workable solutions for others. Often it comes down to an individual's mindset. Renowned economist and microfinance advocate C. K. Prahalad stated that when outsiders "stop thinking of the poor as victims or as a burden and start recognizing them as resilient and creative entrepreneurs and value-conscious consumers, a whole new world of opportunity will open up."[117] The ability of a developing state requires homegrown local solutions able to link capital to a market economy. Only then will macroeconomic reforms begin to work.

Failures in Peru

Sometimes, the lessons of what works and what does not are best learned through the failure of others. The history of Peru provides numerous examples of the failures of economic plans. Normally, these plans focus primarily on macroeconomic changes that need to occur. Plans such as *Peru's Path to Recovery* by Carlos E. Paredes and Jeffrey Sachs, describe utopian goals of "creating a sound, enduring macroeconomic environment in which resources are allocated efficiently and where the state can secure sufficient resources for redistribution to the poorest members of the society."[118] In broad strokes, 20th century Peru has experienced four roles: market-supporting role under a primary-export-led development model prior to the Great Depression; development role during the post WWII era of import-substituting-industrialization (ISI); direct role during post-debt-crisis retreat; and back to the pre-ISI liberal state meant to bolster private initiative through property rights enforcement and the providing basic public goods.[119] In the realm of expeditionary economics, two areas from Peru's past show that well-intentioned plans can produce disastrous results. Although the intervention came from within, the period of military rule provides lessons for others attempting future expeditionary economics. Additionally, the numerous attempts at land reform exemplify how the concentrations of a state on causes of problems do not always produce desired effects.

The case of the Peruvian military government provides a unique example that deviates from other military governments. One of the greatest differences from other military governments stems from the reasons for the military coup. In 1968, the military leadership felt that the Peruvian government's lack of a coherent economic policy created economic disparity and caused political coalitions to unravel.[120] The military correctly assessed many of the issues with the government at that time and believed that the military possessed the ability to correct Peru's economic and political path. Prior to this decision by the military, a remarkable change occurred within the military that transformed them from the protectors of the country's elites to an organization that believed they were capable of correcting Peru's economic and political woes. This belief stemmed from the training military leaders completed such as the Economic Commission for Latin America and the Caribbean (ECLAC) sponsored courses on structuralist economics and exposure to the main writings of the early dependency school in the Peruvian National War College (CAEM) training programs.[121] From this experience and training, top officers viewed the country's highly underdeveloped political and economic structures as the main threats to national security.[122] This, coupled with poverty-related guerrilla uprisings of the mid-1960s, further reinforced the military's perception that a sweeping socioeconomic reform was essential.[123] Thus, the Peruvian military believed that the situation required and demanded their intervention.

The overall goals of the military government centered on achieving greater national economic integration and reducing Peru's dependence on the world economy through upgrading the state's administrative and personnel practices, faster economic growth and higher levels of employment, and tighter controls on foreign direct investment (FDI) in the extractive sectors.[124] Despite the lofty reformist goals of the military regime, its legacy was just the opposite. In the end, a main legacy of military rule was increased state-led excessive external borrowing, reckless state-owned enterprise (SOE) expansion, heightened conflict between the state and domestic entrepreneurs, and the degenerating poverty and income distribution.[125]

Although the military was well educated and professionally trained, these traits did not translate to economic success for Peru. This lack of success occurred during a period where the military understood the economic problems of Peru. In an effort to address the major economic and political issues, the military took a deliberate state-driven development approach. Yet, many of the reforms did not succeed. For instance, the modern-sector industrial reforms did not quickly absorb the traditional sector into the national economy.[126] Additionally, agrarian reforms failed to work because the government did not accept that people have their own methods of using and exchanging land.[127]

One of the main causes for these failures rests with the use of military officers. Although the officers possessed high levels of education and training, the technical nature of the development program coupled with the managerial requirements did not match with such education and training. For instance, the efforts of a strategically placed military cadre to act quickly in transforming the political economy led to immediate structural imbalances, contradictory development outcomes, the failure to reconcile redistributive goals with the chosen model of capital accumulation, and an ambiguous stance toward domestic and foreign capital.[128]

Additionally, the placement of military officers with a highly capable corps of technocrats caused more problems. Problems manifested themselves in the hasty launch of the development effort, conspicuous lack of clear goals, and the built-in tensions of a convoluted management strategy. This ill-informed strategy merged military and civilian policy makers into a top-down hierarchical relationship that operated within the civilian policy maker's bureaucratic turf.[129] Throughout this period, the military was often its own worst enemy. The military undercut its antioligarchic reforms and alienated the working and middle class that they were trying to help by granting generous industrial incentives and salary increases until the 1974 fiscal crunch.[130] These problems were not isolated incidents. For example, the military government lost the support of entrepreneurs by issuing the 1970 Job Stability Law granting workers virtual job tenure.[131] In the end of the military government era, every major approach the military took resulted in increased tensions. Heavy reliance on state-owned enterprises (SOEs) to develop the country failed because of the tension between the firm's pursuit of microeconomic investment goals and the central government's macroeconomic and social objectives.[132] Capital investment programs appeared to favor urban areas over the rest of the country. Debt-backed consumption reduced from borrowing for productive investments.

By the 1976 debt crisis, these competing policy approaches failed to support Peru's development goals and left the country's economy in disarray. Entrepreneurs certainly emerged no stronger from the experience of the 1970s, and workers emerged much better organized and able to articulate their interests.[133] It is difficult to overlook the distributional shortcomings of the military's program, including the propensity of social subsidies to favor town over country and the near exclusion of the jungle and sierra regions from the capital-investment program.[134] As in the 1970s and the early 1980s, the domestic debate over how to proceed with economic adjustment wavered between a draconian shock treatment and a more gradual approach to stabilization.[135] The military's effort to reorganize society into benign classless units actually resulted in enhancement of class-consciousness and conflict.[136] The military's failure to promote equitable economic growth and mediate societal issues created opportunities for subversive groups to garner support. Although the military turned the government back over to civilian leadership in 1980, Peru's political and economic woes continued. The 1982 debt shocks led to a period of chronic financial insolvency and fiscal retrenchment which prompted a retreat from statist strategies to a more indirect mode of state participation in the 1990s.

Development Economics International Successes

Historically, not all development economic efforts in creating economic growth within a country fails. Although Peru failed to create economic growth through many of its economic policies, other states succeeded using a seemingly similar approach. Chile experienced a seventeen-year military government that abandoned the ISI economic policies and followed a market strategy. The Chilean government provided political freedom to policy makers to experiment with market reform until they obtained the desired results.[137] This Chilean strategy allowed the state to sustain economic growth even after the 1982 debt shocks. The ability to experiment provides a state with one of the best tools for economic change. What works for one state does not become a panacea that works for another state. For instance, the failure of SOEs in Peru does not mean that economic success is impossible when a state supports SOEs. In China, SOEs produced tremendous success and helped drive China's economic growth. The reason for China's success with SOEs originates from their ability to use the SOEs when needed and then gradually reduce them while supporting the privatization of the Chinese economy. This support manifests itself through recognizing property rights and allowing villages to own and operate new firms.[138]

States creating economic growth normally follow a path unique to that state. Successful changes do not result from one state's imitation of another's economic path. The economic history of Western states provides plenty examples for states and international agencies to understand how successful economies occur. The primary factor for states to transition to capitalism originates with laws that adapt to the emerging needs of people. However, the history and process by which laws absorb the practices, customs, and norms of extralegals have been obscured by other historical events.[139]

Throughout United States history, in the absence of inclusive laws, individuals must create and agree upon extralegal rules. The United States government realized the difficulty of enforcing exclusive laws that did not work and the futility of making existing laws more stringent. Therefore, Congress gradually managed to integrate into one system the informal property rules created by millions of immigrants and squatters.[140] By creating laws that absorbed extralegal arrangements, Congress enabled individuals to become more productive and generate economic growth.

Many countries view those operating outside the legal realm as criminals. However, positive change occurs when states view the extralegal sector as providing an opportunity for the state to improve its economy. For example, in the Homestead Act of 1862, the United States government provided settlers with 160 acres of free land if the settlers agreed to develop the land. The government's actions essentially legalized existing extralegal practices that were occurring for decades.[141] Even in the American Colonial period, authorities provided property rights to individuals who improved the land, paid taxes, and followed local arrangements among neighbors.[142] The efforts to embrace many of the settler's extralegal arrangements led the United States Congress to pass more than five hundred different laws to reform the property system between 1785 and 1890.[143] This exemplifies the effort it took to provide inclusive laws that created a powerful economic engine.

Peru's Successes

In the 1990s, Peru provides another example of how states can create economic growth through multiple means. When the Alberto Fujimori administration emerged, fifty percent of the population lived in poverty, half of which lived in extreme poverty.[144] Many leading economists of the time proposed solutions for Peru to create economic growth. Top Peruvian economists teamed with Harvard professor Jeffrey Sachs to generate the macroeconomic plan called "A Plan for Economic Stabilization and Growth."[145] However, the Fujimori administration took a different path. In order to take the country out of hyperinflation and entice foreign investment, Fujimori enacted several macroeconomic reforms that eliminated government controlled prices and subsidies, introduced emergency taxes, established a managed floating-exchange-rate, and reduced tariffs on trade.[146] Although such measures created hardships among the most vulnerable in Peru, Fujimori made efforts to communicate the goals of the central government to discover the desires of the locals and address their needs. By creating the Programa de Emergencia Social (PES) and assembling organizations such as the Catholic Church and Non-governmental Organization (NGOs) to participate in the program, Fijimori established the central coordinating committee and local emergency committees that assisted in creating development solutions.[147] Such organizations provided a voice for grassroots leaders and contributed to the undermining of support for the Shining Path.

President Fujimori relied on market forces for much of the economic recovery. He resisted outside intervention and looked for ways to reform Peruvian society. Property reforms built respect for the law and alleviated many individual's grievances that feared the government's expropriation of their extralegally held land. The Fujimori government made it convenient for people to file complaints about excessive bureaucracy by establishing the Administration Simplification Tribunals. The televised tribunals allowed the people to directly examine improvements in different types of bureaucratic processes.[148] During this time, Peru provides an example of a state that became inclusive to its population. This inclusion also extended to coca farmers. Such inclusion benefitted the state and the farmers. The legal recognition of coca farmers resulted in information that helped the government eliminate many terrorist and drug trafficker sanctuaries.[149] Reducing bureaucracy, eliminating institutions that protect the few, creating agencies to support reforms, providing infrastructure and public services, all worked toward building a stronger economic growth machine.

Emergence of Market Economy

Economic systems are complicated, and no single policy prescription, even if precisely followed, is likely to be sufficient to ensure rapid, sustainable growth over time.[150] Generally, for a state to establish a market economy does not require destruction and rejection of existing arrangements. When intervening in a state's economic system, elites and bureaucracies who benefit from the previous system will resist change. However, in order to improve economic growth within a society, the excluded must be included in the legal system that has traditionally shut them out. The ability to gain acceptance from both groups is extremely difficult to do since most policy makers do not fully understand local level activities. No simple answer exists to bring both sides to a consensus. Creating redistributive expectations or establishing specific goals will exacerbate problems. The free market operates with only general goals.[151] By setting general goals, opportunities emerge where the state can integrate the informal institutions and provide the needed level of protection once made available by the extralegal sector. The state's challenge is to embrace the potential solutions that surface. Markets everywhere emerge in unplanned, spontaneous ways, adapting to local traditions and circumstances, and not through externally designed reforms.[152]

Importance of the Law over Other Variables

Understanding the laws, economic policies, and practices that prevent inclusion provides the first step for a country to change its economic health. Recognizing the approach to take constitutes one of the most difficult aspects of expeditionary economics. Although commanders and planners should understand the historical background of successes and failures of economic intervention, such understanding often fails to provide a good guide for future problems. The responsibility for the macroeconomic policy management rests with the state. However, policies that worked in the past does not translate to the same policies working in the future. When prescribing past successful economic policies, the state assumes that the economies, to which they are applying these policies, will continue to behave or operate in fundamentally the same way as in the past or at least in similar fashion.[153]

Blaming the poor economic growth on historical factors is a similar fallacy as blaming its demise on cultural reasons. While cultural understanding is extremely important to successful expeditionary economics, culture should be viewed as an opportunity to generate economic growth instead of a cause of economic woes. However, David Landes of Harvard University Department of Economics claims that growth is primarily about culture and that some societies have hard-working, enterprising people whereas others do not.[154] This view embodies a very dangerous argument since such arguments concentrate on the differences between people and groups instead of what they have in common. For instance, all cultures have entrepreneurs. However, not all cultures accept such groups and fail to encourage their growth. True, some cultures tend to focus on protecting elites, but this is common across most cultures and must be handled both politically and legally. The legal reform process required to bring the extralegal entrepreneurs into one official legal framework is essentially a cultural exercise: adapting Western market and corporate law to the vibrant cultures and customs of the developing state's new entrepreneurs.[155] This change in culture does not transpire overnight. It takes time for individuals to recognize how cultural arguments provide a shelter for the effects of good political institutions and laws. The arguments made individuals who continue to use culture as a reason for the state's economic success or failures fall short. Prior to the "East Asian miracle," many economists blamed a Confucian culture for the lack of economic success in East Asia, but post-miracle, touted such culture as the catalyst for economic success.[156] All culture can become supportive of economic development. Much behavior that is attributed to cultural heritage is not the inevitable result of people's ethnic or idiosyncratic traits but of their rational evaluation of the relative costs and benefits of entering the legal property system.[157]

The importance of inclusive laws cannot be overemphasized. American economists, Douglass North and Oliver Williamson, argue that favorable economic performance requires the following: a market grounded in a sound set of domestic institutions that includes formal rules such as statutes, common laws, regulations, and property rights embodied in the judicial system; informal rules in the way of conventions, norms, and self-imposed codes of conduct; and a wide range of state and societal organizations.[158] Successful systems embrace many of the social contracts pieced together by knowledgeable people familiar with the local environment. One of the main legal obstacles originates from the law's inability of the official law to maintain pace with popular initiative, causing the government to lose control.[159]

To improve the law to support economic revival, one of the greatest hurdles a state must overcome stems from the legal profession. Although the legal profession perfects all the artifacts of formal property: titles, records, trademarks, copyrights, promissory notes, bills of exchange, patent rights, and shares of corporate stock, few lawyers understand the economic consequences of their work.[160] The political actions that embrace grassroots solutions are vital to create inclusive laws that the majority accepts. Therefore, the state must employ a careful strategy for dealing with the legal profession if the government moves to integrate the extralegal sector. By viewing extralegal individuals as enterprising rather than criminals, the state will begin to integrate them into the formal legal system. The Western experience shows that inclusion is a threefold task: find the real social contracts on property, integrate them into official law, and craft a political strategy that makes reform possible.[161]

When Peru made important parts of the law accessible for all people, the state deprived the Shining Path of fertile ground for its insurgency. In economic matters, people do not rebel because they are poor, rather because they are excluded from the system.[162] While courts can help promote inclusive economic activity, they are not the sole answer to improving the system. The costs of legal action for small transactions often outweigh the benefits gained from the protection of property through the legal process.[163] When politicians respond to society's needs and discover ways to establish more honest courts, judges, and police, economic growth becomes possible.[164]

Conclusion

Commanders and planners face incredible challenges when they engage in expeditionary economics. This immense undertaking requires contextual understanding of the causes of grievances within the state. With this understanding, commanders and planners can influence a state to change laws and economic practices. On account of the political nature of creating change that produces economic growth, the state's leadership cannot focus solely on meeting the demands of the poor or excluded. However, change does occur when the state takes the perspective of the poor, co-opts the elite, and addresses exclusive law and technical bureaucracies that exist only to further the current economic system.[165] This process requires knowledge of not only how markets work from the macroeconomic level, but also entails searching the local level for the social norms that create the extralegal agreements. By incorporating these agreements, the state protects property and person and undercuts the extralegal arrangements that undermine the respect for the rule of law. If the state fails to protect property and person, history shows how even a murderous Mafia can meet a genuine social need when law and order collapse.[166]

This does not imply the necessity to incorporate all local arrangements. In fact, many such arrangements will only benefit the few and therefore, negatively effect economic growth. Instead, the state must utilize what actually works within the extralegal arrangements in order to get extralegal individuals to voluntarily adapt to the new circumstances.[167] The extreme entrepreneurial abilities of individuals in the extralegal sector provide everything from basic road infrastructure, water supply, sewage systems, and electricity to actually administering markets, justice, and laws. When the state creates quality laws that enable the inclusion of the majority of its citizens, the entrepreneurs become a part of a global market that increases the state's economic growth. Politicians should guide the change and give it an appropriate institutional framework so that the people can properly use and govern the changed environment.[168]

When the state's goal is to become a member of the modern market economy, the state's leadership must create a system that gives entrepreneurs access to the legal system. Such a system requires incorporating successful extralegal processes along with ensuring simple entry cost into the new system in both time and money. Additionally, transparency is a crucial aspect to the system's success. In Peru's case, the Fujimori government televised individual cases that showed how the current law changed. The strength of the press and judiciary is important in order to effectively scrutinize the government's actions. However, this is not always possible at the onset of creating change that increases economic growth.

The challenge for those conducting expeditionary economics is to encourage and influence the state to create legal and institutional systems that reflect a new reality. This new reality allows the fledgling economy that spontaneously emerges to function in an orderly fashion and enables competitive formal businessmen and merchants to produce with security.[169] Each state has a unique and complex history, culture, and set of grievances that may seem similar to other situations. However, each state requires an approach that is specific and particular to that state. Commanders and planners should not view aspects culture and history as a barrier to economic development. Rather, they should incorporate such aspects with the intention of supporting economic development. In order to provide successful and workable solutions, it is important to decentralize lawmaking and decision making to local governments. By transferring these responsibilities to local and regional governments, they are better able to enact beneficial laws since they are closer to the local issues, struggles and grievances. Regardless of the method used to create inclusive laws, the central government must find the means to incorporate existing arrangements. The United States Congress provides an excellent historical example of how the United States incorporated land laws through an iterative process of over five hundred laws in a span of over a hundred years. Although not perfect, researchers purport that the bottom-up approach to law is superior for economic development to more top-down approaches.[170]

The subject of expeditionary economics covers an incredible amount of areas for a state. The right plan does not exist and is itself a symptom of a misdirected approach.[171] Although no panacea exists to expertly guide the military in the conduct of expeditionary economics, contextual understanding of the underdeveloped state remains essential. Prior to conducting expeditionary economics in a state, commanders and planners can garner information from aid agencies that have individuals who have gained experience in a particular local setting on a particular problem. These are the individuals who can describe what is and is not working within a local environment. Still, this remains only one piece of an extremely complicated economic problem. Regardless what the military may think of local grievances, the institutions work most effectively, if at all, if they are homegrown. With contextual understanding, the military through expeditionary economics, can assist a state to establish a system that generates an engine of economic growth.

Notes

1. Field Manual 3-07: Stability Operations, October 2008, 2-8 – 2-9.

2. Carl J. Schramm, "Expeditionary Economics: Spurring Growth After Conflicts and Disasters," *Foreign Affairs* 89, no. 3 (May/June 2010): 89.

3. Oxford Dictionaries, http://www.oxforddictionaries.com/view/entry/m_en_us1245619#m_en_us1245619 (accessed August 31, 2010).

4. Oxford Dictionaries, http://www.oxforddictionaries.com/view/entry/m_en_us1243059#m_en_us1243059 (accessed August 31, 2010).

5. Erik S. Reinert, "Increasing Poverty in a Globalized World: Marshall Plans and Morgenthau Plans as Mechanisms of Polarization of World Incomes," In *Rethinking Development Economics*. edited by Ha-Joon Chang (London: Anthem Press, 2003), 455.

6. William Easterly, The White Man's Burden: Why the West's Efforts to Aid the Rest have done so much Ill and so Little Good, (London: Penguin Books Ltd., 2006), 345.

7. Easterly, 14-15.

8. David Scott Palmer, "Introduction: History, Politics, and Shining Path in Peru," In *The Shining Path of Peru*, edited by David Scott Palmer (New York: St. Martin's Press, 1994), 1.

9. Palmer, The Shining Path of Peru, 4.

10. Palmer, 5.

11. Palmer, 7.

12. Hernando de Soto, *The Other Path: The Economic Answer to Terrorism* (New York: Basic Books, 1989), xx.

13. de Soto, *The Other Path*, 235.

14. Palmer, The Shining Path of Peru, 5.

15. Palmer, 7.

16. Palmer, The Shining Path of Peru, 9.

17. Palmer, 11.

18. Palmer, 12.

19. de Soto, *The Other Path*, 232.

20. Palmer, The Shining Path of Peru, 13.

21. Ibid., 14.

22. Martin Khor, "Globalization, Global Governance and the Dilemmas of Development," In *Rethinking Development Economics*, edited by Ha-Joon Chang (London: Anthem Press, 2003), 533.

23. Palmer, The Shining Path of Peru, 14.

24. Patricia Oliart, "Alberto Fujimori: "The Man Peru Needed?"," In *Shining and Other Paths: War and Society in Peru, 1980-1995*, edited by Steve J. Stern (Durham: Duke University Press, 1998), 412.

25. Palmer, The Shining Path of Peru, 14.

26. Erik S. Reinert, How Rich Countries Got Rich and Why Poor Countries Stay Poor (New York: PublicAffairs, 2007), 47.

27. Reinert, 204.

28. William J. Baumol, Robert E. Litan, and Carl J. Schramm, *Good Capitalism, Bad Capitalism, and the Economics of Growth and Prosperity* (New Haven: Yale University Press, 2007), 55.

29. Carol Wise, Reinventing the State: Economic Strategy and Institutional Change in Peru (Ann Arbor: The University of Michigan Press, 2003), 179.

30. Moises Arce, Market Reform in Society: Post-Crisis Politics and Economic Change in Authoritarian Peru (University Park: The Pennsylvania State University Press, 2005), 39.

31. Ibid., 41.

32. Palmer, The Shining Path of Peru, 2.

33. Cynthia McClintock, *Revolutionary Movements in Latin America: El Salvador's FMLN and Peru's Shining Path* (Washington: United States Institute of Peace Press, 1998), 262.

34. Carlos Ivan Degregori, "The Origins and Logic of Shining Path: Two Views," In *The Shining Path of Peru*, edited by David Scott Palmer (New York: St. Martin's Press 1994), 52.

35. Ibid.

36. Gustavo Gorriti, "Shining Path's Stalin and Trotsky," In *The Shining Path of Peru*. edited by David Scott Palmer (New York: St. Martin's Press, 1994), 174.

37. Gorriti, The Shining Path of Peru, 175.

38. Degregori, The Shining Path of Peru, 53.

39. McClintock, Revolutionary Movements in Latin America, 65.

40. Ibid.

41. Gorriti, The Shining Path of Peru, 176.

42. McClintock, Revolutionary Movements in Latin America, 65-66.

43. David Scott Palmer, "Conclusion: The View From the Windows," In *The Shining Path of Peru*, edited by David Scott Palmer (New York: St. Martin's Press, 1994), 262.

44. McClintock, Revolutionary Movements in Latin America, 14.

45. Palmer, The Shining Path of Peru, 20.

46. Cynthia McClintock, "Theories of Revolution and the Case of Peru," In *The Shining Path of Peru*, edited by David Scott Palmer (New York: St. Martin's Press, 1994), 247.

47. Tom Marks, "Making Revolution with the Shining Path," In *The Shining Path of Peru*, edited by David Scott Palmer (New York: St. Martin's Press, 1994), 215.

48. Marks, The Shining Path of Peru, 215.

49. Marks, 213.

50. Billie Jean Isbell, "Shining Path and Peasant Responses in Rural Ayacucho," In *The Shining Path of Peru*, edited by David Scott Palmer (New York: St. Martin's Press, 1994), 90.

51. Palmer, The Shining Path of Peru, 23.

52. Palmer, The Shining Path of Peru, 269.

53. Marks, The Shining Path of Peru, 218.

54. de Soto, *The Other Path,* xxiv.

55. Palmer, The Shining Path of Peru, 22.

56. de Soto, *The Other Path,* xvii.

57. de Soto, *The Other Path,* xix.

58. McClintock, Revolutionary Movements in Latin America, 167.

59. Ronald H. Berg, "Peasant Responses to Shining Path in Andahuaylas," In *The Shining Path of Peru*, edited by David Scott Palmer (New York: St. Martin's Press, 1994), 120.

60. Degregori, The Shining Path of Peru, 60.

61. Degregori, The Shining Path of Peru, 52.

62. Hernando de Soto, The Mystery of Capital: Why Capitalism Triumphs in the West and Fails Everywhere Else (New York: Basic Books, 2000), 81.

63. Michael L. Smith, "Shining Path's Urban Strategy: Ate Vitarte," In *The Shining Path of Peru*, edited by David Scott Palmer (New York: St. Martin's Press, 1994), 155.

64. de Soto, The Mystery of Capital, 154.

65. Smith, "Shining Path's Urban Strategy, 210.

66. Baumol, Litan, and Schramm, 143.

67. Reinert, 47.

68. Baumol, Litan, and Schramm, 6.

69. Baumol, Litan, and Schramm, 25.

70. Baumol, Litan, and Schramm, 15.

71. Baumol, Litan, and Schramm, 7.

72. de Soto, The Mystery of Capital, 62.

73. de Soto, *The Other Path*, 132.

74. de Soto, The Mystery of Capital, 176.

75. de Soto, *The Other Path*, 238.

76. de Soto, The Mystery of Capital, 55.

77. de Soto, The Mystery of Capital, 59.

78. de Soto, *The Other Path*, 11.

79. Baumol, Litan, and Schramm, 75.

80. de Soto, The Mystery of Capital, 69.

81. de Soto, The Mystery of Capital, 174.

82. de Soto, *The Other Path*, 245.

83. de Soto, The Mystery of Capital, 157.

84. de Soto, The Mystery of Capital, 188.

85. de Soto, *The Other Path*, xxi.

86. de Soto, *The Other Path*, 234.

87. de Soto, The Mystery of Capital, 71.

88. de Soto, The Mystery of Capital, 176.

89. de Soto, *The Other Path*, 26.

90. de Soto, The Mystery of Capital, 35.

91. de Soto, The Mystery of Capital, 190-191.

92. de Soto, The Mystery of Capital, 41.

93. de Soto, The Mystery of Capital, 44.

94. de Soto, The Mystery of Capital, 66.

95. de Soto, The Mystery of Capital, 5.

96. de Soto, The Mystery of Capital, 47-48.

97. Baumol, Litan, and Schramm, 3.

98. de Soto, The Mystery of Capital, 34.

99. de Soto, The Mystery of Capital, 71.

100. Baumol, Litan, and Schramm, 87.

101. Baumol, Litan, and Schramm, 187.

102. Jeffrey D. Sachs, *The End of Poverty: Economic Possibilities for Our Time* (New York: Penguin Books, 2005), 3.

103. Easterly, 76.

104. Wise, 38.

105. Easterly, 6.

106. Baumol, Litan, and Schramm, 64.

107. Joseph Stiglitz, *Joseph Stiglitz and the World Bank: The Rebel Within* (London, Wimbledon Publishing Company, 2001), 239.

108. Easterly, 63.

109. Easterly, 77.

110. Easterly, 101.

111. de Soto, The Mystery of Capital, 211.

112. Easterly, 61.

113. Easterly, 18.

114. Easterly, 100.

115. Easterly, 312.

116. Easterly, 335.

117. C. K. Prahalad, *The Fortune at the Bottom of the Pyramid* (Upper Saddle River: Wharton School Publishing, 2006), 1.

118. Carlos E. Paredes and Jeffrey D. Sachs, "Introduction and Summary," In *Peru's Path to Recovery: A Plan for Economic Stabilization and Growth*, edited by Carlos E. Paredes and Jeffrey D. Sachs (Washington: The Brookings Institution, 1991), 38.

119. Wise, 18.

120. Wise, 11.

121. Wise, 83.

122. Wise, 83.

123. Wise, 85.

124. Wise, 96-97.

125. Wise, 84.

126. Wise, 103.

127. de Soto, The Mystery of Capital, 168.

128. Wise, 86.

129. Wise, 92.

130. Wise, 94.

131. Wise, 94.

132. Wise, 107.

133. Wise, 114.

134. Wise, 115.

135. Wise, 175.

136. Wise, 96.

137. Wise, 30-31.

138. Baumol, Litan, and Schramm, 56.

139. de Soto, The Mystery of Capital, 109.

140. de Soto, The Mystery of Capital, 53.

141. de Soto, The Mystery of Capital, 107-108.

142. de Soto, The Mystery of Capital, 119.

143. de Soto, The Mystery of Capital, 128.

144. Wise, 183.

145. Wise.

146. Wise, 184-185.

147. Isabel Coral Cordero, "Women in War: Impact and Responses," In *Shining and Other Paths: War and Society in Peru, 1980 – 1995*, edited by Steve J. Stern (Durham: Duke University Press, 1998), 367.

148. de Soto, *The Other Path*, xxviii.

149. de Soto, *The Other Path*, xxvii.

150. Baumol, Litan, and Schramm, 6.

151. Easterly, 12.

152. Easterly, 61.

153. Baumol, Litan, and Schramm, 43.

154. David S. Landes, The Wealth and Poverty of Nations: Why Some Are So Rich and Some So Poor (New York: W.W. Norton, 1999), 516-517.

155. de Soto, *The Other Path*, xxxvii.

156. Ha-Joon Chang, "The East Asian Development Experience," In *Rethinking Development Economics*. edited by Ha-Joon Chang (London: Anthem Press, 2003), 119.

157. de Soto, The Mystery of Capital, 226.

158. Wise, 4.

159. de Soto, The Mystery of Capital, 149.

160. de Soto, The Mystery of Capital, 199.

161. de Soto, The Mystery of Capital, 151.

162. de Soto, *The Other Path*, xxxv.

163. de Soto, *The Other Path*, 177.

164. Easterly, 117.

165. de Soto, The Mystery of Capital, 190.

166. Easterly, 89.

167. de Soto, *The Other Path*, 245.

168. de Soto, *The Other Path*, 240.

169. de Soto, *The Other Path*, 245-246.

170. Easterly, 97.

171. Easterly, 5.

Comparing Models for the Restoration of Essential Services during Counterinsurgency Operations

by

Major Anthony P. Barbina - United States Army

Abstract

What is the military's most effective model for restoring essential services during counterinsurgency operations? That question drove this monograph to compare the most popular restoration model, the SWEAT Model, against a new model, the Factor-Precedence Model. This monograph explains why the Factor-Precedence Model is more effective than the SWEAT Model for restoring essentials services during past, present, and future counterinsurgency operations.

Counterinsurgency operations include those military, paramilitary, political, economic, psychological, and civic actions taken by a government to defeat an insurgency. During counterinsurgency operations, restoring essential services, the infrastructure and supporting services that provide survival and comfort needs to the people, has become an important way to increase government legitimacy and decrease insurgent support. To leverage the positive impacts of essential services efforts, Department of Defense guidance and resource allocations require military forces to execute restoration of services and infrastructure. Because of the complex interactions required to restore essential services, counterinsurgency practitioners need an effective model to understand the environment, plan and analyze options, and conduct the work.

Military and civilian experts have produced many models to provide simple tools that help practitioners understand, prioritize, and execute essential services restoration. The SWEAT Model has become the most popular of these models because the SWEAT Model provides an easy way to think about infrastructure categories while conducting projects to improve those categories. Many units have used the SWEAT Model in Iraq and Afghanistan since 2004. As an alternative to the SWEAT Model, the author proposes a new model called the Factor-Precedence Model that develops processes for geographic and cultural evaluation of services, prioritization of requirements, and continuous assessment during essential services improvements. The Factor-Precedence Model leverages a whole of government approach to plan and execute improvements within the context of each area's needs.

This monograph assesses the effectiveness of the SWEAT and Factor-Precedence Models using two case studies and five comparison criteria: simplicity, flexibility, reproducibility, sustainability, and links to political and military objectives. In Case A, 1st Cavalry Division and its subordinate units used the SWEAT Model in Baghdad, Iraq (2005). Despite simple application and short term successes after implementation, the SWEAT Model used a cookie-cutter approach throughout Baghdad that limited analysis with regards to cultural, geographical, and regional factors. In Case B, 1st Cavalry Division and its subordinate brigades employed a model similar to the Factor-Precedence Model in Baghdad, Iraq (2009). 1st Cavalry Division's 2009 model applied a holistic outlook and focused on re-assessment, much like the Factor-Precedence Model, to allow for better analysis of needs, facilitate flexible execution across Baghdad, and permit project prioritization to meet local needs. To further evaluate the Factor-Precedence Model's usefulness, this monograph applies the Factor-Precedence Model within 10th Mountain Division's operational framework in

Kandahar, Afghanistan (2010). The Afghanistan illustrative example shows the flexibility and applicability of the Factor-Precedence Model in not only varying geographical and cultural regions but also across the range of military operations.

Results matter. The Factor-Precedence Model provides the most flexibility, allows for execution in a variety of situations, and links better to military objectives. Military planners should adopt a holistic approach like the Factor-Precedence Model and integrate existing planning, intelligence, engineering, and analysis tools into the model. Further research can improve the application of the Factor-Precedence Model for other government agencies and can determine execution techniques during the range of military operations.

Introduction

"Essential though it is, the military action is secondary to the political one, its primary purpose being to afford the political power enough freedom to work safely with the population... 'A revolutionary war is 20 percent military action and 80 percent political' is a formula that reflects the truth."[1]

- David Galula

Counter-Insurgency Warfare: Theory and Practice, 1964

This monograph seeks to find the most effective model for restoring essential services during counterinsurgency operations. Although the restoration of essential services plays an important part in both major combat and humanitarian operations, this monograph will focus on restoration efforts and models used during counterinsurgency operations.[2] As David Galula, French counterinsurgency veteran of the Greek Civil War, Indochina War, and Algerian War, recognized in 1964, winning a counterinsurgency fight requires military organizations to apply military and nonmilitary instruments of power in support of the legitimate host nation government. As shown in historical American counterinsurgency operations, restoring essential services has become one of the primary nonmilitary instruments of power. To execute essential services restoration, military and civilian experts have developed a variety of useful models to help facilitate planning and shape operations. This monograph compares application of the military's most popular restoration model, the Sewer, Water, Electricity, Academics, and Trash (SWEAT) Model, with a new model developed herein called the Factor-Precedence Model. The monograph applies a case study framework that assesses both models in terms of five evaluation criteria: simplicity, flexibility, reproducibility, sustainability, and links to political and military objectives. By the end of this monograph, the reader should have a better appreciation of why essential services models exist and why the Factor-Precedence Model is more effective than the SWEAT Model, or other historical models, for restoring essential services during present and future counterinsurgency operations.

Organization

This monograph includes seven main body sections and five appendices that compare the effectiveness of the SWEAT and Factor-Precedence Models. Section 1 of this monograph introduces the primary research question, provides background on essential services, and discusses the operational and intellectual impetus for the monograph. Section 2 conducts a literature review of the essential services debate and provides an overview of existing models. Section 3 provides an overview of the Army's most utilized essential services restoration model, the SWEAT Model. Section 4 describes the Factor-Precedence Model, a new model based in doctrine, adjusted through the lens of accepted theory, and refined through historical study. Section 5 outlines the case analysis framework and walks through the two similar case studies, set in Baghdad, Iraq, that portray use of the SWEAT and Factor-Precedence Models. Section 6 compares and analyzes the two Iraq case studies to determine the most effective model. The section then applies an illustrative example from Afghanistan that tests the applicability of the Factor-Precedence Model and facilitates inferences about future use and applications of the model. Section 7 concludes this effort by establishing recommendations for future actions and by proposing further research concerning the Factor-Precedence Model. The five appendices provide supporting information including definitions, acronyms, historical examples, model overviews, and a detailed explanation on how to use the Factor-Precedence Model.

Background

The United States (US) and its allies have a long history of conducting operations against insurgencies. According to David Galula's *Counterinsurgency Warfare: Theory and Practice*, insurgency is "a protracted struggle conducted methodically to attain specific intermediate objectives leading finally to the overthrow of the existing order."[3] Similar to Galula, Army *Field Manual (FM) 3-24 Counterinsurgency* defines insurgency as "[a]n organized movement aimed at the overthrow of a constituted government through the use of subversion and armed conflict."[4] Both definitions outline the fact that insurgents counter an existing government order and vie with that government for the support of the people. FM 3-24 logically nests with Galula's thoughts by describing counterinsurgency as "[t]hose military, paramilitary, political, economic, psychological, and civic actions taken by a government to defeat insurgency."[5] The critical lessons from Malaya, Algeria, and Vietnam counterinsurgency efforts outlined in Appendix 3 provide essential foundations for the counterinsurgency techniques in use today and inform practitioners how to effectively use non-military tools like the restoration of essential services.[6]

This monograph focuses on the restoration of essential services. Essential services consist of the infrastructure and supporting services that provide survival and comfort needs to the people while sustaining life. Examples of survival and comfort needs generally include food, water, shelter, basic sanitation, and emergency health care. Essential service requirements vary by population density, historic norms and current state of infrastructure, geographic region and climate, and cultural context.[7] According to Army *FM 3-07 Stability Operations*, restoring essential services within regional context allows the host nation's government to increase support from the population and consolidate control in populated areas. During an insurgency, the people's needs and required government support become much more complex in part because the insurgents act to undermine or subvert the government's efforts to provide or restore essential services.[8]

The current models restoring essential services during counterinsurgency operations have evolved from British, French, and American counterinsurgency experiences over the last seventy years. Appendix 3 not only provides historical counterinsurgency experiences, but the appendix also provides context for modern American essential services efforts. Efforts to restore essential services ultimately contribute to achieving a stable democracy and a sustainable economy while improving the social well-being of the population.[9] This monograph focuses on the restoration of essential services within the context of counterinsurgency as opposed to major combat or nation-building operations.[10] When attempting to restore essential services during an insurgency, counterinsurgents must find the model that provides the most effective representation of components, relationships, and dynamics for effective essential services restoration.

Operational and Intellectual Relevance

While every military mission has unique circumstances, essential services restoration in a counterinsurgency environment challenges practitioners operationally and intellectually in ways important to this monograph. Evaluating the effectiveness of essential services models has usefulness to counterinsurgency's operational and intellectual debates. Operationally, the military has conducted essential services restoration missions in the past and will continue to conduct them in the future. The need for commanders and practitioners to have a solid tool to restore essential services has increased debate on the need for and use of effective models. Intellectually, debate continues concerning the definition of needs, procedures for evaluating geographical and cultural impacts, and potential techniques for prioritization and execution support. Understanding the operational and intellectual relevance of this monograph helps set the tone for the case studies and model evaluation.

Operational Relevance

Essential services restoration presents a mission that has operational relevance to the Army's past, present, and future requirements. Militaries around the world have conducted counterinsurgency operations that included essential services restoration prior to World War II. As outlined in detail by Appendix 3, the restoration of essential services became even more important after World War II based on the increased importance of infrastructure on daily life and on the increased instability around the world. From Great Britain's counterinsurgency effort in Malaya to the America's efforts in Iraq and Afghanistan, history continues to demonstrate the relevance of essential services restoration and the need for effective ways to execute it.[11] Historically, Army active duty, Reserve, and National Guard units have become involved in restoration operations regardless of force structures. In anticipation of future requirements, the Department of Defense has directed the military to plan for, support, and conduct essential services restoration during counterinsurgency operations. *Department of Defense Directive (DoDD) 3000.05: Military Support for Stability, Security, Transition, and Reconstruction (SSTR) Operations* officially elevated stability operations to a "core" military mission on par with offensive and defensive operations and tasked the military to execute restoration of essential services tasks.[12] Government leaders also expect the military to support and restore essential services in specific, often dangerous, areas of operation because of limitations in Department of State's personnel capacity and security capabilities.[13] Based on the recurring theme and guidance to conduct essential services restoration, this monograph analyzes some of the most effective and holistic ways to do it.

This monograph also has relevance to operational commanders because, besides being directed to execute essential services restoration, practitioners can gain support for the host-nation government and decrease support for an insurgency by improving essential services. FM 3-24 encourages counterinsurgents to not only fight insurgents but also to "use their capabilities to meet the local populace's fundamental needs as well."[14] Using the Systems Dynamic Model shown in Figure 1, US Navy Captain Brett Pierson, a member of the Joint Staff's Warfighting Analysis Division, modeled the historical connections between improvements in essential services and the influence on a neutral populace during counterinsurgency operations.[15] In areas where services suffered or where the insurgents successfully denied services to the people and blamed it on the government, counterinsurgents paid the price with less population support and less success. In areas where the legitimate government improved services and increased the population's satisfaction with the provided services, counterinsurgents gained population support and had increased success. Based on Captain Pierson's work and other needs-based studies linking positive outcomes with services improvement, the US has increase the operational significance, resourcing, and support for essential services restoration during counterinsurgency efforts Since essential services prove operationally relevant and since the military has limited resources, time and expertise in essential services, counterinsurgents must develop effective ways to understand and improve services.

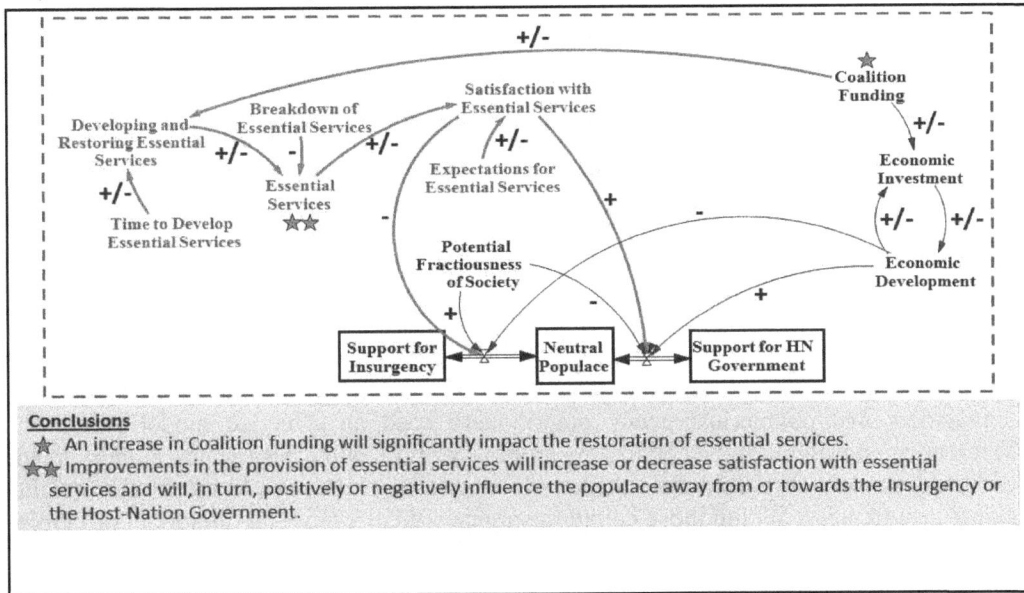

Figure 1: Mapping of Essential Services Impacts Using the Systems Dynamic Model[16]

Intellectual Relevance

A key element of the intellectual debate balances the best techniques to restore services. Based on the operational requirement to restore essential services, concerned commanders and counterinsurgency practitioners need a simple, yet effective, tool to overcome the lack of technical training and experience needed to conduct restoration tasks. A model describes "a set of abstract and general concepts and propositions that integrate those concepts into a meaningful configuration" of components, relationships, and dynamics.[17] The military uses a variety of flexible doctrinal, technical, or conceptual models that allow military members to deal with problems using a variety of techniques. In counterinsurgency model-making, the model usually describes an operational approach that shapes the language and conduct of operations.[18] During essential services restoration, models facilitate planning, analysis, and project selection and help non-technical experts make improvements without the years of training and experience technical provided to professions like engineering. Going without a model would remove an important tool for military and diplomatic practitioners.

In order to best employ limited resources, another important intellectual concern centers on the definition of needs in restoring basic services. The military's doctrinal definition for essential services allows for flexibility in interpretation among practitioners for what people truly need.[19] Due to the differences in geographical and cultural development seen throughout the world, the word *needs* means something different everywhere practitioners operate. According to the National Training Center's *SWEAT Smart Book*, engineers focus on the infrastructure, projects, and capacity improvement to meet needs.[20] According to the Department of State's Post-Conflict Reconstruction Essential Task List, Civil Affairs and Department of State personnel focus on governance, economics, engagement, growth, and development to meet needs.[21] Common vernacular and procedures coupled with an effective model could encourage inter-service and interagency approaches focused not only on projects but also engagements and development. To address the intellectual debate, the literature review in Section 2 helps to define essential services and explain existing approaches to the problem.

2 – Essential Services Literature and Restoration Models

> "The long-term goal is to help develop indigenous capacity for securing essential services, a viable market economy, rule of law, democratic institutions, and a robust civil society... Many stability operations tasks are best performed by indigenous, foreign, or US civilian professionals. Nonetheless, US military forces shall be prepared to perform all tasks necessary to establish or maintain order when civilians cannot do so."[22]

> *- Department of Defense Directive 3000.05*

As shown in Section 1 and the DoDD 3000.05 quote provided above, concerned commanders and counterinsurgency practitioners need an effective model based on valid theory and literature to conduct restoration work. Counterinsurgency authors have developed military and diplomatic theories to enable legitimate governments win a fight against insurgencies. Within those counterinsurgency theories rests an important principle of meeting constituent's needs that contributes to this monograph. To meet population needs and ensure social well-being, the military has conducted operations to restore essential services. Educators, planners, consultants, and engineers have produced many models, to include the SWEAT Model, to provide simple tools that help practitioners understand, prioritize, and execute services restoration. Since 2004, most units have used some form of the SWEAT Model in Iraq and Afghanistan to help them restore essential services and support the host nation government.[23]

Counterinsurgency and Essential Services Literature

Counterinsurgency literature demonstrates how effective counterinsurgents fought against insurgents and provides the historical context for essential services restoration during counterinsurgencies. Since the early 20th Century, winning support of the populace has become a fundamental principle of both insurgency and counterinsurgency literature. In 1937, Chinese revolutionary, guerilla warfare strategist, political theorist, and leader of the Chinese Revolution Mao Tse-Tung wrote that "[b]ecause guerrilla warfare basically derives from the masses and is supported by them, it can neither exist nor flourish if it separates itself from their sympathies and cooperation."[24] In 1952 during the Malayan Emergency, General Sir Gerald Templer, the British High Commissioner and commander of troops in Malaya, linked winning the "hearts and minds" of the Malayan people with improving popular perception and counterinsurgency success. In 1964, after taking part in the Algerian War as a French counterinsurgent, David Galula stated "the support of the population is as important for insurgents as it is for counterinsurgents."[25]

Literature published since the beginning of America's counterinsurgency operations in Afghanistan and Iraq carries the same emphasis on winning support of the population. Dr. Kalev Sepp, senior defense analyst at US Naval Post Graduate School, discussed the importance of the population and the fulfillment of population needs to ensure satisfaction. Dr. John Nagl, former military officer, co-author of the US Army and Marine Corps Counterinsurgency Field Manual, and President for the Center for New American Security, outlined not only the population's importance during counterinsurgency operations but also covered how military units must establish learning organizations to adjust to changing population requirements.[26] FM 3-24 states that "[c]ounterinsurgents often achieve the most meaningful success in garnering public support and legitimacy for the host nation (HN) government with activities that do not involve killing insurgents."[27] Australian counterinsurgency expert, theorist, consultant, and author Dr. David Kilcullen exerted considerable influence on American counterinsurgency operations based on his role as the Senior Counterinsurgency Advisor to General David Petraeus in Iraq from 2007 to 2008. According to Dr. Kilcullen, counterinsurgents should focus on the pillars of counterinsurgency that support government legitimacy and provide for the people's needs.[28] A common idea among modern literature focuses on succeeding in a counterinsurgency campaign by meeting needs and providing basic services to the people in order to increase the host nation's legitimacy and increase chances of success.

Since meeting the population's needs proves important in counterinsurgency, literature outlining methods of meeting needs provides an important foundation for essential services restoration. Abraham Maslow, the American professor of psychology at Brandeis University who founded humanistic psychology and created Maslow's Hierarchy of Needs, provides an excellent theory on human behavior, requirements, and perceptions. Maslow's Hierarchy of Needs has tremendous application in military doctrine because people generally understand his needs pyramid and the requirement to address needs in a population-centric counterinsurgency approach.[29] As depicted in Figure 2, the Maslow's Hierarchy of Needs pyramid on the left shows how humans generally attempt to fulfill the most important physiological needs because they relate to survival. Upon meeting those needs, they can progress up the pyramid to needs more associated with comfort and fulfillment.

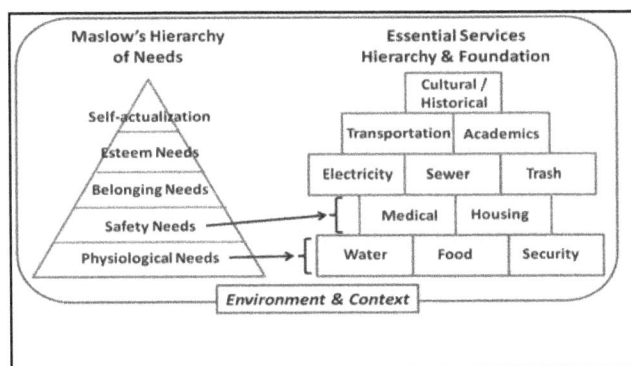

Figure 2: Maslow's Hierarchy of Needs and Essential Services Hierarchy[30]

Because Maslow's studies covered a relatively homogenous group of healthy Americans, practitioners must combine the foundation provided by Maslow's Hierarchy of Needs with ideas from other needs theorists to develop an essential services hierarchy.[31] Complementary analysis provided by Dr. Geert Hofstede and Dr. B.F. Skinner provide depth and context to Maslow's theory. Dr. Hofstede, the Dutch social psychologist, anthropologist, and pioneer in the research of cross-cultural groups and organizations, shows how diversity, geography, government, and economy impact the needs of a group or society. [32] Dr. Skinner, the influential American psychologist, behaviorist, author, and inventor, provides insight into the effects of cultural factors on group and societal needs.[33] Given impacts of geographical, cultural, religious context on societal needs, Figure 2 shows on the right side an essential services and infrastructure hierarchy paired with Maslow's Hierarchy of Needs. In this hierarchy, Naval Post Graduate School student Justin Gorkowski shows the foundational categories and relationships of infrastructure compared to human needs. The two hierarchies show that security becomes an influential force in essential services that may cause higher efforts on the pyramid to fail if security fails. If addressed in the correct context and completed in a relatively secure environment, providing services that support daily life and help people achieve an acceptable level of comfort should assist counterinsurgency practitioners. By connecting doctrinal definitions of essential services with needs-based theory, counterinsurgents can develop a valid categorization of essential services using existing essential services models.

As doctrine points out, the basic premise behind restoring essential services comes from meeting the needs of a population to prevent active or passive insurgent support. Any effective model must assist practitioners in providing population needs while connecting services delivery with the legitimate government. As shown previously in Figure 1, Captain Pierson, like many counterinsurgency authors, outlines the requirements to correlate meeting needs and expectations with increasing government legitimacy.[34] For the purpose of this monograph, relating needs identified in popular theories, literature, and practice with accomplishing military and political objectives helps determine the most effective essential services model.

Literature connecting defined needs with counterinsurgency outcomes provides a critical foundation for military restoration models. Meeting the needs of people can have a great impact on state security and defeating insurgents. Although the military focuses heavily on violence reduction and security improvement as measures of effectiveness, the connection between essential services improvement and changes in violence levels requires additional study outside the scope of this monograph.[35] The debate in essential services literature has not become whether or not to restore essential services but rather how to restore them. Counterinsurgency doctrine focuses the application of essential services restoration in support of government legitimacy using a population centric approach. FM 3-24 outlines essential services as a separate logical line of operations that concentrate on "providing those things needed to sustain life."

The RAND research team of Dr. Todd Helmus, Dr. Christopher Paul, and Dr. Russell Glenn provide compelling evidence that the population centric approach may help prevent deterioration in states bordering on civil violence. They propose that American forces can use stability operations and essential services projects to encourage civilian behavior.[36] Their study states that projects may be allocated or strategically withheld based on adherence to US operational norms. FM 3-07 states that "[t]he greatest threats to our national security will not come from emerging ambitious states but from nations unable or unwilling to meet the basic needs and aspirations of their people."[37] To leverage this technique, practitioners must clearly support the government, identify expectations of the population, and provide that information to the population concerning changes and improvements.[38]

Current Essential Services Models

The operational requirements to restore essential services and the need for models to help understand, prioritize, and execute services restoration have produced multiple models, with the SWEAT Model being the most highly utilized and covered in doctrine. The military uses models to break down problems into visual and understandable parts, facilitate communication between groups, and allow for more effective application of resources. Models help get things "about right" but cannot precisely predict every case. The greatest common factors among military models include keeping concepts simple and allowing maximum flexibility to commanders in the field.

During the last nine years of combat operations, military and diplomatic leaders have searched for the most effective model for restoration of essential services during counterinsurgency operations. In 2004, Marine and Army units began using the SWEAT acronym because restoration operations had no coverage in doctrine or mainstream models.[39] By the end of 2004, several Marine and Army units in Iraq, including the subject of Case A, Multi-National Division – Baghdad (MND-B), employed essential services models focused on SWEAT.[40] In early 2005, the National Training Center (NTC) developed the first essential services restoration model and handbook called the *SWEAT Smart Book: Practical Applications for Deploying Units Version 3.0*. The *SWEAT Smart Book* helped train units on infrastructure reconnaissance and assessments prior to deployments. Also in 2005, a team from the US Military Academy's (USMA) Departments of Systems Engineering and Mathematical Sciences developed the models covered in the *Infrastructure Assessment Methodology*. Colonel (Dr.) Joe Manous and his team provided an operations research-based model that contributed several critical categories and prioritization techniques to later versions of the SWEAT Model.[41]

After a few years of model experimentation in the field, the first essential services model entered doctrine in 2006. In the 2006 version of FM 3-24, and later in the 2008 versions of FM 3-07 and FM 3-34.170, doctrine built on the structure of models from the National Training Center and Army Engineer School to create the "Infrastructure Assessment and Survey Model." Also known by practitioners as the SWEAT Model because it spells out the acronym SWEAT-MSO, the Infrastructure Assessment and Survey Model remains the only essential services model in doctrine and has considerable use among units. Following his work at West Point as an instructor, Major Travis Lindberg introduced the *Critical Infrastructure Portfolio Selection Model (2008)*. This model highlighted critical distinctions between categories and infrastructure purposes. The intent behind Lindberg's models focused on increasing infrastructure security, conducting infrastructure assessments, and completing repairs or re-building to support the achievement of short and long term security goals.[42] In 2010, Professor Dr. John Farr and a small team from USMA traveled to Afghanistan and developed a model for the Department of State in Afghanistan called the *US Embassy (Kabul) Value Model and Project Analysis Tool*.[43] This new model establishes an excellent association between projects and government objectives that had little coverage in doctrine and previous models. Because the model focused on budgeting and action, the tool focused heavily on projects as opposed to holistic assessments of the situation. Appendix 4, Current Essential Services Models, provides more details on popular models including a brief history of each with example pictures.

Despite having several models available, the existing model that has the greatest impact on modern counterinsurgency operations remains the doctrinal SWEAT Model. The ease of use and widespread application of the model made the SWEAT Model the perfect candidate for analysis in this monograph. Using the key lessons and strengths of existing models, this monograph considers the newly created Factor-Precedence Model, which provides an approach that leverages basic needs assessment, establishes basic categories for evaluation and action, and works through project prioritization. Sections 3 and 4 describe the SWEAT Model and the Factor-Precedence Model, respectively, in more detail. Figure 3, Model Comparison Approach, outlines the comparison approach used throughout this monograph.

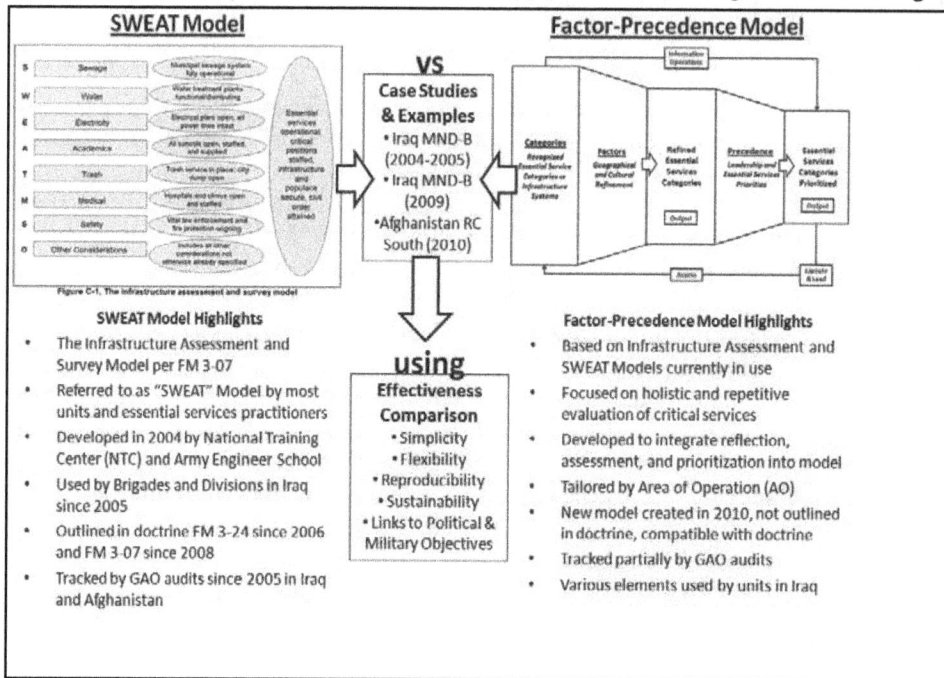

Figure 3: Model Comparison Approach[44]

3 – The SWEAT Model

"A direct correlation existed between the level of local infrastructure status, unemployment figures, and attacks on US Soldiers… The choice was to continue to attrit through direct action or shape the populace to deny sanctuary to the insurgents by giving the populace positive options through clear improvement in quality of life."[45]

- Major General Peter W. Chiarelli
Commander, 1st Cavalry Division
Military Review, 2005

Early in US counterinsurgency efforts in Afghanistan and Iraq, leaders like the commander of 1st Cavalry Division, Major General Chiarelli, identified the improvement of essential services as a key factor in defeating insurgency because it increases support to the legitimate government. As highlighted in Section 2, essential services restoration led to creation of various models to help practitioners understand and improve services. Section 3 provides an overview of the most utilized model, the SWEAT Model, which Army Doctrine describes in FM 3-34.170.[46] To allow for real-world execution, practitioners supplement doctrine with non-doctrinal tools and products like the *SWEAT Smart Book*.[47] Using on this precedent, the SWEAT Model evaluated in this monograph supplements the doctrinal model with Army Engineer School and National Training Center products.

The Army's doctrinal SWEAT Model focuses on infrastructure assessments, data collection, project prioritization, and execution as a way to restore essential services across the lines of effort *SWEAT-MSO*. As shown in Appendix 3, the SWEAT Model emerged after years of the Army conducting essential services restoration during and after combat operations. Tracing fundamental roots to Vietnam-era programs called the Hamlet Evaluation System (HES) and Civil Operations and Revolutionary Development Support (CORDS), the SWEAT Model leverages civilian and military institutions to improve host-nation government services.[48]

By 2004, units like Major General Chiarelli's 1st Cavalry Division used his SWEAT Program to guide the essential services effort.[49] Using field feedback from units like 1st Cavalry Division and combining it with engineering theory, the National Training Center Engineering Team (Sidewinders) developed the first major model for restoration of essential services. NTC not only provided this manual across the military community, NTC teams trained most engineer, civil affairs, and essential services practitioners on the *SWEAT Smart Book* during their training at Ft. Irwin. The Engineer School described the Infrastructure Reconnaissance and Improvement Model in the 2005 document called *The SWEAT/IR Book*.[50] Because it had proprietary photos and information inside the book, *The SWEAT/IR Book* earned an earmark of For Official Use Only (FOUO) that limited the books distribution and impact on the Army. By 2006, the Army had published its first doctrinal essential services restoration model in FM 3-24, which referred to the model as the Infrastructure Assessment and Survey Model. This model outlined the key elements of essential services and focused practitioners on the acronym and memory aid, *SWEAT-MSO*.[51] According to the *SWEAT Smart Book*, units began calling the doctrinal model the SWEAT Model based on the memory aid and in honor of the hard work required to make progress in essential services.[52] Because the infrastructure categories that make up the acronym SWEAT do not always provide the infrastructure solution that a commander needs, the engineer school recommends thirteen "Other" categories for infrastructure support. Figure 4 shows the SWEAT Model used to integrate and synchronize tactical actions, delineate roles and responsibilities, and focus the civil-military efforts in pursuit of related objectives. The following paragraphs provide a brief explanation of the SWEAT Model to facilitate a common understanding.

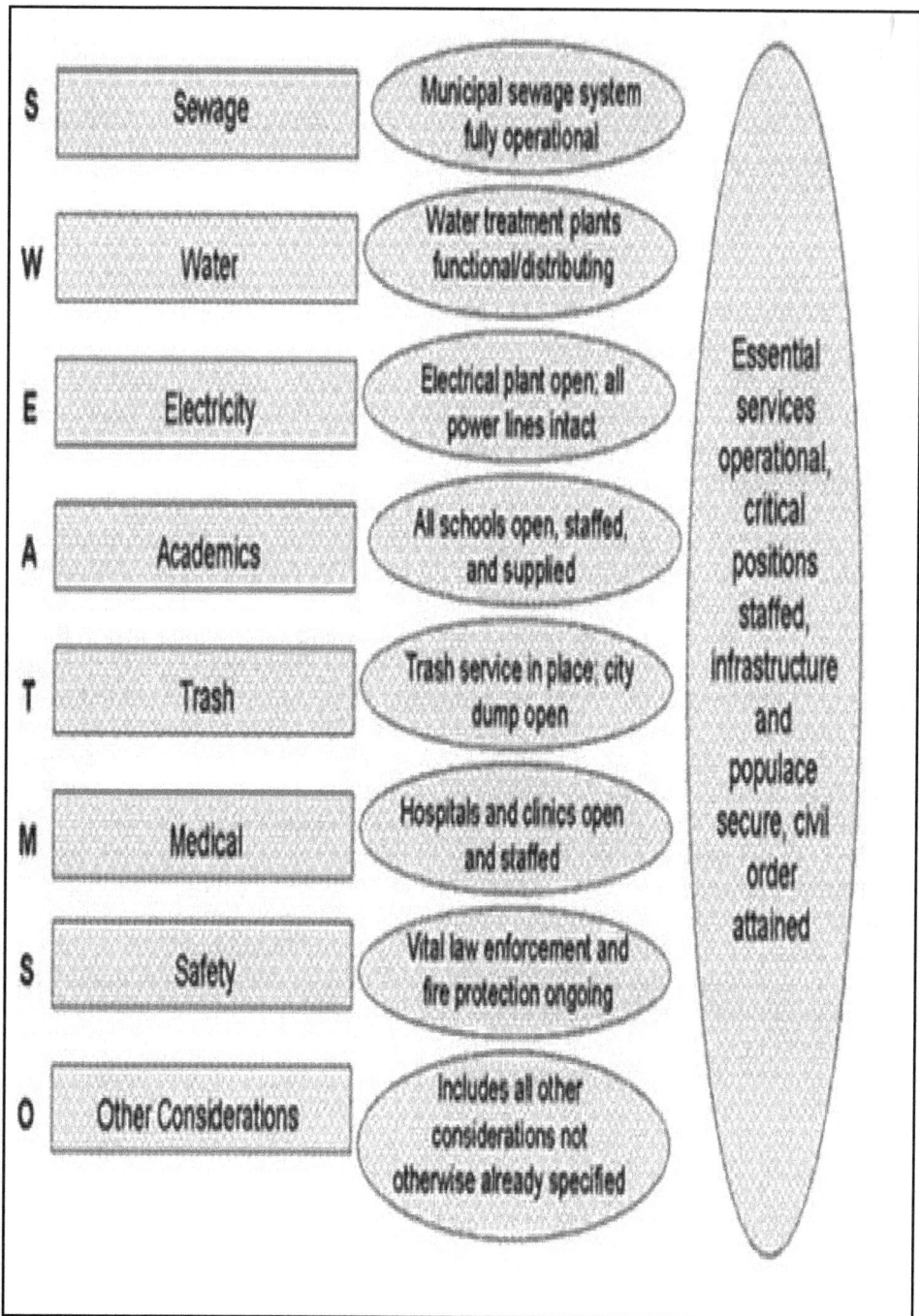

Figure 4: The Infrastructure Assessment and Survey Model (aka SWEAT Model)[53]

Infrastructure Categories and Assessment

The first step of the SWEAT Model requires units to conduct an infrastructure reconnaissance and assessment of existing essential services. The basic services or categories evaluated depend on the situation, mission, and commander's intent. NTC's *SWEAT Smart Book* and the United States Army Engineer School's (USAES's) *The SWEAT/IR Book* provide supplemental references to FM 3-34.170 that outline objectives required to restore essential services. The refinement of infrastructure categories increases the availability of data on SWEAT requirements and helps focus counterinsurgents on the allocation of resources to specific, unprioritized infrastructure categories like sanitation, energy, and agriculture. During the first step, units can ask questions like those in Figure 5 to refine information and understanding of the essential services situation. Infrastructure reconnaissance not only identifies the problems. These questions and the supplemental reconnaissance guides outlined in doctrine provide the relevant information necessary for planning and reconstruction by those skilled in an appropriate specialty.[54]

- **Sewage.** What is the status of the local sewage system? What health and environmental risks exist?
- **Water.** What potable water sources are available? Are they adequate? Have they been tested?
- **Electricity.** What is the status of electrical generation facilities to include availability of generators? What is the status of the transmission infrastructure? What critical facilities to include hospitals, government buildings, and schools are not having their needs met? What is the availability of fuel for transportation, heating, and cooking? Is there an adequate system of distribution?
- **Academics.** What schools are in need of repair and rebuilding?
- **Trash.** Is there a system in place for removing waste? What hazardous waste streams are being generated that may have detrimental impacts on health and the environment? What is the ultimate disposal system for trash?
- **Medical.** Are medical services available and operational? Does an emergency service exist? Are services available for animals?
- **Safety.** Is there a police and fire service? Are UXO or other EHs an issue?

Figure 5: FM 3-34.170 Category Refinement Questions[55]

Essential Services Planning, Objectives, and End States

The second step of the SWEAT Model focuses on the establishment of essential services objectives and end states. After reconnaissance and assessment determine the state of infrastructure, the essential services planning process establishes a feasible road map for action and the best path for improvement. As shown in Figure 4, this path establishes specific tasks, requirements, or objectives for each infrastructure or service category. Both the *SWEAT Smart Book* and *The SWEAT/IR Book* provide useful tools to link assessments with objectives that improve infrastructure.[56] Based on the progression of tasks and objectives during the unit's time in the area, practitioners establish required conditions that qualify the achievement of the commander's end state – they describe what the end state will look like to the host nation. Units plan prioritized projects and infrastructure improvements to increase services, meet emergent needs, and reach the end state for essential services.

Project Prioritization, Execution, and Transformation

The third step of the SWEAT Model provides the platform for practitioners to prioritize their requirements, execute projects, and establish the foundation for long term development. According to the *SWEAT Smart Book*, SWEAT practitioners evaluate each infrastructure category and prioritize actions based on the level of effort required, health concerns, cost, local perception, local involvement, government impact, and interdependence of the structure.[57] Based on priority of need, the SWEAT Model leverages the prioritization of resources and projects to improve unit focus in the counterinsurgency environment.[58] Units execute projects within the SWEAT Model to provide support to governance, economic, and essential services lines of operation. During execution, units track measures at the level of their partnership with host-nation government employees. Since 2005, the Government Accountability Office (GAO) has conducted audits and surveys to track essential services improvements at the national level in Iraq and Afghanistan. Both local and national assessments help monitor improvements, track spending, adjust development plans, and understand on-going transformations in essential services.

In conclusion, the three steps of the SWEAT Model allow practitioners to improve essential services within their time and resource constraints. The doctrinal SWEAT Model focuses on linear improvement over specific lines of effort to meet objectives. The doctrinal model provides no provisions for re-assessment, but commanders and practitioners using the Battle Command Process will conduct continuous evaluation and assessment during operations. The SWEAT Model, when complemented by the *SWEAT Smart Book* and *The SWEAT/IR Book*, becomes a powerful tool for analysis and action. It focuses on action through project execution and host-nation capacity building.

4 – The Factor-Precedence Model

"A victory is not [just] the destruction in a given area of the insurgent's forces and his political organization. It is that, plus the permanent isolation of the insurgent from the population, isolation not enforced upon the population but maintained by and with the population."*[59]*

- David Galula

Counterinsurgency Warfare, 1964

David Galula understood the need for the host nation community to be involved in the planning and performance of the work in order for it to be of lasting impact. The author of this monograph created the Factor-Precedence Model in August 2010 to provide a more holistic approach to restore essential services by working with the local government and through local people to accomplish military objectives. This section provides an overview of the Factor-Precedence Model, a straight-forward model that complements existing counterinsurgency doctrine and incorporates existing tools. Appendix 5 provides a specific, more comprehensive description of how to apply the Factor-Precedence Model.

As shown in Figure 6, the structure of the Factor-Precedence Model consists of sixteen general infrastructure categories that constitute essential services and are common to every global region. Each essential service category represents a service or infrastructure system that provides for the needs of the population. The Army Engineer School and Army doctrine have detailed and refined these categories over the last six years. As a result, practitioners and intelligence specialists understand how to analyze and assess these service systems.[60]

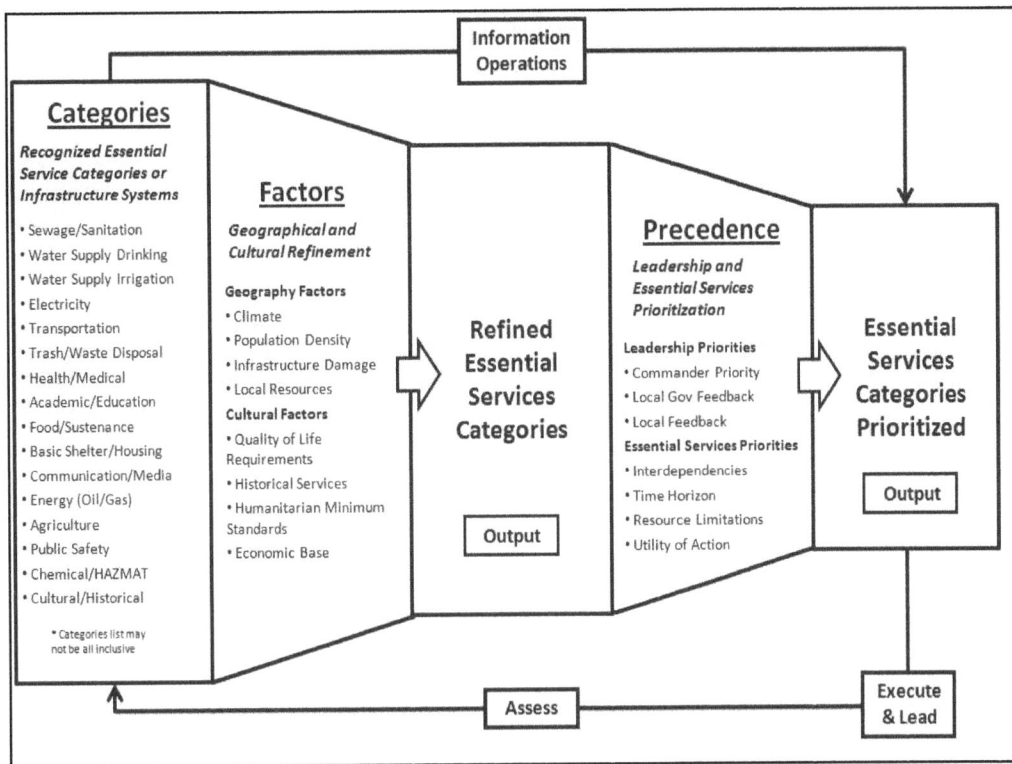

Figure 6: The Factor Precedence Model

Using eight local geographical and cultural factors, the Factor-Precedence Model focuses the existing categories into a manageable list that better represents the needs of the local population. The output of this step reduces to four to seven refined categories that allow practitioners to define essential services lines of effort and provide recommendations for category objectives and end states to their leadership. Using this abbreviated list, units then apply leadership and resource guidance to relate prioritization to both categories and individual projects. Because essential service requirements differ in every geographic location, cultural setting, and unit area of operation, an effective restoration model must first narrow recognized service categories, then allow practitioners to prioritize those selected categories and projects for execution and assessment. Figure 6 shows the Factor-Precedence Model aligned with its complementary tasks of information operations, execution, leadership, and assessment.

Recognized Essential Service Systems or Categories

The first step in the Factor-Precedence Model requires units to analyze the sixteen recognized essential services categories. These categories, ranging from sewage to shelter, provide the required infrastructure to support basic needs for a culturally acceptable quality of life. Appendix 5, How to Apply the Essential Services Factor-Precedence Model, provides a brief explanation of each of these categories. Using the general infrastructure categories recognized by the engineering and international communities, practitioners gain a better understanding of the physical infrastructure and systematic connections. Governments typically align their bureaucratic system to support the sixteen categories with ministries assigned to major areas. Career fields, like engineering, focus on these specific categories for technical licensure and expertise over the life of a career. Because of widespread use, most military units and leaders understand the existing categories and can ascertain initial requirements for action.

Existing tools such as geospatial databases, operational variables analysis, and civil considerations analysis allow the unit to better understand the services system.[61] Infrastructure reconnaissance and assessment of each service category facilitates further application of the Factor-Precedence Model and detailed coverage is provided in *FM 3-34.400 General Engineering*, Appendix C.[62] The analysis of essential services categories establishes a solid baseline for unit intelligence preparation and for government engagement along bureaucratic lines. Essential services reconnaissance, assessment, and analysis also set conditions for the model's second step.

Geographical and Cultural Factors

The second step of the Factor Precedence Model allows units to apply local geographical and cultural factors in order to trim categories to actionable levels. Both geographic and cultural factors force practitioners to think more holistically about the requirements and impact of essential services on the community. The eight geo-cultural factors refine general categories into something specific to a company, battalion, brigade, division, or higher unit's area.[63] Geographical factors filter climate, population density, extent of battle damage, and availability of local resources in order to analyze local weather, terrain, and progress conditions. Cultural factors filter quality of life requirements, historical services, humanitarian minimum standards, and the economic base to focus on local needs, desires, and expectations.

Units gain geographical and cultural information during pre-deployment research, environmental analysis, and during initial reconnaissance. Units then refine these geo-cultural factors using tools such as area and infrastructure assessments, the Engineer Research and Design Center's (ERDC's) *Geo-Cultural Analysis Tools (GCAT)*, and Human Terrain System assessments based on local engagements.[64] The second step of the Factor-Precedence Model outputs four to seven essential services categories on which counterinsurgents can concentrate their efforts for each area of operation. Planners subsequently define the lines of effort (LoE), decisive points, objectives, and end states for each category. Appendix 5 provides a list of examples concerning application of the geo-cultural factors.

Leadership and Mission Precedence Elements[65]

The third step in the Factor-Precedence Model allows units to apply elements of their leader's guidance and essential services technical priorities. Using the refined categorization from the second step, counterinsurgents must utilize elements of precedence to rank order essential service operations and projects. During most military operations, limited time or resources require the commander to prioritize focus and effort before, during, and after operations. Leadership priorities provide focus based on the unit commander's intent and guidance, feedback from concerned government officials, and feedback from local consumers. Essential services priorities tailor the systematic interdependencies, time and resource limitations, and utility of action to balance priorities in terms of wants and needs. Priorities differ within every area based on basic service status, resources available, unit goals, and capabilities of the government entities. The third step of the Factor-Precedence Model outputs a final prioritization that governs specific actions within categories and individual projects to ensure effective and efficient execution of localized essential services operations. Adjustments to funding, resources, or commander's intent can shift the precedence of refined categories. Due to the long-term nature of essential service operations, units should keep adjustments to the minimum necessary.

The effectiveness and flexibility of the Factor-Precedence Model in terms of location, interchangeability, and compatibility demonstrate that the model could work in future counterinsurgency operations. Factor-Precedence Model Figure in Section 4 portrays the interaction of the Factor-Precedence Model with many existing tools used by essential services practitioners. Appendix 5 provides a list of examples concerning application of precedence elements and provides model links to complementary actions like information operations, execution, leadership, and assessment.

In conclusion, the three steps of the Factor-Precedence Model allow practitioners to integrate essential services restoration with the Battle Command Process. The Factor-Precedence Model focuses on holistic improvement within the geographical, cultural, and leadership environment to improve essential services and defeat the insurgency. The integration of provisions for reassessment and information management should help practitioners to continuously develop improvement plans and manage operations.

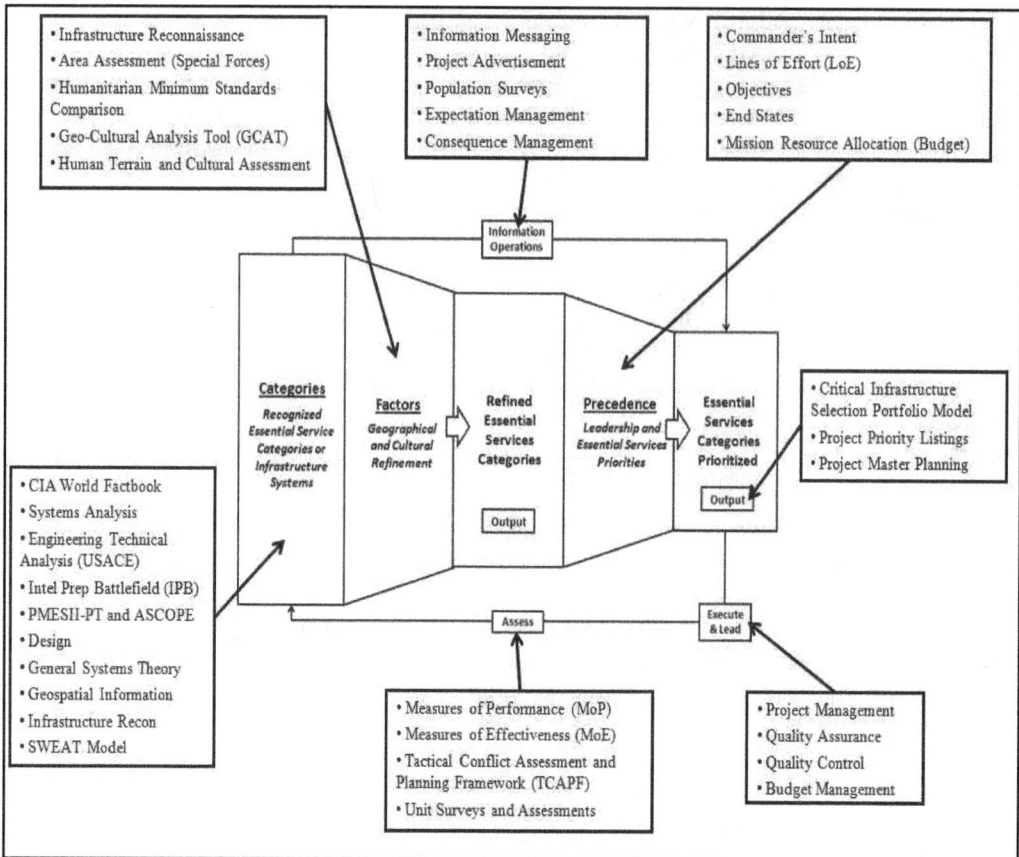

Factor-Precedence Model Figure

Existing Tools and Applicability to the Factor-Precedence Model[66]

5 – Iraq Case Studies

"The answer lies not in pouring more troops into the jungle, but in the hearts and minds of the Malayan People."[67]

- General Sir Gerald Templer,
Director of Operations and High Commissioner for Malaya, 1952

"Military force cannot change opinion. It can only create a framework in which economic reform and government can take effect."[68]

- Major Bill Tee, 1/6 Gurkha Regiment
British District War Executive Committee, 1953

Case Evaluation Framework and Model Effectiveness

The quotes by General Sir Gerald Templer and Major Bill Tee, both British leaders during the Malaya Emergency, illustrate the importance of the defense units working outside narrow security roles by expanding military efforts in social, economic, and government areas. This monograph uses two primary cases from Iraq to compare the effectiveness of the SWEAT and Factor-Precedence Models in situations similar to that faced by General Templer and Major Tee. Case A, Operation IRAQI FREEDOM in 2005, offers an example in which 1st Cavalry Division applied the SWEAT Model to essential services operations. Case B, Operation IRAQI FREEDOM in 2009, offers an example where 1st Cavalry Division applied an essential services model very similar to the Factor-Precedence Model during their counterinsurgency operations.

The case evaluation framework begins with five evaluation criteria that help establish a set of important factors for all effective models.[69] The five evaluation criteria of simplicity, flexibility, reproducibility, sustainability, and links to political and military objectives provide a comparison framework. The evaluation criteria derive from the works of three theorists, Paul Davidson Reynolds, John Lewis Gaddis, and Antoine Bousquet. These theorists have established the primary requirements for evaluation of theories and models. The evaluation criteria draw a comparison between the two models and facilitate inferences from case study analysis by addressing those factors that increase chances of success and those that can cause failure. With slight modifications, these criteria help evaluate model effectiveness within the case studies as outlined in Table 1.[70]

Although restoration of essential services presents a very complex situation, an effective model provides a simple approximation of the real world that American diplomats and Soldiers can understand and apply during counterinsurgency operations. Flexible models allow for deliberate and hasty application across a variety of initial conditions and environmental situations. Reproducible models provide a systematic methodology that allows for application to past and present cases and for execution in nearly any future situation. Sustainable models rely on past experiences as a foundation on which to build. These models last over time, adapt to changing environments, and integrate well into planning and execution tools. Not only do sustainable models facilitate repeated use of the model itself, but they also encourage outcomes that practitioners can pass on to others. In terms of essential services model sustainability, the critical question becomes "can the local people, leadership, or government sustain this project?" Effectively linked models support political and military objectives by applying a holistic cost-benefit approach to informed military thinking in a counterinsurgency environment. Table 1 provides a complete definition, theoretical foundation, and measure for each of the five evaluation criteria.

Table 1: Model Effectiveness and Evaluation Criteria Definitions

Eval Criteria Short Title	Evaluation Criteria Definition	Sources	Measure & (Benchmark)
Simplicity	Simple enough approximation of the real world that American diplomats and Soldiers can understand and apply the model during counterinsurgency operations	- Reynolds[71]	- Number of categories in use (# categories) - Useful to wide spectrum military force (Infantry, Civil Affairs, Engineers, etc)
Flexibility	Flexible models allows for deliberate and hasty model application through a variety of initial conditions and environmental situations	- Reynolds - Gaddis[72]	- Speed capability (fast & slow) - Diversity in areas supported (agricultural, industrial)

Reproducibility	Reproducible models provide a systematic methodology that allows for application to past and present cases and for execution in nearly any future situations	- Gaddis[73] - Bousquet	- Applicable to past cases (Vietnam) - Applicable to current cases (Iraq, Afghanistan) - Useful for future results (Hybrid threat)
* Sustainability	Sustainable models build on past experience, last over time, transform with changing environments, and tie well into planning and execution tools (e.g. can locals sustain the output?)	- Bousquet[74]	- Useful in multiple environments (urban, rural) - Existing tools applicable to model (# applicable) - Immediate vs. long-term perspective (both present)
** Links to Political and Military Objectives	Effectively linked models support political and military objectives by applying a holistic approach to informed military thinking in a counterinsurgency environment (e.g. cost vs. benefit linked militarily and politically)	- Bousquet[75] - Military doctrine	- Nested with higher HQ guidance and objectives - Cost vs. Benefit of action (Measures) - Integration with variety of ministerial or civil service branches (# ministries)

By selecting two similar case studies that occur in the same area, with the same combat unit, and under the same central government and supporting ministries, this case analysis generally controls the comparison framework between past and present restoration operations. In both cases, leadership took into consideration the experience of their force, the technical capacity available for missions, and available opportunities when selecting the appropriate restoration model. Similarities between cases support the appraisal of each model's effectiveness using the five evaluation criteria. Table 2 provides an overview of the primary similarities between Case A and Case B that facilitate direct comparison.

By selecting two case studies with minor differences including the time period, surge effects, Iraqi government capability, and violence levels, this case analysis incorporates adequate controls that differentiate the specific capabilities for each model. As shown in Table 2, the eight minor differences between the two cases link the two similar situations and facilitate comparison of actions and outcomes. The implementation of a new counterinsurgency approach by General Petraeus and his theater command, Multi-National Forces – Iraq (MNF-I), combined with the increased experience of the combat and technical experts, has significant impacts when compared to the 2005 case. As many practitioners on the ground have pointed out, by the time of the 2009 surge, force leaders, staff, commanders, and troops in the field typically brought with them significant previous Iraq experience to the mission. Most leaders and commanders have served at least one previous tour in Iraq, and their familiarity with Iraqi governing structures, basic laws, and customs is markedly greater than the limited knowledge the first coalition teams brought to the Baghdad, Iraq case. However, the differences still facilitate comparison between the two cases.[76]

Table 2: Cases A and B Comparison Controls

Case Similarities	Case Differences
- Area & Time of Year (Geography and cultural breakdown) - Established Central Government - Central government services (Ministries, Civil Service) - Religious apportionment (Shia and Sunni split) - Division in command (MND-B) - Detailed unclassified command reports available (1 CAV) - Detailed 3rd party audit information available (SIGIR and GAO) - Essential services conditions (Damage pre-surge, limited maintenance) - Resourcing priority and support (Pre-OEF Surge) - Focused on non-lethal operations - Command focus on essential services - Engineer technical forces (MND-B and USACE) - Iraqi government revenues (Oil Prices ~ $75/barrel)	- Time period (2005 and 2009) - Surge effects (Forces redeployed in early 2009) * - Violence levels (2009 half of 2005 levels) * - New COIN focus from MNF-I (General Petraeus, Ambassador Crocker, and Dr. Kilcullen) - People with more experience (Combat, Technical) - Different leadership focus (Provincial Reconstruction Teams [PRTs] available, Department of State priority and resource allocation) - Iraqi government more capable (Capacity growth) * - Doctrine and essential services models (Updates) * Differences minimal and facilitate case comparison

Case A: SWEAT Model in Baghdad, Iraq (2005)

Case Context and Unit Approach

In Case A, the context for 1st Cavalry Division's operations in Baghdad evolved from the initial combat focused invasion of Iraq in 2003 into stability operations focused on government and infrastructure reconstruction by 2005. Operation IRAQI FREEDOM (OIF) began on March 20, 2003 with an invasion by a multinational coalition led by the US military. Following a speedy completion of major combat operations that climaxed in the overthrow of Saddam Hussein's regime, the Coalition and allied Iraqi forces established a Coalition Provisional Authority (CPA) to rule Iraq, assist in reconstruction, and set conditions for a "transfer of sovereignty" back to a legitimate Iraqi government. By June 2003, Combined Joint Task Force 7 (CJTF-7) assumed control of the military component of operations and focused on the political (governance), economic, essential services, and security lines of operation.[77] Amid a growing trend in violence and an emerging insurgency in 2004, the CPA transitioned authority to the Interim Government of Iraq.[78]

To support the Interim Government by late 2004, CJTF-7 reorganized into a joint, combined force known as MNF-I and began managing combat operations throughout Iraq.[79] After a review of the military strategy at the end of 2004, the MNF-I Commander concluded that the Iraqi civilians all over the country wanted and needed basic essential services restored or even created. To jump start the rebuilding process, MNF-I distributed funds called Commander's Emergency Relief Program (CERP) Funds to US Coalition Forces for projects and local support.[80] Focus on reconstruction and funding for local projects helped set the context for this case study. The US Coalition commanders directed their maneuver operations to disrupt the enemy and used non-maneuver capabilities like the restoration of essential services to assist the local population.

To narrow more closely into the subject of Case A, 1st Cavalry Division took command and control in April 2004 of Task Force Baghdad, also called Multi-National Division – Baghdad (MND-B).[81] Through their relief in place in February 2005, the MND-B's operational campaign plan balanced five integrated conceptual lines of operations (LOOs) shown in Figure 7: 1) conducting combat operations, 2) training and employing security forces, 3) promoting essential services, 4) establishing a capable, legitimate government, and 5) creating opportunities for economic independence through a free market system.[82] Each LOO had a close relationship with information operations (IO) that communicated positive messages to the Iraqi populace, international community, and American base. With improvement in each line, the Task Force planned to meet the end state, or ultimate goal, of building a legitimate Baghdad government while shifting the city away from instability.[83]

A major part of the instability in Baghdad came from the difference between conditions in 2004 compared with conditions during Saddam Hussein's reign over Iraq. During Saddam's regime from 1979 to 2003, Hussein focused much of his government funding and support to the capital region. Baghdad received fifty percent of the available power despite having only thirty percent of the populace. Saddam built drinking water, trash collection, and irrigations systems in and around Baghdad that far surpassed the quality of those in the rest of the country. Following the coalition invasion, many of these formerly well off Iraqi neighborhoods now had no potable drinking water, continuous electrical blackouts, no evidence of trash collection, high unemployment, and a genuine mistrust of the newly formed Iraqi government. The $30 billion in aid and development spent in the two and one-half years after the end of major combat operations focused on country-wide electrical and water projects that did little to change the situation on the ground, especially in Baghdad.[85]

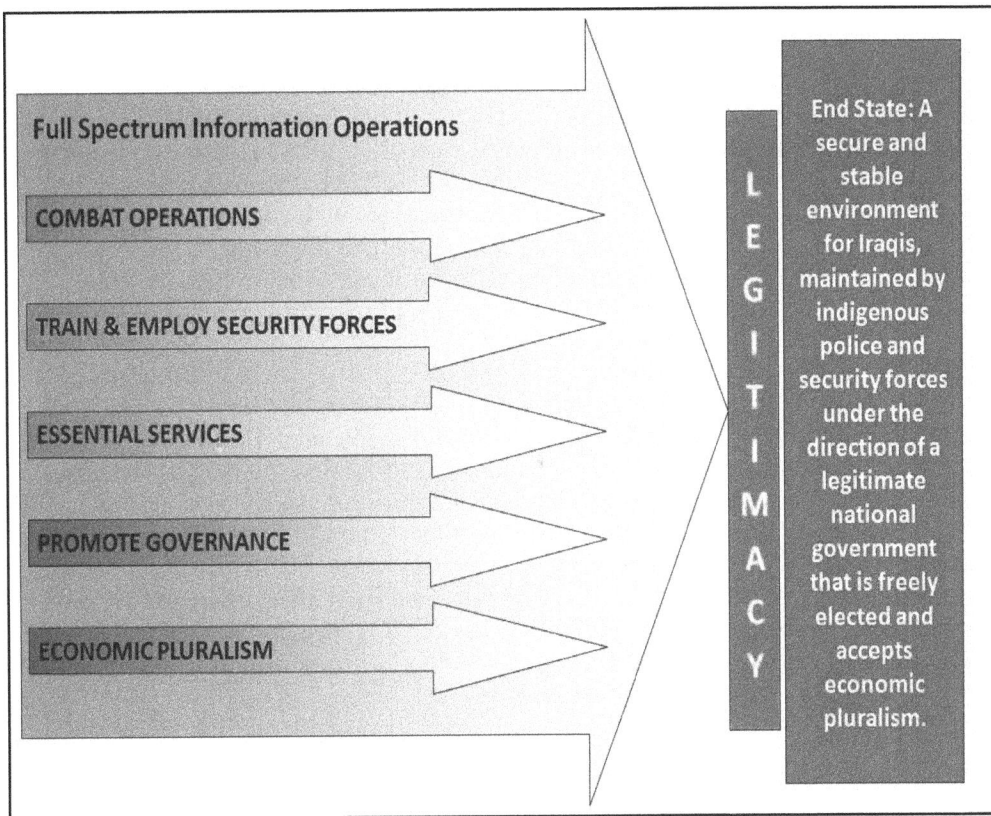

Figure 7: Task Force (TF) Baghdad (1st Cavalry Division) Lines of Operation (LOO)[84]

Essential Services Operations and the SWEAT Model

To support the six million people in Baghdad, 1st Cavalry Division focused immediately on the line of operation for essential services as the "first among equals." When NTC and the Army Engineer School published their SWEAT books, the division refined their approach and became the first unit to officially use a SWEAT Model to restore essential services LOO.[86] Within the essential services line of operation, the division staff organized the Division Engineer Section and 9th Engineer Battalion assets to direct planning, design, and execution towards projects that improved the quality of life for the Iraqi people. The new SWEAT Model helped the division refine their focus, develop a restoration execution plan, determine how to monitor improvement metrics, and provide guidance to subordinate units in order to focus on security and essential services.[87] The 1st Cavalry Division's Brigade Combat Teams now had their areas of operation underpinned with a clear direction and focus, which was on rebuilding, repairing, and eventually monitoring the essential service infrastructure in Iraq.

At a more micro level, 1st Cavalry Division's subordinate units focused on the "first among equals" line of operation as an opportunity to use CERP through local contractors and labor to repair or create basic services while creating jobs. One subordinate unit, the Brigade Troops Battalion (BTB), 2nd Brigade, 3rd Infantry Division partnered with the 20th

Engineer Brigade on the division's main effort in eastern Baghdad's Sadr City.[88] Based on the specific SWEAT Model provided by 1st Cavalry Division, the requirements to plan and manage essential services required engineer expertise. To address this need, the BTB and 20th Engineer Brigade created a SWEAT Shop in which they partnered with local advisory and engineering committees to determine needs, conduct infrastructure reconnaissance, scope requirements, and design projects within the SWEAT categories. As outlined by Major Alexander Fullerton, the BTB SWEAT Shop worked with city engineers to establish basic local services and to provide employment within neighborhoods ripe for insurgent recruitment, both of which directly undermined the insurgent base of support.[89]

Results and Evaluation

During the 1st Cavalry Division's time as MND-B, the division, assigned units, and the supporting 20th Engineer Brigade invested over $200 million into specific SWEAT improvements and essential services restoration. To supplement 1st Cavalry Division's efforts, the United States Army Corps of Engineers Gulf Region Central District provided engineering design, planning, and contract oversight on over 500 SWEAT projects worth $500 million inside Baghdad with most spending allocated toward seven water plants, four waste water plants, 807 school renovations, and 15 major electrical projects.[90] Units focused projects on highly populated urban areas and relegated rural areas to second priority. As shown in the Government Accountability Office's (GAO) spending in narrow categories correlated almost exactly to the SWEAT Model with prioritization coming more from cost of projects than from focus on specific categories.

Despite providing temporary jobs and improving service conditions in Baghdad, Iraqi opinion of services and support remained low. Task Force Baghdad SWEAT Model proponents believed that projects would not only provide jobs and empower the Iraqi government, but essential services efforts would stimulate the economy, improve quality of life, and prevent people from joining the insurgency. As more Iraqis purchased cars and electrical equipment that Saddam had banned during his regime, Iraqi demand for public services increased exponentially and hindered the planned quality of life impacts from Task Force Baghdad projects. Because Iraqis could not complete training and preparation to operate and maintain the power plants, water and sewage treatment facilities, and health care centers the US had rebuilt or restored, projects brought on an initial change until facilities fell into disrepair.[92]

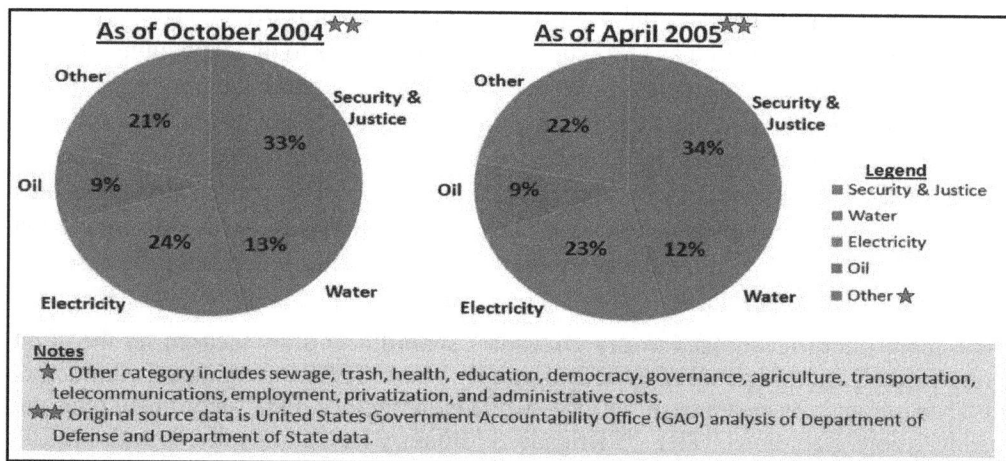

Figure 8: Reconstruction Funds Distributed by Sector for 2004 and 2005[91]

As shown in Figure 9, surveys in the summer of 2006 by US Joint Warfare Analysis Center researchers Frederick Barton and Bathsheba Barton show decreasing satisfaction with new Iraqi Government and US-led Coalition Force (CF) performance. By interviewing large portions of the local population in each Iraqi province, Barton and Crocker determined that techniques for restoration of essential services and the methods communicating positive changes to the population had little positive impact on the population's opinion.[93] Comments revealed that both the CF and the Iraqi Government failed to address priority needs and concerns of these residents.

Perception or Response Availability of...	Improved	Same	Worse	Comments
Sanitation (Sewer)	5%	30%	65%	75% of sewage flows into rivers, damaged and dilapidated infrastructure
Water (Water)	20%	60%	20%	170% increase in potable water from prewar levels, hightened expectations
Power (Electricity)	31%	23%	46%	Higher demand, perceived shortage, highest infrastructure priority
Sanitation (Trash)	5%	30%	65%	Not separated from sewage in survey
Transport (Transportation)	15%	60%	25%	Generally split, attacks on bridges and roads decreased satisfaction
Fuel (Oil/Gas)	20%	40%	40%	Crude production lower, larger imports, attacks on shipments, long lines
Communication (Comm/Media)	60%	30%	10%	Cell phones banned during Saddam regime, becoming available
Jobs	26%	24%	50%	General displeasure about jobs and government spending
Products and services beyond basic needs	50%	30%	20%	Many products not available during Saddam regime

Figure 9: Measuring Iraq's Reconstruction Effort and Population Satisfaction[94]

Perhaps the greatest disappointment came in 2005 and early 2006 when the security situation deteriorated despite huge investments in infrastructure and essential services around Baghdad. Using the SWEAT Model and government feedback, Task Force Baghdad implemented a process that invested heavily into the perceived needs and wants of the Iraqi people. SWEAT Model implementation injected money into the economy and repaired much of the dilapidated infrastructure, but it missed many critical requirements requested by the people. In addition, corruption by contractors, ineptitude within the Iraqi Ministries, and focus on easy projects like school construction reduced the positive impacts of CERP.[95] By early 2006, the United States Army Corps of Engineers reported drops to 6.4 hours of electricity in Baghdad per day versus 11 hours outside Baghdad.[96] After reaching a low point of 1,500 monthly attacks in early 2005, attacks increased through 2005 to a high of nearly 3,000 by September 2005.[97]

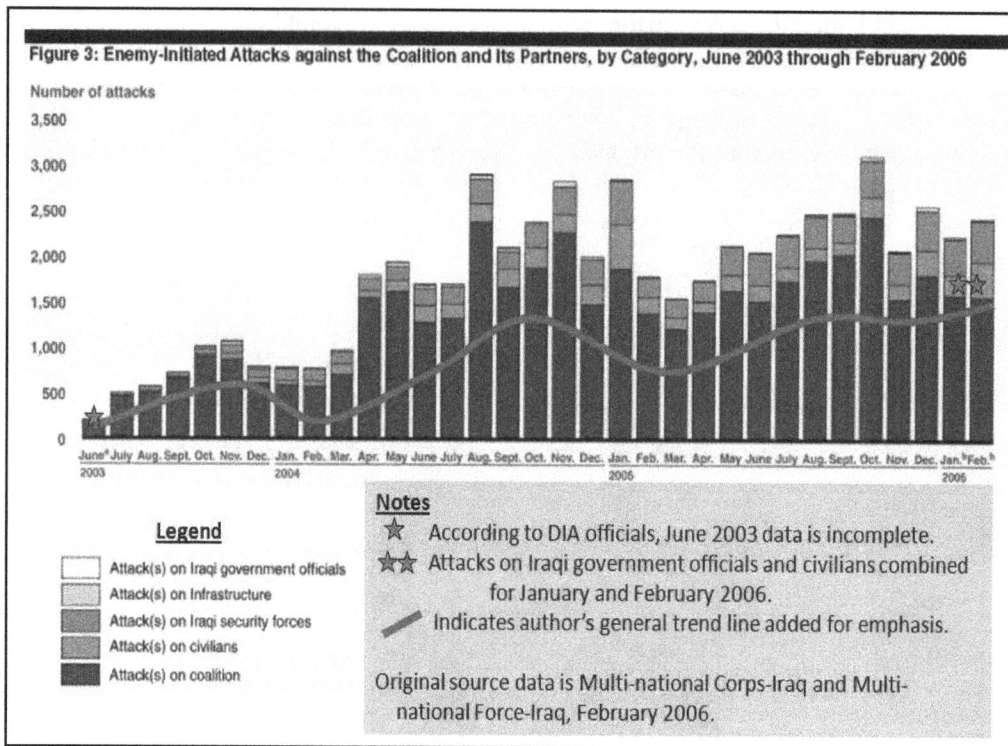

Figure 3: Enemy-Initiated Attacks against the Coalition and Its Partners, by Category, June 2003 through February 2006

Number of attacks

Legend
- Attack(s) on Iraqi government officials
- Attack(s) on Infrastructure
- Attack(s) on Iraqi security forces
- Attack(s) on civilians
- Attack(s) on coalition

Notes

☆ According to DIA officials, June 2003 data is incomplete.

☆☆ Attacks on Iraqi government officials and civilians combined for January and February 2006.

╱ Indicates author's general trend line added for emphasis.

Original source data is Multi-national Corps-Iraq and Multi-national Force-Iraq, February 2006.

Figure 10: GAO 2005/2006 Report on Enemy Initiated Violence[98]

Simplicity

The SWEAT Model's eight categories provide a simple framework, which facilitates restoration actions with limited technical experience Units have used the SWEAT Model for six years now because the model seems simple. As a caution shown in Figure 8, 1st Cavalry Division's use of the SWEAT Model focused support into narrow categories. To overcome technical limitations, the command executed easier projects that required less technical expertise. These factors prevented holistic solutions and discriminated against rural areas around the city of Baghdad. The SWEAT Model's focus on how to think about categories of projects has prevented effort and support to different areas like Northern Baghdad's rural districts or Qadas that need categories other than SWEAT. Although the SWEAT Model allows many non-engineers to apply funds in restoration categories, the SWEAT Model provides little to the no process non-technical branches to plan, resource, and manage improvements.

Flexibility

The SWEAT Model allows for hasty and deliberate application. Although the SWEAT Model is simple, easy to teach, and quick to execute, using a countrywide model for categories limits geo-cultural analysis and prevents nesting with local and national priorities. Based on its urban focus, the model has limited effectiveness through many environmental conditions including rural or agricultural areas. In 1st Cavalry Division's case, this drawback balanced the fact that one third of the country's population lived in Baghdad's urban areas.

Reproducibility

The SWEAT Model uses the infrastructure categories generally applicable to past military operations. The SWEAT Model used by 1st Cavalry Division could find valuable lessons from historic operations like Vietnam. Marine and Army units in early Operation IRAQI FREEDOM used the SWEAT Model with positive results. Because the generic "other" category prevents holistic focus on other services and application of cultural analysis limits full understanding of needs, the SWEAT Model might be difficult to apply effectively to future areas of operation. In the case of 1st Cavalry Division, the SWEAT Model failed to support rural requirements therefore allowing insurgency to build and affect the urban centers.

Sustainability

Unlike most other essential services models, the SWEAT Model has wide use and documentation in doctrine. To its detriment, effective use of the doctrinal model requires integration of outside technical manuals and reconnaissance tools. The Department of State and other US government entities understand and use variants of the SWEAT Model in their own analysis. The model integrates well into reconnaissance tools and project management capabilities within SWEAT categories; however, the static SWEAT-MSO categories prevent units from capturing the feedback from Intelligence Preparation of the Battlefield (IPB) products like the operational variables political, military, economic, social, infrastructure, information, physical environment, and time (PMESII-PT). Using intelligence to better pinpoint populace needs may help locals sustain the output because they received something they needed. The 1st Cavalry Division used the model to focus on and gain many short term wins, but a similar, national-level focus on SWEAT categories prevented a long term tailoring of essential services to Iraq regions. The model considers only specific categories for project prioritization, which means that anything outside the categories are excluded from the list. For long term use, units must adapt the SWEAT Model to local tailoring, modification, prioritization, and assessment.

Links to Political and Military Objectives

As shown by Case A, the SWEAT Model and its application by 1st Cavalry Division generally supported the essential services line of effort established by the Bush Administration, CJTF-7, MNF-I, and MNC-I. The 1st Cavalry Division applied a comprehensive cost versus benefit analysis of area requirements. Essential services became a priority for MND-B, allowing them to apply considerable manpower, technical expertise, and resources towards accomplishing their objectives. Despite MND-B placing a priority on essential service operations, prescriptive SWEAT guidance forced subordinates into a narrow focus. The lack of analysis in categories outside SWEAT resulted in many key Iraqi Government Ministries and Civil Service Directorates having limited interaction with US forces and receiving no assistance in their area.

Case B: Factor-Precedence Model in Baghdad, Iraq (2009)

Case Context and Unit Approach

In Case B, 1st Cavalry Division's return to Baghdad in 2009 came within the context of President Bush's "surge" of combat forces into Iraq. In President Bush's January 10, 2007 address to the nation, he announced that implementation of a "New Way Forward" would deploy additional military units to Iraq, primarily to Baghdad. President Bush's surge forces would, in a paraphrase of the "clear, hold, build" language from 2006, "help Iraqis clear and secure neighborhoods, help them protect the local population, and help ensure that the Iraqi forces left behind are capable of providing the security that Baghdad needs."[99] When General David H. Petraeus and his MNF-I planning team developed the military campaign plan to leverage the surge's additional troops, break the cycle of sectarian violence, and implement the "clear, hold, build" strategy, they made protecting the population the military's top priority in Iraq. Leveraging Dr. Kilcullen's counterinsurgency designs and synchronizing military efforts with US Ambassador to Iraq Ryan Crocker's diplomatic missions, MNF-I set the conditions for military and diplomatic success using Operation FARDH AL-QANOON, Iraqi Arabic for Operation TOGETHER FORWARD.[100] On September 16, 2008, General Petraeus relinquished command of MNF-I to Army General Raymond Odierno, a former Commanding General of Multi-National Corps-Iraq (MNC-I).[101] On November 17, 2008, Ambassador Crocker and General Odierno signed the Iraq Security Agreement with their Iraqi counterparts that changed counterinsurgency techniques and partnership requirements across Iraq.[102]

The new Iraq Security Agreement required Multi-National Division - Baghdad (MND-B) to take a partnered approach in all areas, especially essential services, and forced a review of the Baghdad Campaign Plan. When the 1st US Cavalry Division assumed command and control of MND-B on February 10, 2009, the division received requirements to protect the people of Baghdad, to implement the Security Agreement's demands for partnered operations, and to withdraw all US combat forces from Iraqi "cities, villages, and localities" by June 30, 2009.[103] By March 2009, most Coalition "surge" forces had redeployed leaving MND-B with six brigades of 35,000 personnel, thirteen larger Forward Operating Bases (FOB), fifty-five Joint Security Stations (JSS), and seven small Combat Outposts (COP) throughout Baghdad.[104]

Aware of Baghdad's importance as a microcosm of Iraq for the overall security and stability of the country, Major General Daniel P. Bolger, commander of the 1st Cavalry Division and MND-B, emphasized partnership with the Iraqi Security Forces as the cornerstone for his campaign concept with three lines of effort (LOEs) including Iraqi Security Force (ISF) Partnership, Targeting and Security, and Civil Capacity.[105] Figure 11 shows MND-B's Campaign Design established by Major General Bolger to secure the population and increase Iraqi government legitimacy. Within the MND-B Campaign Design, Major General Bolger clearly expressed his mission statement and intent to establish an environment of sustainable security in Baghdad from which the sustaining LOE, Civil Capacity, could gain the strength and momentum necessary to increase government legitimacy.[106] Key Civil Capacity goals included assisting the Government of Iraq (GoI)'s rule of law initiatives, supporting the election process, mentoring GoI departments with budget execution, and helping to improve essential services. Essential services would serve MND-B as an important sustaining operation within the Civil Capacity LOE.

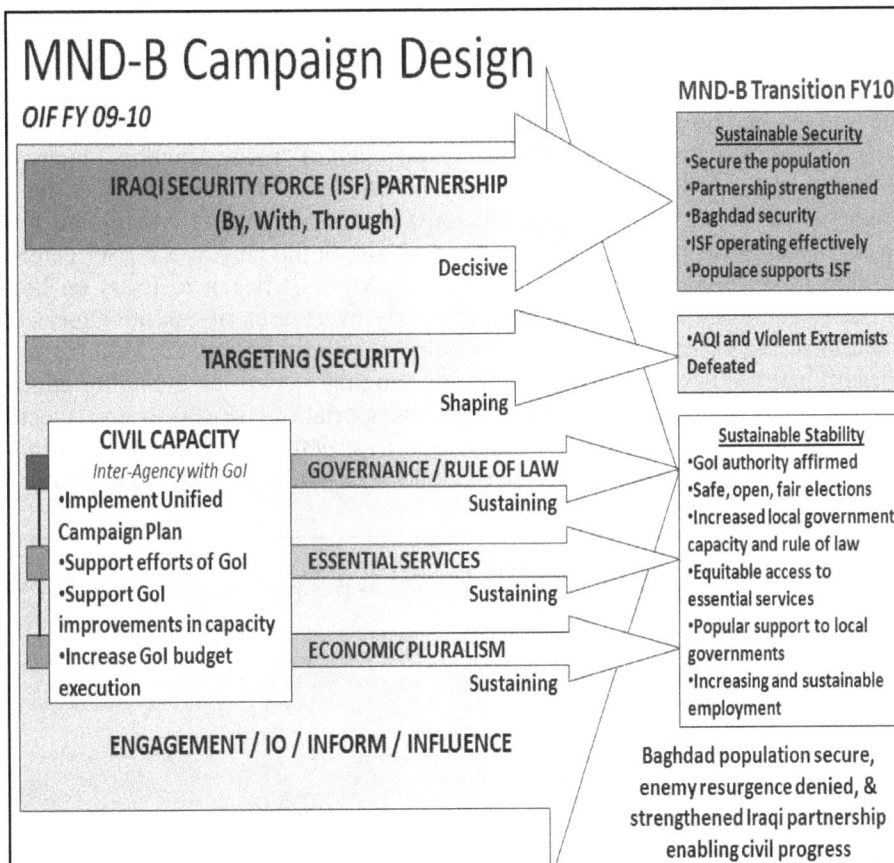

MND-B Campaign Design
OIF FY 09-10

IRAQI SECURITY FORCE (ISF) PARTNERSHIP (By, With, Through)

Decisive

TARGETING (SECURITY)

Shaping

CIVIL CAPACITY
Inter-Agency with GoI
- Implement Unified Campaign Plan
- Support efforts of GoI
- Support GoI improvements in capacity
- Increase GoI budget execution

GOVERNANCE / RULE OF LAW
Sustaining

ESSENTIAL SERVICES
Sustaining

ECONOMIC PLURALISM
Sustaining

ENGAGEMENT / IO / INFORM / INFLUENCE

MND-B Transition FY10

Sustainable Security
- Secure the population
- Partnership strengthened
- Baghdad security
- ISF operating effectively
- Populace supports ISF

- AQI and Violent Extremists Defeated

Sustainable Stability
- GoI authority affirmed
- Safe, open, fair elections
- Increased local government capacity and rule of law
- Equitable access to essential services
- Popular support to local governments
- Increasing and sustainable employment

Baghdad population secure, enemy resurgence denied, & strengthened Iraqi partnership enabling civil progress

Figure 11: MND-B (1st Cavalry Division) Campaign Design and Lines of Effort[107]

Essential Services Operations and the Factor-Precedence Model

Implementation of the Iraq Security Agreement combined with 1st Cavalry Division's arrival to Baghdad caused many changes within MND-B's essential services operations in 2009. Requirements to turn bases within the city over to Iraqi Security Forces forced MND-B to shift essential services focus away from traditional SWEAT Model categories into a broader set of categories and support based on geographical and cultural factors in both the city and in the surrounding agricultural areas.[108] New restrictions on spending and the requirements to work with Provincial Reconstruction Team – Baghdad (PRT-B) leading reconstruction working groups forced MND-B to reassess leadership and essential services priorities.[109] MND-B adjusted procedures to evaluate the longer-term time horizons, compare interdependencies of unit options, and recalculate the utility of critical actions based on PRT-B feedback. To comply with new integration rules within the Security Agreement, MND-B began working all actions through the appropriate levels of

Iraqi government to integrate local priorities and cultural requirements into the essential services model. As a result of Security Agreement's deadlines to move out of the cities, restrictions on spending, and requirements to work through the local governments, the 1st Cavalry Division adopted an essential services restoration approach that exhibited many components of the Factor-Precedence Model.

Requirements to move out of city bases helped MND-B shift essential services focus away from the traditional SWEAT Model categories into a broader set of categories and support based on geographical and cultural factors. The 1st Cavalry Division Essential Services (ESS) Section assessed that despite seven years of "reconstruction," many of the infrastructure systems failed to meet minimum international standards or meet the needs of the Iraqi people.[110] As shown in Case A, units using the SWEAT Model had focused on repairing urban infrastructure and conducted repairs in the narrow SWEAT categories. After moving to bases and camps outside the city, MND-B began to focus on both the city and the surrounding agricultural areas in nearly every area of essential services. As highlighted in the MND-B's 2010 CERP spending shown in Figure 12, MND-B focused outside traditional SWEAT categories into wide ranging categories including education, telecommunications, humanitarian assistance, transportation, sewer, water, electricity, trash, agriculture, and health. MND-B's expanded infrastructure category focus exemplified nearly all of the recognized essential service categories espoused by the Factor Precedence Model.

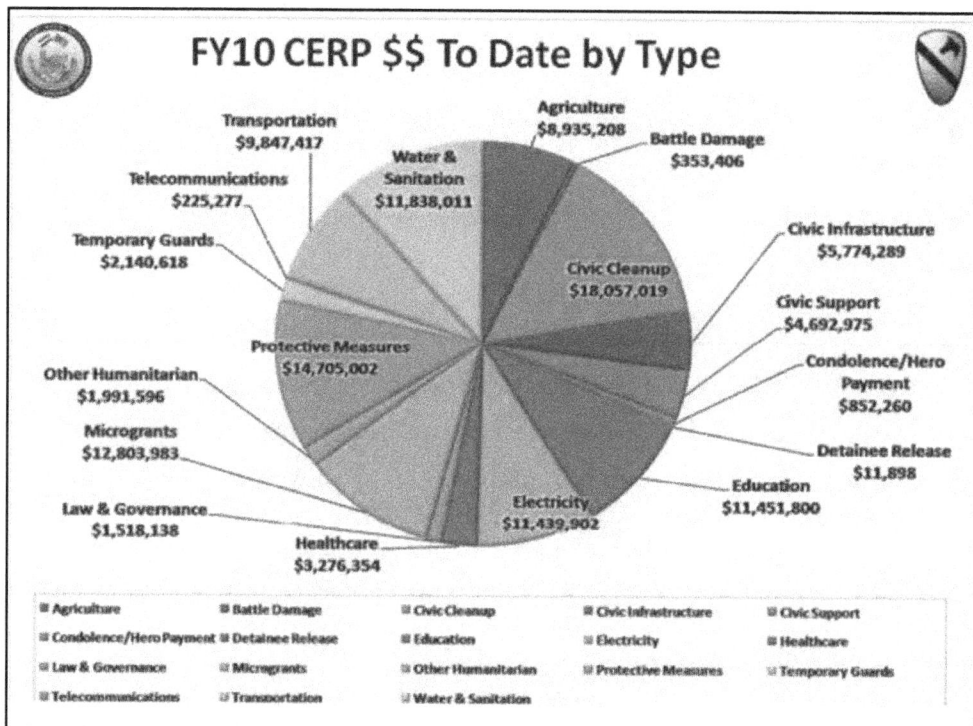

Figure 12: Distribution of CERP Funs by MND-B in Fiscal Year 2010[111]

In addition to deviating from the old SWEAT Model's category focus, the 1st Cavalry ESS Section and subordinate essential services practitioners concentrated on improving the essential services within Baghdad's geographical and cultural factors. As US combat forces transitioned out of Baghdad, they shifted focus to more geographically varying terrain much different from the city. Rural governments, called Qadas, had limited population densities and urban infrastructure like sewers, but they had significant irrigation and drainage infrastructure to facilitate an agricultural economy and apply local resources.[112] These agricultural areas like Taji and Tarmiyah Qadas supported the city with food and offered areas where insurgents could hide if supported by the population. By adopting a model similar to the Factor-Precedence Model, 1st Cavalry Division supported agricultural projects in the outlying areas of Baghdad Province while focusing on urban-based projects like electricity and sewage inside the city.[113] To address cultural factors within the quickly changing operating environment, MND-B established cultural measures for improvement within each category focused on meeting minimum humanitarian standards, achieving the quality of life acceptable to the people in and around Baghdad, and restoring services required to make any modern society function. Similar to the recommendations provided by the Factor-Precedence Model, subordinate brigades modified SWEAT categories to meet the constituent's geographical and cultural factors.

While moving out of the city shifted MND-B focus into broader categories, geographical factors, and cultural factors, new restrictions on spending and the requirement to work with the PRT-B leading reconstruction working groups forced MND-B to reassess leadership and essential services priorities.[114] On 1 May 2009, a new CERP Standard Operating Procedure (SOP) for projects in the Baghdad Amanat went into effect.[115] The new SOP required a Memorandum of Agreement (MOA) approved by the end using Iraqi government entity like the Amanat, Governorate, or Ministry before any project could proceed. The new process increased the coordination process between American and Iraqi essential services practitioners and ensured that the GoI would take over all projects, operations, and maintenance when completed.[116] To comply with the new CERP SOP, MND-B and subordinate essential service practitioners integrated local government and local leadership priority elements of the Factor-Precedence Model into project planning and prioritization.

To support PRT-B's leadership role in Iraqi stability operations and reconstruction, MND-B adjusted procedures to integrate projects with long-term time horizons. Before 2009, the Department of State and the United States Agency for International Development (USAID) had generally focused on services and governance capacity development. In essential services, this capacity development included long-duration, large-scale, strategic-level projects. The long timelines made these larger projects impractical for MND-B or subordinate brigade involvement because of timelines and expertise. To close the gap between large projects favored by diplomatic practitioners with the small projects favored by military practitioners, PRT-B and MND-B involved experts from both organizations to work beside military units and ensure short, mid, and long-term projects made it into planning and funding priorities.[117] MND-B and PRT-B's use of time horizon as an important component of prioritization highlighted another component of the Factor-Precedence Model.

To balance military operations with holistic Iraqi requirements, MND-B began to compare interdependencies of unit options and recalculate the utility of critical actions based on PRT-B feedback. To allow the subordinate brigades the freedom to decide where and how they wanted to perform restoration operations, the Division abolished the centralized priority list of the ten most important projects that the 4th Infantry Division had used to divide resources. The new list of combined political and military services priorities allowed

MND-B's subordinate brigades and partnered embedded Provincial Reconstruction Teams (ePRTs) to begin developing priorities using systems analysis and utility assessments.[118] This new technique allowed personnel on the ground to investigate the interdependencies between essential services and recommend actions or projects to improve the situation. With the units that lived in the affected areas and knew best when, where, and how to perform restoration providing feedback on the utility of actions, MND-B better allocated limited resources and effort in Baghdad's rural and urban areas.

Because the Security Agreement required Coalition Forces to work all actions through Iraqi government officials, MND-B and PRT-B utilized more local and city government feedback to prioritize actions and expenditures. To gain the appropriate approvals on new projects, MND-B and PRT-B had to establish connections with every level of executive and legislative leadership. A critical connection came when leadership broke from the SWEAT Model to align support with government ministries in every category of infrastructure. MND-B's G-9 section, responsible for Civil Military Operations (CMO) that included oversight of the CERP, reconstruction activities, infrastructure repair, economic assistance, support to civil administration, and humanitarian assistance, reapportioned money and priorities based on the feedback coming from units and from the Iraqi government.[119] Division and brigade practitioners engaged and mentored government officials, studied the existing service categories, and promoted Iraqi government activities by providing resources, when needed, through CERP projects. The new cooperation led to better connections between projects and efforts. As an example, during meetings with Ministry of Water Resources (MoWR) representatives, MND-B G-9 identified two major irrigation projects in Mahmodiyah Qada that would help alleviate water shortage for both irrigation and drinking needs. One of these projects, the repair of the Latifeeyah boost water pump and construction of associated irrigation canals, affected between 125,000 to 150,000 farmers in the area south east of Baghdad. This area had experienced little essential services support in the past and had suffered as an insurgent safe-haven for years.[120] Much like the tenets of the Factor-Precedence Model, MND-B's revived connection with Iraqi leaders helped integrate local priorities and culture back into the essential services model.

Results and Evaluation

As a result of the adoption of the new counterinsurgency approach, security in Baghdad and its environs improved dramatically.[121] 1st Cavalry Division's time as MND-B laid the ground work for the enlargement of the division's area of responsibility including Anbar Province and further reduction of forces in Baghdad. In January 2010, the Division handed over authority of Multi-National Division Baghdad, now renamed US Division Central, to the 1st Armored Division.[122] Another area of focus was shaping the Brigade Combat Teams (BCT) battle space through legitimate local leadership and CERP funding.[123] That gradual growth was punctuated by sharp upward spikes at key Iraqi political junctures, including the January 2005 elections and the October 2005 constitutional referendum, and, less sharply, during Ramadan each year. After July 2007, the overall level of attacks declined sharply, punctuated by a spike during Iraqi and coalition operations in Basra and Sadr City, in March 2008. By late 2008, the level of attacks had fallen to well under 200 per week – levels last witnessed at the beginning of 2004 – and those gains held through February 2009.[124] The following sections provide a brief overview of each evaluation criteria based on the case study.

ESSENTIAL SERVICES							
METRIC	PRE-INVASION	POST-INVASION	CPA TRANSITION	NEGROPONTE ERA	KHALILZAD ERA	SURGE ENDS	END OF COMBAT OPERATIONS
Electricity Production[a]							
Megawatts	4,075	711	3,621	4,262	3,475	4,400	6,540
Oil Production							
Million Barrels per Day	2.58	0.30	2.16	2.13	1.95	2.43	2.33
Iraq Security Forces (Cumulative)							
Assigned Soldiers and Police	1,300,000	7,000–9,000	87,000	171,300	328,700	478,500	793,289
Telecommunications							
Landline Subscribers	833,000	0	791,000	998,000	1,111,000	1,200,000	Not available
Mobile Subscribers	80,000	0	461,000	2,422,000	8,720,000	~13,000,000	22,551,000
Human Toll (Cumulative)							
U.S. Troop Fatalities		139	862	1,745	3,248	4,115	4,415
Civilian Contractors		1	46	217	916	1,229	1,507[b]
U.S. Civilians		~9	52	113	224	271	310
Iraqi Civilians		7,413	16,848	29,155	72,858	95,236	113,701
Financial Cost ($ Billions, Cumulative)							
U.S. Funding		$3.45	$22.93	$29.21	$36.96	$50.46	$56.81
Iraqi Funding		$0.00	$16.00	$21.03	$37.27	$50.33	$85.31[c]
International Funding		$0.00	$13.60	$13.87	$15.20	$17.00	$12.01[d]
Total Funding		$3.45	$52.53	$64.11	$89.43	$117.79	$154.12

Figure 13: SIGIR US Reconstruction Effort Metrics as of October 30, 2010[125]

Simplicity

The Factor-Precedence Model's initial sixteen categories require detailed and time consuming analysis. Although slightly more complex than the SWEAT Model, the Factor-Precedence Model increases in simplicity after the initial evaluation of local needs and services. Once established, the Factor-Precedence Model's focus on four to seven categories after refinement step keeps prioritization and restoration work relatively simple. Based on 1st Cavalry Division and their subordinate brigade's success in using the model, the process seems useful to all branches tasked with civil-military support.

Flexibility

The Factor-Precedence Model allows for hasty and deliberate application during operations. The Factor-Precedence Model provides focus on geographical and cultural factors allowing support to wide areas. 1st Cavalry Division's surges in urban areas like Abu Ghraib Qada and rural areas like Tarmiyah Qada provide evidence of the model's flexibility. The Factor-Precedence Model offers a holistic perspective that tailors focus within each area of operation and continuously assesses needs compared with local feedback. The Factor-Precedence Model user could focus on agricultural support in one area while building humanitarian assistance and housing capacity in another area. Because the Factor-Precedence Model allows diverse approaches at Division and Brigade levels, it is critical that headquarters synchronize their infrastructure master plans for long-term effectiveness and overall sustainability.

Reproducibility

Like the SWEAT Model, the Factor-Precedence model can apply to both historical and contemporary essential services efforts. The Factor-Precedence Model seems exceptionally useful in Iraq and could fare well in Afghanistan due to holistic nature of model. Based on limited case analysis, the holistic nature and flexibility of the Factor-Precedence Model seems uniquely capable of supporting future counterinsurgencies against hybrid threats. Circumstantial evidence also indicates that the Factor-Precedence Model could find use restoring essential services in conflict outside of insurgencies.

Sustainability

The Factor-Precedence Model provides focus on geographical and cultural factors allowing support to both rural and urban areas. The model ties in with nearly any existing intelligence, engineering, or management tool. Despite having no major conceptual issues, the model needs refinement for long term use and integration with emerging command and control techniques, namely mission command.

Links to Political and Military Objectives

The Factor-Precedence Model facilitated focus on the critical problems while taking into consideration higher headquarters' guidance. When 1st Cavalry Division needed to move outside of urban areas, their Factor-Precedence-like approach proved useful in treating the local issues and focusing on changing needs. The model also facilitated ties into ministries at Baghdad level and allowed subordinate units to integrate with available local directorates. As mentioned earlier, the differing focus between government levels and geographic make-up requires synchronization between headquarters elements to prevent disconnects in support.

6 – Comparison and Afghanistan Example

"SWEAT is a great acronym. It has caught on and is in widespread use. Those infrastructure categories that make up the acronym SWEAT, however, do not always provide the infrastructure solution that the commander needs... As with any mission a prioritization of tasks must be made and using SWEAT alone cannot be relied upon in every scenario."[126]

- The SWEAT/IR Book

Based on the data provided by the primary case studies, this section compares the important variables of model effectiveness and variable applicability between the SWEAT Model and the Factor-Precedence Model. The primary case studies from the 1st Cavalry Division in Baghdad, Iraq provide an interesting comparison between two different essential services models at work in similar situations. The comparison concludes, similar to the quote above, that the SWEAT Model provides a great acronym and has widespread use, but that the model's limitations prevent solutions that the commander and local populace need. To make the comparisons between the primary cases more relevant to current operations, this section introduces an illustrative example of the Factor-Precedence Model applied to 10th Mountain Division as Regional Command (RC) South in Kandahar, Afghanistan (2010). Adding this illustrative example facilitates conclusions on model applicability, effectiveness, and inferences for future actions not just in Iraq but in other places around the world.

Comparison of Case Studies

When comparing the two models using the Iraq case studies, the Factor-Precedence Model emerges as more effective. The major advantages of the Factor-Precedence Model come because the model offers a more holistic perspective, allows for constant assessment and re-categorization, facilitates reprioritization, and focuses on the full range of military operations. Because the Factor-Precedence avoids the one size fits all categorization of the SWEAT Model, the Factor-Precedence Model can focus more on local needs and capacity thus increasing the sustainability by local leaders and government after improvements. Since case evidence shows that all branches can execute the model, the model can also help synchronize military and political elements on projects, support, and engagements that improve essential services. Most importantly, the Factor-Precedence Model allows for prioritization of effort, shifting priorities within unit areas of operations, or even project prioritization to meet needs of local areas.

The major disadvantage of the Factor-Precedence Model remains the fact that it is a new model not covered in doctrine. Based on the Iraq case studies, the SWEAT model has usefulness and has documentation in doctrine. Because units have used the SWEAT Model for over six years, the simple, easy to remember, and narrowly focused SWEAT Model has positive feedback from practitioners. Because the Factor-Precedence Model has more components than the existing SWEAT Model, units may have a natural aversion against using it. The drawbacks from the SWEAT Model come from the limitations on analysis, especially when concerning culture, climate, and regional factors. Also, the SWEAT Model focuses on urban infrastructure categories like sewage and electricity. The effectiveness and applicability of both models in non-developed, rural areas like Afghanistan require additional analysis. Table 3 provides a brief summary of the comparison between the SWEAT Model and the Factor Precedence Model.

Table 3: Summary of Case A to Case B Comparison between Essential Services Models

	Case A - SWEAT Model	Case B - Factor-Precedence Model	
Eval Criteria Short Title	Rating	Rating	Remarks
Simplicity	+	-	SWEAT Model simple and used throughout military since 2004; units could learn the Factor-Precedence Model quickly and apply
Flexibility	-	+	Factor-Precedence Model much more flexible to environment, geography, and culture
Reproducibility	+	+	Both models allow for systematic application
Sustainability	-	+	Factor-Precedence Model holistic approach builds on past models, offers assessment for changes, and ties into all existing tools; Factor-Precedence Model appears more sustainable by local leaders and government after improvements

Links to Political and Military Objectives	+	+	Both models support lines of effort, objectives, and end state formulation; both models balance the costs and benefits of resources and combat power; Factor-Precedence Models feedback look may synchronize analysis, reprioritization faster

The Iraq case study's outcomes indicate that the Factor-Precedence Model could also prove effective in Afghanistan and future counterinsurgency operations. To make the best conclusions possible about the viability of the Factor-Precedence Model outside Iraq, an illustrative example from Kandahar, Afghanistan provides a hypothetical application of the Factor-Precedence Model and compares it against the effectiveness evaluation criteria.

Illustrative Example: Factor-Precedence Model in Kandahar, Afghanistan (2010)

Example Evaluation Framework and Model Effectiveness

The evaluation of operations in Iraq shows a considerable difference between the effectiveness of the Factor-Precedence and SWEAT Models. By comparing use of the Factor-Precedence Model in Baghdad, Iraq with a hypothetical application of the Factor-Precedence Model in Kandahar, Afghanistan, an illustrative example facilitates universal conclusions on model applicability. Table 4 provides an outline of the controls, similarities, and differences between the two locations that facilitate comparison. Similarities between Iraq and Afghanistan such as general time period, use of full spectrum operations, experience of American Soldiers, and models available facilitate comparison between the two very different political and geographic areas. The similarities provide a point of reference and specific connections between the case study and the illustrative example. On the other hand, the two situations have enough differences to test the Factor-Precedence Model against varying environments, different military situations, and dissimilar initial conditions. Situational differences such as the initial infrastructure levels, level of decentralization and tribal impact, and geography help to strengthen the inferences about the Factor-Precedence Model's applicability outside Iraq.

140

Table 4: Controls Baghdad, Iraq (2009) to Kandahar, Afghanistan (2010)

Situational Similarities	Situational Differences
- Time Period (between 2009 and 2010) - Level of Command (MND-B equivalent [1st Cavalry] to RC-South [10th Mountain]) - Balancing of resource priority (post-Iraq surge equal to pre-Afghanistan surge) - Command balance of full spectrum operations (FSO) - Essential services initial conditions (Damage pre-surge, limited maintenance) - Requirement to restore essential services - External influence and competition - International reconstruction funds - Same doctrine and models available - Religious impacts (Influence of Islam)	- Government Type and History (centralized vs. regional control) - Decentralization (national perspective vs. tribal focus) - Leadership (US vs. Multi-National [ISAF]) - Previous infrastructure levels (initial infrastructure high vs. low) - Education Levels to sustain projects - Area (geography and landscape) - Culture (urban vs. rural culture) ** Major differences between case and illustrative example can be accounted for during comparison and assist in evaluation

Context and Approach

This illustrative example focuses on the hypothetical applicability of the Factor-Precedence Model in Kandahar, Afghanistan. As 2009 drew to a close, American President Barack Obama increased the priority, troop, and resource support to Afghanistan. For the six previous years, the priority of effort and resources focused on Iraq. The drawdown of troops in Iraq facilitated the President's shift of focus and attention. To complement an American "surge" of effort, the President and Secretary of Defense petitioned and received additional support from International Security Assistance Force (ISAF) - Afghanistan partners. To complement growing ISAF and American support, President Karzai outlined his *2010 National Development Strategy* to provide basic services and sustainable development. ISAF, the US Department of State, and subordinate American headquarters updated their counterinsurgency approach to reflect civilian and military integration in support of Afghanistan's government.[127] As outlined by Captain Pierson, ISAFs new approach led to refined lines of effort, shown below in Figure 14, and provided a guide for political and military actions. Essential services remained a major component of military operations against the insurgent and set the conditions for hypothetical application of the Factor-Precedence Model.

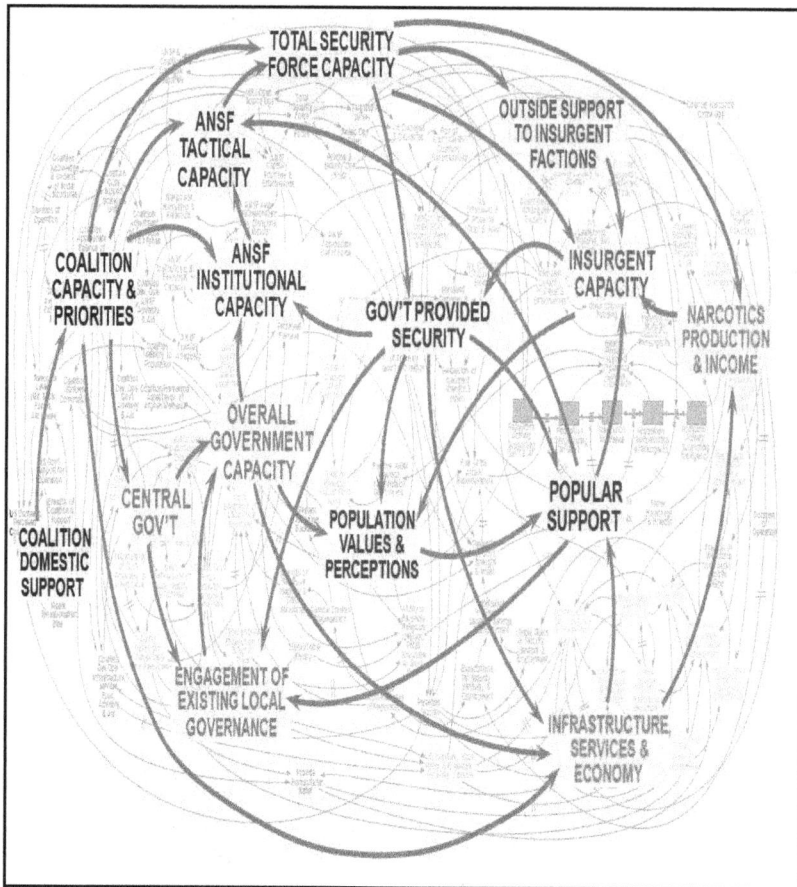

Figure14: ISAF Counterinsurgency Approach for 2009 and 2010[128]

Essential Services Operations and the Factor-Precedence Model

Applying the Factor-Precedence Model to Regional Command - South operations in Kandahar, Afghanistan requires a compatible operational approach. Much like the ISAF lines of effort, the Operating Framework breaks down into six sectors including Rule of Law, Governance, Health and Education, Agriculture and Econ, Infrastructure, and Security.[129] To support infrastructure an essential services work, most units have used the SWEAT Model in different forms throughout Afghanistan since 2004 with varying levels of success. Because Afghanistan has limited cities and because the rural population has different needs than the specific SWEAT categories, the 16 categories offered by the Factor-Precedence Model provide an excellent starting point for reconnaissance and assessment by region. Based on the limited success of the SWEAT Model, Regional Command - South began implementation of a new Stabilization Approach in 2010 so integration of the Factor-Precedence model could prove timely.[130] Regional Command - South's Stabilization Approach provides a framework for alignment and coordination with the Government of the Islamic Republic of Afghanistan (GIRoA). Direct coordination with the local governments simplifies the application of geographical and cultural refinement factors. Climate, population density, and economic base concerns can integrate into GIRoA regional development plans to establish the essential services situation for each province and major city.

142

To ensure resources and priorities within the Regional Command – South area of operation meet needs, the precedence elements of the Factor-Precedence Model can help prioritize effort then monitor for adjustments to the commands actions. Figure 15 provides an example of Agriculture and Economic Growth Line of Operation in terms of needs, end states, actions, and priority concepts. Development in this line moves through the established phases of Shape, Clear, Hold A, Hold B, Build, and Transfer.[131] The command could establish an end state that takes into account current conditions outlined by the Factor-Precedence Model then prioritize projects, engagements, or local emphasis. After establishing an integrated plan, RC South could use the Factor-Precedence Model and existing tools to execute, lead, and assess progress. Based on this example, the current Regional Command South Operating Framework supports application of an essential services model like the Factor-Precedence Model.

Agriculture and Economic Growth						
Grievance: Inability to meet basic household needs and lack of viable agricultural economic opportunity.						
Endstate: People have access to sustainable livelihoods. Employment opportunities are created in urban agricultural, agricultural value-added industry, public works, and municipal services enabled by reliable municipal infrastructure, vocational training and freedom of movement between rural areas and city. Economic opportunities increase the appeal of insurgent reintegration into communities.						
CONCEPT	The municipality will lead city-wide public works projects that build on existing plans to improve city-wide infrastructure including power, water, drainage, and roads. This work will create immediate stabilization effects by improving expectations for the future while contributing to longer-term growth in support of the economic growth sector strategy.					
Priority Actions	**Sub-Actions/Activites**	Afghan Lead	RC South Lead	Geographic Focus	Status	
Work with leaders to determine local project requests	Review Afghan government plan					
	Link plan with government meetings and population needs					
	Finalize plans and put information out to the community					
Maximize power generation to key locations in city	Increase total generator capacity (fuel)					
	Maximize existing power production through repair and maintenance					
	Evaluate new, sustainable power production options					
	Implement plan, hire workers, maintain for long term					
Expand municipal water infrastructure	Dig community wells at points with no water access					
	Repair existing water infrastructure					
	Upgrade potable water infrastructure					
	Replace existing infrastructure					
Improve local road network in conjuction with local gov plan	Repair existing priority roads					
	Replace existing infrastructure					
	Upgrade roads using labor-intensive method					
	Increase access					
	Pass out information on road and rebuilding efforts					
Indicators	Indicators and Measurements of Success					
	% of citizens who feel that local govt. can solve their problems					
	% of citizens who feel that local govt. is addressing their priority concerns					

Figure 15: Regional Command (RC) South Stabilization Approach[132]

Results and Evaluation

Since national Afghanistan statistics on government and essential services show limited growth despite huge investments, the need for a new essential services model becomes clear. Through 2009, the SIGAR reports show that $17.7 Billion from the Departments of Defense and State focused on narrow SWEAT-MSO categories between 2003 and 2009.[133] In Nangarhar alone, only 1 of 26 projects existed on the provincial development plan so projects had little support or interest from the local government.[134] Despite an annual increase in reconstruction dollars, a 300% increase in troop strength, and continued focus on critical lines of SWEAT-MSO, basic services do not meet the minimum standards or provide support to the legitimate government.[135] Afghan crops peaked in 2005/2006 falling since, electricity jumped 400% but supports only 15% of the population, and less than 12% of the population has safe drinking water and sanitation.[136] Use of the Factor-Precedence Model in Regional Command - South's area of operations could improve

143

model performance in each of the evaluation areas and help improve the focus local efforts and spending.

Simplicity

The Factor-Precedence Model's implementation through the evaluation of local needs and services could improve the simplicity of essential services interactions with the Regional Command – South's Stabilization Approach. Once established, the Factor-Precedence Model could become simpler for units to execute and could tie into the existing Stabilization Approach. In Afghanistan like in Iraq, the Factor-Precedence Model could become useful to all military branches and governmental agencies tasked with civil-military support.

Flexibility

The Factor-Precedence Model could allow for hasty and deliberate application during operations, a critical factor for Afghanistan. Because Regional Command - South does not use the SWEAT Model, their Stabilization Approach could benefit from integration with a holistic essential services model like the Factor-Precedence Model. The Factor-Precedence Model provides focus on geographical and cultural factors allowing support to wide areas. Factor-Precedence Model users could focus on agricultural support in one rural area of Afghanistan while providing humanitarian assistance and building housing capacity in another urban area.

Reproducibility

Like in Iraq, the Factor-Precedence model seems reproducible in Afghanistan. Regional Command – South's integration with local government agencies increases the options for systematic execution and reduces inconsistencies in application. Since implementing their Stabilization Approach, RC South has leveled spending on infrastructure outside the SWEAT-MSO categories.[137] Diversification of spending and project prioritization has increased the ability to focus on critical needs and expectations of the public.

Sustainability

The Factor-Precedence Model could provide focus on geographical and cultural factors allowing support to both rural and urban areas in Afghanistan. The model could readily integrate into the existing Regional Command – South's Stabilization Approach and with Region South's diplomatic *Unified Plan*. Because Regional Command – South already integrates with local government and leaders, those leaders can motivation for Afghani government employees and contract workers to learn the systems and maintain them properly. The chances of sustainable improvements over time increases greatly with local interest and buy in.

Links to Political and Military Objectives

The Factor-Precedence Model could facilitate focus on the critical problems identified by both the political and military leadership. In this Afghanistan example, the Factor-Precedence Model could help integrate essential services objectives related to the ISAF Operational Approach, President Karzai's *National Development Strategy*, and Regional Command – South's Stabilization Approach. The cost-benefit analysis conducted using the Factor-Precedence Model could also prove useful in political end state assessment and adjustments to military actions.

Inferences for Future Factor-Precedence Model Application

Can these two case studies and the illustrative example facilitate inferences for the future? Yes, the examples show that the Factor-Precedence Model not only proves more effective than existing models, but the Factor-Precedence Model can also apply in locations the SWEAT Model could not support. Military units must use a valid and effective model that applies historical and regional factors early in the process for a locally refined categorization, allows for a fluid prioritization of the refined categories, and facilitates a continuous assessment of the model to link needs and changes to military objectives. Despite the differences in culture, government, geography, and requirements between Iraq and Afghanistan, the holistic nature of the Factor-Precedence Model could facilitate effective essential services improvements in both locations. The fact that the Factor-Precedence Model can apply in a variety of locations bodes well for future application.

In addition to demonstrating effectiveness in multiple locations, the case studies show that the Factor-Precedence Model could work with military tools during current and future operations. A variety of existing military tools tie directly into the Factor-Precedence model during execution. Factor-Precedence Model Figure (Section 4) shows the nesting of existing tools with the primary components of the Factor-Precedence Model. Refined categorization directly links to establishing lines of effort within the essential services or economic lines of operation. Each refined categorization directly supports establishment of decisive points, key tasks, or key events required to meet end states and unit objectives. Using the categories within the Factor-Precedence Model, engineers, civil affairs, and diplomatic specialists can conduct long-term, mid-term, and short-term master planning of budgets, projects, and efforts to restore essential services more effectively. The Factor-Precedence model provides priority by essential service category and can thus assist in the development of projects lists along with the subsequent prioritization and budgeting of said projects. Continuous assessment within the model allows for adjustment of categories, use of military provided assessment tools, and reprioritization of effort.

7 – Conclusions and Recommendations

"Success will be less a matter of imposing one's will and more a function of shaping behavior of friends, adversaries, and most importantly, the people in between."[138]

- Robert Gates, US Secretary of Defense
October 10, 2007

"If you know the enemy and know yourself you need not fear the results of a hundred battles."[139]

- Sun Tzu

Results matter. The model that provides more flexibility, allows for repetition in a variety of situations, and links better to military objectives will prove more effective during counterinsurgency operations. Not only does the Factor-Precedence Model perform better than the SWEAT and other models in Iraq and Afghanistan's counterinsurgency fights, but the Factor-Precedence model seems more effective in future fights as well. Because future requirements will undoubtedly develop, military planners should adopt a holistic approach like the Factor-Precedence Model and incorporate existing intelligence and analysis tools into the model. Further research can improve the application of culture, climate, and geography factors. Commander requirements can guide the prioritization elements within the Factor-Precedence model, and practitioners can incorporate existing project and area assessment capabilities into model execution.

Conclusions

The SWEAT Model has provided a valuable tool for essential services restoration since 2004, but the military requires change to improve counterinsurgency outcomes. Since the SWEAT Model has widespread use, many commanders, practitioners, and even doctrine confuse the SWEAT Model categories with the exact meaning of essential services. The existing infrastructure categories provided by the SWEAT Model form an excellent foundation for essential services analysis, but a new model and updated doctrine can leverage the best parts of the SWEAT Model to increase effectiveness of restoration operations. Because the SWEAT Model's categories align with existing engineer career fields and because they represent the civil service offices formed in most countries, future essential services models should encourage category use and analysis.[140] Essential services and basic needs differ for each geographical region and cultural area. Understanding and focusing on area-specific needs has become a major weakness of the SWEAT Model and should become an important part of any essential services model placed in future doctrine.

Based on the five evaluation criteria for model effectiveness, the Factor-Precedence Model proves more effective than existing models. The Factor-Precedence Model has grounding in doctrine, takes into consideration the local environment, and fits well into existing operations processes. The Factor-Precedence Model utilizes many of the strong points of existing models to make an effective model that works in both Iraq and Afghanistan. Given the case studies and examples covered in this monograph, there seems a good chance that the Factor-Precedence Model could prove effective in future counterinsurgencies against "hybrid threats" and, with minor model adjustments, could work in situations other than counterinsurgency.[141]

Recommendations for Future Action

- As outlined earlier, many practitioners think SWEAT means essential services. Leaders should avoid confusing the SWEAT acronym with the real definition of essential services by discontinuing the use of the SWEAT family of acronyms.

- The essential services definition seems very vague. Doctrine writers should refine the definition of essential services in FM 3-07 and FM 3-24 to encourage a holistic approach to meeting people's needs while implementing the essential services tasks and logical line of operation.

- The current SWEAT Model, along with the other primary existing essential services and infrastructure models, focuses exclusively on infrastructure repair and project execution. These models exclude Civil Affairs and interagency partners who prefer to address capacity and development in restoration models. To increase the military inter-branch and government interagency applicability of essential services restoration, leaders should:

- Implement a more holistic approach like the Factor-Precedence Model to facilitate synergy between Engineer and Civil Affairs approaches.

- Incorporate the Factor-Precedence Model into doctrine and training for Army and Marine Reserve and National Guard force structures to leverage their unique capabilities and civilian experience. In addition, the new model could encourage an interagency approach focused not only on projects but also actions, engagements, and development.

Department of State guidance could integrate the new model.

- Many tools exist that could work with the Factor-Precedence Model. Military planners should adopt a holistic approach like the Factor-Precedence Model and incorporate existing intelligence and analysis tools into the model. Over time, practitioners could improve the application of existing tools with Factor-Precedence Model.

- Since the scope of this monograph focused on counterinsurgency operations, practitioners should conduct further research to improve the application of culture, climate, and geography factors for all essential services model. Additional research could identify ways to modify the Factor-Precedence Model to meet interagency guidance along with emerging doctrinal requirements.

- After additional research, refinement, and study by US Army Engineer School and Engineer Research and Design Center, units can assess the benefits of the Factor-Precedence Model and integrate the model into their operational approach.

Appendix 1: Definitions and Terms

The following appendix provides definitions for key words and phrases contained in this monograph. To provide a common point of reference for readers, most terms begin with the military's doctrinal definition and refine the use in this monograph.

Civil Considerations – areas, structures, capabilities, organizations, people, events (ASCOPE) within a commander's battlespace that are not normally considered militarily significant. (Field Manual [FM] 5-0, pg C-7)

Counterinsurgency (COIN) – those military, paramilitary, political, economic, psychological, and civic actions taken by a government to defeat insurgency. (FM 3-24, Glossary 4) Comprehensive civilian and military efforts taken to defeat an insurgency and to address any core grievances. Also called **COIN**. (Joint Publication [JP] 1-02, pg 108) Counterinsurgency or counterinsurgents can refer to the group itself.

Essential Services – those things needed to sustain life, such as food, water, clothing, shelter, and medical treatment. Stabilizing a population requires meeting these needs. People pursue essential needs until they are met, at any cost and from any source. People support the source that meets their needs. If it is an insurgent source, the population is likely to support the insurgency. If the host nation government provides reliable essential services, the population is more likely to support it. Commanders therefore identify who provides essential services to each group within the population. (FM 3-24, pg 3-11) Also called ESS by practitioners.

Guerilla – person who engages in irregular warfare (guerilla warfare) especially as a member of an independent unit carrying out harassment and sabotage. (Trinquier, pg 6). Although used interchangeably to describe insurgents or terrorists during the Malaya Emergency and other conflicts, a guerilla is specifically one who engages specifically in guerilla warfare to achieve his or her goals. Guerillas could fight during insurgencies or major combat operations.

Host nation – a nation which receives the forces and/or supplies of allied nations and/or NATO organizations to be located on, to operate in, or to transit through its territory.

Also called **HN.** (JP 1-02, pg 212)

Infrastructure – includes all "real property" (i.e., buildings, roads, facilities, etc) constructed to support a society. Infrastructure spans the spectrum of those structures and services that enhance a life style to those that make survival possible. (NTC SWEAT Smart Book, pg 3)

Insurgency – the organized use of subversion and violence by a group or movement that seeks to overthrow or force change of a governing authority. Insurgency can also refer to the group itself. (JP 1-02, pg 229) An organized movement aimed at the overthrow of a constituted government through the use of subversion and armed conflict. (FM 3-24, pg Glossary 5)

Lines of Effort – a useful tool for framing the concept of operations when stability or civil support operations dominate. Lines of effort link multiple tasks with goal-oriented objectives that focus efforts toward establishing end state conditions. (FM 5-0, pg 2-17) Also called LOEs.

Mission Variables – mission, enemy, terrain and weather, troops available and support available, time available, and civil considerations (METT-TC) provide categories of relevant information to synthesize operational variables and tactical-level information with local knowledge about conditions relevant to their mission. (FM 5-0, pgs 1-21 and 1-71)

Nation-Building – involves the use of armed force as part of a broader effort to promote political and economic reforms with the objective of transforming a society emerging from conflict into one at peace with itself and its neighbors. (Dobbins, pg xvii)

Operational Variables – political, military, economic, social, infrastructure, information, physical environment, and time (PMESII-PT) factors describe the commander's understanding of the battlefield. (FM 5-0, pg 1-6)

Practitioner – for the purpose of this monograph, the term practitioner refers to someone, either military or diplomat, who engages in the study, improvement, or management of essential services. The term unit and practitioner are used interchangeably in this monograph. In the military, most essential services practitioners come from engineer or civil affairs fields.

Reconstruction – the process of rebuilding degraded, damaged, or destroyed political, socioeconomic, and physical infrastructure of a country or territory to create the foundation for long-term development. (FM 3-07, pg 1-12)

Smart Book (also Smartbook) – a useful resource document or reference guide that informs the reader and thus increases his or her ability to accomplish a task in the military. Readers should not confuse the military smart book with electronic smart books, smart phones, or electronic mobile devices.

Stability Operations – Stability operations is defined as an overarching term encompassing various military missions, tasks, and activities conducted outside the United States in coordination with other instruments of national power to maintain or reestablish a safe and secure environment, provide essential governmental services, emergency infrastructure reconstruction, and humanitarian relief." (*DoDD 3000.05*, pg 4) Stability operations encompass the various military missions, tasks, and activities conducted outside the United States in coordination with other instruments of national power to reestablish or maintain secure environment, provide essential governmental services, emergency infrastructure reconstruction, and humanitarian relief. (FM 3-07, pg Glossary-9)

Stabilization – the process by which underlying tensions that might lead to resurgence in violence and a breakdown in law and order are managed and reduced, while efforts are made to support preconditions for successful long-term development. Together, reconstruction and stabilization comprise the broad range of activities defined by the Department of Defense as stability operations. (FM 3-07, pg 1-12)

Terrorism – terrorism is politically-motivated violence, directed primarily against civilians or non-combatants, undertaken with the intention to coerce societies through fear. (Kilcullen, *Countering Global Insurgency, pg* Appendix D-1)

Appendix 2: Acronyms in Essential Services

AR	Army Regulation
ASCOPE	areas, structures, capabilities, organizations, people, events
BCT	Brigade Combat Team
CCIR	commander's critical information requirement
CERP	commander's emergency relief program
CERL	Construction Engineering Research Laboratory
CMO	civil-military operations
COCOM	combatant command
COIN	counterinsurgency
CORDS	Civil Operations and Revolutionary Development Support
DA	Department of the Army
DoD	Department of Defense
DoDD	Department of Defense Directive
DoDI	Department of Defense Instruction
ERDC	Engineer Research and Development Center
ESS	essential services
FM	Field Manual
FMI	Field Manual Interim
GAO	Government Accounting Office
GCAT	Geo-Cultural Assessment Tool
GIRoA	Government of the Islamic Republic of Afghanistan
GOI (or GoI)	Government of Iraq
HES	Hamlet Evaluation System
HIC	high intensity conflict
IO	information operations
IPB	intelligence preparation of the battlefield
IR	infrastructure reconnaissance
ISAF	International Security Assistance Force
ISR	intelligence, surveillance, and reconnaissance
JOPP	Joint Operation Planning Process
JP	Joint Publication
LIC	low intensity conflict
LOE (or LoE)	lines of effort
LOO (or LoO)	lines of operation

MDMP	military decision making process METT-TC mission, enemy, terrain and weather, troops available and support available, time available, and civil considerations
MCWP	Marine Corps Warfighter Pamphlet
MNC-I	Multi-National Corps - Iraq
MND-B	Multi-National Division - Baghdad
MND-N	Multi-National Division - North
MNF-I	Multi-National Force - Iraq
MOE	measure of effectiveness
MOOTW	military operations other than war
MOP	measure of performance
OSD	Office of the Secretary of Defense
PIR	priority intelligence requirement
PMESII-PT	political, military, economic, social, infrastructure, information, physical environment, and time
PRT	Provincial Reconstruction Team
RC-E or RC(E)	Regional Command – East
RC-S or RC(S)	Regional Command – South
SBCT	Stryker Brigade Combat Team
S/CRS	Office of the Coordinator for Reconstruction and Stabilization
SIGAR	Special Inspector General for Afghanistan Reconstruction
SIGIR	Special Inspector General for Iraq Reconstruction
SF	Special Forces
SSTR	stability, security, transition, and reconstruction
SWEAT	sewer/sewage/sanitation, water, electricity, academics, trash
SWEAT-MSO	sewer, water, electricity, academics, trash, medical, safety, other considerations
SWET-H	sewer, water, electricity, trash, health
TCAPF	Tactical Conflict Assessment and Planning Framework
TO	Theater of Operations
US	United States
USACE	United States Army Corps of Engineers
USAES	United States Army Engineer School
USAID	United States Agency for International Development

Appendix 3: Modern Counterinsurgency Operations and Essential Services Key Events

In the modern era, insurgency actions by China and counterinsurgency actions by the United States, France, and Great Britain highlight the development of counterinsurgency thought, techniques, and doctrine. Each counterinsurgency conflict offers lessons to military planners, doctrine writers, and essential services practitioners. By 2006, the American Army had taken critical lessons learned and formulated them into a coherent doctrine in the form of *FM 3-24 Counterinsurgency* and *FM 3-07 Stability Operations*. Both of these manuals focus considerable effort on the restoration of essential services to support the host nation government and gain the support of the population. The first section of this appendix provides an overview of foreign counterinsurgency lessons that helped counterinsurgency literature and doctrine evolve over time. Table 5 provides a historical overview of lessons learned from foreign counterinsurgency involvement.

Table 5: Modern (Post 1942) Foreign Counterinsurgency Lessons

Years	Conflict	Historical Relevance
1927-1950	Chinese Civil War	Since the early 20th Century, winning support of the populace has become a fundamental principle in counterinsurgency literature. In 1937, while developing his theories of Chinese Communism, Mao Tse-Tung stated that "[b]ecause guerrilla warfare basically derives from the masses and is supported by them, it can neither exist nor flourish if it separates itself from their sympathies and cooperation."[142] He later successfully applied these principles during the Chinese Civil War that led to the overthrow of the Republic of China and instatement of Communism.
1948 to 1960	Malayan Emergency	Great Britain waged a low cost, long term counterinsurgency effort in Malaya. Great Britain's comprehensive essential services program tied into comprehensive security efforts, helped lead to a stable Malaysian government, and cost less than $800 million.[143]In 1952, while fighting communist insurgents during the Malayan Emergency , General Sir Gerald Templer linked winning the "hearts and minds" of the Malayan people with improving popular perception and counterinsurgency success.
1954 to 1962	Algerian War	France conducted an unsuccessful counterinsurgency effort in Algeria. French forces failed to gain popular support because they focused too heavily on harsh security tactics and had limited "Special Administration Sections" aimed at improving conditions. [144] In 1966, after taking part in the Algerian War as a counterinsurgent, David Galula stated "the support of the population is as important for insurgents as it is for counterinsurgents."[145] Literature published since the beginning of America's conflicts in Afghanistan and Iraq carries the same theme. In 1966, after taking part in the Algerian War as a counterinsurgent, David Galula stated "the support of the population is as important for insurgents as it is for counterinsurgents."[146] Literature published since the beginning of America's conflicts in Afghanistan and Iraq carries the same theme.
1957	Foreign COIN Review	FM 41-10, *Civil Affairs Military Government Operations*, proposed that insurgencies flourished in conditions of "disorder and socioeconomic hardship" therefore military units must help restore basic infrastructure, services, and humanitarian standards. FM 41-10 estimated that restoring basic services would "win public support for the government and the Army."147

The second section of this appendix relates America's involvement in conducting restoration or provision of essential services to the prevention or counteraction of an insurgency. Table 6 provides a historical overview of American involvement in essential services restoration during and after World War II. These experiences highlight not only the historical precedence of essential services restoration, but they also show the evolution to modern essential services models.

Table 6: Modern (Post 1942) American Essential Services Efforts during Counterinsurgency Operations

Years	Conflict	Historical Relevance
1944-1946	World War II Germany and Japan	Starting heavily in 1945, the United States Army built a history of doctrine and missions that focused on meeting needs and fixing basic services. Lieutenant General Lucius D. Clay in Germany and General of the Army Douglas MacArthur in Japan received the requirements as soldier-diplomats to restore and provide basic governmental services to prevent growth of a Communist insurgency.[148]
1959	Cuba and Columbia	Starting in 1959, President Eisenhower responded to political and social unrest in Cuba and Columbia by appropriating $500 Million and military support to restoring health, education, and agrarian conditions in both countries.[149] These interventions focused on supporting the host-nation government's legitimacy and maintaining a stable partner.
1965	Dominican Republic	In 1965, 1,600 Soldiers from the 82nd Airborne Division deployed in a multi-national effort to the Dominican Republic to restore municipal services, repair roads, build schools, and assist with medical care in the face of an insurgency there.[150] The focus of preventing the spread of Communist insurgencies and Communist rule in South America increased in the Dominican Republic based on the island nation's proximity to the United States.
1955 to 1975	Vietnam War	The United States fought in the Vietnam War against Communist conventional troops and guerrilla forces. The US Army implemented two systems, the Hamlet Evaluation System (HES) and the Civil Operations and Revolutionary Development Support (CORDS), which had positive infrastructure impacts and would establish the foundation for future counterinsurgency and essential services models.[151] Success in meeting basic needs of the populace led, in turn, to improved intelligence that facilitated an assault on the Viet Cong political infrastructure. By early 1970, statistics indicated that 93 percent of South Vietnamese lived in "relatively secure" villages, an increase of almost 20 percent from the middle of 1968. By 1972, pacification had largely uprooted the insurgency from among the South Vietnamese population and forced the communists to rely more heavily on infiltrating conventional forces from North Vietnam and employing them in irregular and conventional operations.[152]
2001 to present	Operation ENDURING FREEDOM (OEF)	Counterinsurgency operations in Afghanistan continued to show the relevance of essential services restoration and the need for effective ways to improve it. In Afghanistan, the limited initial infrastructure, tribal focus, and the cultural self-sufficiency of Afghani populace limited the impact of services restoration and support to the central government.[153] Based on the reoccurring theme and guidance to conduct stability operations, the restoration of essential services will remain a future mission.
2003 to 2010	Operation IRAQI FREEDOM (OIF)	Essential services restoration became a major line of effort for forces in Iraq. Many units like 1st Cavalry Division in 2005 put non-kinetics efforts like essential services above kinetic requirements to defeat insurgents. A variety of models emerged during operations including the most frequently used, the SWEAT Model.[154] This monograph outlines the Factor-Precedence Model which closely resembles 1st Cavalry Division's model used in 2009 near the end of the surge.

Years	Conflict	Historical Relevance
2010 to present	Operation NEW DAWN (OND)	As operations shift in Iraq to advise and assist tasks, the need for essential services restoration and support continues to develop. Effective military models will need to act in support of host nation and Department of State efforts. These efforts will have limited resources for action.

Figure 16: See Factor-Precedence Model Figure in Section 4.

Figure 17 provides additional examples from Australian counterinsurgency specialist David Kilcullen on useful counterinsurgency programs and efforts by the British and United States that shaped thinking today.

<table>
<tr><td colspan="4" align="center">Figure 6
Summary of Historical Case Studies</td></tr>
<tr><th>Insurgency</th><th>Counterinsurgency methods</th><th>Types of attack</th><th>Comments</th></tr>
<tr>
<td>Malaya 1948-60</td>
<td>Resettlement program
Use of surrendered enemy personnel (SEPs)
Special forces deep penetration patrols
Framework security operations
Key infrastructure protection
Hearts and Minds Program
Political concessions to independence</td>
<td>3, 4, 5
1, 2
1,2,3
4,5,6
4
5,6
5</td>
<td>Measures covered a good spread of methods. These were initially ill coordinated but improved dramatically with central coordination. Socio-political measures became effective once security measures began to 'bite'.</td>
</tr>
<tr>
<td>Darul Islam, Indonesia 1948-62</td>
<td>Pagar betis (civilian cordon operations)
Village Defence Organisation
P4K (pacification) strategy
Civic action programs
Decapitation strikes
RPKAD deep penetration patrols
Infrastructure/route security ops</td>
<td>2,3,4,5,6
3,4,5
1,2,3,4,5
5,6
1
1,2
2,3,4</td>
<td>Measures addressed most areas, with a preference for coopting civil populations, harsh collective punishments and decapitation strikes. Most successful in 1959-62 when integrated at theatre level.</td>
</tr>
<tr>
<td>Vietnam 1959-73</td>
<td>Strategic hamlet program
Phoenix Program
CORDS program
Combined Action Platoons (CAP)
Search and Destroy / Sweep and Clear ops
Interdiction of supply routes (HCM trail, Rung Sat, Mekong Delta)
Sanctuary denial ops (DMZ, Cambodia)
Montagnard Strike force operations
Pacification operations
Winning Hearts and Minds (WHAM)</td>
<td>3,4,5,
1,2
2,3,4,5
3,4,5,6
1,2
2, 5
5
1,2,3,4,5
3,4,5,6
5,6</td>
<td>Somewhat counter-intuitively, Vietnam War methods appear to address the full spread of attack methods, with those actions (CORDS, CAP, Montagnard ops) that address most issues being most effective. Coordination was initially poor but improved dramatically in 1968-72.</td>
</tr>
</table>

Figure 17: Kilcullen's Summary of Historical Counterinsurgencies[155]

Appendix 4: Current Essential Services Models

This appendix outlines the major essential services restoration models available at the time of this monograph. Models under development have draft information highlighted. Figures 18 to 22 outline the major models used by practitioners to restore essential services in a counterinsurgency environment. Each figure contains details on the model, a picture of the model's cover page, and examples of critical elements of the model.

SWEAT Smart Book

National Training Center (NTC) Practical Applications for Deploying Units V3.0

Year: 2005

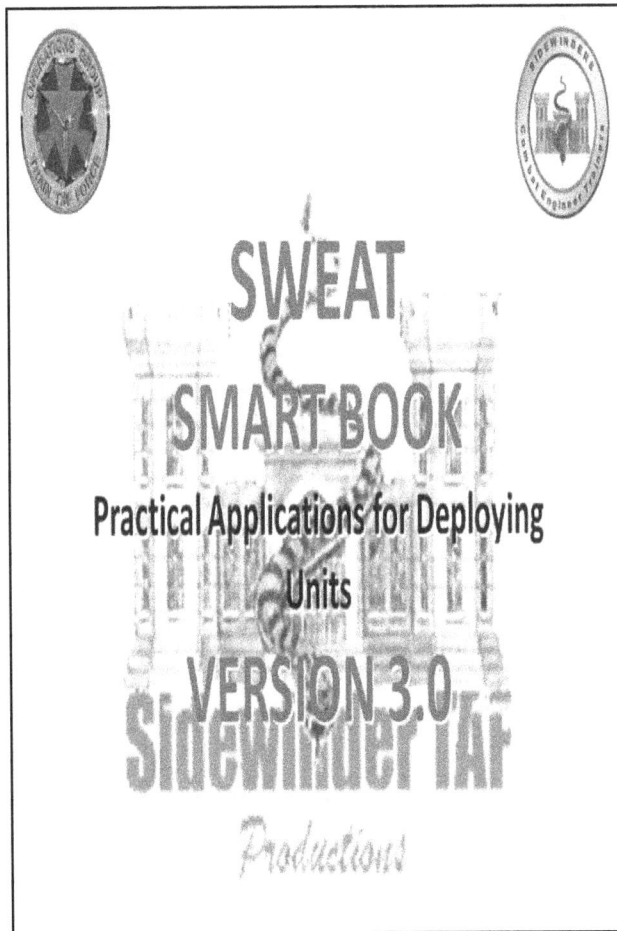

Figure 18: NTC SWEAT Smart Book Cover[156]

Model Summary:

Developed by the NTC Engineer Sidewinder Team between 2004 and 2005 to train deploying units on SWEAT applications in a deployed environment

One of the first publications covering a version of the SWEAT Model

Stand alone Smart Book to facilitate infrastructure reconnaissance and data collection

Prioritization of issues and projects became critical to model's success

Heavily used in development of doctrinal SWEAT Model

Refined many of the categories still in use today

INFRASTRUCTURE INFORMATION & DATA COLLECTION (I²DC)

Purpose

This document provides a basic understanding of the major infrastructure components involved with recovery and sustainability operations. It is intended for use as a "stand alone" instrument by individuals not trained in engineering or recovery operations. Through an awareness of "infrastructure", based on use of this document, any individual in an area of operations becomes a potential reconnaissance asset.

The value of infrastructure reconnaissance is not only the identification of a problem, but providing the relevant information necessary for planning and reconstruction by those skilled in an appropriate specialty. In addition to information gathering, a basic understanding of how infrastructure operates and the associated difficulties in repair can guide tactical operations and operational decision making so as to minimize the resources (time, people, funds) required to reestablish "normalcy" upon the conclusion of hostilities.

This document provides an "initial" data collection standard corresponding to an individual with little experience with the design and function of infrastructure. Consequently, the recipient of the collected infrastructure data (brigade or higher headquarters) should possess a basic level of infrastructure understanding to efficiently prioritize, request, and interpret data collected.

Infrastructure Categories

Infrastructure includes all "real property" (i.e., buildings, roads, facilities, etc) constructed to support a society. Infrastructure spans the spectrum of those structures and services that enhance a life style to those that make survival possible. Within this spectrum, infrastructure can be subdivided into the following unprioritized categories.

- Sanitation (WW) (Wastewater Treatment)
- Water Supply (WS)
- Energy (EN) (electrical power production, bulk fuel storage and distribution)
- Trash (SW) (Solid and Hazardous Waste Disposal)
- Transportation (TR) (highways, railroads, airports, waterways)
- Telecommunications and Media (TM) (cellular service, telephone service, commercial radio, television)
- Agriculture (AF) (farmland, irrigation systems, distribution systems)
- Buildings and Structures (BS) (political offices, records facilities, financial institutions, academic buildings, police stations, industry complexes, public housing)
- Chemical Industry and HAZMAT (HA)

- Cultural or Historical (CH) (places of worship, locations of historical or cultural significance)
- Public Health and Safety (PH) (hospitals, clinics, firefighting)

Prioritization

Resources to deal with infrastructure issues are always in short supply. Whether the issue is time and people to conduct a reconnaissance or funding for materials to restore a facility, prioritization of effort is necessary. Final prioritization is always governed by the specifics of a given situation, but in the absence of detailed analyses, the following prioritized general criteria can be applied.

1. Effort – The amount of expertise required to repair or replace a facility or operation; or the availability and transportation required for repair or replacement of specialty equipment.
2. Health and Safety – The magnitude of impact a task has on the health and safety of a population.
3. Cost – The monetary cost to repair or replace a particular type of facility or operation.
4. Local Perception – Perceived importance by the local population.
5. Self-governance – The level of impact that the loss of function by a facility or operation has on the continued or resumption of self-governance (e.g., municipal facilities, medical facilities, police stations, media centers, etc) in an area.
6. Interdependence – The interdependence of this item with the completion of other tasks, subcategories, or categories of infrastructure activities.

The application of these criteria within the infrastructure categories presented yields the following prioritized list of infrastructure components. The acronym LSC refers to the specific action(s) required, where L is locate, S is secure, and C is collect data.

1. Bridges or tunnels with no bypass (L,S,C)
2. Electrical Power Generation (L,S,C)
3. Potable water supply (L,C)
4. Religious Centers (L)
5. Trash Removal
6. Airports/Airfields/Heliports (L,S,C)
7. Sewage treatment (L,C)

Assessment

The process of assessing the condition, adequacy, and repair requirements for infrastructure is complicated and requires technical expertise and experience. The use of the following infrastructure descriptions and checklists do not provide these prerequisites.

This document does provide a guideline for data collection that can facilitate a technical evaluation of an infrastructure's condition and adequacy. However, the final determination of

Figure 19: NTC SWEAT Smart Book Overview[157]

Developed an infrastructure rating scheme for measures of performance, priority, and effectiveness

Infrastructure Rating Scheme
(2 of 5)

Area	Green	Amber	Red	Black
Power	power system works; only black outs are planned	power system works; black outs unplanned	power system not reliable, broken	power system destroyed
	electric lines are up 100%, no damage, no energy loss	electric lines are up at least 50%, some damage, some line deterioration, can't determine pwr loss	Some electric lines down greater then 50%; majority of lines deteriorated; power loss seen	Electric lines are all down; hot wires; power loss
	Power grid station intact; secureable	Power grid station working; not securable	power grid station not working; not securable; looted	power grid station stripped; destroyed
Trash	trash collection system exists; works	trash collection exists but limited	no formal trash collection	no trash collection; trash stays
	trash put in an area that is not a health issue	not known where trash is dumped	trash is consolidated in a place that could be a health issue	trash is consolidated in a place that is a health issue
	public facilities do not have a trash problem	public facilities do have trash; but it is cleaned-limited	public facilities have no means to remove trash	public facilities have trash; not removed
Housing	residences are structural sound and offer protection from the environment	residences are damaged, need eval for structural; limited protection from environment	residences are damaged; not structural sound; should not be occupied	residences destroyed; not habitable
	utilites are working; reliable	utilities work over 50% of time; not reliable	utilities work under 50% of time; broken	utilities destroyed

Figure 20: NTC SWEAT Smart Book Overview[158]

Infrastructure Assessment Methodology

United States Military Academy (USMA) Infrastructure Assessment Methodology

Year: 2005

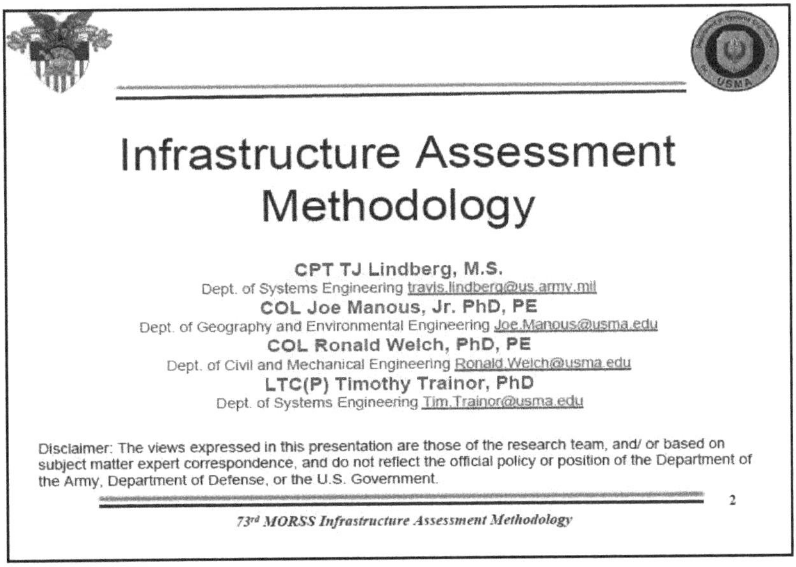

Infrastructure Assessment Methodology

CPT TJ Lindberg, M.S.
Dept. of Systems Engineering travis.lindberg@us.army.mil
COL Joe Manous, Jr. PhD, PE
Dept. of Geography and Environmental Engineering Joe.Manous@usma.edu
COL Ronald Welch, PhD, PE
Dept. of Civil and Mechanical Engineering Ronald.Welch@usma.edu
LTC(P) Timothy Trainor, PhD
Dept. of Systems Engineering Tim.Trainor@usma.edu

Disclaimer: The views expressed in this presentation are those of the research team, and/ or based on subject matter expert correspondence, and do not reflect the official policy or position of the Department of the Army, Department of Defense, or the U.S. Government.

2

73rd MORSS Infrastructure Assessment Methodology

Figure 21: USMA Infrastructure Assessment Methodology Cover Page[159]

Model Summary:

Developed by USMA Department of Systems Engineering in concert with the USAES and ERDC's Construction Engineering Research Laboratory (CERL)

Team focused on "Theater of Operations (TO) infrastructure security, assessment, and repair (re-build)"(MORRS, 12)

Original analysis based on study of domestic critical infrastructure

Flexible, adaptable, scalable tool for use on contingency operations worldwide.

Placed emphasis of the process on infrastructure projects and priority.

Recommended categories used in The SWEAT/IR and NTC SWEAT Smart Book

Became critical in the development of the doctrinal SWEAT Model

Figure 22 shows the major contribution of the team's research: a revised infrastructure category list

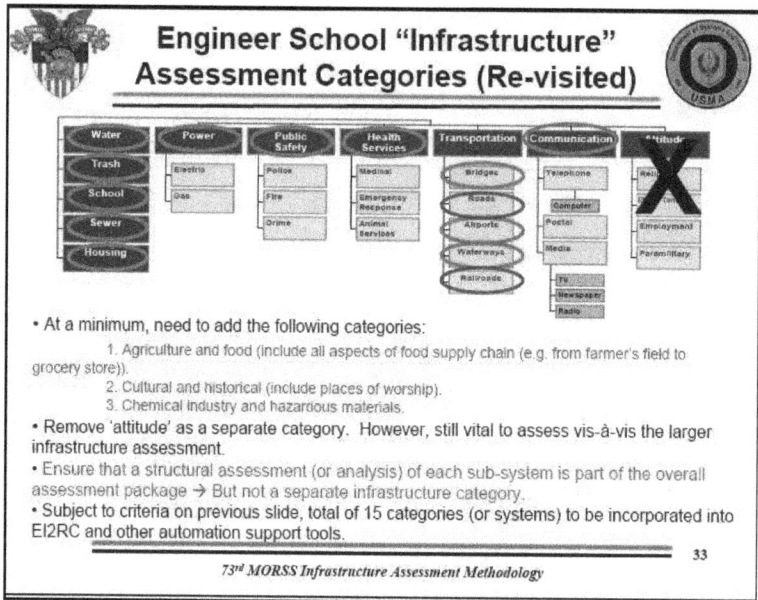

Figure 22: USMA Infrastructure Assessment Methodology Cover Page[160]

The SWEAT/IR Book

United States Army Engineer School (USAES) Infrastructure Reconnaissance Version 2.1

Note: Version 2.1 of The SWEAT/IR Book is unclassified but marked For Official Use Only (FOUO). To maintain a fully unclassified monograph, this appendix will only cover the book's origination and generic content.

Year: 2005

Cover:

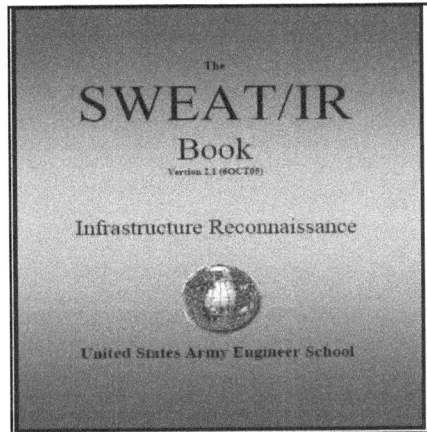

Figure 23: USAES SWEAT/IR Book Cover[161]

Model Summary

USAES developed the book and the book's included model in cooperation with engineers and contractors from ERDC-CERL.

Book's purpose was make up for the widely used SWEAT Model by providing more technical information on categories and giving commanders tools to execute recon and repair

Although classified FOUO due to propriety photographs and figures, the manual gained distribution throughout military and diplomatic engineering units

Along with the NTC and USMA models, this book supplements the doctrinal SWEAT Model and its categories

Expanded the use of the term infrastructure reconnaissance (IR)

The SWEAT Model

The Infrastructure Assessment and Survey Model

Year: 2006

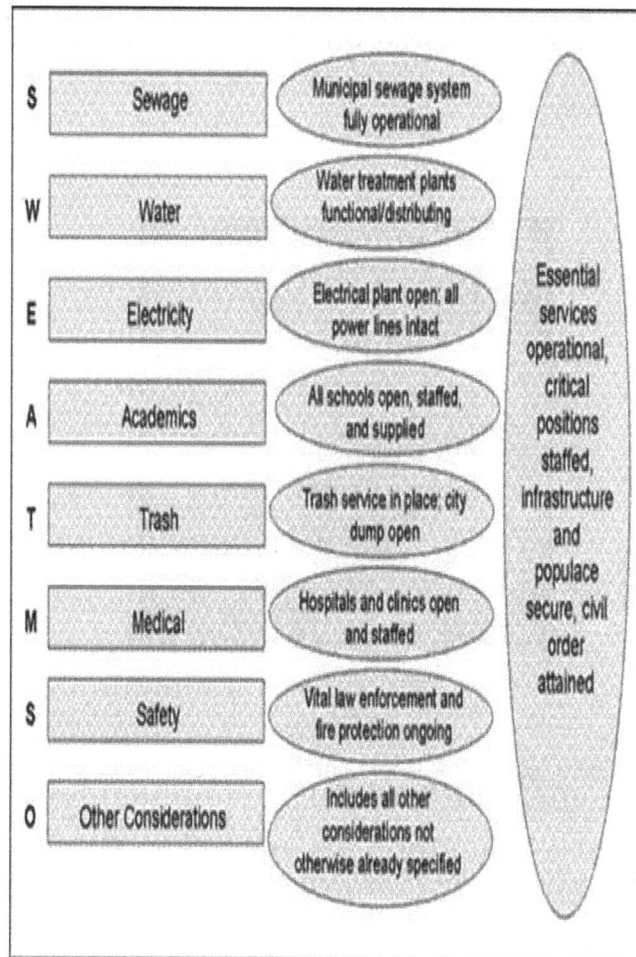

Figure 24: The Infrastructure Assessment and Survey Model aka SWEAT Model[162]

Model Summary

Officially known as the Infrastructure Assessment and Survey Model

Referred to as "SWEAT" Model by most units and essential services practitioners

Initial Model Concepts designed in 2004 by NTC and the Army Engineer School

Used in Iraq since 2005

Outlined in doctrine FM 3-24 since 2006, FM 3-07 since 2008, and FM 3-34.170 since 2008

Tracked by GAO audits since 2005 in Iraq and Afghanistan

Popular model still in use by many units as of 2010

Figure 24 shows one of the most popular interpretations of the model when applied to stability ops

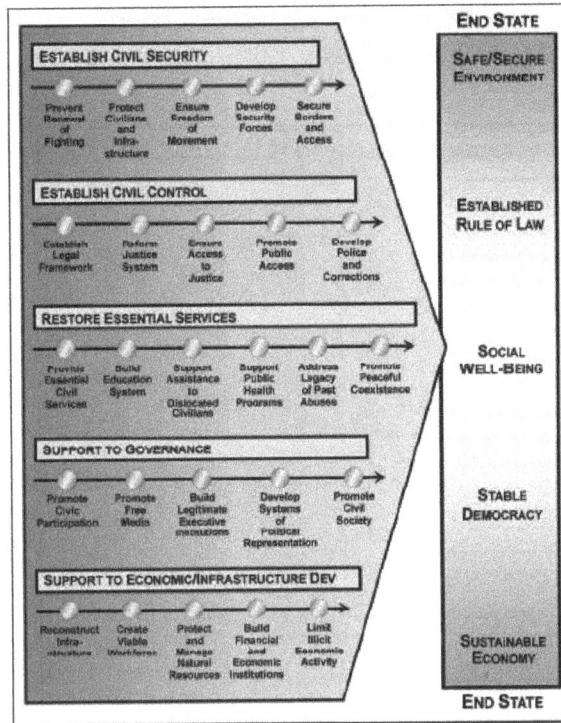

Figure 25: Restoration of Essential Services Line of Effort (LOE)[163]

The Factor-Precedence Model

Holistic Restoration of Essential Services V 1.0

Year: 2010

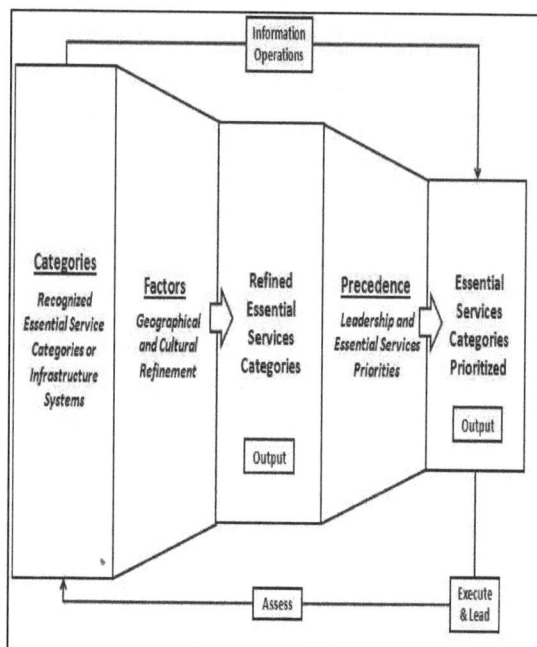

Figure 26: Proposed Factor-Precedence Model[164]

Model Summary

Based on Infrastructure Assessment and SWEAT Models currently in use

Focused on holistic and repetitive evaluation of critical categories

Developed to integrate execution, leadership, and assessment into model

Tailored by Area of Operation (AO) at any military level

Tracked partially by past and current GAO audits

Used in various forms by units in Iraq

Compatible with doctrine and with many existing planning, intelligence, engineering, and analysis tools, see Figure 27

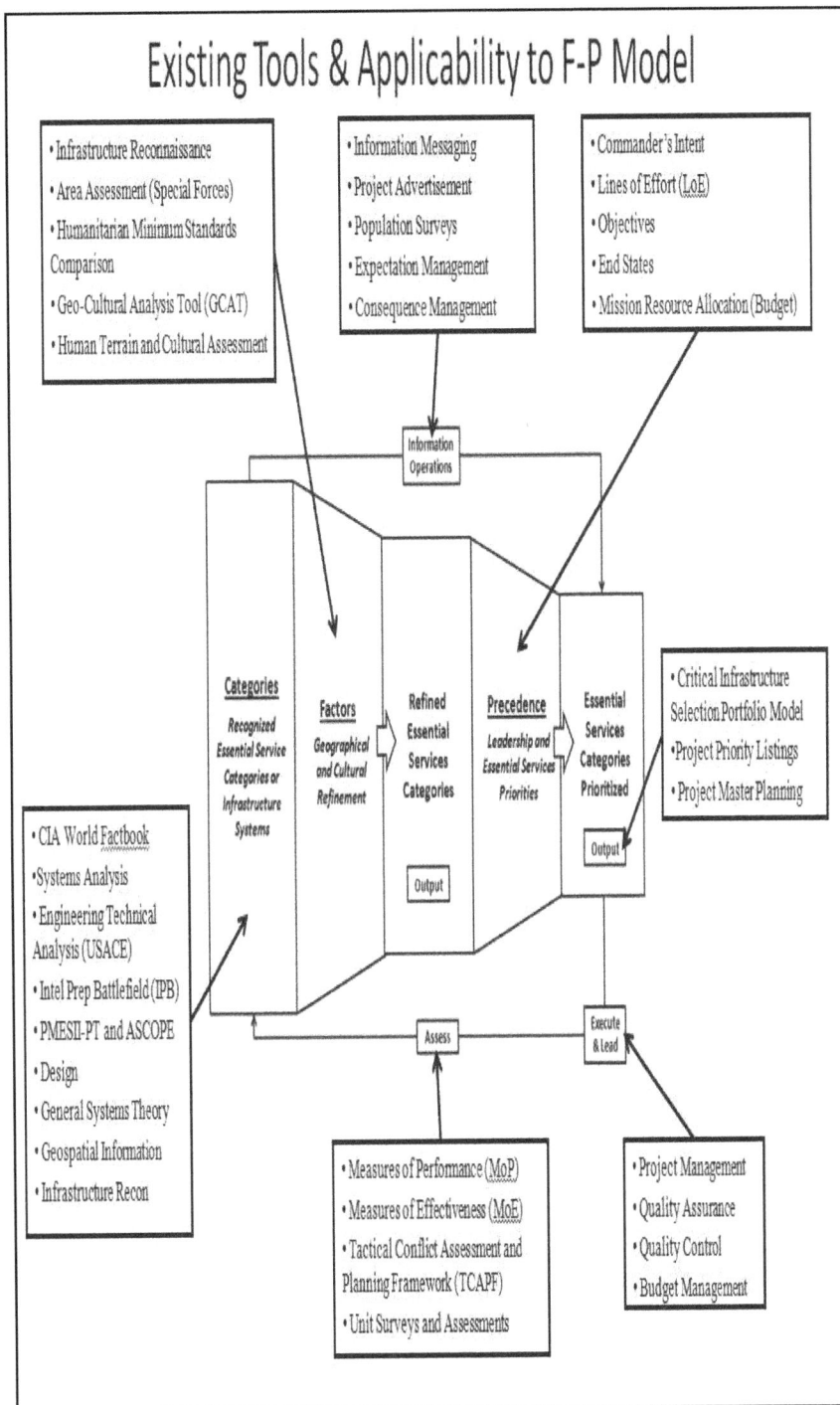

Figure 27: Factor-Precedence Model Interaction with other Military Tools & Programs[165]

Appendix 5: How to Apply the Essential Services Factor-Precedence Model

This appendix provides a detailed description of the steps of the Factor-Precedence Model.[166] Figure 28 presents an overview of the Factor-Precedence Model aligned with its complementary tasks of information operations, execution, leadership, and assessment.

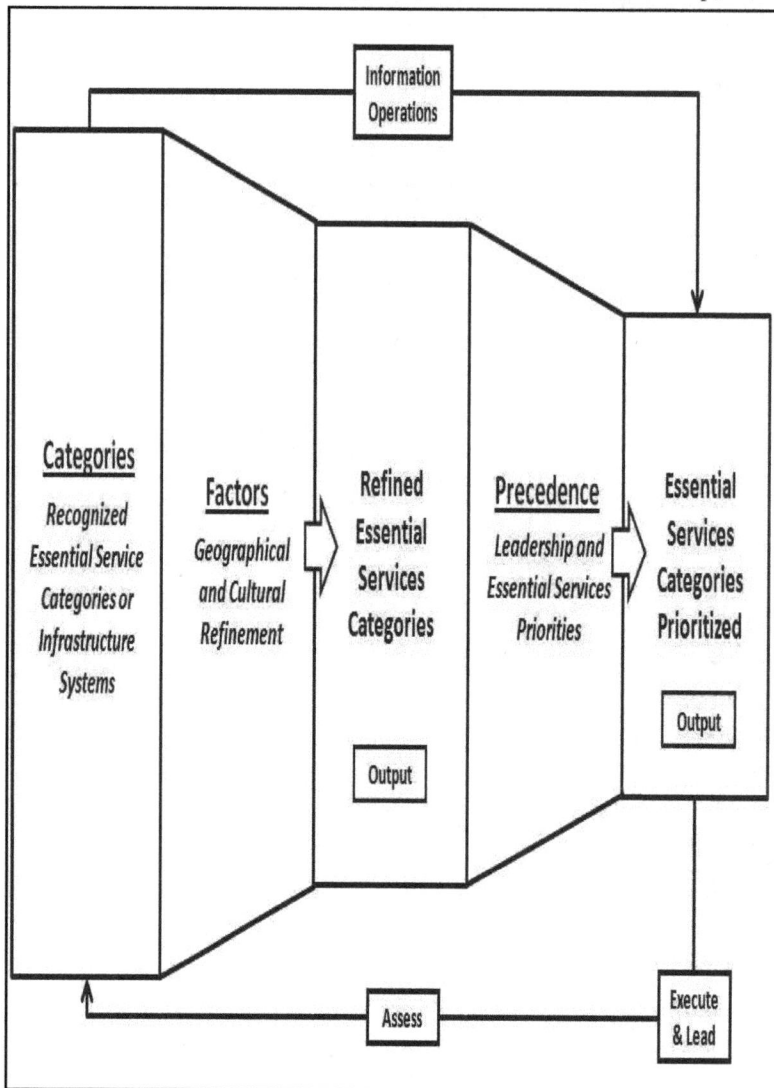

Figure 28: The Factor-Precedence Model

Step 1: Form the Foundation using Recognized Essential Service Categories or Infrastructure Systems

The first step in the Factor-Precedence Model requires units to analyze the sixteen globally-recognized essential services categories that are needed to support basic needs for a culturally acceptable quality of life. The establishment of common categories forms a solid baseline for intelligence preparation, planning, and government engagement along bureaucracy lines. Because of widespread use and existing tools, most military units and leaders understand the categories and can ascertain initial requirements for action.[167] Figure 29 presents the categories identified in the first step of the Factor Precedence Model.

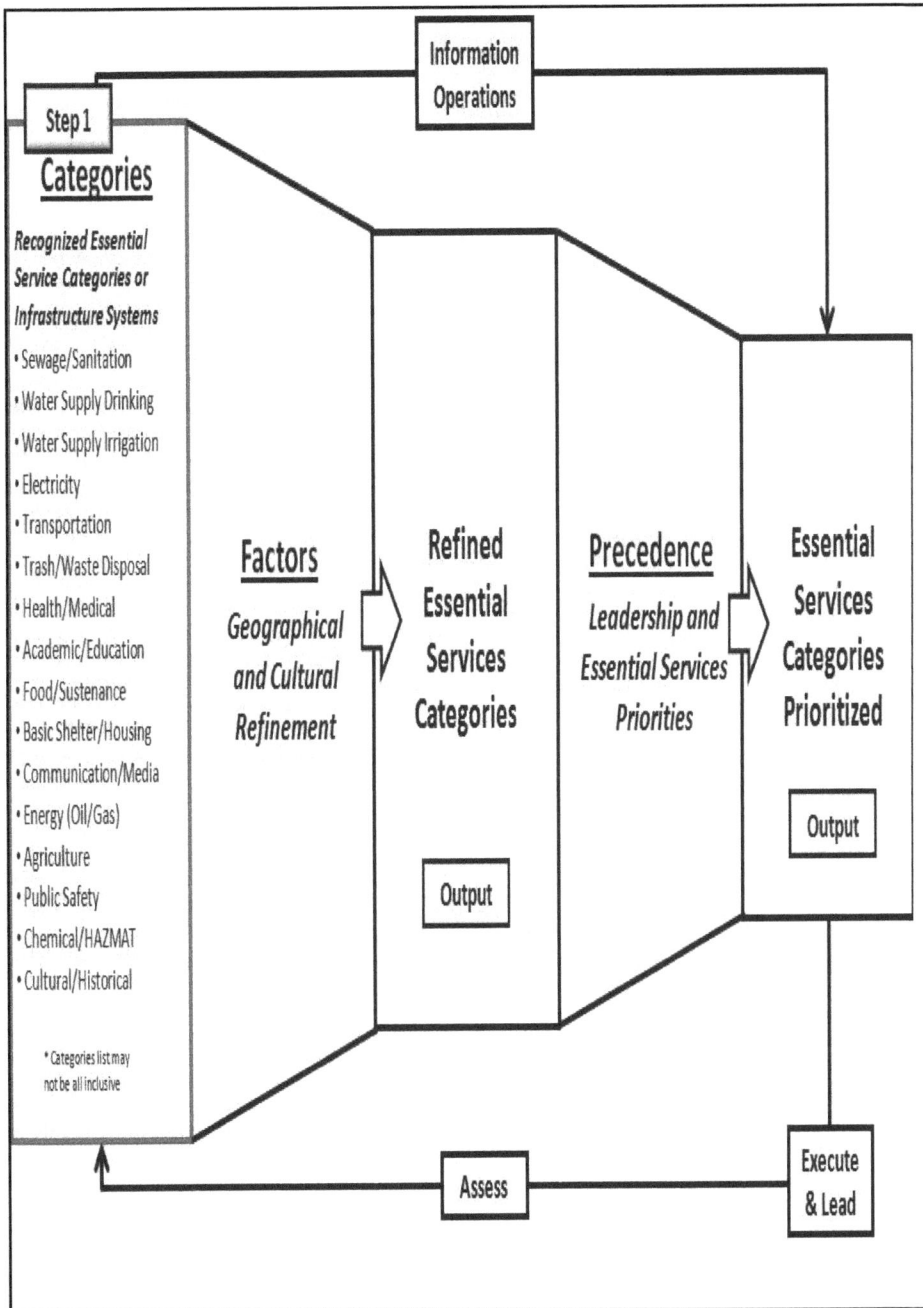

Figure 29: Step 1 of Factor-Precedence Model – Essential Service Categories

Table 7 provides a summary of the sixteen essential services categories identified and assessed during step 1.[168]

Table 7: Essential Services Recognized Categories

Essential Services Category	Purpose/Description
Sewage/Sanitation	Provides wastewater treatment to replicate the natural cleansing process by containment and treatment of water-saturated waste.
Water Supply - Drinking	Provides water at adequate pressure for use in residential or industrial applications. In short term situations, appropriate quantities of treated water may meet health requirement.
Water Supply - Irrigation	Provides certain non-potable water sources as irrigation for crops; may convert to drinking water sources after treatment.
Electricity	Provides the production, distribution, and consumption of electricity for light, information technology (IT), heating or cooling, and industrial production. Most industrialized or IT-based societies require power to function and regain footing.
Transportation	Provides waterways, roads, bridges, airports, and railroad networks to move goods and people and conduct military operations. The movement of goods and people is crucial to the functioning of civilian and military operations. The bulk of the populace and the economic activity will use street systems to support automobile traffic, commercial traffic, and public transportation. Road networks also prove essential for law enforcement and emergency response.
Trash/Waste Disposal	Provides for transportation and disposal of wastes, ranging from municipal garbage to industrial wastes, in a controlled manner to ensure public health and safety. May sometimes include hazardous substances.
Health/Medical	Primary purpose: Provides short and long-term health needs of a population. Secondary purpose: Provides emergency response capabilities which are maintained and coordinated with other agencies.
Academic/Education	Provides the activities of educating, instructing, or imparting knowledge or skill. Usually refers to the physical infrastructure and supporting services that allow educational requirements to take place.
Food/Sustenance	Provides nutrients in solid form that sustain growth, furnish energy, and maintain life; a basic human need.
Basic Shelter/Housing	Provides public housing, private housing, commercial buildings & structures, and governmental buildings & structures.
Communication/Media	Provides for the flow of information between people and institutions. Essential to the proper functioning of a society and becomes progressively more important as the society becomes more developed.
Energy (Oil/Gas)	Provides all power sources required for an industrialized or IT-based society to function or for developing countries to become industrialized or IT based, heat production for warmth and food preparation, electricity for light, heating or cooling, and industrial production, and internal combustion for either industrial purposes or vehicle operation.

Agriculture	Provides a wide range of industries to include livestock, orchards, aqua farming, and traditional planted crops. Performs functions of food sourcing and economic strength.
Public Safety	Provides organizations and institutions that are employed to save lives and property in the event of an accident, natural disaster, or terrorist incident, and to ensure that good order and discipline is maintained. Includes police, fire, rescue, emergency medical services (EMS), and prisons per NTC *SWEAT Smart Book*.
Chemical/HAZMAT	Provides products that are essential to [a state's] economy and standard of living such as fertilizer for agriculture, chlorine for water purification, and polymers that create plastics.
Cultural/Historical	Provides places of worship; also includes locations of historical or cultural significance. Such locations often generate strong emotional sentiments among various groups and can carry significance in terms of collective images of self, sources of great and often times competing pride, and may serve as physical manifestations of a populations' identity.

Step 2: Refine the Categories using Geographical and Cultural Factors

The second step of the Factor Precedence Model is to refine the essential services categories by applying eight local geographical and cultural factors, as presented in Figure 30 and Table 8. The output of this step is four to seven refined categories that represent the local population's needs and are at actionable levels for counterinsurgents. Units may refine geo-cultural factors with tools such as area and infrastructure assessments, Engineering Research and Development Center's (ERDC's) Geo-Cultural Analysis Tools (GCAT), and Human Terrain System assessments based on local engagements.[169]

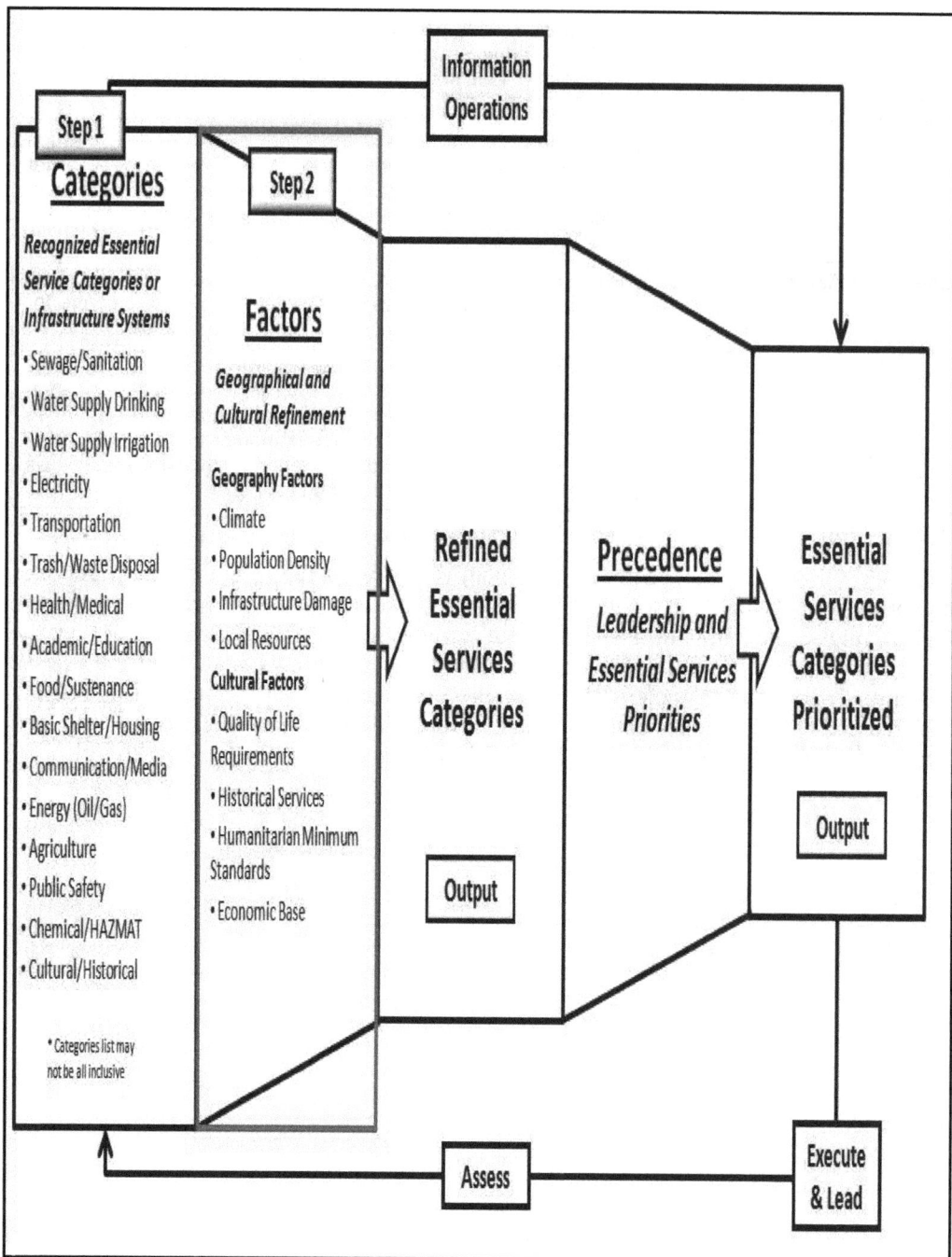

Figure 30: Step 2 of Factor-Precedence Model – Geo-Cultural Factors

Table 8 provides a summary of the eight geo-cultural factors identified and assessed during step 2.

Table 8: Factor-Precedence Model Geo-Cultural Factors

Geographical Factor	Description
Climate	The five primary climate zones, Tropical, Dry, Temperate, Cold, and Polar represent the 30-year characteristic conditions of an area in terms of air temperature and precipitation. Seasonal shifts are also considered.
Population Density	Urban populations comprised of 2,500 or more people living in a single area often show typical built-up conditions and industrialization. Populations not classified as urban compose the rural population. Urban populations require more focus on sewage and trash services due to health requirements in close quarters. Rural populations often focus more on irrigation water and transportation to facilitate farming and trade. Density factors may also guide prioritization of assisting more people.[170]
Extent of Damage to Infrastructure	Violence and infrastructure damage often come before or result from counterinsurgency operations. Measuring the extent of damage resulting from conflict can help counterinsurgents provide a visual means of restoring essential services.
Local Resources Available	Construction and management capabilities, raw materials, and host government capacity to manage services make up the most important local resource factors to improve essential services. This factor may also describe allocation of unit resources like money, personnel, or training that prove critical to restoration efforts.
Cultural Factor (needs, desires, expectations)	Description
Cultural Environment	Quality of life requirements determine the critical needs of the populace and differ in every culture based on the culture's individualism and religious focus. According to Hofstede, individualistic cultures require more personal support, and collectivistic cultures require more support to the tribe, group, or organizational culture. Religion also plays heavily into the cultural context in many areas around the world.[171]
Historical Services Standards	Historical service standards provide an important factor that dictates the essential services expectations of people in the area. Past performance and services of great expectations manage the people's expectation and needs. Flows from the level of development experienced by the area.[172]
Humanitarian Minimum Standards (United Nations)	Based on Maslow's Hierarchy of Needs and basic medical information, the United Nations developed the basic requirements for sustaining the lives and dignity of those affected by calamity or conflict. The Minimum Standards which follow aim to quantify these requirements with regard to people's need for water, sanitation, nutrition, food, shelter and health care.[173]
Economic Base	The growth, decline, or stagnation of the local community rests upon basic economic activity, which integrates local needs and sustains buying power. Agricultural, market, service, and production-based economies are affected most heavily by this factor.

Step 3: Establish Precedence using Leadership and Essential Services Priorities

Using the refined categories from the second step, the third step in the Factor-Precedence Model allows units to apply leadership and essential services priorities, as shown in Figure 31 and listed in Table 9, to rank order essential services operations and projects. The output of this step is a final prioritization that governs specific actions within categories and within individual projects to ensure effective and efficient execution of area essential services operations. Adjustments to funding, resources, or commander's intent can shift the precedence of refined categories. Due to the long-term nature of essential service operations, units should keep adjustments to the minimum necessary.

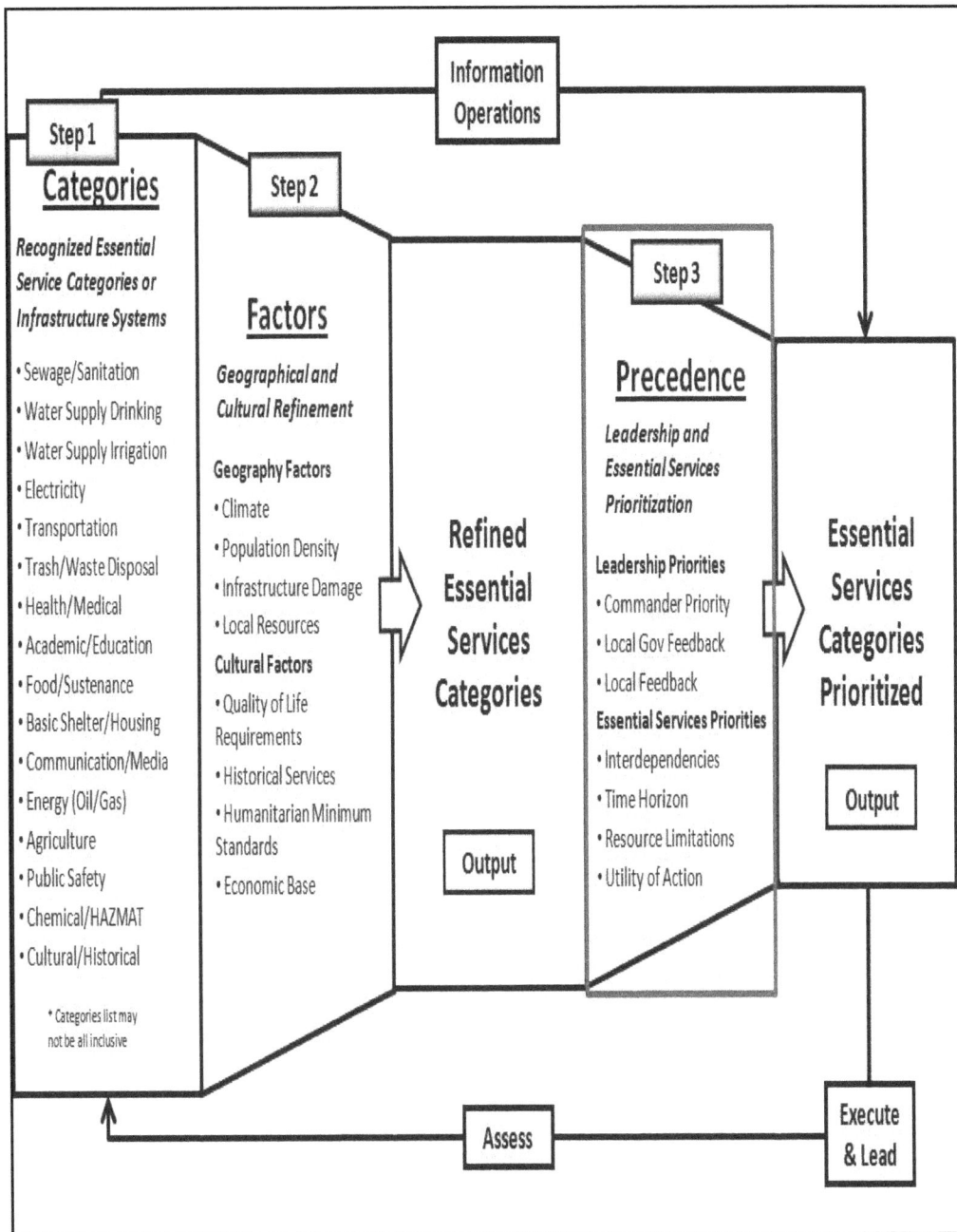

Figure 31: Step 3 of Factor-Precedence Model – Precedence Elements

171

Table 9: Factor-Precedence Model Leadership and Essential Services Precedence Elements

Leadership Priorities	Description
Commander Priority	Commander priority provides a critical element that leverages leadership guidance and mission focus. Planners must meet the Commander's Intent by implementing his prioritization while ensuring that actions nest with higher headquarters priorities. Maintaining consistent priorities in essential service assists in consistent growth and improvement.
Local Government Feedback	Local government feedback incorporates local leadership's assessments and existing plans. The integration of the government's funding, operations, and maintenance capability into restoration activities proves critical into understanding individual and Group needs.[174]
Local Population Feedback	Local feedback in terms of surveys and assessments provide a relative perspective on what they desire or want. Understanding the local feedback helps build prioritization before action and helps inform messages needed during and after execution.[175]
Essential Services Priorities	Description
Interdependencies	Systemic connections between essential services have synergistic effects when critical nodes either improve or decline. Interdependence, described as the "Tailored Network" of related services by 2/25 Stryker Brigade Combat Team, informs critical categories and helps pinpoint critical projects.[176]
Time Horizon	Time horizon balances the short and long-term needs with the operational timeframe of the unit. Certain categories, like electricity, have long-term impacts and have long-lasting projects. Practitioners should also be aware of connections between long-term projects and short-term projects. Again, electricity provides an example with long-term projects in power production needing connection to short-term projects like power sub-stations. Without a systematic connection between projects, power produced would never make it to the end user. Essential services short-term fixes must maintain balance with long-term effects.[177]
Resource Limitations	Unit resources such as budget, personnel, and technical expertise, may limit certain actions while facilitating others. Specific budget cut lines may adjust priority of individual categories and specific projects during resource constrained periods.[178]
Utility of Action	The utility of each balances the cost-benefit analysis, or bang for the buck, with the requirements to fairly meet essentials service needs.[179]

Notes

1. David Galula, *Counterinsurgency Warfare: Theory and Practice* (New York, NY: Praeger, 1964), 89. David Galula, French military officer and scholar, proved influential in developing the theory and practice of counterinsurgency warfare in the late 1960s and early 1970s. Galula participated in or directly studied the Chinese Communist Revolution, the Greek Civil War, the Indochina War, and the Algerian War. His work's popularity has surged since the 2006 version of *Field Manual (FM) 3-34 Counterinsurgency* cited his *Counterinsurgency Warfare: Theory and Practice* several times. This quote highlights the importance of kinetic and non-kinetic operations during counterinsurgency operations.

2. Author's Note: To focus the scope of this monograph, the analysis within focuses on models used during counterinsurgency operations. Restoring essential services may help forestall insurgency following major combat operations. Restoring essential services may also decrease human suffering and improve government effectiveness during humanitarian operations in the United States and overseas. Appendix 1 and 2 offer a comprehensive guide to the acronyms, terms, and definitions in this monograph.

3. Galula, 4. Galula refined his definition of insurgency based on his experiences in Algeria combined with his detailed study of historical guerilla and insurgency movements. See Appendix 1 for more information on definitions and terms used throughout this monograph.

4. United States (US) Department of Defense, *US Army Field Manual (FM) 3-24 / Marine Corps Warfighters Pamphlet (MCWP) 3-33.5, Counterinsurgency* (Washington, DC: Government Printing Office, 2006), Glossary 5. FM 3-24 cites Galula extensively throughout the manual showing the close connection between prevailing theoretical and doctrinal definitions for insurgency.

5. (US) Department of Defense, *US Army Field Manual*, 1-1. Both Army and Joint doctrine define counterinsurgency as, the "[c]omprehensive civilian and military efforts taken to defeat an insurgency and to address any core grievances." As a note, practitioners often refer to counterinsurgency as COIN. See also US Department of Defense, *Joint Publication 1-02, Department of Defense Dictionary of Military and Associated Terms.* Washington, DC: Government Printing Office, 2010, 108.

6. Appendix 3, Modern Counterinsurgency Operations and Essential Services Key Events, provides a comprehensive list of key insurgencies and counterinsurgencies after World War II. Appendix 3 also highlights American involvement in the restoration of essential services during counterinsurgency operations since WWII.

7. US Department of Defense, *US Army FM 3-07, Stability Operations* (Washington, DC: Government Printing Office, 2008), 1-17. FM 3-07 provides a comprehensive relationship between population needs, government support, and effective counterinsurgency efforts. This monograph will expand on the geographical, cultural, and regional factors that influence essential services.

8. FM 3-24, 3-11. According to FM 3-24, stabilizing a population requires meeting their needs. People pursue essential needs until they are met, at any cost and from any source. People support the source that meets their needs, whether those needs be security or physiological requirements. If needs provisions come from an insurgent source, the population is likely to support the insurgency. If the HN government provides reliable essential services, the population is more likely to support the government.

9. FM 3-24, 3-11, 2-11. FM 3-07 proposes that during counterinsurgency operations, gaining support of the populace and increasing the legitimacy of the host nation government become the military's highest priorities. Military and diplomatic efforts in political, economic, and service areas compliment direct military actions.

10. James Dobbins, Seth G. Jones, Keith Krane, and Beth Cole DeGrasse, *The Beginner's Guide to Nation-Building* (Santa Monica: RAND Corporation, 2007), xxxiii. Major combat operations and nation-building establish a different set of initial conditions. Appendix 1, Definitions and Terms, provides a definition of nation-building. According to Dobbins and his co-writers, "[t]he prime objective of any nation-building operation is to make violent societies peaceful, not to make poor ones prosperous, or authoritarian ones democratic."

11. See Appendix 3, Modern Counterinsurgency and Essential Services Key Events. Appendix 3 outlines the major insurgencies and counterinsurgency events since 1942. Each event has a timeline and historical relevance. Due to the detail available for American counterinsurgency and essential services efforts, citations for each event within Appendix 3 accompany the write up to facilitate additional research.

12. US Department of Defense, Department of Defense Directive (DoDD) 3000.05: Military Support for Stability, Security, Transition, and Reconstruction (SSTR) Operations (DoDD 3000.05, November 28, 2005) (Washington, DC: Secretary of Defense for Policy, 2005), 1-2. DoDD 3000.05 directs military units to conduct stability operations outside the United States in coordination with other government elements and focus on tasks to "maintain or reestablish a safe and secure environment, provide essential governmental services, emergency infrastructure reconstruction, and humanitarian relief." See Appendix 1 for a more detailed definitions for stability operations, stabilization, infrastructure, reconstruction, and nation building.

13. FM 3-07, 2-11 – 2-12. FM 3-07 provides detailed guidance on supporting essential services as a primary logical line of operation and an Essential Stability Task in support of stability operations. The essential stability task matrix is an evolving interagency document to help planners identify specific requirements to support countries in transition from armed conflict or civil strife to sustaining stability. Military assets compliment other government agencies. In practical application, essential services may have its own line of effort. In other applications, units may make essential services a component of the governance, economics, or civil capacity lines of effort.

14. FM 3-24, 2-1.

15. Brett Pierson, "A System Dynamics Model of the FM 3-24 COIN Manual," 76th Military Operations Research Society Symposium (MORSS) (June 10-12, 2008) (Washington, DC: Warfighting Analysis Division, 2008) http://www.mors.org/UserFiles/file/meetings/07ic/Pierson.pdf (accessed on December 7, 2010), slide 16. According to Captain Pierson, Systems Dynamics Modeling provides a technique for modeling complex systems, framing issues, showing interdependencies, and portraying the impact of initiatives. Figure 1 graphically depicts the essential services and economic interactions during a counterinsurgency as well as the interaction's impact on a neutral populace. Pierson's analysis shows the effects of critical actions directed by Army FM 3-24's population-centric approach.

16. Pierson, "A System Dynamics Model of the FM 3-24 COIN Manual," Figure 1 shows the author's recreation of Captain Pierson's Systems Dynamic Model. Captain Pierson's model depicts systematic connection between essential services, needs, expectations, and satisfaction related to the positive or negative impacts actions have on a neutral populace. The dotted boundary symbolizes the open nature of the counterinsurgency system where other factors and actions impact the neutral populace, insurgency, and host nation government. The arrows show connections between actions

and outcomes. Pluses (+) denote a positive change or reinforcing relationship caused by one variable on the next. Minuses (-) denote a negative change or balancing relationship caused by one variable on the next. A plus and minus (+/-) denotes a relationship going either direction based on performance. Two critical counterinsurgent activities, economic investment and restoring essential services, greatly increase the support for the host nation government.

17. Gordon L. Lippitt, *Visualizing Change Model Building and the Change Process* (Fairfax, VA: NTL Learning Resources, 1973), 2. http://nationalforum.com/Electronic%20Journal%20 Volumes%5CKritsonis,%20Alicia%20Comparison %20of%20Change%20Theories.pdf (accessed on November 26, 2010). Lippitt's simple definition sets the tone for key elements of any model (components, relationships, and dynamics). Theoretically, a model can represent anything in the world, but models must meet certain criteria to remain effective. According to Lippitt, models must be clear, concise, simple, and flexible; See also George E. P. Box and Norman R. Draper. *Empirical Model-Building and Response Surfaces (Wiley Series on Probability and Statistics)* (New York, NY: John Wiley and Sons, Inc., 1987), 10.

18. FM 3-24, 4-3. Paragraph 4-12 covers the techniques for model making and application during conduct (planning, preparation, execution, and assessment) of counterinsurgency operations. During the last nine years of combat operations in Iraq and Afghanistan, military and diplomatic leaders have used a variety of models for restoration of essential services during counterinsurgency operations.

19. FM 3-24, 3-11. This section provides a general definition with supplemental information in Appendix 1. Doctrine for essential services provides little guidance in how to assess and meet the needs of the people to reinforce a host-nation government in a counterinsurgency environment.

20. Operations Group Sidewinder Team, SWEAT Smart Book: Practical Applications For Deploying Units Version 3.0, Fort Irwin, CA: National Training Center (NTC), 2005. http://www. irwin.army.mil/Units/Operations+Group/Sidewinder/default.htm (accessed on August 28, 2010), 3. Engineers tend to focus on the structures and capacity to manage the structures. Key tasks for engineers include maintenance, construction, and repair for facilities and infrastructure.

21. US Department of State, Office of the Coordinator for Reconstruction and Stabilization, "Post-Conflict Reconstruction Essential Tasks (April 2005)." http://www.crs.state.gov/index. cfm?fuseaction=public.display&shortcut=J7R3 (accessed on November 20, 2010), iii. In a very different outlook to the military, especially engineers, the Department of State connects the restoration of essential services with government and economic systems. Diplomats use this outlook to focus on dialogue, budgeting, the political process, and long term aspects of political development.

22. DoDD 3000.05, 2. DoDD 3000.05 sets the tone for the importance and operational relevance of essential services to the military.

23. Both Section 1 and Appendix 3 address the application of counterinsurgency and essential services efforts before and after 2004. Section 3 will provide additional information about the SWEAT Model and its use in Iraq and Afghanistan.

24. Samuel Griffith, Mao Tse-Tung On Guerrilla Warfare (Baltimore, MD: The Nautical & Aviation Publishing Company of America, 1992), 71. Mao Tse-Tung, also Mao Zedong, wrote one of the first complete manuals on insurgency and guerilla warfare. Over the next ten years, he would execute his doctrine helping to establish the People's Republic of China (PRC) after overthrowing the existing regime.

25. Galula, 74.

26. Kalev Sepp, "Best Practices in Counterinsurgency." Military Review (May-June 2005): 10. See also John A. Nagl, Learning to Eat Soup With a Knife: Counterinsurgency Lessons from Malaya and Vietnam (Chicago, IL: University of Chicago Press, 2005), 22.

27. FM 3-24, 1-27.

28. David J. Kilcullen, "Three Pillars of Counterinsurgency," Remarks delivered at the US Government Counterinsurgency Conference on September 28, 2006, Washington, DC: Office of the Coordinator for Counterterrorism, 2006. www.au.af.mil/au/awc/awcgate/uscoin/3pillars_of_counterinsurgency.pdf (accessed December 4, 2010), 4. Dr. Kilcullen, Australian counterinsurgency consultant, co-author of FM 3-24, and the Senior Counterinsurgency Advisor to General David Petraeus in Iraq from 2007 to 2008, placed many of these population-centric counterinsurgency designs into the 2007-2008 Iraq Campaign Plan and Counterinsurgency Policy. Based on the perceived success of the "surge's" approach, he taught his approach in Iraq to incoming commanders, including the author, and during conferences with the Army and Marines following his OIF experience.

29. Abraham H. Maslow, Motivation and Personality, Third Edition (New York, NY: Addison Wesley Educational Publishers, 1987), 15-22. Abraham Maslow provides the best and most commonly referenced outline of needs known as Maslow's Hierarchy of Needs. As shown by Figure 2, the requirements that form the bottom two sections of the pyramid establish the baseline standards for human physiological and safety needs. Maslow proposed that humans must meet basic needs then they gain motivation and access to progress higher on the hierarchy. According to FM 3-24 section C-7, military practitioners "must focus on meeting basic needs first, and then progress up Maslow's hierarchy as each successive need is met."

30. Justin B. Gorkowski, "A Penny for Your Thoughts, a Nickel for Your Heart: The Influence of the Commander's Emergency Response Program on Insurgency" (Master's thesis, Naval Post Graduate School, 2009), 32. Figure 2 is the author's interpretation of Maslow's Hierarchy of Needs aligned against the categories of infrastructure and essential services. Although Maslow did not draw this pyramid in his own work, his detailed descriptions combined with the progressive nature of his hierarchy make the pyramid a popular interpretation of his ideas. Justin Gorkowski created a figure similar to Figure 2 in his work and compared it with needs of the Kirkuk Iraqis.

31. Gambrel R Ciani, "Maslow's hierarchy of needs: Does it apply in a collectivist culture," Journal of Applied Management and Entrepreneurship, 8 (2003), 143.

32. Geert Hofstede, "The Cultural Relativity of the Quality of Life Concept." Academy of Management Review 9 (July 1984): 389–398. http://www.nyegaards.com/yansafiles/Geert%20Hofstede%20cultural%20attitudes.pdf (accessed on November 20, 2010), 390. Hofstede took into account cultural and environmental factors such as power distance, masculinity, and that help add to the utility of Maslow's work.

33. B.F. Skinner, Science and Human Behavior: Behaviorism. (New York, NY: The Free Press, 1953), 9-10. Skinner focused on environment, conditioning, and learning curves associated with cultural norms.

34. Pierson, 7 and 16.

35. The effect of specific restoration actions or projects on violence levels exists outside the scope of this monograph. On-going systems and mathematical modeling studies by the United States Military Academy Department of Systems Engineering may help to refine ideas on this topic in the future.

36. Todd Helmus, Christopher Paul, and Russell Glenn. Enlisting Madison Avenue: The Marketing Approach to Earning Popular Support in Theaters of Operation (Santa Monica: RAND Corporation, 2007), 139.

37. FM 3-07, vi. People who do not have their needs met look to alternate sources like insurgents or alternate organizations that may have hostile intentions towards the US

38. FM 3-07, 50. Helmus, Paul, and Glenn encourage the use of civilian and military rewards to highlight the benefits of popular compliance. Focus by the authors on the incentive nature of such projects is critical and they go on to warn of the potential danger if insurgent groups become familiar with the process and deliberately take action to deny aid.

39. Alexander Fullerton and Garth Myers, "Fitting into the Fight – An Engineer's Dream From a Brigade Troops Battalion S3," Small Wars Journal (2009). Richmond, VA: Small Wars Foundation LLC, 2004. http://smallwarsjournal.com/blog/journal/docs-temp/221-fullerton.pdf (accessed on January 25, 2011), 4-5.

40. Dawson Plummer, "Examining the Effectiveness of SWET and the Sons of SWET in OIF." (Master's monograph, School for Advanced Military Studies (SAMS), Command and General Staff College, 2007), 30. Plummer's SAMS monograph shows both Marine and Army application in late 2004. He reviews the different versions of the SWEAT family of acronyms that units have developed over time including SWEAT, SWEAT-MSO, SWET-H, SWET-MS, and others. Plummer calls the SWEAT family of acronyms the "sons of SWEAT."

41. Travis Lindberg, et al., Infrastructure Assessment Methodology, 73rd Military Operations Research Society Symposium (MORSS) (21-23 June 2005) (West Point, NY: Department of Systems Engineering United States Military Academy, 2005), 12. Dr. Manous led the team, but then-Captain TJ Lindberg provided the briefing and outlined most of the research data. The team developed "checklists" to support the assessment, built models based on American domestic infrastructure, and then inferred values for host-nation infrastructure in the Theater of Operations (TO) effort.

42. Travis Lindberg, "The Critical Infrastructure Portfolio Selection Model" (Master's thesis, Command and General Staff College, 2008), iii.

43. John V. Farr and Brian D. Sawser, US Embassy (Kabul) Value Model and Project Analysis Tool (West Point, NY: Department of Systems Engineering, 2010), 'Intro' Tab and 'How to Use' page. The program provided useful context for individual project impact and project prioritization techniques.

44. Author's Note: Figure 3 provides a graphical representation of the comparison technique used in this monograph. Using three modern examples compared against five comparison criteria, this monograph attempts to determine the most effective model during a counterinsurgency. Section 3 and 4 will present an in-depth review of each model and will expand on the highlights shown in Figure 3.

45. Peter Chiarelli and Patrick Michaelis, "Winning the Peace: The Requirement for Full Spectrum Operations." Military Review (Jul-Aug 2005): 4–17, 10. Major General Chiarelli makes a solid case for the relationship between status of infrastructure and essential services and insurgent support by the populace.

46. US Department of Army and US Marine Corps, US Army FM 3-34.170/ MCWP 3-17.4 Engineer Reconnaissance (Washington, DC: Government Printing Office, 2008), C-1. FM 3-24, FM 3-07, and FM 3-34.170 all cover important aspects of the Army's SWEAT Model. FM 3-34.170 shows the SWEAT Model as a way to think about categories of projects and support.

47. SWEAT Smart Book, 3. The National Training Center's (NTC) SWEAT Smart Book provides an effective training tool for engineers and SWEAT practitioners. The majority of deployed units have received training on one or both of the essential service support products. The SWEAT/ IR Book provides excellent references for reconnaissance, assessments, and prioritization. See Appendix 4 for additional information on both products.

48. See Appendix 3 for additional information on historical programs and services models. Although HES and CORDS form some of the early roots to infrastructure assessment, reconnaissance, and repair, this monograph will focus only on the relationship between essential services models and the Vietnam-era HES and CORDS programs.

49. Chiarelli and Michaelis, 9. The first fully documented use of the SWEAT Model in a counterinsurgency environment came from the Military Review article written by Major General Chiarelli and MAJ Patrick Michaelis. The article and division history also refer to the program as "sewage, water, electricity, and solid waste" with a minor concentrations on "hospitals, schools, communications, and emergency response networks."

50. FM 3-34.170, C-1. Like doctrine, the United States Army Engineer School (USAES) would rather practitioners call the SWEAT Model by the name Infrastructure Reconnaissance to prevent units from focusing too narrowly on sewage, water, electricity, academic, and trash (SWEAT) categories. In their own words, units currently use SWEAT because "SWEAT is a great acronym. It has caught on and is in widespread use." FM 3-34.170 provides a detailed discussion on the infrastructure reconnaissance and assessment process.

51. FM 3-07, 4-11. SWEAT-MSO stands for sewage, water, electricity, academics, trash, medical, safety, and other considerations.

52. SWEAT Smart Book, 5.

53. FM 3-34.170, C-1. FM 3-34.170 provides doctrinal guidance for engineer reconnaissance across the full spectrum of operations. The manual introduces engineer technical reconnaissance support and infrastructure reconnaissance. Doctrine officially names the essential services restoration model the 'Infrastructure Assessment and Survey Model' but recognizes that most practitioners call it the 'SWEAT Model.' The doctrinal SWEAT Model provides a basic understanding of the essential services categories, conditions, and end states required for success. Doctrine provides key tasks required in a typical restoration landscape and expects practitioners to use engineering references and smart books to increase effectiveness.

54. US Department of the Army, US Army FM 3-0 Operations (Washington, DC: Government Printing Office, 2008), 6-7. Commanders and staffs analyze civil considerations in terms of the categories expressed in the memory aid ASCOPE (areas, structures, capabilities, organizations, people, and events). Civil considerations help commanders develop an understanding of the social, political, and cultural variables within the area of operations and how these affect the mission.

55. FM 3-34.170, C-2.

56. SWEAT Smart Book, 108-112. The assessment and measurement techniques provided by the SWEAT Smart Book outlined measuring service levels using the green, amber, yellow, black system. The infrastructure category tables provide a description of status. Based on the assessed status of infrastructure, practitioners can establish required tasks or objectives needed to reach long-term objectives.

57. SWEAT Smart Book., 120 (References). The SWEAT Smart Book focuses on use of resource and project prioritization to meet unit objectives. The general criteria of effort, health

and safety, cost, local perception, self-governance, and infrastructure interdependence help units and commanders understand local needs and develop their final prioritization. The SWEAT Smart Book credits the United States Military Academy with developing the exact same categories. "The United States Military Academy has developed criteria to assist the commander in determining the prioritization of infrastructure within his area. The following are general criteria to assist the commander and his staff."

58.   SWEAT Smart Book., 3-5.

59.   Galula, 54-56.

60.   FM 3-34.170 / MCWP 3-17.4, 170 and C-2.

61.   US Department of the Army, US Army FM 5-0 The Operations Process (Washington, DC: Government Printing Office, 2010), 1-5 and C-7. Operational variables, PMESII-PT, and civil considerations, ASCOPE, represent tools that allow commanders to understand and visualize the battlefield. Both variables provide valuable information on essential services.

62.   US Department of the Army, US Army FM 3-34.400 General Engineering (Washington, DC: Government Printing Office, 2008), Appendix C. Appendix C provides a complete explanation of rating systems and category color coding based on outcomes of the engineer technical assessment.

63.   Author's Note: Factor in this monograph literally means 'who or which acts' and highlights the importance of using geography and culture to filter the basic essential services into a refined focus. In the Factor-Precedence model's application, factors differ from area to area, but subordinate units should nest their analysis with conclusions and guidance from their higher headquarters.

64.   Dan A. Morrison, Geo-Cultural Analysis ToolTM (GCAT). Remarks and presentation delivered at the US DoD Modeling and Simulation (M&S) Conference in Orlando, FL on March 10, 2008. Champagne, IL: US Army Research & Development Center (ERDC), 2008, 26. In 2008, ERDC proposed a complete Geo-Cultural Analysis Tool (GCAT) to "put people back into the picture, put socio-culture in its place on the map."

65.   Author's Note: Precedence in this monograph literally means the condition of being considered more important than someone or something else; priority in rank; the right to precede in order, rank, importance, or priority.

66.   Author's Note: The Factor-Precedence Model can easily accommodate use of and interaction with all of the programs, models, tools, and techniques listed in Factor-Precedence Model Figure.

67.   David J. Kilcullen, "Counterinsurgency in Iraq: Theory and Practice, 2007," Small Wars Center of Excellence Counterinsurgency Seminar 07 (CS 07 – 26 September 2007), Quantico, VA: Marine Corps Warfighting Laboratory, 2007. Report written by Mr. David Dilegge. http:// smallwarsjournal.com/documents/COINSeminarSummaryReport.doc (accessed on December 4, 2010), 53. David Kilcullen provides this direct quote in his presentation. See also John A Nagl, Learning to Eat Soup With a Knife: Counterinsurgency Lessons from Malaya and Vietnam (Chicago, IL: University of Chicago Press, 2005), 91. Under Templer, the British developed a successful counterinsurgency doctrine that their military used throughout the rest of the campaign. Templer instilled his emphasis on innovation and honest assessment throughout the British Army in Malaya. Templer's efforts allowed the British Army to adapt to the insurgents over the following years.

68.   Nagl, 101. Major Bill Tee, an army officer working with Templer in Malaya, noticed positive impacts of working military and political agendas together to provide water, electricity, and other essential services in areas where security forces set the right conditions.

69.   Author's Note: The author served during Operation IRAQI FREEDOM (OIF) from 2007 to 2009 in one of MND-B's subordinate units, 2/25 Stryker Brigade Combat Team (SBCT). Although the Factor-Precedence Model did not exist at the time, the 1st Cavalry Division deviated so much from existing SWEAT Models and focused so heavily on assessments, reconnaissance, holistic prioritization, and constant re-evaluation that the 2009 case study provides a framework for showing key elements of the Factor-Precedence Model. The military's use

70.   Author's Note: The Army also uses evaluation (eval) criteria to compare feasible courses of action (COAs) during the detailed planning process known as the Military Decision Making Process (MDMP). The case evaluation framework builds on both political science's comparative politics methodology and the Army's course of action evaluation criteria to compare the SWEAT Model and the Factor-Precedence Model. More details on the evaluation criteria follow in Table 1.

71.   Paul Davidson Reynolds, A Primer on Theory Construction (Boston, MA: Allyn & Bacon, 1971), 135. According to Reynolds, keeping things simple remains an important part of effective theory or models. He stated that, "[t]wo 'easy' concepts may be considered 'simpler' than one 'difficult' concept."

72.   John Lewis Gaddis, The Landscape of History: How Historians Map the Past (New York, NY: Oxford University Press, 2002), 79. According to Gaddis, effective models adapt to sensitive or fast changing initial conditions. Most establish common categories then applying screening factors to situations.

73.   Gaddis, 107-108. Gaddis wrote that reproducibility means that repeated application of a model or theory to past, present, and future cases will match closely with reality. Effective models for essential services must match not only the past, but they need to predict with some level of certainty the future.

74.   Antoine Bousquet, The Scientific Way of Warfare. (New York, NY: Columbia University Press, 2009), 21. a model or scientific discourse's "ability to transform radically its constitutive theories and frameworks while still claiming a single corpus and methodology. It is this ability to remould [sic] itself that has secured science's lasting legitimacy as the central authoritative discourse in the Western World."

75.   Bousquet, The Scientific Way of Warfare, 4. Linking "The scientific way of warfare therefore refers to an array of scientific rationalities, techniques, frameworks of interpretation, and intellectual dispositions which have characterised [sic] the approach to the application of socially organised [sic] violence in the modern era."

76.   Catherine Dale, Operation IRAQI FREEDOM: Strategies, Approaches, Results, and Issues for Congress – RL34387. Washington, DC: Congressional Research Service, 2009. http://www.fas.org/sgp/crs/mideast/RL34387.pdf (accessed on January 25, 2011), 140.

77.   Dale, Operation IRAQI FREEDOM., 62. CJTF-7 planned to lead the security line and provide support to CPA efforts in other areas. Almost immediately, CJTF-7 began fighting a stronger-than-expected Iraqi insurgency. These lines of operation, also called categories of effort at the time, evolved greatly over time as leaders and commanders in the field interacted with decision makers in Washington, DC In the absence of a comprehensive reconstruction plan, dialogue continued about the best ways to achieve security and while improving the complex lines of politics, economics, and essential services.

78.   Dale, Operation IRAQI FREEDOM, 32-42. The new US Embassy, led by Ambassador John Negroponte, had no direct rule requirements from the CPA. Instead, the Iraq Embassy only had only responsibility for representing American interests and coordinating efforts with the military.

See also, Chiarelli and Michaelis, 6. Throughout 2004, Marine attacks in Fallujah, just west of Baghdad, and militia leader Muqtada al-Sadr's grass roots movement in Baghdad's Sadr City cause increased violence and spillover issues in the streets of Baghdad. The insurgents deftly placed blame for the "lack of power" squarely on the impotence of the fledgling Iraqi Government and supporting coalition forces, citing the historical truth of power always being available under the Saddam regime.

79.   Dale, Operation IRAQI FREEDOM, 48-49. To support and partner with the military components of the Interim Government of Iraq, MNF-I gained command and control responsibility for the Multi-National Corps-Iraq (MNC-I), also located in Baghdad. MNC-I became the operational-level headquarters reporting to MNF-I and had responsibility for synchronizing coalition forces actions throughout Iraq. The overall strategy focused on defeating insurgents and terrorists conventionally. Then, Coalition Forces could eliminate unconventional support to the enemy from the local population while increasing legitimacy of the Iraqi government.

80.   Frederick Barton and Bathsheba Crocker, Progress or Peril? Measuring Iraq's Reconstruction (Washington, DC: Center for Strategic and International Studies, 2004), 52. Reconstruction of infrastructure had progressed slowly after the invasion. Problems with corruption, increasing demand, and unreasonably high expectations of coalition forces ability to immediately provide services decreased population support for the Iraqi government and American counterinsurgency support. Combat battalions, along with their Iraqi district and city engineer counterparts, identified many shortfalls and projects. Until ERP became available, they lacked the funds and manpower to execute improvements.

81.   Steven C. Draper, 1st Cavalry Division Museum Director, "1st Cavalry Division History - GWOT History." Fort Hood, TX: 2010 1st Cavalry Division Museum. http://www.hood.army. mil/1stcavdiv/about/history/gwot.htm (accessed on January 25, 2011), 2-5. Mr. Draper provided a variety of unclassified documents outlining the efforts and accomplishments of 1st Cavalry Division in 2005. Upon taking command in Iraq, the division gained direct control of more than 39,000 uniformed members and 62 battalions of active duty, reserve, and National Guard Soldiers, Marines, and international coalition partners.

82.   Chiarelli and Michaelis, 7. According to Major General Chiarelli, the Division engaged in multiple lines of operations simultaneously to defeat the enemy and win the support of the Iraqi people. Combat Operations, Train & employ Security Forces, Essential Services, Promote Governance, and Economic Pluralism) while mutual supporting, were discrete, the sixth – Information Operations.

83.   Bruce Pirnie and Edward O'Connell, Counterinsurgency in Iraq (2003-2006) (Santa Monica, CA: RAND National Defense Research Institute, 2008), 41-42.

84.   Chiarelli and Michaelis, 6. Figure 7 shows the author's recreation of Major General Chiarelli and TF Baghdad's lines of operation (LOO). General Chiarelli established his LOOs to focus his forces on securing and stabilizing the Iraqi environment to facilitate a legitimate, freely elected city government that accepts economic pluralism. Essential services would become a major part of Chiarelli's Campaign Plan.

85.   Plummer, 2. Plummer's monograph lays out the differences between essential services in Baghdad before and after the war. By 2005, the difference between the Iraqi populace's expectations of what American forces could provide in essential services versus the actual amount of change on the ground caused a great deal of tension and violence in Baghdad and in neighboring provinces.

86.   Plummer, 1-2. 1st Cavalry Division written orders and after-action-reports outline the division's essential services restoration approach as the SWET, SWET-H, or SWET-MSO Model. For simplification, this monograph will refer to these approaches as the SWEAT Model.

87. Chiarelli and Michaelis, 10. The division dedicated the expertise of the engineer corps and established a cooperative effort with the University of Baghdad to identify, fund, and work with local government officials, contractors. They also worked with the US Department of State and the US Agency for International Development (USAID) to provide the essential services critical to demonstrating those visible first-mile signs of progress in areas most likely to produce insurgent activity.

88. Fullerton and Myers, 7. According to Fullerton and Myers, the Brigade Troops Battalion (BTB) usually provides a Brigade Combat Team with intelligence, engineering, military police, administrative, and management support during required contingency missions or operations.

89. Plummer, 11.

90. Office of the Assistant Secretary of the Army (Acquisition, Logistics, & Technology) and the US Army Corps of Engineers, "Iraq Reconstruction Report: Focusing on Construction and Sustainment, 12.08.06" Arlington, VA: Strategic Communications Office, 2006. http://www. dvidshub.net/index.php?script=pubs/pubs_show.php&id=18&name=Iraq%20Reconstruction%20 Report (accessed on January 25, 2011), 2-3.

91. Joseph A. Christoff, "Rebuilding Iraq: Status of Funding and Reconstruction Efforts," Report to Congressional Committees - GAO-05-876 (July 2005), United States Government Accountability Office (GAO): Washington, DC, 2005, http://www.gao.gov/new.items/d05876.pdf (accessed on January 25, 2011), 7. This chart highlights use of the SWEAT Model throughout Iraq. The figure also shows that little change took place in spending during 2004 and 2005. Spending focused on the SWEAT-MSO categories and dwarfed security and justice spending. The report makes the critical note, almost foreshadowing, that without security all essential services will ultimately fail.

92. Joseph A. Christoff, Rebuilding Iraq: Stabilization, Reconstruction, and Financing Challenges - GAO-06-428T, Testimony before the Committee on Foreign Relations, United States Senate (February 8, 2006), United States Government Accountability Office (GAO): Washington, DC, 2006, http://www.gao.gov/new.items/d06428t.pdf (accessed on January 25, 2011), 19.

93. Barton and Crocker, 45-55. This national survey of Iraq shows the importance of jobs and basic needs to the people. By the end of 2005, the survey shows a growing trend of displeasure with Government of Iraq (GoI) and Coalition Force (CF) performance based on the limited services and growing violence.

94. Barton and Crocker, 52-64. This table outlines the author's interpretation of Iraqi services satisfaction at the time of Barton and Crocker's survey. The percentages outline general percentage of people surveyed who met each criteria or category. Barton and Crocker show that most perceptions actually decreased between 2004 and 2006 because of the Coalition's inability to deliver goods and services at a rate higher than Saddam's regime and because of the Iraqi populace's heightened expectations for services and support.

95. Christoff, 15-25. The results of the US Joint Warfare Analysis Center's summer of 2006 survey of some of the local population in Iraq will reveal that the majority of their higher priority needs and concerns were not being addressed or met by the US Coalition forces or the Iraqi government.

96. Office of the Assistant Secretary of the Army (Acquisition, Logistics, & Technology) and the US Army Corps of Engineers, 6. This 2006 report shows drops in almost all essential services areas between 2004 and 2006. Based on enemy attacks and project delays, the real and perceived restoration of essential services failed to help the people of Baghdad and improve their support to the Iraqi Government.

97. Dale, 136. Graphic portrays the number of attacks in Iraq by month on Coalition Forces and their partners. The 1st Cavalry Division transferred authority to the 3d Infantry Division in February 2005 and completed redeployment in April 2005. Dale points out that after a large drop in late 2004, early 2005, attacks steadily increased through the "surge." See also Figure 10 for a graphical representation.

98. Christoff, 6 and 15. Although the direct correlation between essential services and violence exists outside the scope of this monograph, the GAO's data shows that project completion helped decrease violence in early 2005. Violence escalated as the security situation deteriorated and Coalition Forces projects began to fail due to lack of maintenance.

99. Dale, 67-70. Dale provides a comprehensive outline of the Bush Administration's "clear, hold, build" approach and language that led up to continued after the "surge." Dale found most of his information in the White House Fact Sheet: "Strategy for Victory – Clear, Hold, Build" dated March 20, 2006.

100. Bianka J. Adams, Command Report, 2009 Multi-National Division Baghdad, 1st US Cavalry Division (Fort Hood, TX: Division Historian Publications, 2010), http://www.ndia.org/ Divisions/Divisions/SOLIC/Documents/Command_Report_12-10-10.pdf (accessed on January 25, 2011), 7. Often called the Baghdad Security Plan, Operation FARDH AL QANOON displayed an offensive nature and established security sites and operating bases in the Iraqi community. Within the Baghdad area of operations, the Department of State embedded civilian-heavy PRTs with military units at the brigade level, ePRTs, and division level, PRT-B, to assist with humanitarian aid and reconstruction projects. See also Dale, 73-74.

101. Author's Note: MNC-I forms the operational-level command under MNF-I so General Odierno already had intimate knowledge of the area and understood the inner-workings of General Petraeus' plan.

102. Adams, 8. The Security Agreement's Articles 4 and 22 took effect in January 1, 2009 and established the parameters within which the US forces could conduct operations.

103. Adams, 6.

104. Adams, 6 and 14. In February 2009, MND-B was an organization of six Brigade Combat Teams (BCTs) including 1st and 3d Brigade Combat Teams (BCT), 4th Infantry Division; 3rd BCT, 82nd Airborne Division; 2nd Stryker Brigade Combat Team (SBCT), 25th Infantry Division; BCT, 1st Infantry Division; and the 2nd BCT, 1st Armored Division. The 4th Combat Aviation Brigade provided air support.

105. Adams, 11. The Commander's Intent published by Major General Bolger stated that MND-B would "[p]rotect the people of Baghdad – that's why we're here. Operating by, with, and through our Iraqi Security partners, we isolate the enemy (AQI, VE, others as designated) intimidating the people. Combined offensive operations provide the sustainable security that permits continued Iraqi political and economic growth. As Iraqi civil capacity expands our emphasis on stability operations increases proportionately. Throughout, we'll fight to see Baghdad as it is: the people, the enemy, and our combined forces. Success equals the Baghdad population secure, the enemy resurgence denied, and our partnership with the Iraqis strengthened."

106. Adams, 8. Adams provides a quote taken from OPORD 09-01A. The unit's overview of mission, intent, and end state provided italics for emphasis in the original operations order. The commander's intent stated that "[s]uccess equals the Baghdad population secure, the enemy resurgence denied, and our partnership with the Iraqis strengthened." The end state envisioned the affirmation of GoI authority, increased local government capacity and the rule of law, open and fair elections, equitable access to essential services, and increasing and sustaining employment.

107. Adams, 34 and 47. This figure shows the author's interpretation and summary of the 1st Cavalry's Campaign Plan portrayed in the 2009 Command Report.

108. Adams, 12. The brigades supported the division's capacity building efforts through Commanders' Emergency Response Program funding critical projects.

109. Adams, 40-41. Based on MNF-I guidance to place PRT-B in the lead for actions within Baghdad Province, Colonel Timothy Parks, MND-B Chief of Staff, adopted a no-traditional staff structure consisting of centers, cells, and working groups to streamline the decision making process and connect actions with both PRT-B and Iraqi counterparts. There were four division centers, Current Operations, Future Operations, G5 Plans, and Assessments supported by four cells, Iraqi Security Forces Cell, Targeting, Civil Capacity, and Engagements.

110. Adams, 74.

111. Adams, 71.

112. Author's Note: Rural government structures around Baghdad, Iraq started at the local level with Nahias. A Nahia equates roughly to a town or city council in the United States. The Nahias answered to the next level of rural government, the Qada. A Qada equates roughly to a District or county in the United States. Each Qada reported directly to the Governorate led by the Governor of Baghdad. The Amanat, or literally city hall, ran the metropolitan region of Baghdad as an equivalent to a national ministry. Baghdad Amanat approved and managed all operations and projects inside the city limits.

113. Adams, 40-41.

114. Adams. Based on MNF-I guidance to place PRT-B in the lead for actions within Baghdad Province, Colonel Timothy Parks, MND-B Chief of Staff, adopted a no-traditional staff structure consisting of centers, cells, and working groups to streamline the decision making process and connect actions with both PRT-B and Iraqi counterparts. There were four division centers, Current Operations, Future Operations, G5 Plans, and Assessments supported by four cells, Iraqi Security Forces Cell, Targeting, Civil Capacity, and Engagements.

115. Adams. 68. The GOI and the Coalition Forces had originally agreed on the new procedure in October 2008, but neither side had applied it.

116. Adams. In practice, it had an unintended side effect of slowing down projects which the BCTs wanted to perform because most projects now required Amanat, Governorate, or Ministerial approval. Iraqi project verification and approval could take weeks, if not months before an authorized official signed the approval documents.

117. Norris Jones, "Upgrading Baghdad Essential Services." Iraq Reconstruction Report (December 2006). Baghdad, Iraq: United States Army Corps of Engineers, 2006, 2. In addition to taking too long for military units to execute, strategic level and long duration projects typically required more expertise than MND-B or its subordinate brigades could provide. Large scale project responsibilities shifted to entities such as the Iraqi Transition Assistance Office for the Department of State and the US Army Corps of Engineers (USACE) for the Department of Defense. The USACE International Zone office took over 150 projects worth $500 million to upgrade essential services in Baghdad.

118. Author's Note: As mentioned earlier, the Department of State provided ePRTs to work with many of the brigades who owned important areas of operations. These ePRTs worked on important political and economic missions alongside the combat brigades and eventually took the lead on operations after the Security Agreement went into effect.

119. Adams, 71.

120. Adams, 78.

121. Adams, 7.

122. Adams, 67.

123. Special Inspector General for Iraq Reconstruction (SIGIR), "October 2010 Quarterly Report to Congress." http://www.sigir.mil/publications/quarterlyreports/index.html (accessed on November 20, 2010), 20-22.

124. Dale, 137.

125. SIGIR, "October 2010 Quarterly Report to Congress," 22.

126. The SWEAT/IR Book, 5.

127. US Department of State and US Department of Defense, "United States Government Integrated Civilian – Military Campaign Plan (ICMCP) for Support to Afghanistan – Revision 1," Kabul, Afghanistan: US Embassy Office, 2011. http://ccoportal.org/file/2238/download/3208 (accessed on February 23, 2011), 4-8.

128. Pierson, 41. According to Captain Pierson's outline, essential services fell under the Infrastructure, Services, and Economy line of effort. The essential services line of effort received direct inputs from the security, host-nation government capacity, and coalition capacity lines of effort. The essential services line of effort contributed directly to the influence of the narcotics industry and the balance of popular support for the host nation.

129. US Department of State and US Department of Defense, "ICMCP," 32-33. According to the ICMCP, the new RC South Stabilization approach and operating framework utilizes the RC South Headquarters at Kandahar along with three Provincial Construction Teams (PRTs), 6 District Stabilization Teams (DSTs), and 12 Key Terrain Districts (KTDs) to cover a large portion of the south and central part of the country.

130. Regional Command - South also has names such as Region Command - South, RC South, or RC(S) in different Afghanistan War documents. The 10th Mountain Division assumed command of the Regional Command – South area of operations in November 2010.

131. Regional Command - South. Figure 15 shows how the Factor-Precedence Model can integrate results from local reconnaissance, needs assessment, and factor refinement with existing products in Regional Command -South. Practitioners can monitor execution of projects just like RC South already does, then the practitioner can tie his or her assessment criteria into re-evaluation of local needs. Fusing the existing development plan with Factor-Precedence Model capabilities can increase sustainability with local leaders.

132. Regional Command - South. The author created this product to consolidate many of RC-South's ideas and tracking products into a generic example.

133. Special Inspector General for Afghanistan Reconstruction (SIGAR), "October 2010 Quarterly Report to Congress," http://www.sigar.mil/pdf/quarterlyreports/Oct2010/Lores/SIGAR4Q_2010Book.pdf (accessed on November 20, 2010), 20.

134. SIGAR, 24.

135. SIGAR, 58, 82, 97-102.

136. Islamic Republic of Afghanistan, Afghanistan National Development Strategy (2008-2013): A Strategy for Security, Governance, Economic Growth, and Poverty Reduction (Kabul, Afghanistan: Afghanistan National Development Strategy Secretariat, 2009), 10-15.

137. SIGAR, 97.

138. Robert Gates, "Landon Lecture Series Secretary of Defense Speech," Kansas State University Landon Lecture (26 November 2007). Washington, DC: Office of the Assistant Secretary of Defense (Public Affairs), 2007, 1. http://www.defense.gov/Speeches/Speech.aspx?SpeechID=1199 (accessed December 7, 2010).

139. Valentina Taddeo, "US Response to Terrorism: A Strategic Analysis of the Afghanistan Campaign," Journal of Strategic Security, 3 (2010): 27-38. http://scholarcommons.usf.edu/cgi/viewcontent.cgi?article=1010&context=jss (accessed January 25, 2011), 27.

140. Michael R. Lindeburg, Civil Engineering Reference Manual for the PE Exam, 11th Edition. Belmont, CA: Professional Publications, Inc. (PPI), 2008, Introduction.

141. FM 3-07, 1-20. Hybrid threats use a variety of approaches to fighting. According to the FM, the Second Lebanon War of 2006 highlighted hybrid warfare by Hezbollah against Israel. A key take-away, against outside the scope of this monograph, is that the restoration of essential services exists during major combat, counterinsurgency, or humanitarian assistance operations; therefore, the Factor-Precedence model could prove useful in situations other than counterinsurgency.

142. Samuel Griffith, Mao Tse-Tung On Guerrilla Warfare (Baltimore, MD: The Nautical & Aviation Publishing Company of America, 1992), 71.

143. Kalev Sepp and John Nagl provide outlines of British efforts in Malaya, the history, and lessons learned. See Kalev Sepp, "Best Practices in Counterinsurgency." Military Review (May-June 2005): 10 for a conflict review and best practices. See also John A. Nagl, Learning to Eat Soup With a Knife: Counterinsurgency Lessons from Malaya and Vietnam. Chicago, IL: University of Chicago Press, 2005 for a comprehensive book on the conflict and French lessons learned.

144. Bertrand Valeyre and Alexandre Guerin, "From Galula to Petraeus: The French Legacy in the US Counterinsurgency Doctrine." Cahier de la Recherché Doctrinale (Christine Valley, France: Centre de Doctrine d'Emploi des Forces (CDEF), 2010), 10-12; Galula, 89. Frenchmen Bertrand Valeyre, Alendre Guerin, and David Galula provide great information on France's efforts in Algeria. Both books provided critical lessons information concerning the conflict along with French military and political lessons learned.

145. Galula, 74.

146. Galula.

147. Andrew J. Birtle, US Army Counterinsurgency and Contingency Operations Doctrine 1942-1976. Washington, DC: Center of Military History, 2007, 148. CMH outlines the history of recent US Counterinsurgency operations and doctrine. Throughout the book, it refers to guerillas in the same way modern doctrine refers to insurgents.

148. Birtle, 14.

149. Birtle, 291 and 299.

150. Birtle, 208-209.

151. A. J. Langguth, Our Vietnam: The War, 1954-1975 (New York, NY: Simon and Schuster, 2000), 15; Jacob Kipp, "The Human Terrain System a CORDS for the 21st Century." Military Review 86, no. 5 (September-October 2006): 8-15, 11. American stability and essential services operations in Vietnam played a large part in modern counterinsurgency operations. CORDS and HES became components of an effective pacification campaign that improved late-war situations but failed to overcome political pressure for withdrawal.

152. FM 3-24, 2-13.

153. SIGAR, 97.

154. Fullerton and Myers, 4-5.

155. Kilcullen, "Countering Global Insurgency," Small Wars Journal (NOV 04), Richmond, VA: Small Wars Foundation LLC, 2004. Available at http://smallwarsjournal.com/documents/ kilcullen.pdf. Accessed on 20 NOV 10, 33.

156. SWEAT Smart Book, 1-33. Figure 18 shows the NTC SWEAT Smart Book's digital cover.

157. SWEAT Smart Book, 3.

158. SWEAT Smart Book, 109. The SWEAT Smart Book provides several measures of performance that compare the specified infrastructure category with generally acceptable levels of performance or output.

159. Lindberg, et al, 2-33.

160. Lindberg, et al, 33.

161. The SWEAT/IR Book, 1-8. Because the USAES has deemed the technical contents and several images within this book Unclassified – For Official Use Only (FOUO), the author has limited the use of the use of this source. This monograph contains no FOUO information. Because the SWEAT/IR Book provides such utility in the field, practitioners can find digital copies of this document online or through the USAES.

162. FM 3-07, Figure 4-2, 4-11; see also FM 3-34.170, C-1.

163. FM 3-07, Figure 4-1, 4-10.

164. Author's Note: Proposed in late 2010, the Factor-Precedence Model walks practitioners through geo-cultural screening of infrastructure categories then helps establish prioritization for execution.

165. Author's Note: As outlined earlier, the Factor-Precedence Model is a way to develop reflection and prioritization on essential services restoration within the context of existing environments and tools.

166. Precedence Defined: See Appendix 1. The condition of being considered more important than someone or something else; priority in rank. The right to precede in order, rank, or importance; priority.

167. FM 5-0, 1-5 and C-7. Operational variables, PMESII-PT, and civil considerations, ASCOPE, represent tools that allow commanders to understand and visualize the battlefield.

168. SWEAT Smart Book, 1-52. The book dedicates considerable time to providing a comprehensive outline of each essential services category. Each category had detailed descriptions, system explanations, and reconnaissance forms for practitioners. Table 7 provides a summary of key elements of reach category as they integrate into the Factor-Precedence Model. For additional information, see the SWEAT Smart Book. The SWEAT/IR Book also goes into considerable detail on each category.

169. Dan A Morrison, Geo-Cultural Analysis ToolTM (GCAT). Remarks and presentation delivered at the US DoD Modeling and Simulation (M&S) Conference in Orlando, FL on March 10, 2008. Champagne, IL: US Army Research & Development Center (ERDC), 2008, 26. In 2008, ERDC proposed a complete Geo-Cultural Analysis Tool (GCAT) to "put people back into the picture, put socio-culture in its place on the map."

170. Jeffrey Herbst, States and Power in Africa: Comparative Lessons in Authority and Control (Princeton, NJ: Princeton University Press, 2000), 45.

171. Hofstede, 21.

172. Maslow, 195; Malinowski, 23.

173. The Sphere Project, Humanitarian Charter and Minimum Standards in Disaster Response. (Oxford, England: Oxfam Publishing, 2004), 16.

174. Maslow, 195; see also Hofstede, 21.

175. Skinner, 1-26; see also Gorkowski, 45.

176. Kilcullen, 16.

177. SWEAT Smart Book, 3-5.

178. SWEAT Smart Book.

179. Skinner, 1-26; see also Gorkowski, 45.

Shari'a Compliant Finance
The Overlooked Element for Developing an Effective Financial System in Afghanistan
by
Lieutenant Colonel Jan Willem Maas - Royal Netherlands Army
Abstract

An effective financial system is essential to economic development. US Army doctrine acknowledges that military forces play an important role in supporting economic stabilization and infrastructure development. A specific task is to support the financial system. However, stability operations have not always been successful. First, Western stability operations have constrained economic development because the cultural paradigms of the Western actors and the local population have not fit. Second, segments of the Muslim community perceive Islamic banks as more reliable than other banks. Both reasons endanger the trust of Muslims in the financial system, which limits bank penetration and therefore hampers economic development.

This monograph argues that the application of *Shari'a* Compliant Finance (SCF) increases bank penetration and thereby improves economic development during stability operations in Afghanistan. Research found that Western organizations mainly used Western financial principles to develop the financial system in Afghanistan, while neglecting positive effects of SCF. The best way to apply SCF in order to improve the development of a financial system during stability operations is by facilitating local efforts that make use of religious reasoning and the social environment in order to gain and maintain subjective confidence. In order to mitigate the risk for sustainability of SCF on the longer term, international organizations like the World Bank and the IMF should maintain their focus on how to evolve a SCF system into a system that is still *Shari'a* compliant but also fulfills internationally recognized financial standards.

To support the development of a financial system successfully, commanders need to understand the implications of SCF. By appreciating and applying SCF, commanders can increase the trust of the population in their financial system resulting in increased bank penetration and economic development. This leads to five lessons for military commanders. The first lesson is that SCF is an alternative or at least a valuable complement for the development of a financial system in Afghanistan. The second lesson is that commanders should question and challenge the Western paradigm by a Muslim paradigm in order to prevent that the military commander develops a deficient operational approach. The third lesson is that the military has to invest in basic knowledge of the Afghan society, Islam, and SCF. The fourth lesson is that the military should start building partnerships with other organizations to enable unified action. The final lesson is that the military commander should focus on facilitating local efforts instead of providing a solution for the development of the financial system in order to achieve the maximum development results.

Introduction

According to the President of the Kauffman Foundation, a country can only have peace and prosperity when its people truly own their economy.[1]

US Army doctrine acknowledges that military forces play an important role in supporting economic stabilization and infrastructure development.[2] A specific task is to support strengthening the local economy. This includes support of the financial system.[3] To be successful in supporting a financial system, commanders need a complete and thorough understanding of the operational environment.[4] Because Islamic finance is part of an Islamic society, it is important that commanders understand the implications of *Shari'a* compliant finance (SCF), especially when supporting the financial system in an Islamic country like Afghanistan. Understanding SCF can help to establish confidence of Muslims in their financial system in order to increase bank penetration and thereby improve economic development. Bank penetration is the percentage of firms or people in a specific area that use banks or other financial institutions to fulfill financial services.

Until recently, the international community did not even consider Islam when developing the economy in Afghanistan. For example, in a report of the World Bank published in December 2005 the World Bank assessed the investment climate in Afghanistan.[5] The World Bank published the report four years after the start of the stabilization operation in Afghanistan.[6] They acknowledged the importance of an effective financial system and even stated that access to finance was severely constrained for companies. However, not once did the World Bank refer to SCF.[7] The negligence of SCF is probably one of the reasons why the World Bank and others developed in Afghanistan a financial system based solely on Western principles. Only in 2010 and 2011 did the Afghan legislature draft an Islamic banking law to enable SCF.[8]

The literature mentions two main reasons why the development of a Western financial system in an Islamic country is not successful. First, Western stability operations constrain economic development because Western development organizations and the local population have different cultural paradigms.[9] This occurs because a segment of the Muslim population perceives conventional banks as un-Islamic because of the application of interest.[10] In addition, conventional financial products do not fulfill the needs of the population because they are not *Shari'a* compliant.[11] Second, a part of the Muslim community has no or very limited confidence in the imposed Western financial system because they believe that Islamic banks are more reliable and more stable than other banks.[12] This monograph defines this kind of confidence as subjective confidence, which means the way Muslims, individually or as a group, perceive their confidence in the financial system. This is different from objective confidence. There is objective confidence when banks fulfill the internationally recognized standards for financial institutions. The disconnect between the Western and Islamic paradigm and the perceived reliability of Islamic banks constrains bank penetration and therefore endangers economic development.

By neglecting SCF during planning and execution, stability operations do not take into account the presumed positive effects of SCF as an alternative to economic development. A Malaysian study showed a positive correlation between Islamic banking and economic development.[13] According to other literature, the Islamic financial system facilitates economic development because it promotes socio-economic goals: applying SCF promotes social justice, equity, poverty alleviation, and human well-being. By achieving these goals, SCF copes with financial and social exclusion and, therefore, increases the number of people that can benefit from economic growth.[14]

This monograph will argue that the application of SCF increases bank penetration and thereby improves economic development during stability operations in Afghanistan. Although some scientists claim that SCF products are only Islamic in form but not in content and SCF institutions have objective confidence shortcomings, the evidence will show that SCF improves subjective confidence and fulfills the needs of Muslims.

To substantiate this thesis, the monograph consists of five sections. The first section uses Afghanistan as a case study to determine the level of effectiveness of the Afghan financial system. The second section defines SCF and describes the sources, principles, products, and standards of SCF. The third section describes the possible ways SCF can facilitate the development of the formal financial system as claimed in predominantly Islamic literature. The fourth section applies elements of SCF to the financial system of Afghanistan. The fifth section describes the lessons military commanders at the operational level can learn when they support the development of a financial system in an Islamic society.

In order to conduct successful stability tasks, commanders must take into account that each country has its own unique characteristics that guide economic development.[15] By understanding the implications of SCF, military efforts to support the development of a financial system can improve. Therefore, this monograph creates a nuanced and culturally sensitive solution, which will contribute to a successful result of a stability operation in an Islamic country such as Afghanistan.

Afghan Financial Development Results

This subsection reviews the development of the Afghan financial system as a contemporary example of developing a financial system during stability operations. This review shows that Western organizations developed the financial system in Afghanistan using mainly Western principles while neglecting the positive effects of SCF.

To provide a complete overview, this subsection will first describe the confidence necessary for the financial system to be effective. Second, this subsection will describe the major organizations and the ways in which they provided support for the development of the financial system. This subsection will conclude with the results of the development of the financial system in Afghanistan as assessed by the World Bank, as well as by the central Bank of Afghanistan, *Da Afghanistan Bank* (DAB). This provides an external and internal assessment of the Afghan financial system.

A financial system can only be effective if there is some degree of confidence in the financial system.[16] However, confidence has both subjective and objective elements.[17] It is subjective because it is up to the people to judge whether the system is reliable and whether they are willing to invest and deposit funds in the bank. If subjective confidence is low, people will avoid the formal financial system and local currency.[18] On the other hand, confidence has an objective element that correlates to accountability according to internationally recognized standards. The World Bank emphasized the importance of accountability and transparency for a financial system.[19] An effective financial system that satisfies both subjective and objective confidence helps to reduce risks and lowers the costs of financial transactions in order to facilitate sustainable economic development.

The first organization that supported Afghanistan was the World Bank. They provided technical assistance for the development of the infrastructure and the capacity of the DAB. The World Bank also provided assistance to implement changes in the financial sector. They assisted in improving human resource management, accounting and auditing, and in developing a system to supervise commercial banks according to international standards. An additional task was to improve credit risk assessments in order to reduce risk and increase credit based lending. Finally, the World Bank assisted the DAB and the Afghanistan Bank Association in the development of bankers training.[20] These programs focused on improving the efficiency and reliability of the banking system based on Western standards.

The second organization to offer support to Afghanistan was the International Monetary Fund (IMF). They provided assistance with currency reform, central bank modernization, and new financial and banking legislation.[21] Additionally, an IMF staff team assisted the authorities in developing "a macroeconomic framework to guide economic decision-making" in order to achieve sustainable economic growth.[22] In 2003, the IMF prepared new banking and central bank laws, new payment laws, currency laws, and financial services laws.[23] The IMF also provided technical assistance for the organization, accounting, financial reporting, internal auditing, and an appropriate central bank facility.[24] The IMF also based their support on Western standards.

The third organization that provided support was the United States Agency for International Development (USAID). They focused on four main areas within the financial sector: central bank oversight, retail banking, small and medium enterprise finance, and microfinance. USAID also provided advice on how to implement on-site examinations of commercial banks using trend analysis and methods to bring the accounting system in line with internationally recognized standards. To develop retail banking and small and medium enterprise finance, USAID assisted in the enactment of financial laws and regulations. To facilitate growth of small and medium enterprises, USAID supported the bank's ability to provide loans to these enterprises. As part of microfinance, USAID programs also provided capital and technical assistance in order to facilitate the banking system and to develop *Shari'a* compliant loans and transactions.[25]

With assistance from the World Bank, IMF, and USAID, the government of the Islamic Republic of Afghanistan enacted the DAB Law of 2003. By implementing this law, Afghanistan created an autonomous central bank for Afghanistan.[26] Its tasks, as formulated in Article 2 of DAB Law, are in line with the five internationally recognized standards for a proper functioning central bank. These tasks are control over the local network of banking services or banks, the pursuit of price stability, the facilitation of a stable system of payments, the ability to provide independent economic advice to the government, and the capability to ensure that commercial banks have sufficient financial funds to meet their obligations. According to USAID, DAB accounting and reporting in 2009 and 2010 remains consistent with International Financial Reporting Standards, as prescribed by the International Accounting Standards Board. Therefore, DAB formally fulfills the international recognized standards for a central bank and achieves objective confidence.

Bank penetration and subjective confidence in the financial system in Afghanistan and its region is inadequate. According to the Enterprise Analysis Unit of the World Bank, only 3.4 percent of the firms have a line of credit with a financial institution compared to 8.6 percent in Pakistan and 10.5 percent in Uzbekistan. Among all firms in Afghanistan, 91.6 percent use internal means to finance working capital. In Pakistan, Tajikistan and Uzbekistan it is respectively 86.3 percent, 90.0 percent, and 94.4 percent. Only 1 percent of the Afghan firms use banks to finance working capital, against 1.6 percent in Pakistan, 1.3 percent in Tajikistan, and 3.6 percent in Uzbekistan. If a firm in Afghanistan needs a loan, collateral requirements equal 254 percent of the loan. That is almost twice the average percentage of Tajikistan. Finally, 36.6 percent of the businesses identify access to finance as a major constraint, while the next highest score is only 17.7 in Pakistan (see Table 1). Although the figures show similarities among the four nations, Afghanistan has the lowest level of bank penetration.

Table 1: Bank Penetration in Afghan Region

	Afghanistan (2008)	Pakistan (2007)	Tajikistan (2005)	Uzbekistan (2005)
% of firms that have a line of credit with or loans from financial institution	3.4	8.6	-	10.5
% of firms using internal financed working capital	91.6	86.3	90.0	94.4
% of firms using banks to finance working capital	1.0	1.6	1.3	3.6
% of firms using supplier/customer credit to finance working capital	3.7	11.9	5.0	1.0
% of firms using other means to finance working capital	3.7	0.2	3.7	1.0
Value of collateral as % of loan	253.5	67.7	145.2	122.2
% of firms who identify finance as a major constraint	36.6	17.7	4.4	11.6

Source: World Bank, "Enterprise Surveys," https://www.enterprisesurveys.org/CustomQuery/ Indicators.as px?characteristic=size&indicator=51 (accessed 14 August 2011).

The World Bank described an inadequate level of bank penetration and subjective confidence in the formal financial system of Afghanistan. The local Afghan reports of the DAB describe a different perspective. The DAB confirms in its Strategic Plan 2009–2014 the problem concerning bank penetration in Afghanistan.[27] According to the DAB, there is still a vast number of people, potential entrepreneurs, and small enterprises excluded from the services of the financial system in Afghanistan. Although the DAB does not quantify the problem, the bank confirms that a substantial number of firms are dependent on an informal financial system, like internal ways to finance investments and working capital. This constrains the possibilities for economic growth because capital for expansion is limited.[28] The DAB acknowledges the importance of an effective financial system and formulates the objectives in the strategic plan to promote possibilities for savings, access to credit, and the development of the necessary financial institutions.[29] The DAB specifically mentions the importance of accountability and transparency of the financial system to give customers, investors, and entrepreneur's confidence in the system.[30]

Although the World Bank and the Strategic Plan describe the problems concerning bank penetration, the annual financial report 2008–2009 of the DAB describes a slightly different perspective. The total amount of assets of the Afghan banking system increased by 73.4 percent from March 2008 until March 2009. According to the DAB, this is a sign of increased confidence in the Afghan financial system. The total amount of loans increased over the same period by 25 percent and the deposits increased by 86 percent.[31] However, it is not clear whether there is a correlation between the increase of assets, loans, and deposits and increased bank penetration and confidence. First, the return on assets decreased from 1.8 percent to 1.7 percent.[32] That means that the financial system was less profitable. Based on efficiency, one would expect an increase in profitability when more people use the formal financial system. Second, the DAB does not provide any insight in the amount of individual accounts. This means that it is not possible to estimate whether more people or firms used the formal financial system. It only shows an increased value of assets, loans, and deposits. Third, half of the deposits are in US Dollars.[33] This means that local currency is still not very popular and could indicate a lack of confidence in the financial system and limited bank penetration.[34] It is therefore unlikely that there is an increase in bank penetration and confidence in the Afghan financial system.

Afghanistan received considerable support from very capable financial and development organizations to develop its financial system. However, all three organizations used Western principles to support the development of the Afghan financial system. This support led to objective confidence in the financial system, because the financial system fulfilled the internationally recognized financial standards. However, the support did not secure subjective confidence. Based on data of the World Bank and the DAB, it is justified to conclude that bank penetration and subjective confidence is still extremely low.

Shari'a Compliant Finance

Muslims claim SCF is a valuable alternative to conventional banking.[35] Although the literature mentions the Igibi Bank of Babylon in 575 BC as one of the first Islamic banks, the modern Islamic banking sector is a rather young industry.[36] Modern Islamic finance has existed since 1970.[37] In addition, the first all-embracing Islamic bank was the Dubai Islamic Bank, established in 1975.[38] Since then, the Islamic financial sector has grown enormously. According to a report by Standard and Poor's, Islamic bank assets increased from $639 billion in 2008 to $822 billion in 2009, a total increase of 28.6 percent.[39] Despite the Islamic claims and the growth of the industry, it is not clear what Islamic finance encompasses. Therefore, this section defines SCF – its sources, principles, products, and standards – to create an understanding of the concepts of SCF. This will enable the reader to understand the latter parts in this monograph.

Definition of SCF

There is no precise definition of SCF. Therefore, this monograph will delineate its own definition and starts with a short literature review of SCF definitions. Defining SCF as interest free banking is an example of a narrow definition, while describing SCF as a financial operation conducted by Muslims is too broad.[40] However, there are definitions that are more concise. The first defines SCF as a financial system based on the principles of the *Quran*.[41] Although not very detailed, this definition creates a distinction between a conventional or Western financial system and SCF. Other scholars define SCF as "a system that adheres strictly to the rulings of *Shari'a* in the fields of finance and other dealings."[42] This definition expands it to issues other than financial products. A more comprehensive definition of SCF is:

A non-interest based financial institution, which complies fully with Islamic laws and has creative and progressive financial engineering to offer efficient and competitive banking, investment, trade finance, commercial, and real estate financing services.[43]

This definition encompasses not only the application of Islamic laws but also refers to non-interest based finance as a basic principle of SCF. By mentioning progressive financial engineering, the definition seems to recognize the essential balance between the conformity with Islam and the financial needs of Muslims. A final example of a definition of SCF is a financial system that executes finance in consonance with the ethos of Islam and which is governed by *Shari'a* principles.[44] This definition perfectly describes the intent of SCF.

This monograph defines SCF as a financial system based on Islamic principles and values that offers Muslims a possibility to fulfill their financial needs within the limits of Islam. For further clarification of this definition, values are the beliefs people have about what is right and wrong, what is most important in life, and which control their behavior.[45] The following sections describe the sources, principles, and products of SCF in order to put this definition into perspective.

Sources of SCF

The basis of Islam is that the individual obeys the rules of *Shari'a* because the individual has an agreement or contract with Allah. The rules describe unity and oneness on earth as well as in the hereafter. By obeying the rules, men establish social unity and cohesion. According to the Islam, all conduct contrary to *Shari'a* leads to disunity and disintegration. Final judgment before Allah is as an individual as well as a part of the collective.[46] Therefore, there is an individual as well as a collective motivation to adhere to the rules of *Shari'a*. Although Islam has primary and secondary sources, there are also some major differences between the implementation of Islam because of different schools of thought, movements, and regional customs.

Islamic law has three primary sources and three secondary sources. A pyramid is an allegory for the primary and secondary sources. The first primary source, at the top of the pyramid, is the *Quran*. According to Muslims, this is the Holy Book, the word of God as conveyed to the Prophet Mohammed.[47] The second layer from the top consists of the *Hadith* and the *Sunna,* both primary sources. The *Hadith* are short texts and refer to the words and deeds of the Prophet Mohammed.[48] The *Sunna* explains and analyzes the *Quran* as well as the *Hadith* and consists of the practices and rulings deduced from the *Quran* and the *Hadith.*[49] The third layer of the pyramid consists of secondary sources. These sources are *Ijtihad, Ijma,* and *Qiyas. Ijtihad* refers to the activities of legal scholars to find solutions for emerging problems in a society where the *Quran,* the *Hadith,* and *Sunna* do not provide a solution. *Ijma* and *Qiyas* are the ways legal scholars exercise *Ijtihad.*[50] *Ijma* refers to problem solving by consensus. Muslims believe that consensus by a group of legal scholars in a certain society prevents men from failures to make the right decisions. *Qiyas* provides solutions by analogy or logical inference when the other sources such as the *Quran,* the *Hadith, Sunna,* and *Ijma* do not provide a workable solution for a problem. The legal scholars try to determine how the Prophet Mohammed would have acted in a specific case.[51]

SCF Principles

According to Islamic law, Allah created the universe and controls it. To control life on earth, Allah delegated stewardship to men. However, *Allah* also realized that humans are not without faults. Therefore, Allah provided rules and guidance to men in every part of their life. Because of the contract between Allah and men, men must obey these rules even when these rules go against their personal interests, because adhering to the rules is in the public's interest. Applying the rules brings unity and social cohesion because they take the welfare and well-being of others specifically into account.[52]

The pursuit of unity, cohesion, and the well-being of others is also visible in the four main SCF principles. The first principle is the ban on *Riba*, an amount of money that a borrower must pay to a lender for the use of money and for which the rate is determined beforehand. Islam considers *Riba* as a form of excess. According to some Muslim scientists, the Quran forbids *Riba* because it enslaves the debtor.[53] Other scientists argue that the *Quran* only forbids excessive *Riba*. The *Quran* only forbids charging interest when it brings injustice.[54] The reality is that most Muslims feel uncomfortable when charging or receiving interest. Secondly, money is not an asset in its own right; it is a means to exchange goods. Tangible assets must always back money.[55] This prevents the growth of debt and, therefore, social injustice. The third principle is the avoidance of *Gharar*, failure to disclose information needed to make a decision. The avoidance of *Gharar* means that people must avoid every uncertainty or ambiguity when they trade.[56] The fourth principle, *Haram,* refers to investments that should enhance society. The *Quran* prohibits consuming goods or services such as alcohol, pornography, gambling, and products made of pork.[57] All these principles promote the social unity and cohesion within Islamic societies.

196

SCF Products

To pursue social unity, cohesion, and the well-being of others, SCF created some very specific SCF products. The SCF products of *Mudarabah*, *Musharaka*, and *Murabaha* are not the only SCF products but they are the most common. These SCF products also show how previously mentioned principles work in SCF. *Mudarabah* and *Musharaka* are two profit-and-loss sharing (PLS) products. *Murabaha* is an example of how banks can offer financial products despite the ban on *Riba* (interest). *Mudarabah* is a financial construction based on profit sharing. Within this construction, the bank provides money and the borrower or, more specifically, the entrepreneur does the work. The bank and the entrepreneur share the profit based on a pre-determined ratio. The profit sharing continues as long as there is a debt. When the entrepreneur has repaid the debt, the profit sharing ceases. In the event that the entrepreneur goes bankrupt, the bank shoulders the costs. No one compensates the bank for its losses.[58] *Musharaka* is similar, although, in this construction, the bank as well as the entrepreneur shares the losses in proportion to their investment of finances and work. The bank and the entrepreneur determine the ratio in advance. *Musharaka* is an example of PLS.[59] *Murabaha* is an example how to deal with the ban on Riba in SCF. *Murabaha* is a financial construction in which the bank buys goods and services for the borrower. In this way, the bank does not officially lend money to the borrower; the bank makes a profit on the investment by marking up the prices of the goods or services. Therefore, the borrower has to repay more than the initial costs of the bank's purchase.[60]

Standards of SCF

Three main organizations set the standards and safeguard *Shari'a* character of SCF. The first organization is the Islamic Financial Services Board (IFSB). In 2002, the IMF assisted in founding the IFSB. Its task is supervision and regulation of SCF. Its goal is to complement the work of the Basel Committee on Bank Supervision, which is the organization that sets the standards for internationally recognized banking standards.[61] The second organization is the Accounting and Auditing Organization for Islamic Financial Institutions (AAOIFI). This organization focuses on accounting, auditing, solvency, and the application of *Shari'a*. The AAOIFI issues certifications for SCF institutions and has a *Shari'a* board that tries to unify all the rulings of the individual *Shari'a* boards.[62] The AAOIFI and IFSB are overarching organizations that concentrate on setting the standards for SCF. However, banks do not universally apply those standards and the organizations have no power to enforce the standards.[63] The third organization is the *Shari'a* Supervisory Board (SSB) of each individual bank. These boards consist of at least three Islamic scholars who direct, review, and supervise the activities of the Islamic financial institution in order to ensure *Shari'a* compliance.[64] These boards can issue *Fatwas* to declare financial products are *Shari'a* compliant.

This subsection described the way in which SCF conducts business within the SCF principles and manages the ban on *Riba*. This subsection also described the way in which the Islamic financial system ensures *Shari'a* compliance within the financial system. The SCF products are logical from an Islamic perspective and fit the SCF principles. This does not automatically mean that SCF also improves bank penetration. The following subsection will therefore describe how, according to Islamic literature, SCF can improve bank penetration.

Islamic Proposed Ways to Facilitate Bank Penetration

The function of a financial system is to reduce the risk for investors and to create financial possibilities for entrepreneurs, regardless of whether the financial system is based on religious principles.[65] This subsection describes the possible ways for SCF to facilitate bank penetration in order to bring investors and entrepreneurs together within the financial system.[66] According to the literature, SCF has at least four positive ways to facilitate bank penetration. First, SCF establishes just and equitable distribution of resources. Second, SCF fulfills the specific financial needs of Muslims. Third, SCF is more reliable compared to conventional financial systems. Finally, SCF development depends, for its development, less on a well-functioning rule of law than a conventional financial system.

SCF focuses on just and equitable distribution of resources. The primary focus of SCF is not profit maximization but to enable Muslims to conduct financial transactions in adherence to *Shari'a*.[67] SCF is a welfare system, which focuses on economic development in order to facilitate societal benefits such as just and equitable distribution of resources. The evidence for this statement is the use of PLS and the ban on *Riba* instead of focus on profit maximization like conventional financial systems.[68] A study conducted in Pakistan confirms the welfare aspect of SCF and its contributions to economic development for society as a whole. The research also found that SCF contributes to a higher level of customer satisfaction because of these effects. Therefore, an increased satisfaction of customers contributes to a higher bank penetration.[69] According to the United States Institute of Peace, this means that SCF should be more tolerant of low-income customers and should be prepared to take more risks to provide these customers the financial assets they need.[70] By applying SCF, Islam creates cohesion and social unity as described in the *Quran*. According to Muslims Islam is a comprehensive and all-encompassing system that focuses on sustainable, ethical, and socially responsible behavior on earth as well as in the hereafter.[71]

SCF fulfills the specific financial needs of Muslims. The fact that financial institutions offer SCF can increase bank penetration for Muslims. There will always be Muslims who do not want to participate in a financial system, which is not *Shari'a* compliant.[72] The application of SCF for religious reasons can be that single, important incentive to attract Muslims to the formal financial system in a country.[73] The government of Turkey provided an example when they used SCF in 1983 to attract people to the formal financial system.[74] Although Turkey focused on taming the effects on political Islamists, it shows that emotion can be a reason to use a formal banking system even in a secular state like Turkey. To offer SCF in order to attract Muslims to the formal financial system and increase bank penetration seems even more important in non-secular societies. Afghanistan is an example of a non-secular state. The Director General of the Financial Supervision Department of the Afghan Central Bank, Da Afghanistan Bank (DAB) iterates that the most important reason for Afghans not to participate in the formal banking system is that the financial system is not *Shari'a* compliant.[75] Applying SCF can increase bank penetration among Muslims and therefore improve economic development. The application of SCF can therefore enhance accessibility in a larger area and for a larger group of people that would normally exclude themselves, from a formal non-*Shari'a* compliant financial system.

SCF is more reliable compared to conventional banking for three reasons. The first reason is that SCF is based on PLS. As mentioned previously, the function of the financial system is to reduce risk for investors and to create financial possibilities for entrepreneurs.[76] PLS means that a depositor of money shares in the profit as well as in the losses of the financial institution. Therefore, the financial institution is not the only one that runs the risk when investing money. A SCF institution has less risk for insolvency and can be more reliable than a conventional financial institution.[77] A prerequisite for the depositor is that he has access to information to make a reasonable estimate of his risk.[78] Although PLS can definitely enhance bank penetration, PLS requires a fine balance between the risk for the financial institution and the depositor.[79] When balance of risk is too heavily shifted to the depositor, the flow of money available for investments will decline. This will constrain economic development, especially during stability operations.

The second reason is that SCF is asset backed. This means that tangible goods always back money. A legal right, such as a loan is therefore not enough to back money. As a result, the growth of the total amount of money is limited, as well as the total amount of debt and inflation.[80] Therefore, asset backed money has a positive effect on economic development and on social justice within society.[81]

The third reason is that SCF systems have a rigorous method of self-regulation. The literature refers to the SSB's of each individual bank in conjunction with the Islamic paradigm concerning social behavior. These supervisory boards direct, review and supervise the activities of the Islamic financial institutions in order to ensure sound *Shari'a* compliant finance.[82] Because the paradigm of Islam is that the financial system should be sustainable and ethical, Muslims expect SCF to strengthen internal control of the financial system and therefore facilitate sustainability and reliability of the SCF system.[83]

SCF depends less on a well-functioning rule of law than a conventional financial system. Research conducted in low-income countries, stated that there is a positive correlation between presence of rule of law and development of financial institutions. The rule of law protects the rights of people and therefore limits the costs of doing business. The availability of rule of law therefore enhances the efficiency of the financial system.[84] However, other research found that Islamic banks depend less on the quality of institutions that facilitate rule of law.[85] It highlights a different influence of the rule of law on Islamic banks. The main reason for the limited dependency on rule of law is the strict application of *Shari'a* law. This prevents people's dependence solely on the formal judicial system to protect their rights. Muslim scholars or clerks settle disputes.[86] Therefore, Islamic banks do not depend as much as conventional financial institutions on the availability of a well-functioning rule of law. This should have a positive influence on the level of bank penetration in developing countries where rule of law is often lacking or insufficient.

Application of SCF in Afghanistan

So far, this monograph has described the current effectiveness of the Afghan financial system. The analysis of the development of the Afghan financial system showed that the World Bank, IMF and USAID mainly applied Western financial principles and neglected SCF as an alternative or complementary system to facilitate bank penetration. The literature provided examples of the positive effects of SCF to facilitate bank penetration. The current section focuses on the effectiveness of the application of SCF for the specific situation in Afghanistan. The question is whether the application of SCF could have improved bank penetration in Afghanistan.

The first subsection analyzes whether the application of SCF would attract enough Muslims to make a difference in facilitating bank penetration. Because SCF is inseparably linked to *Shari'a*, the second subsection analyzes the reasons for Muslims to select SCF. The third subsection analyzes whether SCF is reliable in order to increase bank penetration in Afghanistan. The fourth subsection will do the same for sustainability. The fifth subsection analyzes whether applying SCF will actually improve the development of the financial system because SCF depends less on conventional financial institutions as on the availability of a well-functioning rule of law. This section will end with a conclusion.

Quantitative Preference for SCF

According to Islamic law, applying Islamic rules brings unity and social cohesion because it creates welfare and well-being for others. [87] This implies that there should be a relatively large number of Muslims who prefer SCF over a conventional financial system in order to adhere to the contract between Allah and men. Therefore, religious reasons should be one of the most important reasons to choose SCF. This subsection analyzes the percentage of Muslims that choose to use SCF to fulfill their financial needs.

The monograph uses the results of the analysis to determine the percentage of Muslims in Afghanistan that would prefer SCF because there is no specific data for Afghanistan. In addition, every research has its own focus. It is also difficult to exclude external factors that influence the choice of Muslims who prefer SCF. These external factors can be poverty, availability of infrastructure, knowledge of SCF, or differences between secular and non-secular societies.

To estimate the potential size of the group of Muslims that prefers SCF in Afghanistan, this subsection uses research conducted in Central Java and Yogyakarta, as part of the Republic of Indonesia, Syrian Arab Republic (Syria), West Bank and Gaza Strip as part of the Palestinian territories, Pakistan, and Yemen. In order to extrapolate the results to Afghanistan, all countries have a similar percentage of Muslims in their population as Afghanistan. The percentage of Muslims ranges between 92 percent in Syria and 99.7 percent in Afghanistan.[88]

Research conducted by The Indonesia Bank and the University of Semarang in 2000 in Central Java and Yogyakarta showed that 48.3 percent of the Muslim population would choose SCF because they perceived interest as forbidden within Islamic Law.[89] In July 2008, the World Bank conducted a microfinance market assessment in Syria and found that

43.2 percent of the population only wanted to use SCF because they perceived conventional banking as incompatible with Islamic law.[90] It is difficult to determine how the lack of knowledge of financial services influences choice, because research also pointed out that 20.9 percent were not aware of the possibilities to acquire loans from a formal financial system like a bank.[91] In May 2007, the World Bank conducted a survey on the West Bank and in Gaza Strip.[92] Research showed that 55 percent of the entrepreneurs on the West Bank and 61 percent in Gaza Strip would choose SCF if they had had a choice.[93] In 2010, research in Pakistan found that 52.6 percent of the population preferred SCF as their way to fulfill financial services. At the same time awareness of different SCF products ranged from 13.5 percent to 66.7 percent.[94] The conclusion was that SCF has an enormous potential for further development. However, SCF institutions have to improve awareness among their customers.[95] Research conducted in Yemen estimated that 40 percent of the population in Yemen preferred SCF, even if it were more expensive than conventional financial services. [96] However, the expectation is that, based on research in Syria and Pakistan, awareness of SCF among the population of Yemen is relatively low.

Based on the aforementioned research (see Table 2), between 40 and 61 percent of the population of the countries surveyed prefer SCF if they have a choice. It is therefore reasonable to conclude that, based on extrapolation, at least 50 percent of the Muslims in Afghanistan should have a strong preference for SCF. At the same time, research pointed out that awareness of SCF products is in some cases low. Therefore, the percentage of a preference for SCF can increase when financial institutions inform people about the possibilities of SCF.

When 50 percent of the people prefer SCF, it is reasonable to conclude that a substantial part of the population chooses SCF. In addition, this percentage could be even higher if the population has enough knowledge and information about SCF to make a choice. However, the percentage of Muslims choosing SCF does not give any insight into the actual reasons for choosing SCF. The next subsection will analyze whether religion is an important selection criterion or whether there are other reasons to choose SCF.

Table 2: Quantitative Preference for SCF

	Java	Syria	West Bank	Gaza Strip	Pakistan	Yemen
Percentage of Muslims preferring SCF	48.3	43.2	55	61	52.6	40

Source: See footnotes in the text.

Qualitative Preference for SCF

It is also important to know why Muslims choose SCF. As explained earlier, Islamic literature links the characteristics of SCF to Islam and states that it promotes unity and social cohesion; SCF fulfills the needs of the people and, therefore, facilitates bank penetration. This subsection analyzes the reasons why Muslims choose SCF. The analysis uses international research conducted in Kuwait, Libya, Jordan, Bangladesh, Malaysia, and Pakistan.

The most frequently mentioned reason in the literature to choose SCF is the fact that the conventional financial system is un-Islamic because of the application of interest. This refers to the ban on *Riba* as explained in this monograph.[97] The reference to the ban on interest is a misperception because the statement neglects the interpretation possibilities within SCF as conducted by the SSB of each individual bank. If the SSB does not interpret the interest as excessive, they can issue a fatwa to declare a financial product *Shari'a* compliant. Although it is not a broad interpretation of *Shari'a*, it is a legitimate interpretation.[98]

Local circumstances can differ and each research has its own focus. However, there are some similarities for the reasons why Muslims choose SCF. Research in Kuwait found that reliability of the financial institutions and the diversity of services were the most important reasons to choose a financial institution. SCF principles and products were only fifth on the list of the selection criteria. The research also stated that the population of Kuwait is multi-bank users. They use the financial institution that best fulfills their needs. Religion is not an important selection criterion in Kuwait.[99] It is important to mention that Kuwait deviates from the rest of the countries because the average income of Kuwaitis is considerably higher.

A survey conducted in 2007 and 2008 in Libya showed that the most important reason to choose SCF was that entrepreneurs perceived more encouragement for business expansion and the willingness of SCF institutions to share risk with them. Interest free banking provided less motivation for Libyan entrepreneurs.[100] This research indicates an opposite effect compared to the Kuwait research. It also seems to indicate that perception of SCF is more important than facts. Not statistical evidence, but personal opinions of the entrepreneurs were the most important source of the research.

Research conducted in Jordan found four main reasons for choosing SCF. The first reason was the profitability of the bank. Although this can refer to PLS between banks and depositors, it can also refer to reliability and sustainability. The research does not clarify this issue. The second reason was the influence of friends and relatives. The third reason was religion and the fourth reason was the image and reputation of the financial institution.[101] It is not clear whether the fourth reason refers to the marketing image of a financial institution, the religious image, or the reliability and sustainability of the institution. The research also does not prioritize the reasons, but there is more emphasis on religion and social aspects such as peer influence.[102]

Research in Bangladesh found three main reasons why people in Bangladesh choose SCF. The first and most important reason was that the bank follows the SCF principles as described in this monograph. The second reason was that a bank should be at a convenient location for the customer. The third reason was the influence of family and friends.[103] This research provides a similar perspective as the research conducted in Jordan. Religion is an important reason and family and friends influence others when choosing a financial institution.

A study conducted in Pakistan in 2010 analyzed bank customers' behavior. Research found four main reasons why people chose SCF. The first reason was adherence to Islamic principles. The second reason was the influence of family and friends. The third reason was the profitability of the bank and the last reason was easy access to the bank.[104] This research supports the results in Jordan and Bangladesh. Religion and the adherence to the Islamic principles are the most important reasons to choose SCF. The next important reason is the influence of family and friends. Profitability is the third, and convenience last.

The studies show that most of the arguments are based on subjective confidence of Muslims in the SCF system, because facts are hardly mentioned or taken into consideration to determine the preferences. The studies also confirm the importance of religion and social influences in the way in which Muslims choose their financial institution. Because most of the studies focused on perception and not on facts, the results show the importance of subjective confidence that people have in a system. Religion and social influence are important factors for selection. Because only SCF can provide financial services in accordance with *Shari'a*, SCF is an important way to fulfill the needs of Muslims. This knowledge creates opportunities to attract Muslims towards the formal financial system in Afghanistan.

Reliability of SCF

Reliability of SCF is the perception of people to trust SCF because the system behaves and works in the way people expect it to behave.[105] Perception facilitates subjective confidence. Reliability has a major influence on the success of SCF. An example is the success of the *Hawala* system, a system based on honor and trust. In the absence of a formal financial system, money exchange dealers provide a well-organized, reliable, convenient, safe, and cost-effective means of making international and domestic payments.[106] Because the Afghans lacked a formal banking system for a very long time, they relied solely on this informal system for their financial needs.[107]

In the first place, reliability is primarily a subjective value judgment of the financial system, based on an individual's thoughts and observations. Reliability judgment is therefore closely linked to the two previous subsections. When at least 50 percent of the Muslims prefer SCF, and religious reasons and peer influence are the most important reasons to select SCF, it is an indicator that Muslims perceive SCF as reliable. It does not mean that bankruptcy of the Kabul Bank because of corruption did not damage trust in the financial system in Afghanistan.[108] However, bankruptcy and corruption are not restricted to Islam.

The second reason why Afghans perceive SCF as reliable refers to the growing demand for SCF.[109] Although this is an implied conclusion, growing demand implies the perception that the system will act and behave as customers expect. The DAB, as well as the Afghan government, recognized this trend, enacted an Islamic Banking Law in 2010, and prepared the financial system to offer SCF. In addition, the reliability of SCF is stronger in non-secular societies because of the tight link between state, society, and religion.[110] Research also found that smaller firms with less business experience, smaller assets and employees, fewer owners, and less outstanding debts, are more willing to use SCF to fulfill their financial needs.[111]

The factor that could constrain reliability is the existence of the SSB.[112] Because each financial institution has its own religious board, there is no uniformity in its financial products and control mechanisms.[113] Because the interpretation of *Shari'a* differs, it increases uncertainty and therefore decreases the reliability of SCF products and control mechanisms at the macro level.[114] Sometimes financial institutions do not even accept each other's SCF products. This could further constrain objective confidence because the financial institutions do not completely fulfill the internationally recognized standards for banks anymore. At the same time, a SSB can increase reliability. Especially in Afghanistan, where the formal financial system was destroyed, a *Fatwa* of the SSB can persuade people to participate in SCF and strengthen bank penetration. Therefore, SCF can transform a disadvantage into an advantage in Afghanistan.

To conclude, reliability is an expression of subjective confidence and is important for increasing bank penetration. The experience with the *Hawala* system, the growing demand for SCF, the religious nature of Afghan society, and the smaller firms that require finance and feel attracted to SCF all support the conclusion that applying SCF will increase subjective confidence and therefore will increase bank penetration, although the influence of the different Islamic interpretations could constrain reliability. The question whether this also restricts the sustainability of SCF in Afghanistan will be the subject of the next subsection.

Sustainability of SCF

Sustainability of SCF in Afghanistan is the ability to continue the system over a longer period of time.[115] To estimate the sustainability of an Afghan SCF system, this subsection describes the Afghan consequences for the application of PLS and asset backed finances. This subsection also describes the specific challenges in Afghanistan that constrain the sustainability of an SCF system.

PLS requires a fine balance of risk between the lender and the financial institution. However, when SCF applies PLS in a strict Islamic manner, borrowers are only interested in PLS when the risk of the enterprise is high because that creates the need to mitigate the negative financial effects of risk. If the borrower has a positive expectation, the conventional financial system that has fixed interest rates is more profitable for the borrower.[116] This requires exchange of information among borrower, financial institution, and lender in order to prevent *Gharar*.[117] The lender can only estimate risk and willingness to invest when information is available to conduct the financial analysis. Although PLS can have its positive effects, in the specific case of Afghanistan it is difficult to exchange information. First, because information exchange is not part of the normal procedures of smaller firms and they lack the knowledge how to exchange information. Second, Afghanistan lacks the infrastructure in the remote areas to exchange information in a timely and organized manner. As a result, there is risk-sharing but dismal information exchange.

Asset backed finance is problematic during a stability operation, but especially in Afghanistan because people simply lack the assets to back up their loans. This negates the positive effects of asset-backed finance as explained earlier in this monograph, but also increases the risk for financial institutions and lenders. This is one of the reasons why the collateral for loans is 253.5 percent as depicted in Table 1.

The challenges to apply PLS and asset-backed finance are reasons that the SCF system creates financial products that are *Shari'a* compliant in form, but are less *Shari'a* compliant in content. An example is when a depositor participates in a PLS construction and the bank provides the depositor a fixed return on investment instead of a return based on the profit of the activities of the entrepreneur. Banks sometimes do this to compete with conventional banks that provide a fixed interest rate. The bank provides a product that is *Shari'a* compliant in form but not in content by defining the return on investment as compensation and not as interest. This is a method of financial engineering that mimics conventional financial products without violating the formal SCF regulations like *Riba*.[118] The SSB of each financial institution determines whether a financial product fulfills the requirements of SCF.[119] It all depends on how to define the return on investment. Although the literature mentions this as a disadvantage of SCF, it is a practical solution for the Afghans to apply SCF. Therefore, the best compromise is to engineer financial products in such a way that they fulfill the SCF religious requirements and fulfill the required financial function and balance of risk.[120]

The challenges to sustain a SCF system in Afghanistan are a consequence of infrastructure that years of war destroyed and continuity of insecurity. Therefore, financial institutions will have to invest in security as well as in infrastructure to enable them to develop their financial system outside the major cities. The current financial system is highly centralized and 75 percent of all loans arise in Kabul.[121] Therefore, providing financial services is expensive outside Kabul because population density is low, infrastructure is poor, and loans are small.[122] In addition, Afghanistan lacks qualified professionals that have knowledge of *Shari'a,* finance, and economics. This means that financial institutions have additional expenses to hire expensive expatriate staff that has the capabilities and knowledge needed to operate the financial system.[123]

To conclude, the best compromise between religion and functionality is to create a SCF system that establishes legitimacy based on religion, but uses conventional finance to be functional. This means that financial engineering within SCF is not a negative characteristic, but a practical compromise to facilitate bank penetration and develop economic growth in Afghanistan.

Rule of Law

As previously described, SCF depends less on conventional levels of rule of law because of the strict application of *Shari'a* law. Therefore, people do not depend on the conventional judicial system but adhere to the verdicts of Islamic scholars and clerks to settle disputes.[124] Additionally, the long-term positive results of the Hawala system in areas where there was no formal rule of law implies that SCF can survive and grow under such circumstances. However, depending on *Shari'a* for the implementation of SCF has both short term and long-term effects.

The short-term effect is positive for bank penetration and the economic development of an Islamic region. Using the Islamic system will facilitate bank penetration because it gives people the possibility to protect their property rights, which is a prerequisite for business. Properties rights are important, especially in low-income countries. Effective property rights limit uncertainty and makes doing business more efficient and less expensive.[125] However, depending on local justice will decrease uniform rights in Afghanistan because the interpretation of *Shari'a* differs per region or school of thought. Nevertheless, it will facilitate subjective confidence in the regions.

The long-term effect is that it will be extremely difficult to create a uniform Afghan financial system that adheres to the international recognized standards for finance because interpretation and application of rules and regulations will differ per region. However, the IMF can prevent this problem by continuing and intensifying its support and cooperation with the IFSB to supervise and regulate SCF in Afghanistan. This should not be difficult because the IMF is already supporting the IFSB.[126]

Applying SCF can facilitate Afghan bank penetration because it does not need the same level of rule of law as a conventional financial system. Therefore, subjective confidence in the SCF system will increase. The only long-term point of concern is that there should be a plan for evolving into a system that adheres to the internationally recognized standards of finance and, therefore, establishing objective confidence.

Bank Penetration

The application of SCF can facilitate bank penetration in Afghanistan by improving subjective confidence without having to violate objective confidence. Currently, bank penetration is low in Afghanistan. The international development community missed an opportunity to attract at least 50 percent of the Muslims in Afghanistan to the formal financial system by making the population aware of SCF. By developing a financial system that based on a Western financial paradigm, the Western organizations neglected the preferences of the local population as well as the possibilities of SCF to facilitate bank penetration.

The analysis also found that religion and social influences are the most important reasons why people choose SCF as the preferred way to fulfill financial needs. Although most of the studies focused on perception and not on facts, the results indicate the importance of subjective confidence that people have in a financial system. In addition, the fact that Afghanistan is relatively poor and has an Islamic society helps to attract people to SCF and, therefore, facilitates bank penetration in Afghanistan.

Literature implies financial engineering as a negative characteristic of SCF. However, the analysis in this monograph found that financial engineering could be a practical solution for the situation in Afghanistan. Establishing legitimacy based on religion and using conventional finance creates a functional system that fulfills profitability and, therefore, sustainability. SCF is a way to establish a practical compromise to facilitate bank penetration and develop economic growth in Afghanistan.

Applying SCF can facilitate Afghan bank penetration because it uses local Islamic judicial systems to settle disputes and protect property rights. The effect is also that it facilitates subjective confidence in SCF. SCF is local and people are familiar with the system. The only point of concern is that in the longer term Afghanistan needs a plan of how to evolve into a system that adheres to the internationally recognized standards of finance to establish objective confidence.

Significance for the Military Commander

Operational art promotes unified action and supports the commander in achieving the strategic objective by integrating the elements of national power as well as the efforts of multinational partners. Operational art is commander centric and enables the commander to link the ends, ways, and means in order to achieve the desired military end state.[127] Therefore, the commander designs an operational approach that describes the broad actions the force must achieve.[128] To develop an operational approach the commander must understand the strategic direction and the operational environment, and the commander must define the problem.[129] As stated in the introduction of this monograph, military forces play an important role in supporting economic stabilization and infrastructure development and the support for the development of a financial system.[130] However, besides some security and logistical tasks, there is no evidence that the military provided any substantial support for the development of the financial system in Afghanistan.[131] Previous discussion showed that SCF could facilitate bank penetration by improving subjective confidence without compromising on objective confidence in order to develop the financial system as part of the economic development of Afghanistan. This section describes five lessons the military commander at the operational level can learn from this knowledge to assist in achieving the military end state.

Lessons Learned

The first lesson is that this monograph found that SCF is an alternative or at least a valuable complement to the development of a financial system in Afghanistan. Commanders should consider this when planning, preparing, executing, and assessing a stability operation in a country with a Muslim majority. This leads to four addition lessons.

The second lesson is that the commander should challenge and compare the Western definition of the operational environment, the problem and the operational approach with a Muslim paradigm. Although the military commander is in a supporting role when developing a financial system, commanders should realize that a Western paradigm could hinder their analysis of the operational environment and development of an operational approach. Previous subsections have shown that the social, economic, and financial elements of the operational environments in Afghanistan are different from a Western environment. For example, Muslims focus more on the hereafter than non-Muslims do, Muslims consider just and equitable distribution of resources as important functions of their economic system, and Muslims cannot invest in *Haram* goods and services. Although previous subsections showed that the function of a financial system is to reduce the risk for investors and to create financial possibilities for entrepreneurs, regardless of whether the financial system is based on religious principles, the operational approach supporting SCF system can be different from supporting a Western financial system.[132] Different paradigms will influence the perspective of an operational environment and the operational approach achieving the military end state. Challenging our Western paradigm prevents the military commander from pursuing the wrong military tasks in time, space and purpose.

The third lesson is that the military must invest in basic knowledge of Islam, SCF, and Afghan society in order to effectively support the development of a financial system in Afghanistan. This goes further than cultural awareness. The monograph described the sources, principles, products, and standards of SCF, and described positive Islamic ways to facilitate bank penetration. The previous sections showed that Islam and the SCF system are different from our Western, primarily Christian, society and financial system. These differences require that the military obtain additional knowledge in order to prepare, plan, execute, and assess the support of an SCF system during stability operations in Afghanistan. This knowledge enables the military commander to mitigate weaknesses and threats; it also enables the commander to use the strengths and opportunities of the SCF system. An example is the use of religious reasoning and social influences to increase subjective confidence in the SCF system in order to facilitate bank penetration. A conventional Western approach would probably have focused on rationale, to convince the population. Previous subsections showed that Muslims have different considerations deciding which financial system to choose.

The fourth lesson is that the military should start building partnerships with other organizations that could facilitate the development of a financial system. The military can build partnerships with interagency organizations such as USAID. USAID has considerable experience in providing microfinance in Afghanistan. Additionally, USAID not only provides financial and local Afghan information, but also can integrate and synchronize its activities as an interagency organization with the military. An example is USAID providing microfinance based on SCF principles, standards, and products to local entrepreneurs and integrating the Commander's Emergency Response Program Funds into SCF. This also means spending the funds in accordance with SCF principles.

A second group with whom to build a partnership is an international organization such as the IMF. The IMF has a wealth of expertise and experience. The military could use this information to improve its own effectiveness. An example of cooperation with the IMF is the use of knowledge they have in regard to their support of the IFSB.

A third group with whom to build partnerships are the local Islamic scholars and clerks. Local scholars and clerks can support the military commander's understanding of the operational environment and provide information to develop an operational approach. Their knowledge can provide insight into local circumstances because, as described earlier, Islam is not a monolith. SCF can differ per region, per school of thought, or even because of different local interpretation. Previous subsections also showed the importance of religious arguments in building subjective confidence. Local scholars and clerks can facilitate the improvement of subjective confidence in the SCF system because they can explain and convince the local Muslim population by using religious reasoning that fits local circumstances.

The fifth and final lesson is that the military commander should focus on facilitating local efforts instead of providing a solution for the development of the local financial system. The World Bank, the IMF, and USAID provided mainly top-down support to the financial system. However, religious arguments and social influences are the most important reasons to choose SCF. Facilitating local Muslim efforts better supports subjective confidence than providing them a Western based system. A bottom-up approach seems to be more promising compared to previous efforts by the World Bank, IMF and USAID. Although there are some shortcomings in SCF principles, products and standards, SCF is able to attract a substantial percentage of Muslims to the formal financial system. Therefore, during preparing, planning, executing and assessing a stability operation, the military commander should not only focus on the disadvantages of SCF, but also on how to combine the positive effects of SCF with conventional finance in order to achieve a maximum development effect on the financial system. Examples of this combination are the SCF products that are Islamic in form and conventional in content. The military commander should not judge a financial product when it fulfills the needs of Muslims and fits into the international financial system. Another example is to enable the local population to use *Shari'a* to develop their financial system or to settle their disputes, especially in Afghanistan, where the informal *Hawala* system replaced a destroyed financial system. Bank penetration can benefit from SCF.

Summary

SCF can facilitate bank penetration in order to develop the financial system in Afghanistan. However, using SCF provides the military commander five lessons. The first lesson is that SCF is an alternative or at least a valuable complement for the development of a financial system in Afghanistan. The second lesson is that the military commander must challenge and compare the Western paradigm with a Muslim paradigm in order to prevent to develop a deficient operational approach. The third lesson is that the military has to invest in basic knowledge of the Afghan society, Islam, and SCF in order to mitigate weaknesses and threats and to use the strengths and opportunities of the SCF system. The fourth lesson is that the military should start building partnerships with other organizations to enable unified action. The final lesson is that the military commander should focus on facilitating local efforts instead of providing a solution for the development of the financial system in order to achieve the maximum development results.

Conclusion

This monograph challenged the generally accepted way of developing the financial system in Afghanistan. SCF improves the development of a financial system during stability operations by increasing subjective confidence in the financial system and therefore increasing bank penetration in Afghanistan.

Development of the Afghan financial system focused on Western financial principles and neglected SCF to facilitate the development of the financial system. As a result, the World Bank, IMF and USAID, as main contributors, established the internationally recognized standards for a financial system in Afghanistan. However, based on World Bank and DAB data, bank penetration was inadequate. These organizations managed to achieve objective confidence, but failed to establish subjective confidence in the financial system in Afghanistan.

The second part of the monograph defined SCF as a financial system based on Islamic principles and values that offers Muslims a possibility to fulfill their financial needs within the limits of Islam. This part also described the sources, principles, products and standards of SCF which research used to analyze whether SCF could have been an alternative for the development of the financial system in Afghanistan. Based on the assessment of the available information, research found that an estimated 50 percent of the Afghan population would choose SCF if they had a choice and that religion and social influence are the most important reasons for SCF selection.

Reliability of SCF is closely linked to subjective confidence: the perception of people to trust SCF because the system behaves and works in the way people expect it to behave. Although research did not find data that could objectively validate the reliability of SCF, the number of Muslims preferring SCF and the growing demand for SCF provided the basis for the conclusion that reliability of SCF is high among Muslims. However, the existence of an SSB could constrain objective confidence while at the same time an SSB can also pursue subjective confidence because they have the legitimacy in a Muslim society to determine financial products as *Shari'a* compliant.

Sustainability of the SCF system is problematic in the Afghan situation, especially when applied a strict manner. It was therefore remarkable to discover that there is some level of adaptability in SCF systems because Muslims do not always apply PLS, asset backed finance, and other SCF products in a strict manner. Financial engineering is a way to fulfill Islamic needs and requirements, while simultaneously establishing sustainable financial products. The best compromise between religion and functionality is to have an SCF system that uses religion to establish legitimacy but uses conventional finance to be functional. Therefore, the disadvantage of SCF is mitigated by creating SCF products that are *Shari'a* compliant in form but not necessarily in content.

A lack of rule of law is not always problematic for the development of SCF because it uses the local Islamic judicial system of scholars and clerks to settle disputes and protect property rights. Using the local system even facilitates subjective confidence in the financial system. The only point of concern is that in the longer term there Afghanistan needs a plan to evolve into a system that adheres to the internationally recognized standards of finance and therefore establishes objective confidence.

The third part of the monograph described the lessons for a military commander when tasked to support the development of a financial system. Research found five main lessons. The first and foremost lesson is that SCF is an alternative or a valuable complement to a conventional financial system in Afghanistan. The military commander should not limit himself to analyzing and acting only in accordance with a Western paradigm. The force also needs additional knowledge about Islam and local Afghan financial customs. The military should invest in partnerships with interagency, international, and local Afghan organizations and entities such as Islamic scholars and clerks. The last and most important lesson is that the military should facilitate local efforts instead of imposing a solution. When the military supports and encourages locals, they can increase subjective confidence and improve bank penetration.

To conclude, the best way to apply SCF in order to improve the development of a financial system in Afghanistan during stability operations is by facilitating local efforts, which facilitates subjective confidence and therefore increases bank penetration. In order to mitigate the risk for sustainability in the longer term, the World Bank and especially the IMF should maintain their focus on how to evolve an SCF system into a system that is still *Shari'a* compliant but also fulfills all internationally recognized financial standards. This is not a major challenge because the IMF is already engaged in providing support to the IFSB, and maybe this is a first step to enable the local population to truly own their economy.

Notes

1. Rebecca Patterson and Dane Stangler, *Building Expeditionary Economics: Understanding the Field and Setting forth a Research Agenda* (Kansas City, MO: Ewing Marion Kauffman Foundation, November 2010), 12.

2. US Army, *Field Manual 3-07, Stability Operations* (Washington, DC: Headquarters, Department of the Army, October 2008), 3-14–5.

3. *Stability Operation.*, 3-16.

4. US Army, *Field Manual 3-0, Operations* (Washington, DC: Headquarters, Department of the Army, February 2011), 7-1.

5. World Bank, *The Investment Climate in Afghanistan* (Washington, DC: The World Bank, December 2005), 1.

6. US Department of State, "Background Note: Afghanistan," 6 December 2010, http://www. state. gov/r/pa/ei/bgn/5380.htm (accessed 9 February 2011).

7. World Bank, *The Investment Climate*, 1, 4, 13.

8. Shaheen Pasha, "Afghan Central Bank Sees Islamic Banking Law Enacted In 2011," *Reuters*, 6 February 2011, http://www.reuters.com/article/2011/02/06/us-afghanistan-islamicbanking-idUSTRE7150 EQ20110206 (accessed 4 August 2011).

9. Patterson and Stangler, *Building Expeditionary Economics*, 8–11.

10. Steven A. Zyck, "The Increasing Role and Potential of Islamic Finance in Afghanistan," Civil-Military Fusion Centre, March 2011, https://www.cimicweb.org/Documents/CFC_AFG_ Economic_ Stabilization_Archive/Contemporary_Economic_Issues_in_Afghanistan-Islamic_ Finance-Mar_2011.pdf (accessed 6 August 2011), 1.

11. Nimrak Karim, Michael Tarazi, and Xavier Reille, "Islamic Microfinance: An Emerging Market Niche," *CGAP Focus Note* no. 47 (August 2008), http://www.cgap.org/gm/ document-1.9.5029/FN49.pdf (accessed 6 August 2011), 5.

12. Zyck, "The Increasing Role," 1.

13. Hafa Furqani and Ratna Mulyany, "Islamic Banking and Economic Growth: Empirical Evidence from Malaysia," *Journal of Economic Cooperation and Development* 30, no. 2 (2009): 70.

14. Salma Sairally, "Community Development Financial Institutions: Lessons in Social Banking for the Islamic Financial Industry," *Kyoto Bulletin of Islamic Area Studies* (2007), http:// www.asafas.kyoto-u.ac.jp/kias/contents/pdf/kb1_2/05salma.pdf (accessed 4 August 2011), 19–20.

15. Patterson and Stangler, *Building Expeditionary Economics,* 8.

16. Ake Lönnberg, "Restoring and Transforming Payments and Banking Systems in Post-Conflict Economies," Washington, DC: International Monetary Fund, May 2002, http://www.imf. org/external/ np/leg/sem/2002/cdmfl/eng/lonnb.pdf (accessed 24 November 2010), 3.

17. Keith Crane, Olga Oliker, Nora Bensahel, Derek Eaton, S. Jamie Gayton, Brooke Stearns Lawson, Jeffrey Martini, John L. Nasir, Sandra Reyna, Michelle Parker, Jerry M. Sollinger, and Kayla M. Williams, "Guidebook for supporting Economic Development in Stability Operations", *Technical Report*, RAND Cooperation, 2009, http://www.rand.org/pubs/technical_reports/2009/ RAND_TR633.pdf (accessed 14 August 2011), 77–9.

18. "Guidebook for supporting Economic Development in Stability Operations", 77.

19. World Bank, *Financial Accountability in Nepal: A Country Assessment*. (Washington, DC: The World Bank, 2003), 107-110.

20. The World Bank, *Financial Sector Strengthening Project*, 17 September 2008, http://www-wds.worldbank.org/external/default/WDSContentServer/WDSP/IB/2008/09/17/0000760 92_20080918160815/Rendered/PDF/Project0Inform1cept0Stage0F0SEPT017.pdf (accessed 14 Augustus 2011), 4–7.

21. *Financial Sector Strengthening Project*, 8.

22. Messrs. A. Bennett (ed.), B. de Schaetzen, R. van Rooden, Dicks-Mireaux, F. Fischer, and T. Kalfon, *Islamic State of Afghanistan: Rebuilding a Macroeconomic Framework for Reconstruction and Growth* (Washington, DC: International Monetary Fund, September 2003), http://www.imf.org/external/ pubs/ft/scr/2003/cr03299.pdf (accessed 14 Augustus 2011), 8.

23. International Monetary Fund, *Country Report No. 02/219, Islamic Republic of Afghanistan: Report on Recent Economic Developments and Prospects, and the Role of the Fund in the in the Reconstruction Process* (Washington, DC: International Monetary Fund, October 2002), http://www.imf. org/external/pubs/ft/scr/2002/cr02219.pdf (accessed 10 February 2011), 39.

24. Staff of the Monetary and Financial Systems Department, *Background Paper for MFD Technical Assistance to Recent Post-conflict Countries* (Washington, DC: International Monetary Fund, 13 December 2004), www.imf.org/external/np/ta/2005/eng/022805.htm (accessed 14 August 2011), 5.

25. United States Agency for International Development, *Fact Sheet Afghanistan* (Washington, DC: USAID, June 2010), http://afghanistan.usaid.gov/documents/document/document/1004 (accessed 14 August 2011).

26. Da Afghanistan Bank, "The Afghanistan Bank Law," *The Official Gazette*, (17 December 2003), *http://www.centralbank.gov.af/pdf/UpdatedOfDaAfghanistan_BankLaw_1_.pdf (accessed 13 Augustus 2011), 1–2.*

27. Da Afghanistan Bank, *Annual Bulletin Da Afghanistan Bank 2008-2009,* Kabul, Afghanistan: Da Afghanistan Bank, August 2009, http://www.centralbank.gov.af/pdf/DAB_QB_ Annual-1387%282008-2009%29.pdf (accessed 13 September 2011), 93–102.

28. Da Afghanistan Bank, *Strategic Plan 2009–2014, Fostering Price Stability and Building a Robust Financial System,* Kabul, Afghanistan: Da Afghanistan Bank, 22 February 2009, http://www.central bank.gov.af/pdf/Strategic_Plan_2009-2014.pdf (accessed 13 September 2011), 24.

29. *Fostering Price Stability and Building a Robust Financial System*, 44.

30. *Fostering Price Stability and Building a Robust Financial System*, 22.

31. Da Afghanistan Bank, *Annual Bulletin Da Afghanistan Bank 2008-2009,* 93–8.

32. *Annual Bulletin Da Afghanistan Bank 2008-2009*, 93.

33. *Annual Bulletin Da Afghanistan Bank 2008-2009*, 98.

34. Crane et al., "Guidebook for supporting Economic Development," 77.

35. Hans Visser, *Islamic Finance: Principles and Practice* (Cheltenham, UK: Edward Elgar Publishing Limited, 2009), ix.

36. Muhammad Ayub, *Understanding Islamic Finance* (West Sussex, UK: John Wiley & Sons, 2007), 179.

37. Shayerah Ilias, "Islamic Finance: Overview and Policy Concerns," *CRS Report for Congress* (9 February 2009), http://assets.opencrs.com/rpts/RS22932_20090209.pdf (accessed 23 August 2011).

38. Visser, *Islamic Finance,* ix.

39. Paul Coughlin, "Islamic Finance Outlook 2010," *Report for Standard & Poor's* (19 April 2011), http://www2.standardandpoors.com/spf/pdf/media/Islamic_Finance_Outlook_2010.pdf (accessed 23 August 2011), 9.

40. Mahmoud A. El-Gamal, *Islamic Finance: Law, Economics, and Practice* (New York: Cambridge University Press, 2006), 2.

41. Ibrahim Warde, *Islamic Finance in the Global Economy* (Edinburgh University Press, 2000), 5.

42. Mehboob ul Hassan, "People's Perceptions towards the Islamic Banking: A Fieldwork Study on Bank Account Holders' Behaviour in Pakistan," *Oikonomika* 43, no. 3(April 2007), http://www.econ.na goya-cu.ac.jp/~oikono/oikono/vol47_34/pdf/vol43_34/09_hassan.pdf (accessed 25 August 2011), 153–176.

43. Abdul Qawi Othman and Lynn Owen, "Adopting and measuring customer Service Quality (SQ) in Islamic Banks: A case study in Kuwait Finance House," *International Journal of Islamic Financial Services* 3 (2001), http://www.iiibf.org/journals/journal9/abdulqawi.pdf (accessed 23 August 2011), 1–26.

44. Muhammad Shehzad Moin, "Performance of Islamic Banking and Conventional Banking in Pakistan: A Comparative Study," *Master Degree Project in Finance Advance Level, University of Skövde* (Spring Term 2008) http://his.diva-portal.org/smash/record.jsf?pid=diva2:113713 (accessed 25 August 2011), 8.

45. Elizabeth Walter ed., *Cambridge Advanced Learner's Dictionary* (Cambridge, UK: University Press, 2008), 753.

46. Zamir Iqbal, and Abbas Mirakhor, *An Introduction to Islamic Finance: Theory and Practice.* (Singapore, Asia: John Wiley & Sons Pte Ltd, 2007), 5–6.

47. Ibrahim Warde, *Islamic Finance in the Global Economy* (Edinburgh, UK: Edinburgh University Press, 2000), 32.

48. Mahmoud A. El-Gamal, *Islamic Finance: Law, Economics, and Practice* (New York: Cambridge University Press, 2006), 27–8.

49. Warde, *Islamic Finance in the Global Economy*, 32.

50. Iqbal and Mirakhor, *An Introduction to Islamic Finance: Theory and Practice*, 13–4.

51. Warde, *Islamic Finance in the Global Economy*, 32.

52. Muhammad Taqi Usmani, *An Introduction to Islamic Finance* (The Hague, NL: Kluwer Law International, 2002), 10–11.

53. Timur Kuran, *Islam and Mammon: The Economic Predicaments of Islamism,* 3rd ed. (Princeton, NJ: Princeton University Press, 2006), 40–1.

54. Imad-ad-Dean Ahmad, "Riba and Interest: Definitions and Implications," *Minaret of Freedom Institute Preprint Series* 96-5, Minaret of Freedom Institute, Bethesda (15–17 October 1993), www.mina ret.org/riba.htm (accessed 25 August 2011).

55.   Kabir M. Hassan, and Mervyn K. Lewis, *"Development of Islamic Economic and Social Thought; Handbook of Islamic Banking,"* (Cheltenham, UK and Northampton, MA, USA: Edward Elgar, 2007), 34.

56.   Iqbal and Mirakhor, *An Introduction to Islamic Finance: Theory and Practice*, 53.

57.   Usmani, *An Introduction to Islamic Finance*, 27.

58.   Linda Eagle, "Banking on Shari'a Principles: Islamic Banking and the Financial Industry," The Edcomm Group Banker's Academy, New York, NY (14 May 2009), http://www. anythingislamicbanking. com/articles/article_2010_002.html (accessed 25 August 2011).

59.   Muhammad Shaukat Malik, Ali Malik, and Waqas Mustafa, "Controversies that make Islamic Banking Controversial: An Analysis of Issues and Challenges," *American Journal of Social and Management Science* 2, no. 1 (2011): 42.

60.   Eagle, http://www.anythingislamicbanking.com/articles/article_2010_002.html.

61.   Visser, *Islamic Finance,* 97.

62.   Ron Terrell, "Islamic Banking: Financing Terrorism or Meeting Economic Demand?" Naval Postgraduate School, 2007, http://edoc.bibliothek.uni-halle.de/servlets/MCRFileNodeServlet/ HALCoRe_d erivate_00003456/Islamic_banking_financing.pdf (accessed 16 August 2011), 65.

63.   Visser, *Islamic Finance,* 95–6.

64.   Hassan and Lewis, *Handbook of Islamic Banking*, 136.

65.   International Finance Cooperation of The World Bank Group, *Afghanistan Country Profile 2008* (Danvers, MA: The World Bank Group, 2008), http://www. enterprisesurveys.org/documents/ EnterpriseSurveys/Reports/Afghanistan-2009.pdf (accessed 14 August 2012), 11.

66.   Bank penetration is the percentage of firms or people in a specific area that use banks or other financial institutions to fulfill financial services.

67.   Ashfaq Ahmad, Asad Afzal Humayoun, and Uzair ul Hassan, "An Analysis of Functions Performed by Islamic Bank: A Case of Pakistan," *European Journal of Social Sciences* 17, no. 1 (October 2010), http://www.eurojournals.com/ejss_17_1.htm (accessed 12 September 2011), 8.

68.   *European Journal of Social Sciences* 17, no. 1.

69.   Ashfaq Ahmad, Kashif ur Rehman, and Muhammad Iqbal Saif, M. I., "Islamic Banking Experience of Pakistan: Comparison of Islamic and Conventional Banks," *International Journal of Business and Management* 5, no. 2 (2010), 141.

70.   Andrew Cunningham, "Are Islamic Banks a More Powerful Force for Post-Conflict Economic Development than Conventional Banks?" United States Institute of Peace, *International Network for Economics and Conflict Blog*, entry posted May 2, 2011, http://inec.usip.org/blog/2011/ may/02/are-islamic-banks-more-powerful-force-post-conflict-economic-development-convention (accessed 12 September 2011).

71.   Konrad Adenauer Stiftung E.V., "Islamic Economic Thought and the Social Market Economy," *Im Plenum Kompakt* (September-October 2010), http://www.kas.de/wf/doc/kas_21925-544-2-30.pdf?11 0216095211 (accessed 10 August 2011), 4.

72.   Islamic Financial Services Industry Development, "Ten Year Framework And Strategies," Islamic Development Bank, Islamic Research And Training Institute, Islamic Financial Services Board, 2007, http://www.ibisonline.net/En/Policy_Dialogue/TenYearFrameworkAndStrategies.pdf (accessed 6 August 2011), 19.

73.   Omer Demir, Mustafa Acar, and Metin Toprak, "Anatolian Tigers or Islamic Capital: Prospects and Challenges," *Middle Eastern Studies* 40, no. 6 (2004): 171.

74.   Ji-Hyang Jang, "Taming Political Islamists by Islamic Capital: The Passions and the Interests in Turkish Islamic Society," *PhD dissertation*, The University of Texas at Austin (2005), www.lib.utexas.edu/ etd/d/2005/jangj05548/jangj05548.pdf, (accessed 12 September 2011), 141.

75.   Pasha, "Afghan Central Bank sees Islamic Banking Law Enacted in 2011."

76.   International Finance Cooperation of The World Bank Group, *Afghanistan Country Profile*.

77.   Visser, *Islamic Finance,* 135.

78.   *Islamic Finance*, 136.

79.   *Islamic Finance*, 138.

80.   Hassan and Lewis, *Handbook of Islamic Banking,* 34.

81.   Shaheed Saleem, "Role of Islamic Banks in Economic Development," Hailey College of Banking and Finance (PAK), C.I.M.A. (UK), 2008, http://mpra.ub.uni-muenchen.de/7332/2/ MPRA_ paper_ 7332.pdf (accessed 16 August 2011), 13.

82.   Hassan and Lewis, *Handbook of Islamic Banking,* 136.

83.   Islamic Financial Services Industry Development, "Ten Year Framework and Strategies," 18.

84.   Enrica Detragiache, Poonam Gupta, and Theirry Tressel, "Finance in Lower-Income Countries: An Empirical Exploration," *Working Paper* 05/167, Washington, DC: International Monetary Fund, August 2005, http://www.econdse.org/faculty/poonam/papers/Finance_21.pdf (accessed 10 September 2011), 21.

85.   Patrick Imam, and Kangni Kpodar, "Islamic Banking: How has it Diffused?" International Monetary Fund, 2010, http://www.imf.org/external/pubs/ft/wp/2010/wp10195.pdf (accessed 16 August 2011), 16.

86.   "Islamic Banking: How has it Diffused?", 20.

87.   Usmani, *An Introduction to Islamic Finance*, 10–11.

88.   Pew Research Center's Forum on Religion & Public Life, "Mapping the Global Muslim Population," *Report on the Size and Distribution of the World's Muslim Population* (October 2009), http://pewforum.org/newassets/images/reports/Muslimpopulation/Muslimpopulation.pdf (accessed 28 September 2011), 28–33.

89.   Bank of Indonesia and Research Center on Development Studies Research Institute Diponegoro University Semarang, "Research on Potency, Preference and Society Behavior Toward Syariah Banking System in Central Java and Yogyakarta Provinces," *Executive Summary* (2000), http://www.bi.go.id/NR/ rdonlyres/4DFA2814-DAF4-4CFC-8D5B-109018D30895/13298/ BPSESJatengenglish.pdf (accessed 28 September 2011), 21.

90.   Grameen-Jameel Pan-Arab Microfinance Limited and the International Finance Corporation, "Syria: Microfinance Market Assessment," *Final Report* (July 2008), http://ebookbrowse.com/ syria-microfinance-market-assessment-final-posted-cgap-july2008-pdf-d45320007 (accessed 29 September 2011), 46.

91.   "Syria: Microfinance Market Assessment," *Final Report* (July 2008).

92. The International Finance Corporation (IFC) and Palestinian Network for Small and Microfinance (PNSMF), "Microfinance Market Survey in the West Bank and the Gaza Strip" (May 2007), http://www.microfinancegateway.org/gm/document-1.9.26182/MicrofinanceMarketSurvey-Final.pdf (accessed 29 September 2011), 3.

93. "Microfinance Market Survey in the West Bank and the Gaza Strip", 10.

94. Naveed Azeem Khattak and Kashif-Ur-Rehman, "Customer Satisfaction and Awareness of Islamic Banking System in Pakistan," *African Journal of Business Management* 4, no. 5 (May 2010): 667.

95. *African Journal of Business Management* 4, no. 5 (May 2010): 670.

96. Karim, Tarazi, and Reille, "Islamic Microfinance: An Emerging Market Niche," 5.

97. See page 9–11 of this monograph.

98. Ahmad, "Riba and Interest: Definitions and Implications."

99. Thabet A., Edris, "Services Considered Important to Business Customer and Determinants of Bank Selection in Kuwait: A Segmentation Analysis," *International Journal of Bank Marketing* 15, no. 4 (1997): 126-133.

100. Alsadek H.Gait, and Andrew C. Worthington, "Libyan Business Firm Attitudes Towards Islamic Methods of Finance," Griffith Business School, Griffith University, 2009, http://www.griffith.edu. au/_data/assets/pdf_file/0009/146871/2009-10-libyan-business-firm-attitudes-towards-islamic-methods-in-finance.pdf (accessed 10 August 2011), 8.

101. Ahasanul Haque, Jamil Osman, and Ahmad Zaki Hj Ismail, "Factor Influences Selection of Islamic Banking: A Study on Malaysian Customer Preferences," *American Journal of Applied Sciences* 6, no. 5 (2009): 924.

102. *American Journal of Applied Sciences* 6, no. 5 (2009): 924..

103. Mohammad Saif Noman Khan, M. Kabir Hassan, and Abdullah Ibneyy Shahid, "Banking Behavior of Islamic Bank Customers in Bangladesh," *Journal of Islamic Economics, Banking and Finance* 3, no. 2 (July–December 2007): 190.

104. Syed Umar Farooq, "A Profile Analysis of the Customers of Islamic Banking in Peshawar, Pukhtunkhwa," *International Journal of Business and Management* 5, no. 11 (November 2010): 116.

105. Walter, *Cambridge Advanced Learner's Dictionary*, 1201.

106. Samuel Munzele Maimbo, "The Money Exchange Dealers of Kabul: A Study of the Hawala System in Afghanistan," Finance and Private Sector Unit, South Asia Region, World Bank (June 2003), http://www.ifc.org/ifcext/gfm.nsf/AttachmentsByTitle/Tool6.13.WorldBankReport-HawalaSystem /$FILE/Tool+6.13.+World+Bank+Report+-+Hawala+System.pdf (accessed 30 September 2011), 5.

107. "The Money Exchange Dealers of Kabul: A Study of the Hawala System in Afghanistan," Finance and Private Sector Unit, South Asia Region, World Bank (June 2003), 12.

108. Steven A. Zyck, "Special Report on Economic Development in Afghanistan The Kabul Bank Crisis: What Happened and What It Means for Development, Governance and Security in Afghanistan." Civil Military Fusion Centre, September 2010, https://www.cimicweb.org/ Documents/CFCAFGEconomic Stabilization_Archive/Econ_Dev_Monthly_Rpt_Sep2010_Kabul_

Bank_Crisis_FINAL.pdf (accessed 30 September 2011), 2–4. The Kabul bank went bankrupt because of corruption and fraud.

109. Mohamed Abdel Hamied Hassan El Biesi, "Foreign Banking, Financial Development and Economic Growth: Recent Evidence from MENA Region," Università Degli Studi di Roma "Tor Vergata," 2010, http://dspace.uniroma2.it/dspace/bitstream/2108/1345/1/El+Biesi_PhD_thesis.pdf (accessed 16 August 2011), 18.

110. Pasha, "Afghan Central Bank sees Islamic Banking Law Enacted in 2011."

111. Gait and Worthington, "Libyan Business Firm Attitudes," 8.

112. Hassan and Lewis, *Handbook of Islamic Banking*, 136.

113. Nazima Ellahi, Tayyab Alam Bukhari, and Mehwish Naeem, "Role of Islamic Modes of Financing for Growth of SME's: a Case Study of Islamabad City," *International Journal of Academic Research* 2. no. 6 (November 2010, part I): 165.

114. Visser, *Islamic Finance,* 79.

115. Walter, *Cambridge Advanced Learner's Dictionary*, 1201-1471.

116. Visser, *Islamic Finance,* 81.

117. *Gharar* is the failure to disclose information needed to make a decision.

118. Visser, *Islamic Finance,* 145–6.

119. Hassan and Lewis, *Handbook of Islamic Banking,* 136.

120. Malik, Malik, and Mustafa, *American Journal of Social and Management Science* 2, no. 1 (2011): 44.

121. US Department of State, "Overview of Foreign Investment Climate," March 2011, http://www.state.gov/e/eeb/rls/othr/ics/2011/157228.htm (accessed 30 September 2011).

122. Maliha Hamid Hussein, "State of Microfinance in Afghanistan," Institute of Microfinance (InM), 2009, http://inm.org.bd/saarc/document/Afghanistan.pdf (accessed 10 August 2011), 26.

123. Malik, Malik, and Mustafa, *American Journal of Social and Management Science* 2, no. 1 (2011): 43.

124. Imam and Kpodar, "Islamic Banking: How Has it Diffused," 20.

125. Enrica Detragiache, Poonam Gupta, and Theirry Tressel, "Finance in Lower-Income Countries: An Empirical Exploration," Working Paper 05/167, (Washington, DC: International Monetary Fund, August 2005), http://www.econdse.org/faculty/ poonam/papers/Finance_21.pdf (accessed 14 December 2010), 1.

126. Visser, *Islamic Finance: Principles and Practice*, 97.

127. Joint Staff, *Joint Publication 5-0, Joint Operation Planning* (Washington, DC: Joint Chiefs of Staff, 11 August 2011), III-1.

128. *Joint Publication 5-0, Joint Operation Planning*, III-5.

129. *Joint Publication 5-0, Joint Operation Planning*, III-7.

130. US Army, *Field Manual 3-07, Stability Operations* (Washington, DC: Headquarters, Department of the Army, October 2008), 3-14–6.

131. Staff of the Monetary and Financial Systems Department, *Background Paper for MFD*, 5.

132. International Finance Cooperation of The World Bank Group, *Afghanistan Country Profile 2008*.

Conclusion
by
Dan G. Cox

Nothing that contains great promise comes free of peril, and the notion of expeditionary economics is no exception. The essays in this volume, written by US Army and foreign officers, explore the specific promises and perils that lie ahead. This honest exploration of the practice of expeditionary economics is in keeping with Carl Schramm's and the Kaufmann Foundation's *initial* promise to explore fully the concept of expeditionary economics. Unfortunately, Carl Schramm left unceremoniously and abruptly in 2011, the Kaufmann Foundation declared that expeditionary economics had won the day, and there was no longer a need for the Kaufmann Foundation to devote resources to a time proven concept with momentum of its own.[1]

While Carl Schramm likely meant what he said at the Kaufmann Foundation's initial conference—that expeditionary economics was a new concept and that, despite writing the initial *Foreign Affairs* article outlining a notional definition, he felt the work of refining the definition and practice of expeditionary economics fell on those interested souls in the audience—it was less clear that the Kaufmann Foundation shared his vision. One of the first indications that Schramm's vision was being contested was the announcement that the Kaufmann Foundation would publish a Field Manual on Expeditionary Economics.

Either the Kaufmann Foundation did not understand Army culture at all or they were signaling that Expeditionary Economics would be foisted upon the Army from on high. The Army produces numerous field manuals on every military topic ranging from leadership to planning and operations. Dubbing the new Expeditionary Economics tome a field manual raised eyebrows and a few hackles.

If this collected work serves no other purpose, it serves to provide that unbiased, academic exploration of the concept and practical application of Expeditionary Economics. Each author approached this topic individually and conducted deep research which produced vast variance in conclusions regarding the viability of the concept and its application. Hopefully, Carl Schramm will find a copy of this someday and realize that the academic examination of his embryonic concept did take place.

Overarching Conclusions

The chapters contained within this edited work are diverse, ranging from case studies of Stability Economics providing an integral part of the solution to the Shining Path problem in Peru to an examination of the doctrinal and strategic implications of the Expeditionary Economics movement. Also, each author ended up drawing widely different conclusions about the prospect of Stability Economics as a viable and practical US Army endeavor. No single author fully embraced or dismissed Stability Economics, but there was great variance in how far each embraced the notion or cast it aside. This made drawing overarching conclusions from all five works difficult but not impossible.

All of the authors acknowledged the importance of Stability Economics to modern warfare. Regardless of whether or not the American military is engaging in a major combat operation, counterinsurgency campaign, or nation-building, all of the authors contained within this volume agree that economic factors play a key role. However, they found the execution of economic warfare to be lacking.

This is important as more publications come out referencing the weaponization of money and as post-conflict reviews of the use of the Commander's Emergency Relief Program (CERP) funds occur. Lessons learned from the recent Afghanistan and Iraq campaigns should not be overemphasized as representative of all efforts on the part of the American military to use economics in war, but neither should these lessons be marginalized, or worse, lost.

Major Marc Pelini posits that there is a growing foundation in recent executive and Department of Defense (DoD) writings placing a greater burden on the US military to carry out stability economics as part of larger stability operations. The 2010 *National Security Strategy* and the DoD's *National Defense Strategy* both layout a larger anticipated role for stability operations in the future. The US military will increasingly be tasked with performing such operations, and while the 2010 *Quadrennial Defense Review* indicates that the Army's Civil Affairs branch will be tasked with supporting economic development efforts with partnering nations, this is indicative of only one aspect of Stability Economics with which the US Army will have to deal.

Pelini concludes that robust economic development can only occur in an environment of stable security, good governance, and the rule of law. These are the foundations he sees the US Army being most able to affect in the early stages of Stability Operations. However, he finds that an uncoordinated effort between the Civilian Response Corps (CRC), USAID, Provisional Reconstruction Teams (PRTs), and other international aid agencies creates confusion that often occurs before the prerequisites of security, good governance, and rule of law are established.

Pelini closely examines the US Army's use of Commander's Emergency Relief Program (CERP) funds and finds that while much of the use of these funds was ineffectual, there were some successes. For Pelini, the problem is that none of the economic lessons learned are being formalized into doctrine or really even saved in any systematic form at all.

In the final analysis, Pelini, like several of the other authors, sees the need to introduce not only new training and doctrine dealing with Stability Economics but a new force structure. Pelini is the most aggressive, suggesting an expansion of Civil Affairs capabilities largely through reorganizing the existing Heavy Combat Brigade Team (HCBT) structure. As will become evident throughout this chapter, Civil Affairs is the most often referred to Army branch in Stability Economics discussions.

One Army practice that needs re-evaluating is the Sewer, Water, Electronic, Academics, and Transportation (SWEAT) construct. The assumption going into Afghanistan and Iraq regarding services and economics was sound: basic services are a battleground between insurgents and counterinsurgents. The one who could provide the most service the quickest was likely to win more support from the local populace. However, it is absolutely true that adherence to the SWEAT concept constrained operational and strategic thinking and forced a pre-conceived notion onto an environment and human domain that perhaps needed something completely different.

So Anthony Barbina's analysis and contribution becomes extremely important, especially at the operational and tactical level, as he finds SWEAT to be lacking in both the Afghanistan and Iraq counterinsurgency campaigns. Major Barbina proposes a very fine-tuned analytical device, the Factor-Precedence Model, to not only offer that there are nineteen broad infrastructure categories the US Army should consider building or rebuilding in a counterinsurgency fight, but also that there are regional factors, perhaps even local factors, that shape the order preference in which the US Army should tackle these infrastructure problems. This is one of the most important insights echoed by several of the other authors. Cultural factors play a big role in the desires of the people and, therefore, on what type of economic development is most appropriate and will be most effective in a country, region, or locality.

Building on this, Lieutenant Colonel J. Willem Maas argues that opportunities were lost in Afghanistan when Western military and international agency efforts, like those initiated by the World Bank, hammered a western style banking system into a fundamentally Islamic populace. Maas argued convincingly that the application of *Shari'a* Compliant Finance (SCF) has increased bank and financial penetration in the Islamic world and would have helped to improve economic development in the Afghanistan counterinsurgency campaign. There are many constraints SCF places on lending, but Maas argues that the overall benefit of lending penetration far outweighs the risks associated with SCF. Further, Maas suggests that Western lenders could meld some Western practices to SCF to create a more palatable hybrid that would accelerate economic development even further. In the final analysis, both Barbina and Maas warn that the US military and its interagency partners must not only collaborate together more efficiently but take time to understand local economic practices and desires before engaging in any Stability Economics endeavor in order to achieve full and effective unity of action.

Major Thomas Archer-Burton warns that millions of dollars in CERP funds and interagency aid has been wasted in Iraq and Afghanistan. Mirroring Major Barbina, Archer-Burton warns that CERP funds and other investments have been used largely to build infrastructure regardless of the local need. Many schools were constructed in Iraq that were later blown up by insurgents without a single student attending. Locals were often not consulted prior to a school being built. Archer-Burton correctly argues that Carl Schramm intended Expeditionary Economics to be entrepreneurial in nature. He sees four major problems with such a proposition. First, outside organizations, be they military or civilian in nature, will be much more adept at dictating changes, e.g. controlling the economy from the Keynesian commanding heights. Engendering the entrepreneurial spirit will be nearly impossible for any organization, but particularly the US Army as it has neither the expertise nor resources to do this while it fights a war or counterinsurgency. Archer-Burton notes that the US Army expended over ten billion dollars on infrastructure development but only a few million to engender an entrepreneurial spirit in either Iraq or Afghanistan. As a side note, such expenditures often undermine local economic development and lead to inflationary trends.

The second major problem is that money dispersed is rarely given with strings attached, strings that would help an entrepreneurial spirit to grow. This means there is no incentive to drive an entrepreneurial shift in economic culture and the results in Iraq show that no such culture has been engendered. Further, even successful projects enacted by Provincial Reconstruction Teams (PRTs) can lead to a culture of dependency rather than development. Currently, scholars are speculating on the ramifications to the Afghan economy that a full Coalition exit will cause.

Archer-Burton notes that when the military correctly focuses on winning short-term loyalty from the people, they miss engendering the long-term economic development that many see as at least part of the long-term solution to the strategic military problem. Too often projects are hastily constructed, funds are corruptly diverted, and no one notices or cares as long as the key leaders and organizations in a commander's area of operations are quiescent during their tour of duty. Archer-Burton has a strong point here that cannot be understated. However, sometimes short-term loyalty buying is necessary. The trick is fitting those short-term economic actions in time, space, and purpose with a larger campaign to develop the economy of a locality, region, or state.

Finally, Archer-Burton argues that the militarization of aid and economic development is sure to bring the ire of international organizations who already engage in this activity. Not only will organizations like the United Nations and, specifically, the United Nations Development Program (UNDP) feel that increasing military aid is an indictment of their past performance but other organizations whose profit or non-profit mandate revolves around international development will feel that their very existence is threatened. This is an insightful point which, to our knowledge, has not been posited previously.

Major James Connally produced some interesting findings from his detailed examination of the Peruvian government's efforts against the Shining Path insurgency. Like many of the other authors in this book, Connally found that economic development only works when a state or external actor understands the local economic culture. However, Connally provides three specific aspects of the human economic domain, which must be understood before successful economic development can occur. First, one must understand that if the poor are excluded, if relative deprivation is allowed to expand, revolt is the most likely outcome. Second, one has to work with or around local customs that allow for extralegal economic transactions or black markets. Third, one cannot hope for reform all at once. If change occurs rapidly, it will create too much shock to the economic system, resulting in sometimes dire unintended consequences. At the very least, quick reform is unlikely to stick or create a lasting entrepreneurial market and culture.

Connally also found that while the Peruvian military correctly deduced that economic concerns produced security concerns, they, despite the best intentions, were not savvy enough to bring about lasting economic change. It was not until the President Fujimori administration that a new and successful path toward economic development was carved. Despite severe economic crisis, President Fujimori resisted the temptation of outside aid, opting for the far more painful path of severing subsidies and many entitlements in order to allow market forces to take over. Short term pain led to long-term gain and ultimately was integral in undermining the Shining Path's raison d'être and leading to this downfall of this insurgency. Connally emphasizes that the rule of law and orderly markets are the key to long-term economic development.

Expeditionary Economics is a relatively new concept that sprang out of the Kaufmann Foundation and has reverberated through academia. While not specifically cited by name in any national security document, the broader concept of Stability Economics is absolutely referred to as an important aspect of stability operations. So, for better or worse, the US military and, most likely, the US Army will be involved with this endeavor for some time to come. We do not mean to imply that the US military has never been involved in economic development in the past, but the explicit emphasis and rising list of tasks associated with a new and higher level of involvement is unique to this point in American history.

The good news is that all of the authors in this volume found utility in at least some aspects of military involvement in economic development. It has been shown to lessen violence and, in at least one case, undermine an insurgency. If the Marshall Plan is any guide, it can also turn bitter enemies into lasting allies but executing successful expeditionary economics is fraught with peril.

It should be clear to the reader at this point that the US Army is not organized to deal with this task effectively. For example, an inability to establish a micro-loan program similar to what Muhammed Yunis established in Bangladesh is a shortcoming. CERP funds can only be given as grants and, as such, can lead to graft or localized inflation. The US Army is predisposed to view money as a weapon and in many cases this is an effective way to use money but this leads to short-sightedness and an overemphasis on gaining loyalty from people rather than producing lasting development. US Army leaders are often not educated properly to accomplish long-term development in the first place. There is a pressing need to coordinate US Army leaders with expertise from civilian interagency partners and international lending and development organizations. There is not even a process to effectively identify and deploy those with economic expertise in a Stability Economics operation.

For all of the promise Expeditionary Economics held and the increasing emphasis on Stability Operations, little has been done to examine the US Army's capabilities or the implications of foisting this new task on a budget constrained organization. This collection of works represents an honest attempt to approach and research this topic. It is our hope that other studies will follow.

Note

1. The editors of this volume had a written agreement granting the Kaufmann Foundation permission to print this book under their own press. In a phone call almost a year after the agreement, it was related to the editors that the Kaufmann Foundation would no longer publish works on expeditionary economics as the concept had been proven and had a life of its own.

Entrepreneurial Expeditionary Economics and the United States Military

Right Task, Wrong Tool?

by

Major Thomas J. Archer-Burton RHG/D - British Army

Bibliography

Alexander, David, "New US military strategy looks beyond Afghan war" *Reuters*, 9 February 2011, http://www.reuters.com/article/2011/02/09/us-usa-military-strategy-idUSTRE71803H20110209 (accessed 18 June 2011).

Allen, Eisendrath. "Why Building Power and Water Utilities Is like Building a National Army: and Why It Is Not." In *Expeditionary Economics: Towards and Doctrine for Enabling Stabilization and Growth.* Proceedings, West Point. June 2010. http://sites.kauffman.org/eee/resources/ee_summit_proceedings.pdf (accessed 30 January 2011).

Bacevich, Andrew J. *Washington Rules: America's Path to Permanent War.* (New York: Metropolitan Henry Holt, 2011).

Bayrasli, Elmira. "Are the Trenches of Entrepreneurship Dug In War?" *Forbes*, March 21, 2011. http://blogs.forbes.com/elmirabayrasli/2011/03/21/are-the-trenches-of-entrepreneurship-dug-in-war/ (accessed March 29, 2011).

Command and General Staff College *Entrepreneurship and Expeditionary Economics: Towards a New Approach to Economic Growth following Conflict or Disaster*, proceedings, Command and General Staff College, Ft. Leavenworth, Kansas http://sites.kauffman.org/eee/resources/ee_summit_proceedings.pdf (accessed 1 April 2011).

Cordesman, Anthony H. *The War after the War: Strategic Lessons of Iraq and Afghanistan.* (Washington, D.C.: CSIS Press, 2004).

Desai, Maghnad, and Robert Skildelsky. "Beyond Keynes and Hayek." *The Guardian*, October 28, 2010. http://www.guardian.co.uk/commentisfree/2010/oct/28/hayek-keynes-third-fourth-way (accessed 1 February 2011).

Desai, Meghnad, and Robert Skidelsky. "Beyond Keynes and Hayek." *The Guardian*, October 28, 2010. http://www.guardian.co.uk/commentisfree/2010/oct/28/hayek-keynes-third-fourth-way (accessed 4 March 2011).

Fearon, J. D. "Primary Commodity Exports and Civil War." *Journal of Conflict Resolution* 49, no. 4 (2005): 483-507.

Ferguson, Niall. *The Ascent of Money: a Financial History of the* World (New York: Penguin Press, 2008).

Flynn, Michael T., Matt Pottinger, and Paul D. Batchelor. *Fixing Intel: A Blueprint for Making Intelligence Relevant in Afghanistan.* Technical paper. January 2010. http://www.cnas.org/files/documents/publications/AfghanIntel_Flynn_Jan2010_code507_voices.pdf (accessed March 5, 2011).

Foust Joshua. "Expeditionary Economics: A New Approach to Post-Crisis

Development." American Security Project. http://americansecurityproject.org/wp-content/uploads/2011/04/Expeditionary-Economics-ExpEcon-Part-One.pdf (accessed 20 May 2011).

Fukuyama, Francis. *Nation-building: beyond Afghanistan and Iraq*. (Baltimore: Johns Hopkins University Press, 2006).

David Galula, Counter-*Insurgency Warfare: Theory and Practice* (New York: Oxford University Press, 1964).

Hirschman, Albert O. *The Strategy of Economic Development* (New Haven: Yale University Press, 1958).

Hunt, Richard A. *Pacification: the American Struggle for Vietnams Hearts and Minds*. (Boulder: Westview Press, 1995).

Johnson Gregory, Ramachandran Vijaya and Walz Julie, "The Commanders Emergency Response Program in Afghanistan & Refining US Military Capabilities in Stability and In-Conflict Development." USMA Senior Conference XLVIII http://www.dean.usma.edu/sosh/senior_conference/sc_papers/Ramachandran%20EE%20final%205%2019%202011.pdf (accessed 12 June 2012).

Kalyvas, Stathis N. *The Logic of Violence in Civil War*. Cambridge: Cambridge University Press, 2006.

Kilcullen, David. "Counterinsurgency in Iraq: Theory and Practice 2007." Noetic. http://www.orgsites.com/va/asis151/CounterinsurgencyinIraqTheoryandPractice2007.pdf (accessed 20 February 2011).

Kilcullen, David, "Small Wars Center of Excellence Counterinsurgency Seminar 07" Small Wars Center. https://jko.harmonieweb.org/coi/iwt/IWed/Document%20Library/Report%20-%20Counterinsurgency%20in%20Iraq%20-%20Theory%20and%20Practice%202007.pdf (accessed 5 May 2011).

Larson, Alan. "US Economic Diplomacy: The Next 50 Years." *Foreign Service Journal* 88, no. 2 (February 2011): 17-24.

Mehta, Aditya, UNAMA, http://unama.unmissions.org/Default.aspx?tabid=1741&ctl=Details&mid=1882&ItemID=7100 (accessed 20 May 2011).

Marron, Donald. "US Military Focuses on Development, but Does It Take the Right Approach?" The Christian Science Monitor. http://www.csmonitor.com/Business/Donald-Marron/2010/0621/US-military-focuses-on-development-but-does-it-take-the-right-approach (accessed 1 March 2011).

Moyo, Dambisa. *Dead Aid: Why Aid Makes Things Worse and How There Is Another Way for Africa* (London: Penguin, 2010).

National Military Strategy of the United States of America, 2011: Redefining America's Leadership. http://www.jcs.mil/content/files/2011-02/020811084800_2011_NMS_-_08_FEB_2011.pdf (accessed April 4, 2011).

Taylor, William, "Opposed Development: Concept and Implications." United States

Institute of Peace. http://www.usip.org/events/opposed-development-concept-and-implications (accessed 4 April 2011).

Oxfam "Quick Impact Quick Collapse: The Dangers of Militarized Aid in Afghanistan," *Oxfam Research*. http://www.oxfam.org/en/policy/quick-impact-quick-collapse (accessed 20 April 2011).

Patterson, Rebecca, and Dane Stangler. *Building Expeditionary Economics: Understanding the Field and Setting Forth a Research Agenda*. Working paper. (Kansas City: Kauffman Foundation, 2010).

Patterson, Rebecca, and Robinson, Jonathan, "The Commander as Investor: Changing CERP Practices." *PRISM* 2, no. 2 (March 2011): 115-26. http://www.ndu.edu/press/lib/images/prism2-2/prism_toc.pdf (accessed April 1, 2011).

Obama, Barack. *National Security Strategy 2010*. http://www.whitehouse.gov/sites/default/files/rss_viewer/national_security_strategy.pdf (accessed 5 February 2011).

Ricks, Thomas E. "Overhauling Intelligence Ops in the Afghan War." FOREIGN POLICY. January 5, 2010. http://ricks.foreignpolicy.com/posts/2010/01/05/overhauling_intelligence_ops_in_the_afghan_war (accessed 14 June 2011).

Riegg, Nicholas, H., "Implementing Expeditionary and Entrepreneurial Economics: Iraq and Afghanistan," *Entrepreneurship and Expeditionary Economics: Towards a New Approach to Economic Growth following Conflict or Disaster*, Command and General Staff College, Ft. Leavenworth, Kansas, http://sites.kauffman.org/eee/resources/ee_summit_proceedings.pdf (accessed 1 April 2011).

Schramm, Carl J., "Expeditionary Economics: Spurring Growth after Conflicts and Disasters." *Foreign Affairs* 89, no. 3 (April/May 2010): 89-102.

Schake, Kori, "Operationalizing Expeditionary Economics," *Entrepreneurship and Expeditionary Economics: Towards a New Approach to Economic Growth following Conflict or Disaster*, Command and General Staff College, Ft. Leavenworth, Kansas, http://sites.kauffman.org/eee/resources/ee_summit_proceedings.pdf (accessed 1 April 2011).

Smith, Rupert. *The Utility of Force: the Art of War in the Modern World*. (New York: Knopf, 2007).

Taylor, John B. *Global Financial Warriors: the Untold Story of International Finance in the Post-9/11 World*. (New York: W.W. Norton, 2007).

United States. USAID. *Development to Counter Insurgency*. Accessed May 1, 2011. http://igcc.ucsd.edu/research/security/DACOR/Evidence%20Summit%20E2COIN%20Evidence%20Packet%20Cluster%203.pdf (accessed 28 May 2011).

US Joint Chiefs of Staff. *National Military Strategy of the United States of America 2011—Redefining America's Military Leadership*. Washington, DC: US Joint Chiefs of Staff, February 8, 2011. http://www.jcs.mil//content/files/2011-02/020811084800_2011_NMS_-_08_FEB_2011.pdf (accessed 25 April 2011).

US Army, *Field Manual (Interim) 3, Operations, 2008* (Washington: Headquarters, Department of the Army, 2008).

Waldman, M. "Caught in the Conflict – Civilians and the International Security Strategy in Afghanistan" *A Briefing Paper for the NATO Heads of State and Government Summit, 3-4 April 2009.* http://www.oxfam.org.uk/resources/policy/conflict_disasters/downloads/bp_caught_in_conflict_afghanistan.pdf (accessed 03 March 2011).

Wilder, Andres, and Stuart Gordon. "Money Can't Buy America Love." Foreign Policy. December 1, 2009. http://www.foreignpolicy.com/articles/2009/12/01/money_cant_buy_america_love (accessed 1 April 2011).

Wilder, Andrew. "A 'weapons System' Based on Wishful Thinking." *Boston Globe* (Boston), September 16, 2009. Accessed March 09, 2011. http://www.boston.com/bostonglobe/editorial_opinion/oped/articles/2009/09/16/a_weapons_system_based_on_wishful_thinking/.

Yergin, Daniel, and Stanislaw, Joseph. *The Commanding Heights: the Battle for the World Economy.* (New York: Simon & Schuster, 2002).

Expeditionary Economics and Its Implications on the United States Army

by

Major Marc E. Pelini - United States Army

Bibliography

Ancker, Clinton J. "How Ideas Become Doctrine: The Evolution of Military Thought in an Era of Complex, Rapid Change." Fort Leavenworth, KS: Combined Arms Doctrine Directorate, US Army Combined Arms Center. 2010.

Baumol, William J., Robert E. Litan, and Carl J. Schramm. *Good Capitalism, Bad Capitalism, and the Economics of Growth and Prosperity*. 1 ed. New Haven: Yale University Press, 2007.

Burke, Edward. "Leaving the Civilians Behind: The 'Soldier-diplomat' in Afghanistan and Iraq." *Prism* 1, no. 2 (March 2010): 26-47.

Carreau, Bernard. "Lessons from USDA in Iraq and Afghanistan." *Prism* 1, no. 3 (June 2010): 139-50.

Casey Jr., George. "SITREP on the Army." Lecture, Command and General Staff College, Fort Leavenworth, KS, April 16, 2010. MP3 file. https://courses.leavenworth. army.mil/webapps/portal/frameset.jsp?tab_id=_18_1 (accessed December 7, 2010).

Chandrasekaran, Rajiv. "Marines seek foothold in Helmand." *The Financial Times*. July 8, 2009.

Chu, Jeff. "Joint Venture." *Fast Company*, May 2010, 73-79.

Cohen, Eliot A., and John Gooch. *Military Misfortunes: The Anatomy of Failure in War*. Illustrated. ed. New York: Anchor, 1991.

Collier, Paul. "Economic Causes of Civil Conflict and their Implications for Policy." University of Oxford, 2006. http://users.ox.ac.uk/...econpco/research/pdfs/ EconomicCausesofCivilConflict-ImplicationsforPolicy.pdf (accessed December 7, 2010).

Cornell, Stephen and Joseph P. Kalt. "Reloading the Dice: Improving the Chances for Economic Development on American Indian Reservations." Los Angeles: American Indian Studies Center, UCLA. 1992.

Crane, Conrad C. "Phase IV Operations: Where Wars are Really Won." *Military Review* (May-June 2007): 11-19.

Department of Defense. Department of Defense Instruction 3000.05. Washington, District of Columbia: United States Department of Defense, 2009.

----------. *National Defense Strategy*. Washington, District of Columbia, 2008.

----------. *Quadrennial Defense Review Report*. Washington, District of Columbia. 2010.

Joint Staff. *Capstone Concept for Joint Operations* [Version 3.0]. Washington, DC: Government Printing Office, 2009.

----------. *Joint Publication 1-02: Dictionary of Military and Associated Terms*: As Amended

Through 31 July 2010. Washington, DC: Government Printing Office, 2010.

----------. *Joint Publication 3.0: Joint Operations*: Incorporating Change 2. Washington, DC: Government Printing Office, 2010.

----------. *Joint Publication 3-07.3 Peace Operations*. Washington, DC: Government Printing Office, 2007.

Driscoll, Gerald P.. *Adam Smith and Modern Political Economy: Bicentennial Essays on The Wealth of Nations*. Ames: Iowa State University Press, 1979.

Gates, Robert M. "Helping Others Defend Themselves." *Foreign Affairs* 89, no. 3 (May/June 2010): 2-6.

Grameen Bank. "Grameen Bank At A Glance: September 2010". http://www.grameen-info.org/index.php?option=com_content&task=view&id=26&Itemid=175 (accessed December 7, 2010).

Grimmett, Richard F. *CRS Report for Congress: Instances of Use of United States Armed Forces Abroad, 1798-2007*. Washington, DC: Congressional Research Service, 2008. http://www.au.af.mil/au/awc/awcgate/crs/rl32170.pdf (accessed December 7, 2010).

Headquarters, Department of the Army, *2010 Army Posture Statement*. Washington, District of Columbia: United States Army, 2010.

----------. "Adapting our Aim: A Balanced Army for a Balanced Strategy." Washington, DC: United States Army, 2009.

----------. *Field Manual 3-05.40: Civil Affairs Operations*. Washington, District of Columbia: Department of the Army, 2006.

----------. *Field Manual: 3-07: Stability Operations*. Washington, DC: Government Printing Office, 2008.

----------. Force Management Memorandum "Organizational Design Paper for Active Army Conventional Forces CA Brigade." Washington, DC February 22, 2010.

----------. *Pamphlet 611-21: Personnel Selection and Classification*. Washington, DC: Government Printing Office, January 22, 2007.

----------. *The Army Strategy 2008*. Washington, DC: Government Printing Office, 2008.

Hoekstra, Robert. "Adjusting to Stabilization and Reconstruction Operations." *PRISM* 1, no. 2 (March 2010): 13-26.

Kolb, Lawrence J. "Fixing the Mix." *Foreign Affairs* 83. no. 2, March 2004.

Kennedy, John F. "Remarks at West Point to the Graduating Class of the US Military Academy." John F. Kennedy Library, June 6, 1962, http://www.jfklibrary.org/Asset+Tree/Asset+Viewers/Audio+Video+Asset+Viewer.htm?guid={71B1B505-C400-4CA5-8CE8-2C36BC2618F0}&type=Audio (accessed December 7, 2010).

Kruzel, John J. "Economic Training for Junior Ranks Resonates with Military Chief." Official Homepage of the United States Army. http://www.army.mil/-news/2010/03/05/35363-economic-training-for-junior-ranks-resonates-with-military-chief/ (accessed December 7, 2010).

Marquis, Jefferson P. *Developing an Army Strategy for Building Partner Capacity for Stability Operations.* Arlington, Virginia: RAND Corporation, 2010.

Mines, Keith W.. "E-Notes: Economic Tools in Counterinsurgency and Postconflict Stabilization: Lessons Learned (and Relearned) in al Anbar, Iraq, 2003" Foreign Policy Research Institute - FPRI. http://www.fpri.org/enotes/20060928.military.mines.economictoolscounterinsurgency.html (accessed December 7, 2010).

Murad, Anatol. *What Keynes Means: A Critical Clarification of the Economic Theories of John Maynard.* New York: Bookman Associates, 1962.

National Public Radio. "Diplomats Pushed to Serve in Iraq." National Public Radio.

http://www.npr.org/templates/story/story.php?storyId=15939537&ft=1&f=1012 (accessed December 7, 2010).

O'Brien, D.P. *Classical Economists.* Oxford: Oxford University Press, 1975.

Office of the President of the United States. *National Security Presidential Directive/ NSPD-44.*

Washington, DC: The White House, 2005.
----------. *National Security Strategy.* Washington, DC: The White House, 2010.

Patil, Sayali Bedekar. "Classical Economics vs Keynesian Economics." Buzzle Web Portal: Intelligent Life on the Web. http://www.buzzle.com/articles/classical-economics-vs-keynesian-economics.html (accessed December 7, 2010).

Schake, Kori. "Operationalizing Expeditionary Economics." Hoover Institution, 2010.

Schramm, Carl. "Expeditionary Economics." *Foreign Affairs*, May - June 2010, 89-99.

United States Department of State. "Office of the Coordinator for Reconstruction and Stabilization (S/CRS): Reserve Component, Civilian Response Corps." Office of the Coordinator for Reconstruction and Stabilization (S/CRS) : Home Page. http://www.crs.state.gov/index.cfm?fuseaction=public.display&shortcut=4B5C (accessed December 7, 2010).

----------. "Reserve Component, Civilian Response Corps." US Department of State.

http://www.crs.state.gov/index.cfm?fuseaction=public.display&shortcut=4B5C (accessed December 7, 2010).

----------. "Secretary Clinton Announces Civilian Response Corps Reaches 1,000 Members at Its Two-Year Anniversary Mark." US Department of State. http://m.state.gov/md144656.htm (accessed December 7, 2010).

----------. "Standby Component Opportunities." US Department of State.

http://www.crs.state.gov/index.cfm?fuseaction=public.display&shortcut=4FPI (accessed December 7, 2010).

United States Institute of Peace. "Embedded Provincial Reconstruction Teams." United States Institute of Peace. http://www.usip.org/publications/embedded-provincial-reconstruction-teams (accessed December 7, 2010).

Simpson, Samual Kyle. "Restructuring Civil Affairs for Persistent Engagement." US Army Command and General Staff College, 2010.

Skidelsky, Robert. *Keynes: The Return of the Master*. New York: PublicAffairs, 2009.

Smith, Rupert. The Utility of Force: The Art of War in the Modern World. New York: Vintage, 2008.

Special Investigator General for Iraqi Reconstruction (SIGR). "SIGR Accomplishments," March

2010, http://www.sigir.mil/files/about/SIGIRaccomplishments.pdf (accessed December 7, 2010).

----------. *Quarterly and Semi-Annual Report to the United States Congress*. Washington DC: SIGR, July 2010.

The Louis Berger Group, Inc., and The Services Group, Inc. "Iraq Private Sector Growth and Employment Generation: The Iraq Microfinance Strategy." Washington, DC: United States Agency for International Development, 2007.

The White House. *The National Security Strategy of the United States of America.* Washington, DC: Government Printing Office, 2010.

Treadgold, Matt. "Fit to Exercise: S/CRS and AFRICOM's Judicious Response Exercise."

Civilian Response no. 11 (Summer 2010): 24.

United Nations Development Programme, (UNDP). *Human Development Report 2002*. New York: Oxford University Press, USA, 2002.

United States Embassy Iraq, "PRT (Provincial Reconstruction Team) Fact Sheet 2008," March 20, 2008.

United States Forces Afghanistan (USFOR-A). *USFOR-A Publication 1-06 (Money As A Weapon System)*. Kabul, Afghanistan, 2007.

United States Institute of Peace and US Peacekeeping and Stability Operations Institute.

Guiding Principles for Stabilization and Reconstruction. Washington, D.C: United States Institute of Peace Press, 2009.

United States Forces Command. "Infantry Warfighting Conference." Presentation at the Infantry Warfighting Conference. US Forces Command. Fort Benning, GA,

September 14, 2010, https://www.benning.army.mil/iwc/2010/...Gen%20Thurman.ppt (accessed December 7, 2010).

----------. "National Guard Association of the United States." Presentation at the National Guard

Association of the United States Conference. US Forces Command. Fort McPherson, GA, August 23, 2010, http://www.ngaus.org/ngaus/files/ccLibraryFiles/ Filename/000000006899/thurman.pdf (accessed December 7, 2010).

United States Joint Forces Command. *Joint Operating Environment: 2010*. Suffolk, VA: Government Printing Office, 2010.

"UT G8 Info. Centre. Genoa Summit 2001. COMMUNIQUÉ." G8 Information Centre. http://www.g8.utoronto.ca/summit/2001genoa/finalcommunique.html (accessed December 7, 2010).

US Army Combined Arms Center. "Commander's Guide to Money as a Weapon System." *Center for Army Lessons Learned Handbook* 09-07 (2009).

----------. "Provencial Reconstruction Teams." *Center for Army Lessons Learned Playbook* 07-34 (2007).

Wright, Donald P., and Timothy R. Reese. *On Point II: Transition to the New Campaign: The United States Army in Operation IRAQI FREEDOM,* May 2003-January 2005. Fort Leavenworth, KS: Department of the Army, 2008.

Yunus, Muhammad. *Banker To The Poor: Micro-Lending and the Battle Against World Poverty.*

Reviewed and updated for the paperback edition. London: PublicAffairs, 2008.

Expeditionary Economics in Turbulent Times
by
Lieutenant Colonel James R. Connally - United States Army

Bibliography

Books

Arce, Moises. Market Reform in Society: Post Crisis Politics and Economic Change in Authoritarian Peru. University Park: The Pennsylvania State University Press, 2005.

Berg, Ronald H. "Peasant Responses to Shining Path in Andahuaylas." In *The Shining Path of Peru*, edited by David Scott Palmer, 101-122. New York: St. Martin's Press, 1994.

Chang, Ha-Joon. "The East Asian Development Experience," In *Rethinking Development Economics*. edited by Ha-Joon Chang, 107-124. London: Anthem Press, 2003.

Cordero, Isabel Coral. "Women in War: Impact and Responses." In *Shining and Other Paths: War and Society in Peru, 1980-1995*, edited by Steve J. Stern, 345-374. Durham: Duke University Press, 1998.

Degregori, Carlos Ivan. "The Origins and Logic of Shining Path: Two Views." In *The Shining Path of Peru*, edited by David Scott Palmer, 51-62. New York: St. Martin's Press, 1994.

de Soto, Hernando. The Mystery of Capital: Why Capitalism Triumphs in the West and Fails Everywhere Else. New York: Basic Books, 2000.

—. The Other Path: The Economic Answer to Terrorism. New York: Basic Books, 1989.

Easterly, William. The White Man's Burden: Why the West's Efforts to Aid the Rest have done so much Ill and so Little Good. London: Penguin Books Ltd., 2006.

Gorriti, Gustavo. "Shining Path's Stalin and Trotsky." In *The Shining Path of Peru*, edited by David Scott Palmer, 167-188. New York: St. Martin's Press, 1994.

Isbell, Billie Jean. "Shining Path and Peasant Responses in Rural Ayachucho." In *The Shining Path of Peru*, edited by David Scott Palmer, 77-99. New York: St. Martin's Press, 1994.

Khor, Martin. "Globalization, Global Governance and the Dilemmas of Development," In *Rethinking Development Economics*. edited by Ha-Joon Chang, 523-544. London: Anthem Press, 533.

Landes, David S. The Wealth and Poverty of Nations: Why Some Are So Rich and Some So Poor. New York: W.W. Norton, 1999.

Marks, Tom. "Making Revolution with the Shining Path." In *The Shining Path of Peru*, edited by David Scott Palmer, 209-223. New York: St. Martin's Press, 1994.

McClintock, Cynthia. Revolutionary Movements in Latin America: El Salvador's

FMLN and Peru's Shining Path. Washington: United States Institute of Peace Press, 1998.

McClintock, Cynthia. "Theories of Revolution and the Case of Peru." In *The Shining Path of Peru*, edited by David Scott Palmer, 243-258. New York: St. Martin's Press, 1994.

Oliart, Patricia. "Alberto Fujimori: "The Man Peru Needed?"," In *Shining and Other Paths: War and Society in Peru, 1980-1995*. edited by Steve J. Stern, 411-424. Durham: Duke University Press, 1998.

Palmer, David Scott. "Conclusion: The View From the Windows." In *The Shining Path of Peru*, edited by David Scott Palmer, 259-273. New York: St. Martin's Press, 1994.

Palmer, David Scott. "Introduction: History, Politics, and Shining Path in Peru." In *The Shining Path of Peru*, edited by David Scott Palmer, 1-32. New York: St. Martin's Press, 1994.

Paredes, Carlos E., and Jeffrey D. Sachs. "Introduction and Summary." In *Peru's Path to Recovery: A Plan for Economic Stabiliztion and Growth*, edited by Carlos E. Paredes and Jeffrey D. Sachs, 13-38. Washington: The Brookings Institution, 1991.

Prahalad, C. K. *The Fortune at the Bottom of the Pyramid*. Upper Saddle River: Wharton School Publishing, 2006.

Reinert, Erik S. How Rich Countries Got Rich and Why Poor Countries Stay Poor. New York: PublicAffairs, 2007.

—. "Increasing Poverty in a Globalized World: Marshall Plans and Morgenthau Plans as Mechanisms of Polarization of World Incomes," In *Rethinking Development Economics*. edited by Ha-Joon Chang (London: Anthem Press, 2003), 453-478.

Sachs, Jeffrey D. The End of Poverty: Economic Possibilities for Our Time. New York: Penguin Books, 2005.

Smith, Michael L. "Shining Path's Urban Strategy: Ate Vitarte." In *The Shining Path of Peru*, edited by David Scott Palmer, 145-165. New York: St. Martin's Press, 1994.

Stiglitz, Joseph. *Joseph Stiglitz and the World Bank: The Rebel Within*. London, Wimbledon Publishing Company, 2001.

Turabian, Kate L. *A Manual for Writers of Research Papers, Theses, and Dissertations*. 7th ed. Chicago: University of Chicago Press, 2007.

William J. Baumol, Robert E. Litan, and Carl J. Schramm. *Good Capitalism, Bad Capitalism, and the Economics of Growth and Prosperity* . New Haven: Yale University Press, 2007.

Wise, Carol. Reinventing the State: Economic Strategy and Institutional Change in Peru. Ann Arbor: The University of Michigan Press, 2003

Journals

Schramm, Carl J. "Expeditionary Economics: Spurring Growth After Conflicts and Disasters." *Foreign Affairs* (Council on Foreign Relations) 89, no. 3 (May/June 2010): 89-99.

Public Documents

US Department of the Army. *Field Manual 3-07: Stability Operations*. Washington, 2008. 2-8 - 2-9.

Web Sites

Oxforddictionaries.com. http://www.oxforddictionaries.com/view/entry/m_en_us1243059#m_en_us1243059 (accessed August 31, 2010).

Oxforddictionaries.com. http://www.oxforddictionaries.com/view/entry/m_en_us1245619#m_en_us1245619 (accessed August 31, 2010).

Comparing Models for the Restoration of Essential Services during Counterinsurgency Operations

by

Major Anthony P. Barbina - United States Army

Bibliography

Adams, Bianka J. *Command Report, 2009 Multi-National Division Baghdad, 1st US Cavalry Division*. Fort Hood, TX: Division Historian Publications, 2010. http://www.ndia. org/Divisions/Divisions/SOLIC/Documents/Command_Report_12-10-10.pdf (accessed on January 25, 2011).

Bar-Yam, Yaneer. Making Things Work: Solving Complex Problems in a Complex World. Cambridge, MA: NECSI Knowledge Press, 2004.

Barton, Frederick, and Bathsheba Crocker. *Progress or Peril? Measuring Iraq's Reconstruction*. Washington, DC: Center for Strategic and International Studies, 2004.

Beckett, I. F. W., and John Pimlott. *Armed Forces and Modern Counter-Insurgency.* London: Croom Helm, 1985.

Berman, Eli, Jacob Shapiro, and Joseph Felter. "Can Hearts and Minds be Bought? The Economics of Counterinsurgency in Iraq." Cambridge, MA: National Bureau of Economics Research (NBER) WP #14606, 2008. http://econ.ucsd.edu/~elib/ham.pdf. (accessed on November 20, 2010).

Birtle, Andrew. J. US Army Counterinsurgency and Contingency Operations Doctrine 1942-1976. Washington, DC: Center of Military History, 2007.

Bousquet, Antoine. *The Scientific Way of Warfare.* New York, NY: Columbia University Press, 2009.

Bowman, Steve and Catherine Dale. *War in Afghanistan: Strategy, Military Operations, and Issues for Congress – R40156*. Congressional Research Service: Washington, DC, 2009. http://www.fas.org/sgp/crs/row/R40156.pdf (accessed on January 25, 2011)

Box, George E. P., and Norman R. Draper. Empirical Model-Building and Response Surfaces (Wiley Series on Probability and Statistics). New York, NY: John Wiley and Sons, Inc., 1987.

Brigham, Erwin. "Pacification Measurement." *Military Review* (May 1970): 47-55.

Brown, Ross A. "Commander's Assessment: South Baghdad." *Military Review* 86, no. 1 (January-February 2007): 27-34.

Center for Army Lessons Learned (CALL). "Seven Months in Ar Ramadi: Observations from: 2d Battalion, 4th Marines." *A Summary of Observations from OIF 04-06*. Fort Leavenworth, KS: Government Printing Office, 2006. FOUO.

Chiarelli, Peter, and Patrick Michaelis. "Winning the Peace: The Requirement for Full Spectrum Operations." *Military Review 85, no. 4 (*July-August 2005): 4–17.

Choueri, Nazli, Daniel Goldsmith, Stuart E. Madnick, et al. "Using System Dynamics to Model and Better Understand State Stability." Cambridge, MA: MIT Sloan School of Management Working Paper 4661-07 (CISL# 2007-03), 2007. http://ssrn.com/ abstract=1011230 (accessed on November 26, 2010).

Christoff, Joseph A. *Rebuilding Iraq: Stabilization, Reconstruction, and Financing Challenges - GAO-06-428T* . Testimony before the Committee on Foreign Relations, United States Senate (February 8, 2006). United States Government Accountability Office (GAO): Washington, DC, 2006. http://www.gao.gov/new.items/d06428t.pdf (accessed on January 25, 2011).

---------------. "Rebuilding Iraq: Status of Funding and Reconstruction Efforts." *Report to Congressional Committees - GAO-05-876* (July 2005). United States Government Accountability Office (GAO): Washington, DC, 2005. http://www.gao.gov/new.items/ d05876.pdf (accessed on January 25, 2011).

Cianci, Gambrel R. "Maslow's hierarchy of needs: Does it apply in a collectivist culture." *Journal of Applied Management and Entrepreneurship*, 8 (2003), 143-161.

Cordesman, Anthony H. *The War After the War: Strategic Lessons of Iraq and Afghanistan.* Washington, DC: CSIS Press, Center for Strategic and International Studies, 2004.

Crane, Keith. Guidebook for Supporting Economic Development in Stability Operations. Santa Monica: RAND Corporation, 2009.

Dale, Catherine. *Operation IRAQI FREEDOM: Strategies, Approaches, Results, and Issues for Congress – RL34387*. Washington, DC: Congressional Research Service, 2009. http://www.fas.org/sgp/crs/mideast/RL34387.pdf (accessed on January 25, 2011).

DeJarnette, John. "Toward a Nation-Building Operating Concept." Master's monograph, School of Advanced Military Studies, Command and General Staff College, 2010.

Dobbins, James, Seth G. Jones, Keith Krane, and Beth Cole DeGrasse . *The Beginner's Guide to Nation-Building*. Santa Monica: RAND Corporation, 2007.

Dodge, Toby. Inventing Iraq: The Failure of Nation-Building and a History Denied. New York, NY: Columbia University Press. 2003.

Draper, Steven C. 1st Cavalry Division Museum Director. "1st Cavalry Division History - GWOT History." Fort Hood, TX: 2010 1st Cavalry Division Museum. http://www.hood. army.mil/1stcavdiv/about/history/gwot.htm (accessed on January 25, 2011).

Fall, Bernard B. *Street Without Joy.* Mechanicsburg, PA: Stackpole Books, 1994.

Farr, John V., and Brian D. Sawser. *US Embassy (Kabul) Value Model and Project Analysis Tool*. West Point, NY: Department of Systems Engineering, 2010.

Feldman, Noah. *What We Owe Iraq: War and the Ethics of Nation Building.* Princeton, NJ: Princeton University Press, 2004.

Fuller, Samuel, and Paul Kremer. *Engineer Infrastructure Assessment and Reconnaissance.* Fort Leonard Wood, MO. United States Army Engineer School, 2005.

Fullerton, Alexander and Garth Myers. "Fitting into the Fight – An Engineer's Dream From a Brigade Troops Battalion S3." *Small Wars Journal (2009)*. Richmond, VA: Small Wars Foundation LLC, 2004. http://smallwarsjournal.com/blog/journal/docs-temp/221-fullerton.pdf (accessed on January 25, 2011).

Gaddis, John Lewis. *The Landscape of History: How Historians Map the Past.* New York, NY: Oxford University Press, 2002.

Galula, David. Counterinsurgency Warfare: Theory and Practice. New York, NY: Praeger, 1964.

--------------. Foreword by Robert R. Bowie. *Counterinsurgency Warfare: Theory and Practice*. St. Petersburg, FL: Hailer Publishing, 2005.

Gates, Robert. "Landon Lecture Series Secretary of Defense Speech." Kansas State University Landon Lecture (26 November 2007). Washington, DC: Office of the Assistant Secretary of Defense (Public Affairs), 2007. http://www.defense.gov/Speeches/Speech. aspx?SpeechID=1199 (accessed December 7, 2010).

Gilley, Bruce. *The Right to Rule*. New York, NY: Colombia University Press, 2009.

Gorkowski, Justin B. "A Penny for Your Thoughts, a Nickel for Your Heart: The Influence of the Commander's Emergency Response Program on Insurgency." Master's thesis, Naval Post Graduate School, 2009.

Griffith, Samuel. *Mao Tse-Tung On Guerrilla Warfare*. Baltimore, MD: The Nautical & Aviation Publishing Company of America, 1992.

Helmus, Todd, Christopher Paul, and Russell Glenn. Enlisting Madison Avenue: The Marketing Approach to Earning Popular Support in Theaters of Operation. Santa Monica, CA: RAND Corporation, 2007.

Herbst, Jeffrey. *States and Power in Africa: Comparative Lessons in Authority and Control*. Princeton, NJ: Princeton University Press, 2000.

Hofstede, Geert. "The Cultural Relativity of the Quality of Life Concept." *Academy of Management Review* 9 (July 1984): 389–398. http://www.nyegaards.com/yansafiles/ Geert%20Hofstede%20cultural%20attitudes.pdf (accessed on November 20, 2010).

Holmes, Barrett L. "Restoring Essential Services in Baghdad During Operation IRAQI FREEDOM II." USAWC Strategy Research Project, US Army War College, 2007.

Islamic Republic of Afghanistan. Afghanistan National Development Strategy (2008-2013): A Strategy for Security, Governance, Economic Growth, and Poverty Reduction. Kabul, Afghanistan: Afghanistan National Development Strategy Secretariat, 2009.

Joes, Anthony J. *Resisting Rebellion: The History and Politics of Counterinsurgency*. Lexington, KY: The University Press of Kentucky, 2004.

Jones, Norris. "Upgrading Baghdad Essential Services." *Iraq Reconstruction Report (December 2006)*. Baghdad, Iraq: United States Army Corps of Engineers, 2006.

Kilcullen, David J. "Countering Global Insurgency." *Small Wars Journal (NOV 04)*. Richmond, VA: Small Wars Foundation LLC, 2004. http://smallwarsjournal.com/ documents/kilcullen.pdf (accessed on November 20, 2010).

--------------. "Counterinsurgency in Iraq: Theory and Practice, 2007." *Small Wars Center of Excellence Counterinsurgency Seminar 07 (CS 07 – 26 September 2007)*. Quantico, VA: Marine Corps Warfighting Laboratory, 2007. Report written by Mr. David Dilegge. http://smallwarsjournal.com/documents/COINSeminarSummaryReport.doc (accessed on December 4, 2010).

--------------. "Three Pillars of Counterinsurgency." Remarks delivered at the US Government Counterinsurgency Conference on September 28, 2006. Washington, DC: Office of the Coordinator for Counterterrorism, 2006. *www.au.af.mil/au/awc/awcgate/ uscoin/3pillars_of_counterinsurgency.pdf* (accessed December 4, 2010).

--------------. "Twenty-Eight Articles: Fundamentals of Company-Level Insurgency."

Military Review (May-June 2006): 103-108.

King, Anthony A. "Maslow: The First Step in COIN." Quantico, VA: Marine Corps University, 2009.

Kipp, Jacob. "The Human Terrain System a CORDS for the 21st Century." *Military Review* 86, no. 5 (September-October 2006): 8-15.

Kirkwood, Craig. Strategic Decision Making: Multiobjective Decision Analysis. Belmont, CA: Wadsworth Publishing, 1997.

Kretchik, Walter E., Robert F. Baumann, and John T. Fishel. *Invasion, Intervention, "Intervasion": A Concise History of the US Army in Operation UPHOLD DEMOCRACY.* Fort Leavenworth, KS: US Army Command and General Staff College Press, 1997.

Kugelman, Michael S. Winning Hearts and Minds Through "Actual Deeds": US Public Diplomacy During the Occupation of the Philippines in Comparison with the American Involvement in Iraq Today. Medford, MA: The Fletcher School Tufts University Press, 2005.

Kuhn, Thomas S. *The Structure of Scientific Revolutions*. Chicago, IL: University of Chicago Press, 1970.

Ladwig, Walter C. III. "Managing Counterinsurgency: Lessons from Malaya" *Military Review (*May-June 2007): 56-66.

Langguth, A. J. *Our Vietnam: The War, 1954-1975*. New York, NY: Simon and Schuster, 2000.

Lewy, Guenter. *America in Vietnam*. New York, NY: Oxford University Press, 1978.

Lindberg, Travis, Joe Manous, Ronald Welch, and Timothy Trainor. *Infrastructure Assessment Methodology*. 73rd Military Operations Research Society Symposium (MORSS) (June 21-23, 2005). West Point, NY: Department of Systems Engineering, United States Military Academy, 2005.

Lindberg, Travis, and David Anderson. "Prioritizing the Reconstruction of Critical Infrastructure with a Stability Operation Environment." *Small Wars Journal* (2008). Available at http://smallwarsjournal.com/blog/journal/docs-temp/94-lindberg.pdf (accessed November 20, 2010).

Lindberg, Travis. "The Critical Infrastructure Portfolio Selection Model." Master's thesis, Command and General Staff College, 2008.

Lindeburg, Michael R. *Civil Engineering Reference Manual for the PE Exam, 11th Edition*. Belmont, CA: Professional Publications, Inc. (PPI), 2008.

Lippitt. Gordon.L. *Visualizing Change Model Building and the Change Process*. Fairfax, VA: NTL Learning Resources, 1973. http://nationalforum.com/Electronic%20Journal%20Volumes%5CKritsonis,%20Alicia%20Comparison%20of%20Change%20Theories.pdf (accessed on November 26, 2010).

Londono, Ernesto. "US 'Money Weapon' Yields Mixed Results." *Washington Post*, July 27, 2009. http://www.washingtonpost.com/wp-dyn/content/article/2009/07/26/AR2009072602833.html (accessed on November 26, 2010).

Manous, Joe, Ronald Welch, Timothy Trainer, and Led Klosky. *A Soldier's Guide For Infrastructure Information and Data Collection (I2DC)*. Department of Geography and Environmental Engineering, United States Military Academy, West Point, NY. June 2005

Martins, Mark. "The Commander's Emergency Response Program." *Joint Forces Quarterly* 37 (2005): 46–52.

Maslow, Abraham H. "A Theory of Human Motivation." *Psychological Review* (50): 370-396. http://psychclassics.yorku.ca/Maslow/motivation.htm (accessed on November 20, 2010).

---------------. "Maslow's hierarchy of needs." W*ikipedia.* Nov 12, 2007. http://en.wikipedia.org/wiki/Maslow's_hierarchy_of_needs, dtd 12 Nov 07 (accessed August 28, 2010).

---------------. *Motivation and Personality.* New York, NY: Harper and Row Publishers, 1954.

---------------. *Motivation and Personality, Third Edition.* New York, NY: Addison Wesley Educational Publishers, 1987.

---------------. *Toward a Psychology of Being.* New York: John Wiley & Sons, 1999.

Morrison, Dan A. *Geo-Cultural Analysis Tool^{TM} (GCAT)*. Remarks and presentation delivered at the US DoD Modeling and Simulation (M&S) Conference in Orlando, FL on March 10, 2008. Champagne, IL: US Army Research & Development Center (ERDC), 2008. *www.msco.mil/files/DMSC/2008/Geo_Cultural_Analysis_Tool.ppt* (accessed on January 25, 2011).

Murray, Williamson, ed. *A Nation at War in an Era of Strategic Change.* Carlisle Barracks, PA: Strategic Studies Institute, US Army War College, 2004.

Nagl, John A. Learning to Eat Soup With a Knife: Counterinsurgency Lessons from Malaya and Vietnam. Chicago, IL: University of Chicago Press, 2005.

Office of the Assistant Secretary of the Army (Acquisition, Logistics, & Technology) and the US Army Corps of Engineers. "Iraq Reconstruction Report: Focusing on Construction and Sustainment, 12.08.06" Arlington, VA: Strategic Communications Office, 2006. http://www.dvidshub.net/index.php?script=pubs/pubs_show.php&id=18&name=Iraq%20Reconstruction%20Report (accessed on January 25, 2011).

O'Neill, Bard E. Insurgency and Terrorism: Inside Modern Revolutionary Warfare. Washington, DC: Brassey's, 1990.

Operations Group Sidewinder Team. *SWEAT Smartbook: Practical Applications For Deploying Units Version 3.0.* Fort Irwin, CA: National Training Center, 2005. http://www.irwin.army.mil/Units/Operations+Group/Sidewinder/default.htm (accessed on August 28, 2010).

Orr, Robert C. Winning the Peace: An American Strategy for Post-Conflict Reconstruction. Washington, DC: The CSIS Press, 2004.

Patai, Raphael. *The Arab Mind.* New York, NY: Hatherleigh Press, 2002.

Pierson, Brett. "A System Dynamics Model of the FM 3-24 COIN Manual." 76th Military Operations Research Society Symposium (MORSS) (June 10-12, 2008). Washington, DC: *Warfighting Analysis Division, 2008.* http://www.mors.org/UserFiles/file/meetings/07ic/Pierson.pdf (accessed on December 7, 2010)

----------------. PA Consulting Group. "Dynamic Planning for COIN in Afghanistan." London, UK: PA Knowledge Limited, 2009.

Pirnie, Bruce, and Edward O'Connell. *Counterinsurgency in Iraq (2003-2006)*. Santa Monica, CA: RAND National Defense Research Institute, 2008.

Plummer, Dawson A. "Examining the Effectiveness of SWET and the Sons of SWET in OIF." Master's monograph, School for Advanced Military Studies, 2007.

Race, Jeffrey. *War Comes to Long An: Revolutionary Conflict in a Vietnamese Province*. Berkeley and Los Angeles, CA: University of California Press, 1972.

Reynolds, Paul Davidson. *A Primer on Theory Construction*. Boston, MA: Allyn & Bacon, 1971.

Robinson, J B Perry. *Transformation in Malaya / J.B. Perry Robinson*. London, England: Secker & Warburg, 1956.

Roush, Maurice. "The Hamlet Evaluation System." *Military Review* (September 1969): 10-17.

Sepp, Kalev. "Best Practices in Counterinsurgency." *Military Review* (May-June 2005): 10.

Skinner, B.F. *Science and Human Behavior: Behaviorism*. New York, NY: The Free Press, 1953.

Special Inspector General for Afghanistan Reconstruction (SIGAR). "October 2010 Quarterly Report to Congress." http://www.sigar.mil/pdf/quarterlyreports/Oct2010/Lores/SIGAR4Q_2010Book.pdf (accessed on November 20, 2010).

Special Inspector General for Iraq Reconstruction (SIGIR). "Management of the Commander's Emergency Response Program in Iraq for Fiscal Year 2006." http://www.sigir.mil/files/audits/07-006.pdf#view=fit (accessed on November 26, 2010).

----------------. "October 2010 Quarterly Report to Congress." http://www.sigir.mil/publications/quarterlyreports/index.html (accessed on November 20, 2010).

----------------. "Tables: Funding for Iraq Reconstruction." http://www.sigir.mil/publications/quarterlyreports/October2010-Tables.html#Section2 (accessed on November 20, 2010).

Stewart, Rory. The Prince of the Marshes: And Other Occupational Hazards of a Year in Iraq. Orlando: Harcourt, Inc., 2006.

Summers, Harry G. *On Strategy: A Critical Analysis of the Vietnam War*. Quoted in Colonel Robert Killebrew's "Winning Wars." *Army Magazine*, April 2005.

Taddeo, Valentina. "US Response to Terrorism: A Strategic Analysis of the Afghanistan Campaign."*Journal of Strategic Security, 3* (2010): 27-38. **http://scholarcommons.usf.edu/cgi/viewcontent.cgi?article=1010&context=jss** (accessed January 25, 2011).

Terrill, W. A., and Conrad C. Crane. *Precedents, Variables, and Options in Planning a US Military Disengagement Strategy from Iraq*. Carlisle Barracks, PA: Strategic Studies Institute, US Army War College, 2005.

The Sphere Project. Humanitarian Charter and Minimum Standards in Disaster Response. Oxford, England: Oxfam Publishing, 2004.

The World Bank. *Post-Conflict Reconstruction: The Role of the World Bank.* Washington DC: The International Bank for Reconstruction and Development, 1998.

Time Magazine Editor. "Battle of Malaya: Smiling Tiger." *Time (December 1952)*: 42-50. www.time.com/time/magazine/article/0,9171,820481,00.html (accessed on December 4, 2009).

Trinquier, Roger. *Modern Warfare: A French View of Counterinsurgency*, translated from French by Daniel Lee. New York, NY: Praeger, 1964. http://carl.army.mil/download/csipubs/trinquier/intro.pdf (accessed on January 25, 2011).

Turabian, Kate L. *A Manual for Writers of Research Papers, Theses, and Dissertations.* 7th ed. Chicago: University of Chicago Press, 2007.

United States Army Engineer School (USAES). *The SWEAT/IR Book: Infrastructure Reconnaissance Version 2.1 (6OCT05).* Fort Leonard Wood, MO: United States Army Engineer School and Engineer Research and Design Center (ERDC), 2005.

United States (US) Congress. Senate. Committee on Foreign Relations. *Civil Operations and Rural Development Support Program*: Hearing before the Committee on Foreign Relations. 91st Cong., 2nd sess., 17-20 February and 3, 4, 17, 19 March 1970. http://homepage.ntlworld.com/jksonc/docs/phoenix-scfr-1970-appx.html (accessed on November 20, 2010).

US Department of Defense. *Department of Defense Directive (DoDD) 3000.05: Military Support for Stability, Security, Transition, and Reconstruction (SSTR) Operations (DoDD 3000.05, November 28, 2005).* Washington, DC: Secretary of Defense for Policy, 2005.

---------------. *Department of Defense Instruction Number (DoDI) 3000.05: Stability Operations (DoDI 3000.05, September 16, 2009).* Washington, DC: Secretary of Defense for Policy, 2009.

---------------. Joint Publication 1-02, Department of Defense Dictionary of Military and Associated Terms. Washington, DC: Government Printing Office, 2010.

---------------. *Joint Publication 5-0, Joint Operations Planning.* Washington, DC: Government Printing Office, 2006.

US Department of State, Bureau of Near Eastern Affairs. "Weekly Reports from August to December 2006." http://www.state.gov/p/nea (accessed on August 28, 2010).

US Department of State, Office of the Coordinator for Reconstruction and Stabilization. "Post-Conflict Reconstruction Essential Tasks (April 2005)." http://www.crs.state.gov/index.cfm?fuseaction=public.display&shortcut=J7R3 (accessed on November 20, 2010).

US Department of State and US Department of Defense. "United States Government Integrated Civilian – Military Campaign Plan for Support to Afghanistan – Revision 1." Kabul, Afghanistan: US Embassy Office, 2011. http://ccoportal.org/file/2238/download/3208 (accessed on February 23, 2011).

US Department of the Army. *US Army Field Manual (FM), 3-0 Operations.* Washington, DC: Government Printing Office, 2008.

---------------. *US Army FM 3-07, Stability Operations.* Washington, DC:

Government Printing Office, 2008.

------------. *US Army FM 3-34.400, General Engineering.* Washington, DC: Government Printing Office, 2008.

------------. *US Army Field Manual 5-0, The Operations Process.* Washington, DC: Government Printing Office, 2010.

US Department of the Army and US Marine Corps. *US Army Field Manual 3-24 / Marine Corps Warfighter Pamphlet (MCWP) 3-33.5, Counterinsurgency.* Washington, DC: Government Printing Office, 2006.

------------. *US Army FM 3-34.170 /* MCWP 3-17.4, *Engineer Reconnaissance.* Washington, DC: Government Printing Office, 2008.

Valdez, Edward M. "Analysis of Change in Population Stance on Infrastructure Using a Cultural Geography Model for Stability Operations." Master's thesis, Naval Post Graduate School, 2009.

Valeyre, Bertrand, and Alexandre Guerin. "From Galula to Petraeus: The French Legacy in the US Counterinsurgency Doctrine." *Cahier de la Recherché Doctrinale.* Christine Valley, France: Centre de Doctrine d'Emploi des Forces (CDEF), 2010.

West, Bing, and Owen West. "Return to Fallujah: City of Discontent." Education for Peace in Iraq Center, September 2005. http://www.slate.com/id/2126905/entry/2126990 (accessed on November 24, 2010).

Williams, Garland H. *Engineering Peace: The Military Role in Postconflict Reconstruction.* Washington, DC: United States Institute of Peace Press, 2005.

Shari'a Compliant Finance

The Overlooked Element for Developing an Effective Financial System in Afghanistan

by

Lieutenant Colonel Jan Willem Maas - Royal Netherlands Army

Bibliography

Abd Rahman, Ust Hj Zaharuddin Hj. "Differences Between Islamic Bank and Conventional." *MohdHafez.net* (March 2007). http://mohdhafez.wordpress.com/2007/03/03/differences-between-islamic-bank-and-conventional/ (accessed 20 July 2011).

Ahmad, Ashfaq, Asad Afzal Humayoun, and Uzair ul Hassan. "An Analysis of Functions Performed by Islamic Bank: A Case of Pakistan." European Journal of Social Sciences 17, no. 1 (October 2010). http://www.eurojournals.com/ejss_17_1.htm (accessed 12 September 2011).

Ahmad, Imad-ad-Dean. "Riba and interest: definitions and implications." *Minaret of Freedom Institute Preprint Series* 96-5, Minaret of Freedom Institute, Bethesda, (15☐17 October 1993), www.minaret.org/riba.htm (accessed 25 August 2011).

Ahmad, Ashfaq, *Kashif ur Rehman, and Muhammad Iqbal Saif*, M. I. "Islamic Banking Experience of Pakistan: Comparison of Islamic and Conventional Banks." *International Journal of Business and Management* 5, no. 2 (2010): 141.

Ansari, Omar M., and Faizan Ahmed Memon. "Islamic Banking: Is it really 'Islamic'?" *Islamic Finance Pakistan* Vol. 2, issue 1 (January 2011). http://www.publicitas.com.pk/ifp/DO WNLOADS/Islamic Finance Pakistan Issue 1 Volume 2.pdf (accessed 10 August 2011).

Ayub, Mohammad. *Understanding Islamic Finance*. West Sussex, UK: John Wiley and Sons Ltd, 2007.

Bank of Indonesia and Research Center on Development Studies Research Institute Diponegoro University Semarang. "Research on Potency, Preference and Society Behavior Toward Syariah Banking System in Central Java and Yogyakarta Provinces," Executive Summary (2000), http://www.bi.go.id/NR/rdonlyres/4DFA2814-DAF4-4CFC-8D5B-109018D30895/13298/BPSESJateng_english.pdf, (accessed 28 September 2011).

Bhala, Raj. *Understanding Islamic Law (Shari'a)*. Dayton, Ohio: LexisNexis, 2011.

Bennett, A. Messrs, B. de Schaetzen, R. van Rooden, L. Dicks-Mireaux, F. Fischer, and T. Kalfon. "Islamic State of Afghanistan: Rebuilding a Macroeconomic Framework for Reconstruction and Growth." *Country Report* No. 03/299, Washington, DC: International Monetary Fund, 2003. http://www.imf.org/external/pubs/ft/scr/2003 /cr03299.pdf (accessed 14 August 2011).

Blachard, Christopher M. "Islam: Sunnis and Shiites. Congressional Research Service," *CRS Report for Congress* (3 March 2010). http://www.dtic.mil/cgi-bin/GetTRDoc?AD= ADA52_1232&Location=U2&doc=GetTRDoc.pdf (accessed 25 August 2011).

Bureau of Economic, Energy and Business Affairs. "2011 Investment Climate Statement – Afghanistan: Overview of Foreign Investment Climate." US Department of State, 2011. http://www.state.gov/e/eeb/rls/othr/ics/2011/157228.htm# (accessed 16 August 2011).

Camacho, Jasper. "Islamic Financing for Large Infrastructure Projects." *International Financial Mgmt*, Section 1 (Fall 2005). http://people.hbs.edu/mdesai/IFM05/Camacho.pdf (accessed 10 August 2011).

Center for International Private Enterprise and Charney Research. "Afghan Business Attitudes on the Economy, Government, and Business Organizations." 2009-2010 Afghan Business Survey Final Report.

Christopoulosa, Dimitris K., and Efthymios G. Tsionas. "Financial Development and Economic Growth: Evidence from Panel Unit Root and Cointegration Tests." *Journal of Development Economics*, no. 73 (2004): 55–74.

Collier, Paul. "Post-Conflict Recovery: How Should Policies Be Distinctive?" Centre for the Study of African Economies, Department of Economics, Oxford University, 2007. http://users.ox.ac.uk/~econpco/research/pdfs/PostConflict-Recovery.pdf (accessed 8 October 2010).

Coughlin, Paul. "Islamic Finance Outlook 2010." *Report for Standard and Poor's* (19 April 2011), http://www2.standardandpoors.com/spf/pdf/media/Islamic_Finance_Outlook _2010.pdf, (accessed 23 August 2011).

Crane, Keith, Olga Oliker, Nora Bensahel, Derek Eaton, S. Jamie Gayton, Brooke Stearns Lawson, Jeffrey Martini, John L. Nasir, Sandra Reyna, Michelle Parker, Jerry M. Sollinger, and Kayla M. Williams. "Guidebook for Supporting Economic Development in Stability Operations." *Technical Report*, RAND Cooperation, 2009. http://www.rand. org/ pubs/technical_reports/2009/RAND_TR633.pdf (accessed 14 August 2011).

Cunningham, Andrew. "Are Islamic Banks a More Powerful Force for Post-Conflict Economic Development than Conventional Banks?" *International Network for Economics and Conflict,* United States Institute of Peace (2 May 2011). http://inec.usip.org/blog/2011 /may/02/are-islamic-banks-more-powerful-force-post-conflict-economic-development-convention (accessed 20 July 2011).

Da Afghanistan Bank. "Annual Bulletin Da Afghanistan Bank 2008-2009." Kabul, Afghanistan: Da Afghanistan Bank, 2009. http://www.centralbank.gov.af/pdf/DAB_QB_ Annual-1387 282008-2009_29.pdf (accessed 9 February 2011).

———. "Licensed Financial Institutions." http://www.centralbank.gov.af/licensed-financial-institutions.php (accessed 9 February 2011).

———. *Strategic Plan 2009–2014, Fostering Price Stability and Building a Robust Financial System.* Kabul, Afghanistan: Da Afghanistan Bank, 22 February 2009. http:// www.central bank.gov.af/pdf/Strategic_Plan_2009-2014.pdf (accessed 13 September 2011).

―――――. The Afghanistan Bank Law. *The Official Gazette*, 17 December 2003. http://www.cen tralbank.gov.af/pdf/UpdatedOfDaAfghanistanBankLaw_1_pdf (accessed 9 February 2011). No writer

Demir, Omer, Mustafa Acar and, Metin Toprak. "Anatolian Tigers or Islamic capital: prospects and challenges." *Middle Eastern Studies* 40, no 6 (2004): 171.

Department for International Development. "The Afghanistan Investment Climate in 2008: Growth Despite Poor Governance, Weak Factor Markets, and Lack of Innovation." The World Bank Finance and Private Sector Development South Asia Region, 2008. http://siteresources.worldbank.org/AFGHANISTANEXTN /Resources/305984-12370850 35526/5919769-1258729848597/1AFInvestment   Climate_surveyReportFinal.pdf (accessed 16 August 2011).

Detragiache, Enrica, Poonam Gupta, and Theirry Tressel. "Finance in Lower-Income Countries: An Empirical Exploration." Working Paper 05/167, Washington, DC: International Monetary Fund, August 2005. http://www.econdse.org/faculty/poonam/papers/Finance_ 21.pdf (accessed 10 September 2011).

Eagle, Linda. "Banking on Sharia Principles: Islamic Banking and the Financial Industry." The Edcomm Group Banker's Academy, New York, NY(14 May 2009). http://www.anything islamicbanking.com/articles/article_2010_002.html (accessed 25 August 2011).

Economy Watch. "Islamic Republic of Afghanistan Economic Statistics and Indicators." *Economy, Investment and Financial Reports*, 9 February 2011. http://www.economy watch.com/economic-statistics/country/Afghanistan/ (accessed 9 February 2011).

El Biesi, Mohamed Abdel Hamied Hassan. "Foreign Banking, Financial Development and Economic Growth: Recent Evidence from MENA Region." Università Degli Studi di Roma "Tor Vergata," 2010. http://dspace.uniroma2.it/dspace/bitstream/ 2108/1345/ 1/ El+Biesi_PhD_thesis.pdf (accessed 16 August 2011).

Edris, Thabet A. "Services considered important to business customer and determinants of bank selection in Kuwait: A segmentation analysis." *International Journal of Bank marketing* 15, no. 4 (1997): 126-133.

El-Gamal, Mahmoud A. *Islamic Finance: Law, Economics, and Practice*. New York: Cambridge University Press, 2006.

Ellahi, Nazima, Dr. Tayyab Alam Bukhari, and Mehwish Naeem. "Role of Islamic Modes of Financing for Growth of SME's; a Case Study of Islamabad City." *International Journal of Academic Research* 2. no. 6 (November 2010, part I): 165.

Farooq, Dr. Syed Umar (Professor). "A Profile Analysis of the Customers of Islamic Banking in Peshawar, Pukhtunkhwa." *International Journal of Business and Management* 5, no. 11 (November 2010): 116.

Fisher, Dr. Irving. *The Purchasing Power of Money, It's Determination and Relation to Credit, Interest, and Crises*. New York: MacMillan Co., 1911. http://www.econlib.org/library/ YPDBooks/Fisher/fshPPM2.html# (accessed 12 December 2010).

Furqani, Hafas, and Ratna Mulyany. "Islamic Banking and Economic Growth: Emperical Evidence from Malaysia." *Journal of Economic Cooperation and Development* 30, 2 (2009): 59–74.

Gait, Alsadek H. and Andrew C. Worthington. "Libyan Business Firm Attitudes Towards Islamic Methods of Finance." Griffith Business School, Griffith University, 2009. http://www.gr iffith.edu.au/_data/assets/pdf_file/0009/146871/2009-10-libyan-business-firm-attitudes-towards-islamic-methods-in-finance.pdf (accessed 10 August 2011).

Gerstle, Tracy, and Timothy Nourse. "Market Development in Crisis Affected Environments: Emerging Lessons for Achieving Pro-poor Economic Reconstruction." 2007. http://www.usaid.gov/iraq/contracts/pdf/Market_development_post-conflict.pdf (accessed 9 October 2010).

Ghannouchi, Dottore Walid. "Banking Productivity and Economic Growth in Emerging Countries." Università Degli Studi di Roma "Tor Vergata," 2010. http://dspace.uniroma 2.it/dspace/bitstream/2108/1311/1/Walid+Ghannouchi+-+Doctorate+Thesis.pdf (accessed 16 August 2011).

Grameen-Jameel Pan-Arab Microfinance Limited and the International Finance Corporation. "Syria: Microfinance Market Assessment," *Final Report* (July 2008), http://ebookbrowse. com/syria-microfinance-market-assessment-final-posted-cgap-july2008-pdf-d45320007 (accessed 29 September 2011).

Hassan, Kabir M. ed., and Mervyn K. Lewis, ed. *Development of Islamic economic and social thought; Handbook of Islamic Banking.* Cheltenham, UK and Northampton, MA, USA: Edward Elgar, 2007.

Hassan, Mehboob ul. "People's Perceptions towards the Islamic Banking: A Fieldwork Study on Bank Account Holders' Behaviour in Pakistan," *Oikonomika* Vol. 43 no. 3 (April 2007), http://www.econ.nagoya-cu.ac.jp/~oikono/oikono/vol47_34/pdf/vol43_34/09_hassan.pdf (accessed 25 August 2011).

Haughton, Jonathan. "The Reconstruction of War-torn Economies." Technical Paper, Harvard Institute for International Development, June 1998. http://citeseerx.ist.psu.edu/viewdoc/ download?doi=10.1.1.116.6026&rep=rep1&type=pdf (accessed 9 October 2010).

Haque, Ahasanul, Jamil Osman and Ahmad Zaki Hj Ismail. "Factor Influences Selection of Islamic Banking: A Study on Malaysian Customer Preferences." *American Journal of Applied Sciences* 6, no.5 (2009): 924.

Hussein, Maliha Hamid. "State of Microfinance in Afghanistan." Institute of Microfinance (InM), 2009. http://inm.org.bd/saarc/document/Afghanistan.pdf (accessed 10 August 2011).

Ilias, Shayerah. "Islamic Finance: Overview and Policy Concerns." *CRS Report for Congress* (29 July 2008). http://www.dtic.mil/cgi-bin/GetTRDoc?Location=U2&doc=Ge tTRDoc. pdf&AD=ADA484714 (accessed 10 August 2011).

Imam, Patrick, and Kangni Kpodar. "Islamic banking: How has it Diffused?" International Monetary Fund, 2010. http://www.imf.org/external/pubs/ft/wp/2010/wp10195.pdf (accessed 16 August 2011).

International Finance Cooperation of The World Bank Group. "Afghanistan Country Profile 2008." Danvers, MA: The World Bank Group, 2008. http://www.enterprisesurveys. org/documents/EnterpriseSurveys/Reports/Afghanistan-2009.pdf (accessed 24 December 2010).

————,and Palestinian Network for Small and Microfinance (PNSMF), "Microfinance Market Survey in the West Bank and the Gaza Strip" (May 2007), http://www. microfinancegate way.org/gm/document-1.9.26182/Micro finance Market Survey-Final. pdf (accessed 29 September 2011).

International Monetary Fund. "About the IMF." http://www.imf.org/external/about. htm (accessed 24 November 2010).

————. Country Report No. 02/219, "Islamic Republic of Afghanistan: Report on Recent Economic Developments and Prospects, and the Role of the Fund in the in the Reconstruction Process." Washington, DC: International Monetary Fund, October 2002. http://www.imf.org/external/pubs/ft/scr/2002/cr02219.pdf (accessed 10 February 2011).

————. Country Report No. 09/319, "Islamic Republic of Afghanistan: Afghanistan National Development Strategy: First Annual Report 2008/09." Washington, DC: International Monetary Fund, November 2009, http://www.imf.org/external/pubs/ft/ scr/2009/cr093 19.pdf (accessed 9 February 2011).

————. "Mission Concluding Statement." 16 September 2009. http://www.imf.org/ external/np /ms/2009/091609.htm (accessed 8 February 2011).

Islamic Financial Services Industry Development. "Ten Year Framework And Strategies," Islamic Development Bank, Islamic Research And Training Institute, Islamic Financial Services Board, 2007. http://www.ibisonline.net/En/Policy_Dialogue/ TenYearFrameworkAndStrategies.pdf (accessed 6 August 2011).

Ivatury, Gautam, and Ignacio Mas. "The Early Experience with Branchless Banking" *CGAP Focus Note* 46 (April 2008). http://www.cgap.org/p/site/c/template.rc/1.9.2640/ (accessed 16 December 2010).

Iqbal, Zamir, and Abbas Mirakhor. *An Introduction to Islamic Finance: Theory and Practice*. Singapore, Asia: John Wiley and Sons Pte Ltd, 2007

Jang, Ji-Hyang. "Taming political Islamists by Islamic capital: the passions and the interests in Turkish Islamic society." *PhD dissertation*, The University of Texas at Austin (2005). www.lib.utexas.edu/etd/d/2005/jangj05548/jangj05548.pdf. (accessed 12 September 2011), 141

Johnson, Ronald W., and Syedur Rahman. "Improved Budgeting and Financial Management as a Tool for Enhancing the Performance of Local Government in Developing Countries." *International Journal of Public Administration* 15, no. 5 (1992): 1241–1261.

Joint Staff. *Joint Publication 5-0, Joint Operation Planning.Washington, DC: Joint Chiefs of Staff,* (11 August 2011). Joint Warfighting Center. *Handbook for Military Support to Economic Stabilization. Washington, DC: US Joint Forces Command,* 27 February 2010.

Joint Warfighting Center. *Handbook for Military Support to Economic Stabilization. Washington, DC: US Joint Forces Command,* 27 February 2010.

Karim, Nimrak, Michael Tarazi and Xavier Reille. "Islamic Microfinance: An Emerging Market Niche," *CGAP Focus Note* no. 47 (August 2008). http://www.cgap.org/gm/document-1.9.5029/FN49.pdf (accessed 6 August 2011).

Khan, Mohammad Saif Noman, M. Kabir Hassan and Abdullah Ibneyy Shahid. "Banking Behavior of Islamic Bank Customers in Bangladesh." *Journal of Islamic Economics, Banking and Finance* 3, no. 2 (July-December 2007): 190.

Khattak, Naveed Azeem, and Kashif-Ur-Rehman. "Customer satisfaction and awareness of Islamic banking system in Pakistan." *African Journal of Business Management* 4, no. 5 (May 2010): 667.

Kiertisak Toh. "South Sudan: Post Conflict Economic Recovery and Recovery and Growth: An Agenda for USAID Engagement." Washington, DC: Management Systems International Office, August 2009. http://pdf.usaid.gov/ pdf_docs/PNADR011.pdf (accessed 12 December 2010).

Konrad Adenauer Stiftung E.V. "Islamic Economic Thought and the Social Market Economy." *Im Plenum Kompakt* (September-October 2010). http://www.kas.de/wf/doc/kas_21925-544-2-30.pdf?110216095211 (accessed 10 August 2011).

Kreimer, Alcira, John Eriksson, Robert Muscat, Margaret Arnold, and Colin Scott. *The World Bank's Experience with Post-Conflict Reconstruction.* Washington, DC: The World Bank, 1998. http://www.wds.worldbank.org/external/default/main?pagePK=64193 7&piPK=64187937&theSitePK=523679&menuPK=64187510&searchMenuPK=64187283&theSitePK=523679&entityID=000178830_98111703551072&searchMenuPK=64187283&theSitePK=523679 (accessed 22 September 2010).

Kuran, Timur. *Islam and Mammon: The Economic Predicaments of Islamism.* Princeton, NJ: Princeton University Press, 3rd edn, 2006.

Levine, Ross. "The Legal Environment, Banks, and Long-Run Economic Growth." *Journal of Money, Credit and Banking* 30, no. 3 (August 1998, Part 2): 596–597.

Levine, Ross, Norman Loayza, and Thorsten Beck. "Financial Intermediation and Growth: Causality and Causes." *Journal of Monetary Economics* 46 (2000): 31–77.

Lönnberg, Ake. *Restoring and Transforming Payments and Banking Systems in Post-Conflict Economies.* Washington, DC: International Monetary Fund, May 2002. http://www.imf.org/external/np/leg/sem/2002/cdmfl/eng/lonnb.pdf (accessed 24 November 2010).

Malik, Muhammad Shaukat, Ali Malik, and Waqas Mustafa. "Controversies that make Islamic banking controversial: An analysis of issues and challenges." *American Journal of Social and Management Science* 2(1) (2011): 43.

Maimbo, Samuel Munzele. "The Money Exchange Dealers of Kabul; A Study of the Hawala System in Afghanistan." Finance and Private Sector Unit, South Asia Region, World Bank (June 2003) http://www.ifc.org/ifcext/gfm.nsf/AttachmentsByTitle/Tool6.13. WorldBankReport-HawalaSystem /$FILE/Tool+6.13.+World+Bank+Report+-+Hawala+System.pdf (accessed 30 September 2011), 5.

Maran Marimuthu, Chan Wai Jing, Lim Phei Gie,Low Pey Mun, Tan Yew Ping. "Islamic Banking: Selection Criteria and Implications." *Global Journal of Human Social Science* 10, no. 4 (September 2010): 57.

Massing, Stephan, and Abdul Bari. "Capacity Development during Political Transition, the Case of Afghanistan." *Bratislava Seminar*, 21-23 November 2005. http://europeandcis.undp.o rg/files/uploads/CDF/Afghanistan-casestudy-final-15-11.doc (accessed 15 September 2010).

Moin, Muhammad Shehzad. "Performance of Islamic Banking and Conventional Banking in Pakistan: A Comparative Study." *Master Degree Project in Finance Advance Level*, *University of Skövde* (Spring Term 2008) http://his.diva-portal.org/smash/record.jsf?pid=diva2:113713, (accessed 25 August 2011).

Nalette, Major Kevin R. "Shari'ah Compliant Finance: Toward Economic Jihad." Monograph, School for Advanced Military Studies, Ft. Leavenworth, KS, 2010.

Nazar, Zarif, and Charles Recknagel. "Kabul Wants To Change The Way Foreign Aid Is Spent." Relief Web, 19 July 2010. http://www.reliefweb.int/rw/rwb.nsf/db900S ID/VVOS-7HL 4N?OpenDocument&RSS20=18-P (accessed 9 February 2011).

NEPAD Secretariat. "African Post-Conflict Reconstruction Policy Framework." June 2005. http://www.reliefweb.int/rw/lib.nsf/db900sid/PANA-794D7A/$file/nepad-jun2005.pdf ?openelement (accessed 11 December 2010).

Nienhaus, Volker. "Islamic Economic System – A Threat to Development?" 2006. http://www.ief pedia.com/english/wp-content/uploads/2009/09/Islamic-Economic-System---A-Threat-to-Development.pdf (accessed 10 August 2011).

North Atlantic Treaty Organization. "A Comprehensive Approach." 3 November 2010. http:// www.nato.int/cps/en/natolive/topics_51633.htm (accessed 17 November 2010).

Ohiorhenuan, John F. E. and Frances Stewart. *Post-Conflict Economic Recovery, Enabling Local Ingenuity.* New York: United States Development Programme, 2008. http://www.undp. org/cpr/content/economic_recovery/PCERreport.pdf (accessed 12 December 2010).

Othman, Abdul Qawi, and Lynn Owen. "Adopting and measuring customer Service Quality (SQ) in Islamic Banks: A case study in Kuwait Finance House." *International Journal of Islamic Financial Services* 3 (2001) 1-26. http://www.iiibf.org/journals/journal9/abdul qawi.pdf (accessed 23 August 2011).

Pasha, Shaheen. "Afghan Central Bank Sees Islamic Banking Law Enacted In 2011," Reuters, 2011. http://www.reuters.com/article/2011/02/06/us-afghanistan-islamicbanking-idUST RE7150EQ20110206 (accessed 4 August 2011).

Patterson, Rebecca, and Dane Stangler. *Building Expeditionary Economics: Understanding the Field and Setting Forth a Research Agenda.* Kansas City, MO: Ewing Marion Kauffman Foundation, 2010.

Pavlović, Jelena, and Joshua Charap. Working Paper 09/150, *Development of the Commercial Banking System in Afghanistan: Risks and Rewards.* Washington, DC: International Monetary Fund, July 2009. http://www.imf.org/external/pubs/ft/wp/2009/wp0915 0.pdf (accessed 9 February 2011).

Pew Research Center's Forum on Religion & Public Life. "Mapping the Global Muslim Population." *Report on the Size and Distribution of the World's Muslim Population*, October 2009. http://pewforum.org/newassets/images/reports/Muslimpopulation/Muslim population.pdf (accessed 28 September 2011).

Policy and Poverty Team South Asia Region. "Afghanistan Economic Update," The World Bank, April 2010. http://siteresources.worldbank.org/AFGHANISTANEXTN/Resources/305 984-1264608805475/Afghanistan_Spring_Brief_April.pdf (accessed 23 February 2011).

Priniotakis, Manolis. *Countering Insurgency and Promoting Democracy.* New York: CENSA, 2007.

Recchia, Giovanni. "Basics of Islamic Banking." US Agency for International Development, 2008. http://pdf.usaid.gov/pdf_docs/PNADQ078.pdf (accessed 16 August 2011).

Sairally, Salma. "Community Development Financial Institutions: Lessons In Social Banking For The Islamic Financial Industry." *Kyoto Bulletin of Islamic Area Studies*, 2007. http://ww w.asafas.kyoto-u.ac.jp/kias/contents/pdf/kb1_2/05 salma.pdf (accessed 4 August 2011).

Saleem, Shahid. "Role of Islamic banks in economic development." Hailey College of banking and finance (PAK), C.I.M.A. (UK), 2008. http://mpra.ub.uni-muenchen.de/7332/2/MPRA_paper_7332.pdf (accessed 16 August 2011).

Schramm, Carl J. 2010. "Expeditionary Economics, Spurring Growth after Conflicts and Disasters." *Foreign Affairs* (May-June): 3.

Shostak, Dr. Frank. *Fractional Reserve Banking and Boom-Bust Cycles.* Ludwig von Mises Institute, August 2009. http://mises.org/journals/scholars/shostak2.pdf (accessed 24 November 2010).

Spiegelglas, Stephen, and Charles J. Welsh, ed. *Economic Development, Challenge and Promise.* Englewood, NJ: Prentice-Hall, 1970.

Staff of the Monetary and Financial Systems Department. *Background Paper for MFD Technical Assistance to Recent Post-Conflict Countries.* Washington, DC: International Monetary Fund, 13 December 2004. http://www.imf.org/external/np/ta/2005/eng/022805a.pdf (accessed 14 August 2011).

Terrell, Ron. "Islamic Banking: Financing Terrorism or Meeting Economic Demand?" Naval Postgraduate School, 2007. http://edoc.bibliothek.uni-halle.de/servlets/MCRFileNodeSer vlet/HALCoRe_derivate_00003456/Islamic_banking_financing.pdf (accessed 16 August 2011).

Timberg, Thomas A. "Risk Management: Islamic Financial Policies: Islamic Banking and its Potential Impact." US Agency for International Development, 2011. http://www.scribd. com/doc/60947811/Islamic-Banking (accessed 16 August 2011).

Turner, Nicholas, Obijiofor Aginam, and Vesselin Popovski. "Post-Conflict Countries and Foreign Investment." *United Nations University Policy Brief,* no. 8, 2008. http://unu.edu/ publications/briefs/policy-briefs/2008/pb08-08.pdf (accessed 15 December 2010).

United Nations. "Emergency Economic Recovery Program." *International Report* 1, no. A1 (3 April 1995). http://www.hartfordhwp.com/archives/43a/050.html (accessed 15 September 2010).

United Nations General Assembly Security Council. "The Situation in Afghanistan and its Implications for International Peace and Security." General Assembly 56th sess., 18 March 2002. http://daccess-dds-ny.un.org/doc/UNDOC/GEN/N02/289/20/PDF/N022892 0.pdf?OpenElement (accessed 9 February 2011).

United States Agency for International Development. "About USAID." November 2010. http://www.usaid.gov/about_usaid (accessed 24 November 2010).

———. "A Guide to Economic Growth in Post-Conflict Countries." Washington, DC: USAID, January 2009. http://pdf.usaid.gov/pdf_docs/PNADO408.pdf (accessed 9 October 2010).

———. "Afghanistan Strategy." Washington, DC: USAID, 9 February 2011. http:// afghanistan. usaid.gov/en/about/country_strategy (accessed 9 February 2011).

———. "Economic Growth." Washington, DC: USAID, June 2010. http://afghanistan. usaid.gov/ en/programs/economic_growth (accessed 15 September 2010).

———. "Fact Sheet Afghanistan." Washington, DC: USAID, June 2010. http://afghanistan. usaid. gov/documents/document/document/1004 (accessed 14 August 2011).

———. "Securing the Future." Washington, DC: USAID, April 2008. http://www.usaid. gov/our _work/economic_growth_and_trade/eg/eg_ strategy/ (accessed 15 September 2010).

US Army, *Field Manual 3-0, Operations. Washington, DC: Headquarters, Department of the Army*, 2008.

———. *Field Manual 3-07, Stability Operations. Washington, DC: Headquarters, Department of the Army*, 2008.

US Department of Defense. "Report on Progress Toward Security and Stability in Afghanistan." Washington, DC: Government Printing Office, November 2010. http://www. defense.gov/ pubs/November_1230_Report_FINAL.pdf (accessed 9 February 2011).

US Department of State. "Background Note: Afghanistan." 6 December 2010. http://www. state. gov /r/pa/ei/bgn/5380.htm (accessed 9 February 2011).

———. "Overview of Foreign Investment Climate." March 2011. http://www.state.gov/e/ eeb/rls/ othr/ics/2011/157228.htm (accessed 30 September 2011).

United States Institute for Peace and United States Army Peacekeeping and Stability Operations Institute. *Guiding Principles for Stabilization and Reconstruction.* Washington, DC: United States Institute of Peace Press, 2009.

Usmani, Muhammad Taqi. *An Introduction to Islamic Finance.* The Hague, NL: Kluwer Law International, 2002.

Visser, Hans. *Islamic Finance: Principles and Practice.* Cheltenham, UK: Edward Elgar Publishing Limited, 2009.

Walter, Elizabeth, ed. Cambridge Advanced Learner's Dictionary (Cambridge, UK: University Press, 2008).

Warde, Ibrahim. *Islamic Finance in the Global Economy.* Edinburgh, UK: Edinburgh University Press, 2000.

Wolfenson, James, D. "Address to the 1997 World Bank Annual Meeting." Speech, Hong Kong, 23 September 1997. http://www.imf.org/external/am/speeches/pdf/ PR04E.pdf (accessed 14 December 2010).

The World Bank. *Financial Accountability in Nepal: A Country Assessment.* Washington, DC: The World Bank, 2003.

The World Bank Group. "About Us." 24 November 2010. http://web.worldbank.org/ WBSITE/   EXTERNAL/EXTABOUTUS/0,,pagePK:50004410~piPK:36602~theSite PK:29708,00.html (accessed 24 November 2010).

———. *Afghanistan World Bank Approach Paper.* November 2001. http://siteresources. world bank.org/INTAFGHANISTAN/Resources/afgApproach.pdf (accessed 9 February 2011).

———. *Afghanistan: Interim Strategy Note.* 5 May 2009. http://www.worldbank.org. af/WBSITE   /EXTERNAL/COUNTRIES/SOUTHASIAEXT/AFGHANISTANEXTN/ 0,,contentMDK:22216104~menuPK:305990~pagePK:2865066~piPK:2865079~theSite PK:305985,00.html (accessed 9 February 2011).

———. "Afghanistan: Supporting State-Building and Development." July 2009. http:// siteresour ces.worldbank.org/IDA/Resources/IDA-Afghanistan.pdf (accessed 9 February 2011).

———. "Enterprise Surveys." 2010. https://www.enterprisesurveys.org/CustomQuery/ View CustomReport.aspx (accessed 8 February 2011).

———. "Financial Sector Strengthening Project." 17 September 2008. http://www-wds. world bank.org/external/default/WDSContentServer/WDSP/IB/2008/09/17/000076092_

20080918160815/Rendered/PDF/Project0Inform1cept0Stage0F0SEPT017.pdf (accessed 14 Augustus 2011),

———. "International Development Association Program Document for a Proposed Credit in the Amount of SDR 54.7 million (US\$ 80 Million Equivalent) to the Islamic Republic of Afghanistan for Programmatic Support for Institution Building." 6 July 2004. http://ww w-wds.worldbank.org/external/default/WDSContentServer/WDSP/IB/2004/07/12/000 160016_20040712102143/Rendered/PDF/281920AF.pdf (accessed 9 February 2011).

———. "The World Bank Should Facilitate, Not Provide." *Beyond Transition* 8, no. 2 (April 1997). http://www.worldbank.org/html/prddr/trans/apr97/pg18.htm (accessed 12 December 2010).

———. "Worldwide Governance Indicators." 2010. http://info.worldbank.org/governance/ wgi/ sc_chart.asp (accessed 8 February 2011).

———. "The Investment Climate In Afghanistan: Exploiting Opportunities in an Uncertain Environment." 2005. http://www-wds.worldbank.org/external/default/WDSContent Server/WDSP/IB/2006/03/22/000160016_20060322131430/Rendered/PDF/355700AF0 white0cover0P0947540ICA01PUBLC1.pdf (accessed 16 August 2011).

Yoshiro, Miwa, and J. Mark Ramseyer. "Banks and Economic Growth: Implications from Japanese History." *Discussion paper no. 289.* Cambridge MA: Harvard Law School, August 2000. http://www.law.harvard.edu/programs/olin_center/papers/pdf/289.pdf (accessed 11 December 2010).

Zyck, Steven A. "Special Report on Economic Development in Afghanistan The Kabul Bank Crisis; What Happened and What It Means for Development, Governance and Security in Afghanistan." Civil-Military Fusion Centre, September 2010. https://www. cimicweb.org/ Documents/CFCAFGEconomicStabilizationArchive/Econ_Dev_Monthly_ Rpt_Sep2010_Kabul_Bank_Crisis_FINAL.pdf (accessed 30 September 2011), 2–4.

———. "The Increasing Role And Potential of Islamic Finance in Afghanistan." Civil-Military Fusion Centre, 2011. https://www.cimicweb.org/Documents/CFC_AFG_ Economic_ Stabilization_Archive/Contemporary_Economic_Issues_in_Afghanistan– Islamic_Finance–Mar_2011.pdf (accessed 6 August 2011).